AMBUSHED!!
IN THE FAMILY ROOM

Other *Baby Blues*® Books from Andrews McMeel Publishing

Guess Who Didn't Take a Nap?
I Thought Labor Ended When the Baby Was Born
We Are Experiencing Parental Difficulties . . . Please Stand By
Night of the Living Dad
I Saw Elvis in My Ultrasound
One More and We're Outnumbered!
Check, Please . . .
threats, bribes & videotape
If I'm a Stay-at-Home Mom, Why Am I Always in the Car?
Lift and Separate
I Shouldn't Have to Scream More Than Once!
Motherhood Is Not for Wimps
Baby Blues®: Unplugged
Dad to the Bone
Never a Dry Moment
Two Plus One Is Enough
Playdate: Category 5
Our Server Is Down
Something Chocolate This Way Comes
Briefcase Full of Baby Blues®
Night Shift
The Day Phonics Kicked In
My Space
The Natural Disorder of Things
We Were Here First

Treasuries

The Super-Absorbent Biodegradable Family-Size Baby Blues®
Baby Blues®: Ten Years and Still in Diapers
Butt-Naked Baby Blues®
Wall-to-Wall Baby Blues®
Driving Under the Influence of Children
Framed!
X-Treme Parenting

Gift Books

It's a Boy
It's a Girl

BABY BLUES® 26 SCRAPBOOK

AMBUSHED!
IN THE FAMILY ROOM

BY RICK KIRKMAN
& JERRY SCOTT

Andrews McMeel
Publishing, LLC

Kansas City • Sydney • London

Baby Blues® is syndicated internationally by King Features Syndicate, Inc. For information, write King Features Syndicate, Inc., 300 West Fifty-Seventh Street, New York, New York 10019.

10 11 12 13 14 RR2 10 9 8 7 6 5 4 3 2 1

ISBN: 978-0-7407-9740-8

Library of Congress Catalog Number: 2010927042

www.andrewsmcmeel.com

Find *Baby Blues*® on the Web at
www.babyblues.com.

——— **ATTENTION: SCHOOLS AND BUSINESSES** ———

Andrews McMeel books are available at quantity discounts with bulk purchase for educational, business, or sales promotional use. For information, please write to: Special Sales Department, Andrews McMeel Publishing, LLC, 1130 Walnut Street, Kansas City, Missouri 64106.

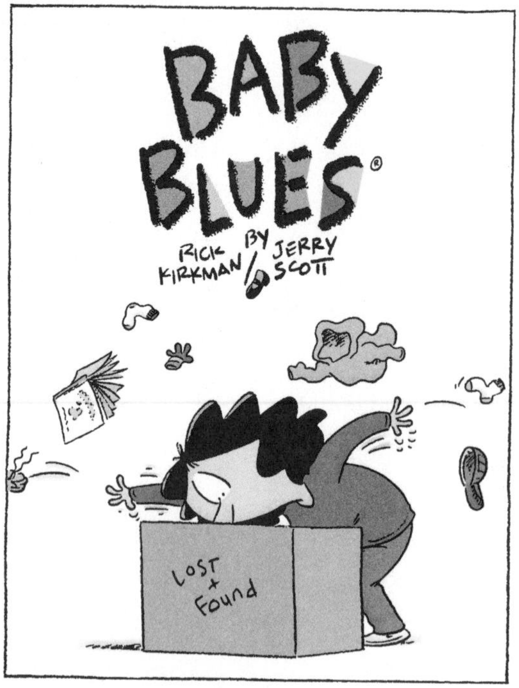
BABY BLUES®
BY
RICK KIRKMAN
JERRY SCOTT
LOST + FOUND

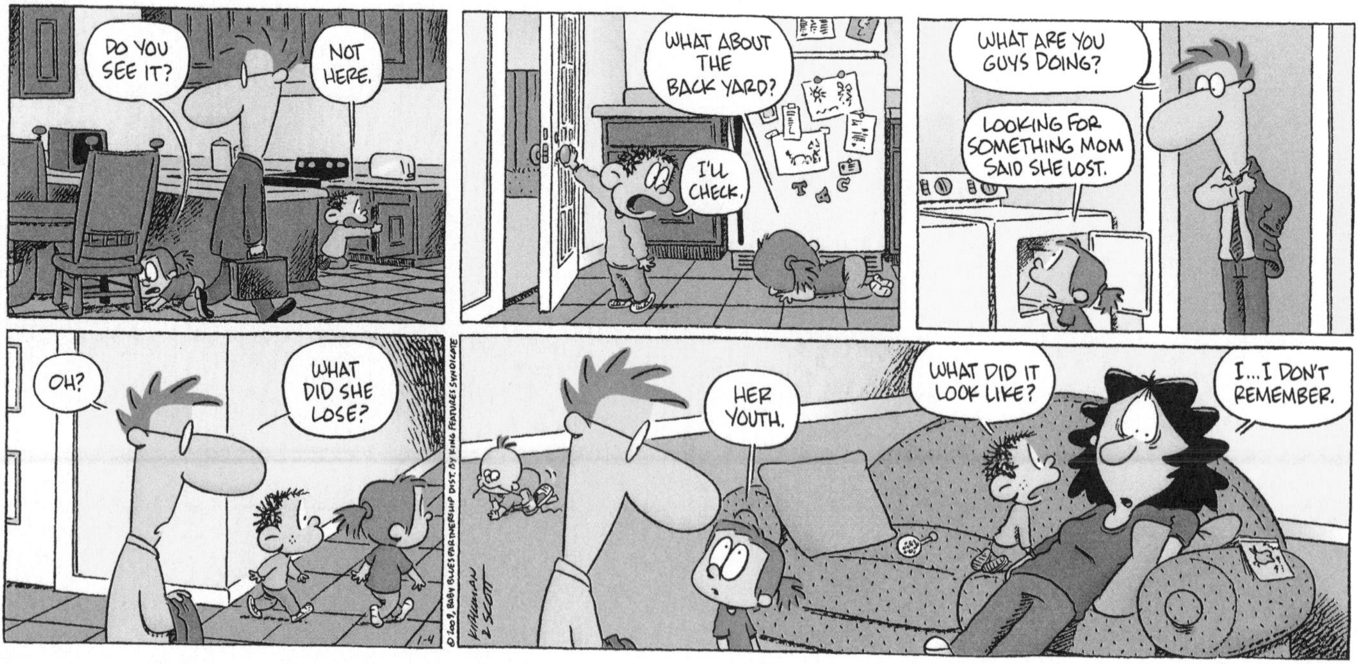
DO YOU SEE IT?
NOT HERE.
WHAT ABOUT THE BACK YARD?
I'LL CHECK.
WHAT ARE YOU GUYS DOING?
LOOKING FOR SOMETHING MOM SAID SHE LOST.
OH?
WHAT DID SHE LOSE?
© 2009, BABY BLUES PARTNERSHIP DIST. BY KING FEATURES SYNDICATE
1-4
KIRKMAN & SCOTT
HER YOUTH.
WHAT DID IT LOOK LIKE?
I... I DON'T REMEMBER.

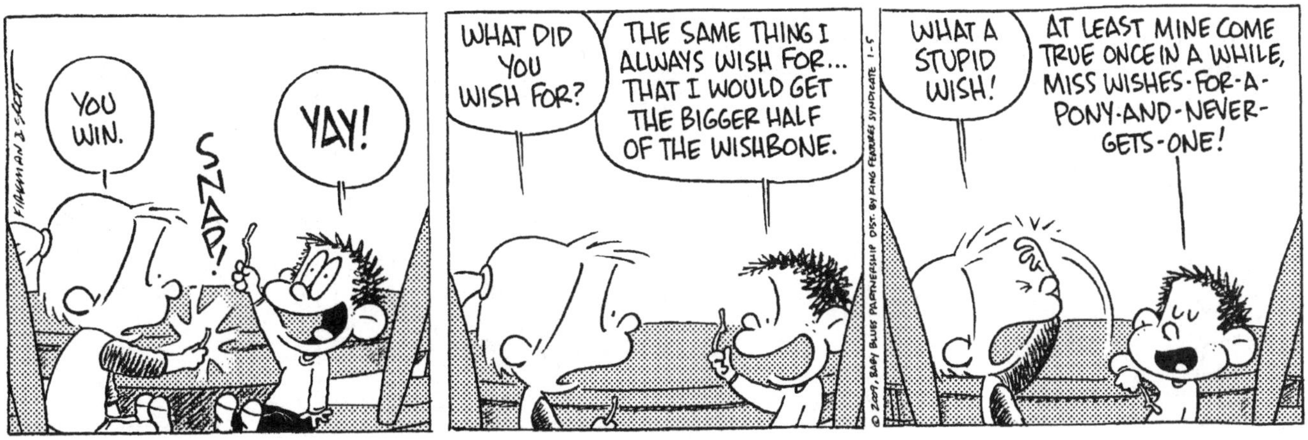
KIRKMAN & SCOTT
YOU WIN.
SNAP!
YAY!
WHAT DID YOU WISH FOR?
THE SAME THING I ALWAYS WISH FOR... THAT I WOULD GET THE BIGGER HALF OF THE WISHBONE.
© 2009, BABY BLUES PARTNERSHIP DIST. BY KING FEATURES SYNDICATE 1-5
WHAT A STUPID WISH!
AT LEAST MINE COME TRUE ONCE IN A WHILE, MISS WISHES-FOR-A-PONY-AND-NEVER-GETS-ONE!

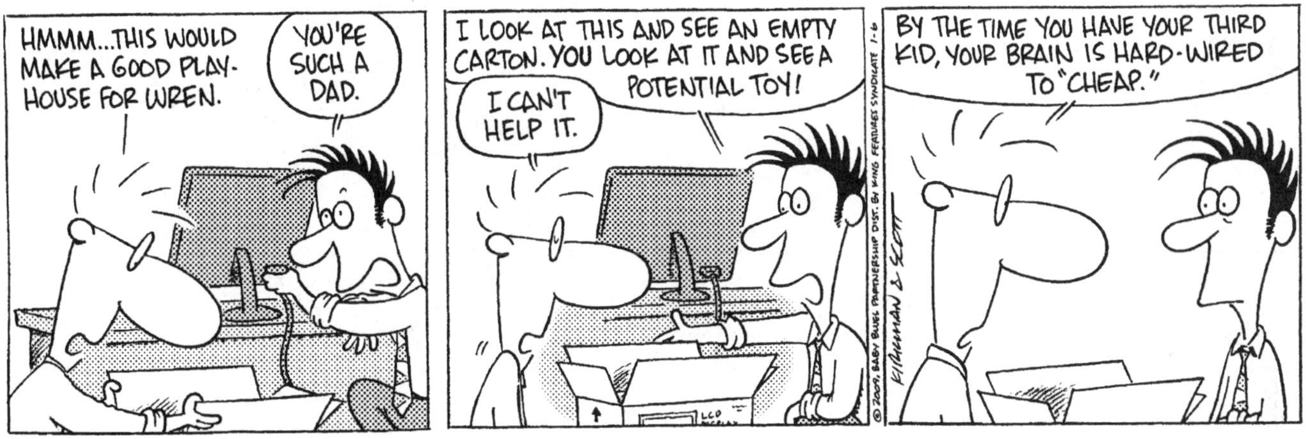
HMMM...THIS WOULD MAKE A GOOD PLAY-HOUSE FOR WREN.
YOU'RE SUCH A DAD.
I LOOK AT THIS AND SEE AN EMPTY CARTON. YOU LOOK AT IT AND SEE A POTENTIAL TOY!
I CAN'T HELP IT.
© 2009, BABY BLUES PARTNERSHIP DIST. BY KING FEATURES SYNDICATE 1-6
KIRKMAN & SCOTT
BY THE TIME YOU HAVE YOUR THIRD KID, YOUR BRAIN IS HARD-WIRED TO "CHEAP."

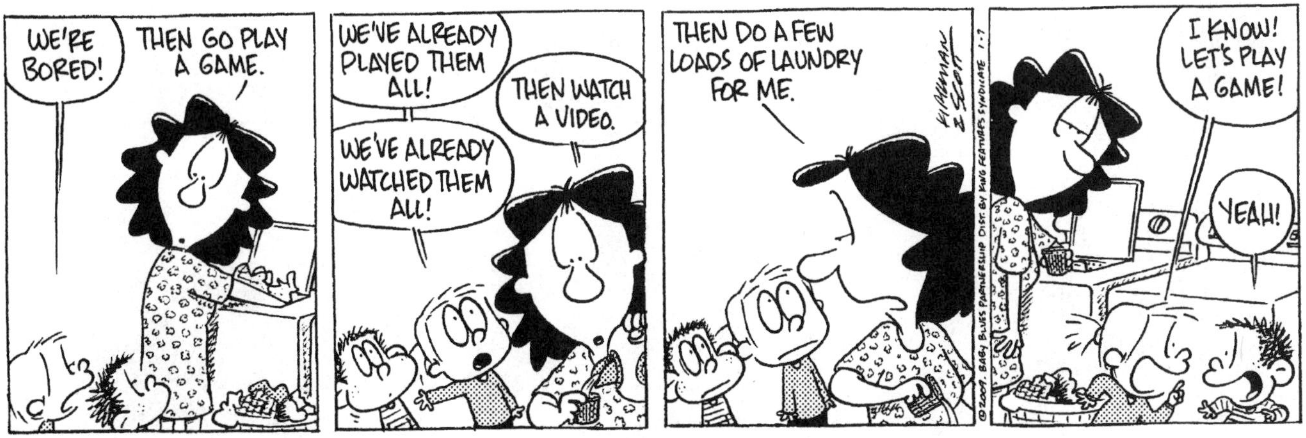
WE'RE BORED!
THEN GO PLAY A GAME.
WE'VE ALREADY PLAYED THEM ALL!
THEN WATCH A VIDEO.
WE'VE ALREADY WATCHED THEM ALL!
THEN DO A FEW LOADS OF LAUNDRY FOR ME.
KIRKMAN & SCOTT
© 2009, BABY BLUES PARTNERSHIP DIST. BY KING FEATURES SYNDICATE 1-7
I KNOW! LET'S PLAY A GAME!
YEAH!

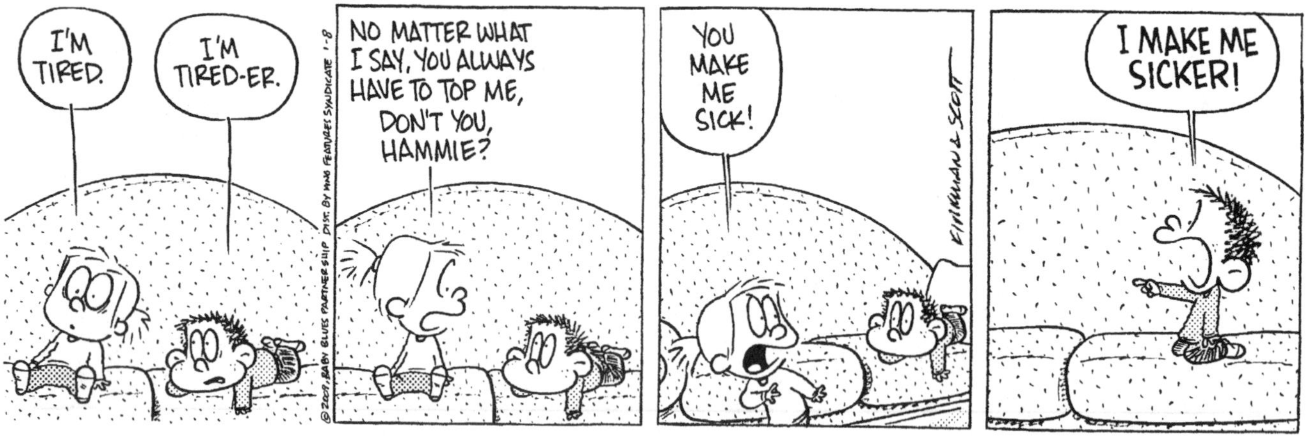
I'M TIRED.
I'M TIRED-ER.
NO MATTER WHAT I SAY, YOU ALWAYS HAVE TO TOP ME, DON'T YOU, HAMMIE?
YOU MAKE ME SICK!
I MAKE ME SICKER!
©2009, BABY BLUES PARTNERSHIP DIST. BY KING FEATURES SYNDICATE 1-8
KIRKMAN & SCOTT

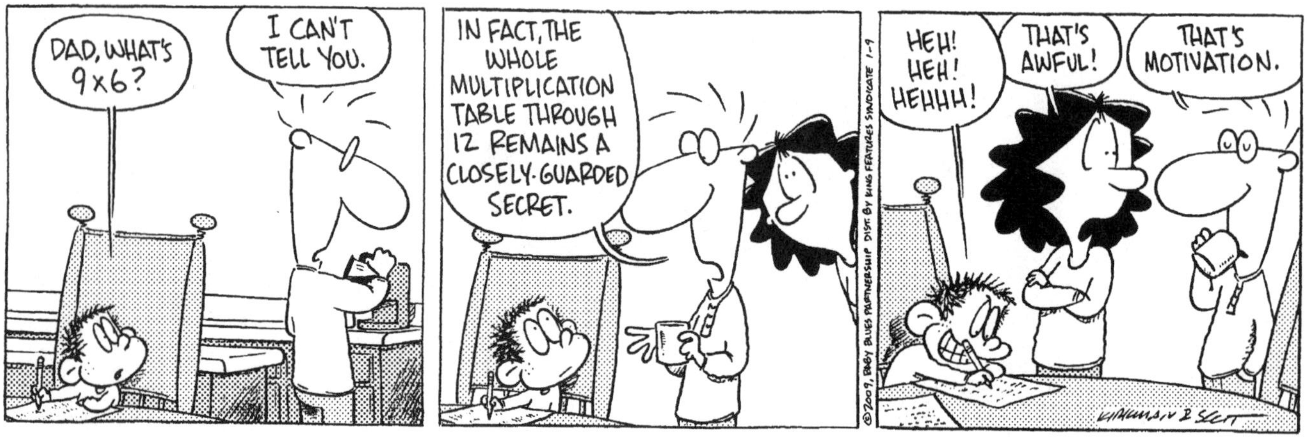
DAD, WHAT'S 9x6?
I CAN'T TELL YOU.
IN FACT, THE WHOLE MULTIPLICATION TABLE THROUGH 12 REMAINS A CLOSELY-GUARDED SECRET.
HEH! HEH! HEHHH!
THAT'S AWFUL!
THAT'S MOTIVATION.
©2009, BABY BLUES PARTNERSHIP DIST. BY KING FEATURES SYNDICATE 1-9
KIRKMAN & SCOTT

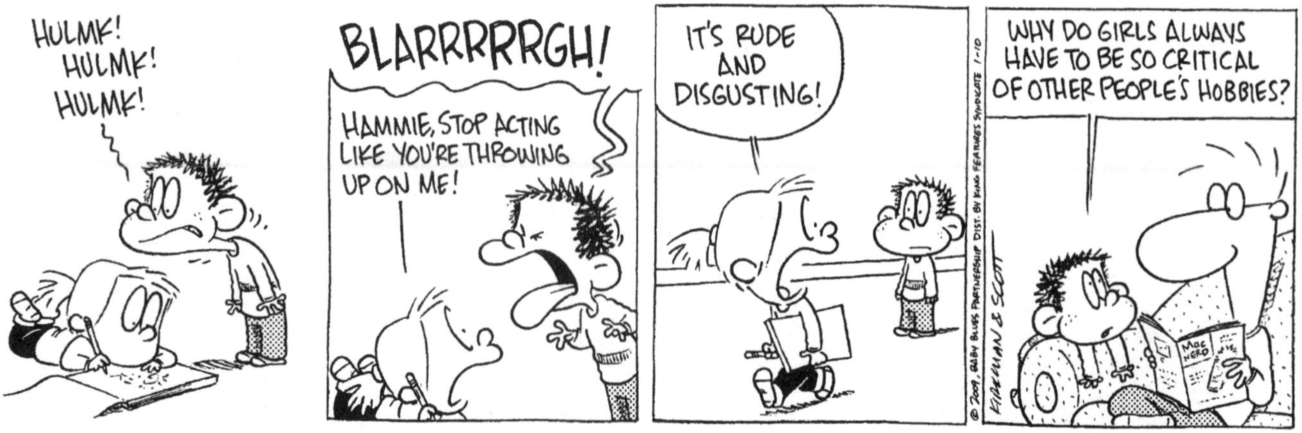
HULMK! HULMK! HULMK!
BLARRRRRGH!
HAMMIE, STOP ACTING LIKE YOU'RE THROWING UP ON ME!
IT'S RUDE AND DISGUSTING!
WHY DO GIRLS ALWAYS HAVE TO BE SO CRITICAL OF OTHER PEOPLE'S HOBBIES?
©2009, BABY BLUES PARTNERSHIP DIST. BY KING FEATURES SYNDICATE 1-10
KIRKMAN & SCOTT

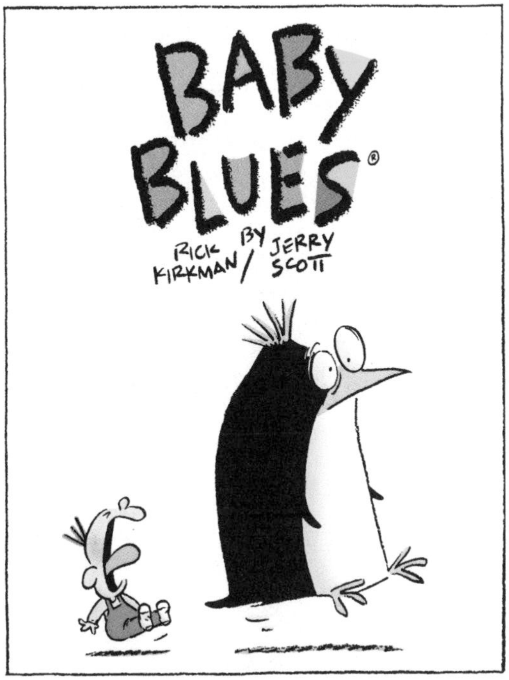
BABY BLUES®
BY
RICK KIRKMAN / JERRY SCOTT

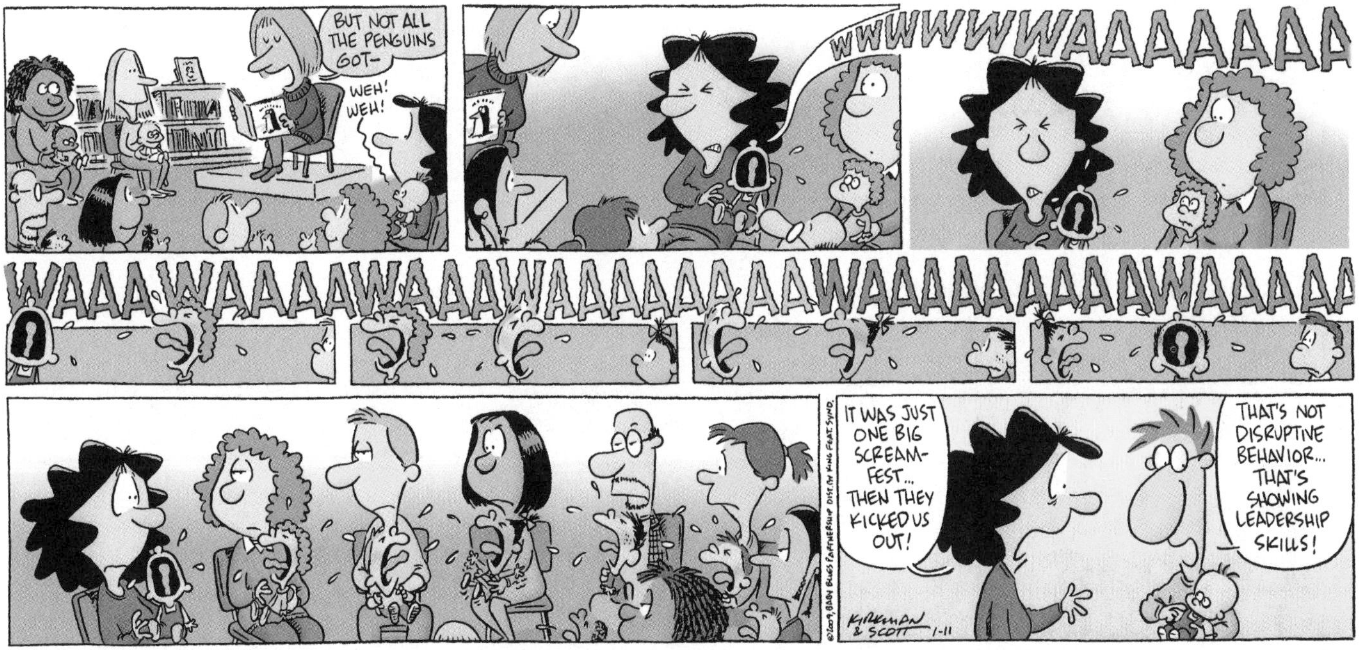
BUT NOT ALL THE PENGUINS GOT–
WEH! WEH!
WWWWWWWAAAAAAAA
WAAAWAAAAWAAAWAAAAAAAAAWAAAAAAAAAAWAAAAA
IT WAS JUST ONE BIG SCREAM-FEST... THEN THEY KICKED US OUT!
THAT'S NOT DISRUPTIVE BEHAVIOR... THAT'S SHOWING LEADERSHIP SKILLS!
KIRKMAN & SCOTT 1-11

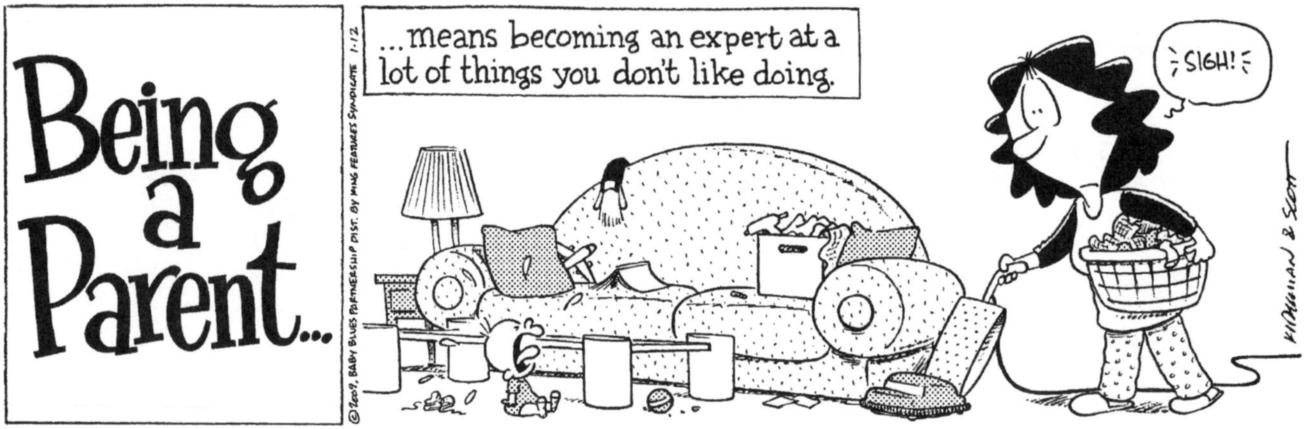
Being a Parent...
...means becoming an expert at a lot of things you don't like doing.
SIGH!
©2009, Baby Blues Partnership Dist. by King Features Syndicate 1-12
KIRKMAN & SCOTT

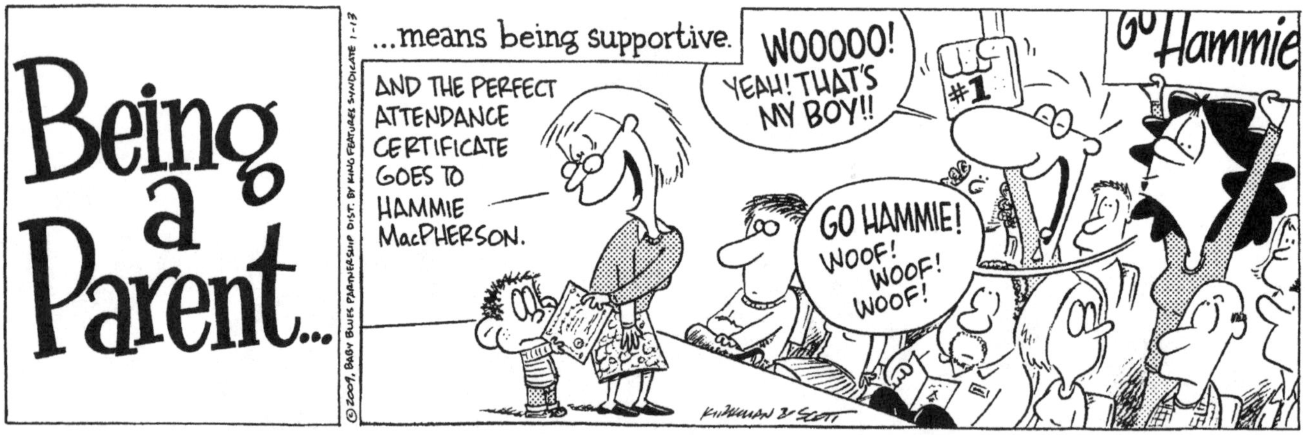
Being a Parent...
...means being supportive.
AND THE PERFECT ATTENDANCE CERTIFICATE GOES TO HAMMIE MacPHERSON.
WOOOOO! YEAH! THAT'S MY BOY!!
GO HAMMIE! WOOF! WOOF! WOOF!
#1
GO Hammie
©2009, Baby Blues Partnership Dist. by King Features Syndicate 1-13
KIRKMAN & SCOTT

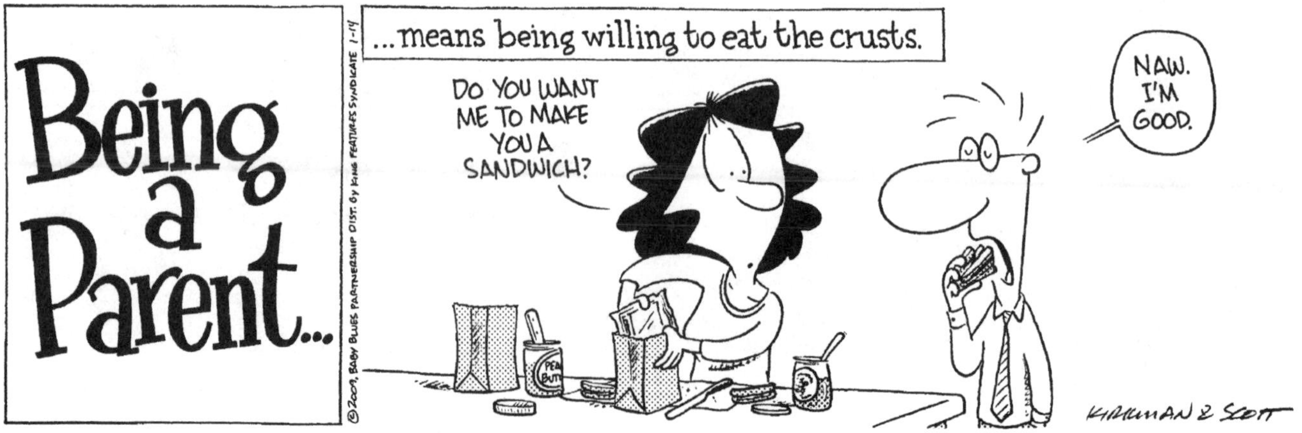
Being a Parent...
...means being willing to eat the crusts.
DO YOU WANT ME TO MAKE YOU A SANDWICH?
NAW. I'M GOOD.
©2009, Baby Blues Partnership Dist. by King Features Syndicate 1-14
KIRKMAN & SCOTT

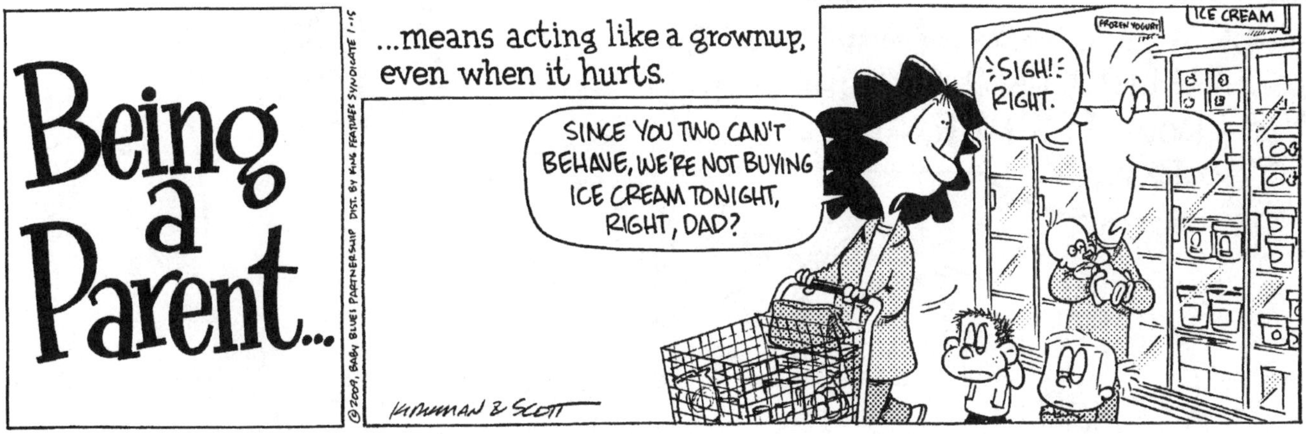
Being a Parent...
©2009, Baby Blues Partnership Dist. by King Features Syndicate 1-15
...means acting like a grownup, even when it hurts.
FROZEN YOGURT
ICE CREAM
SINCE YOU TWO CAN'T BEHAVE, WE'RE NOT BUYING ICE CREAM TONIGHT, RIGHT, DAD?
SIGH! RIGHT.
KIRKMAN & SCOTT

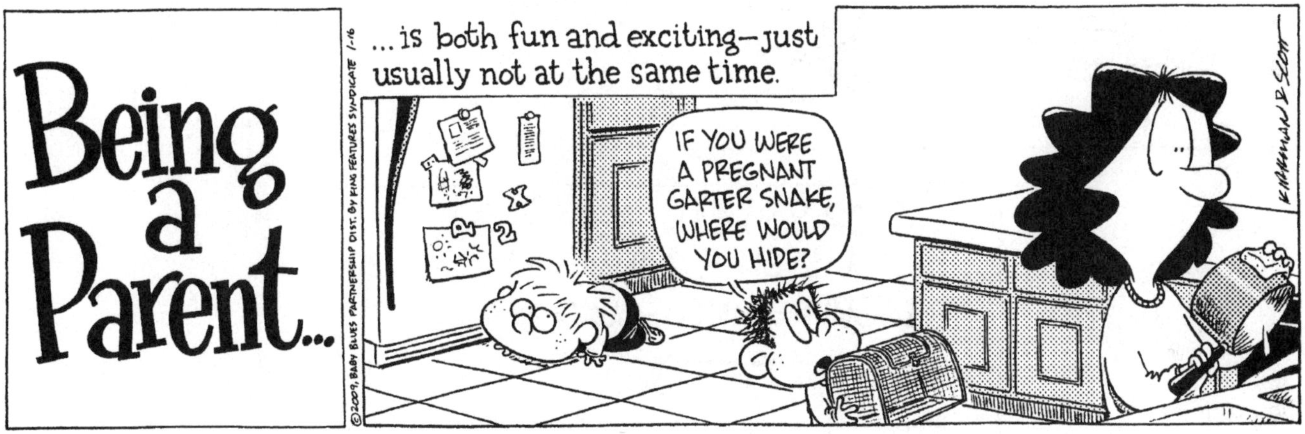
Being a Parent...
©2009, Baby Blues Partnership Dist. by King Features Syndicate 1-16
...is both fun and exciting—just usually not at the same time.
IF YOU WERE A PREGNANT GARTER SNAKE, WHERE WOULD YOU HIDE?
KIRKMAN & SCOTT

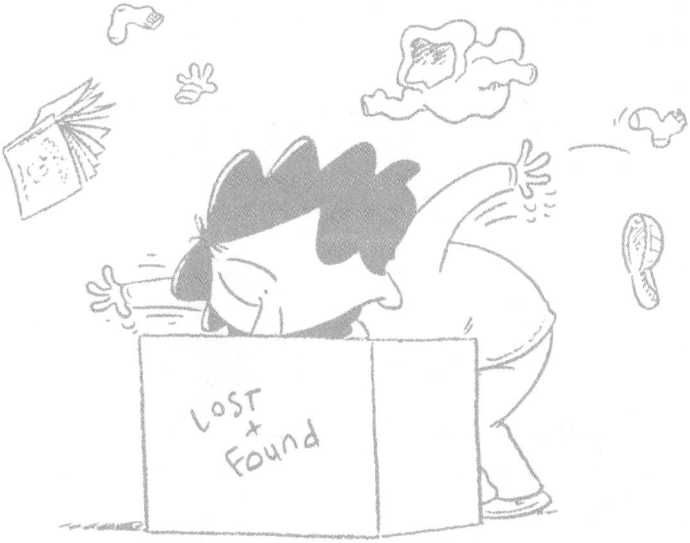
LOST + FOUND

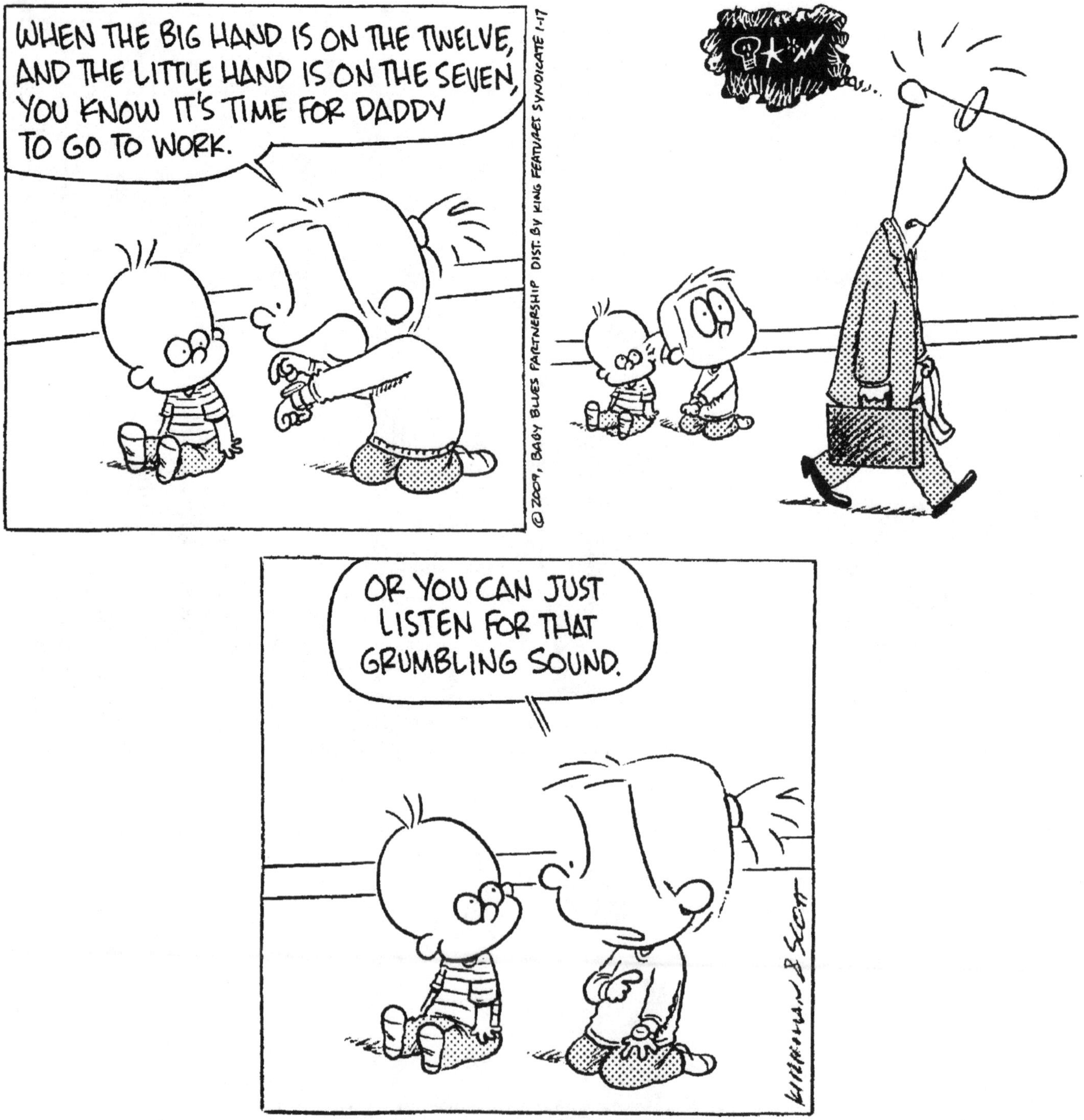
WHEN THE BIG HAND IS ON THE TWELVE, AND THE LITTLE HAND IS ON THE SEVEN, YOU KNOW IT'S TIME FOR DADDY TO GO TO WORK.
© 2009, BABY BLUES PARTNERSHIP DIST. BY KING FEATURES SYNDICATE 1-17
OR YOU CAN JUST LISTEN FOR THAT GRUMBLING SOUND.

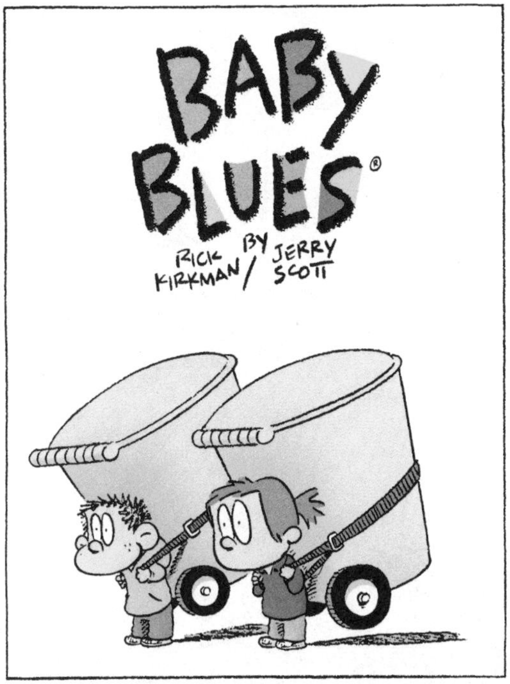
BABY BLUES®
RICK KIRKMAN / BY JERRY SCOTT

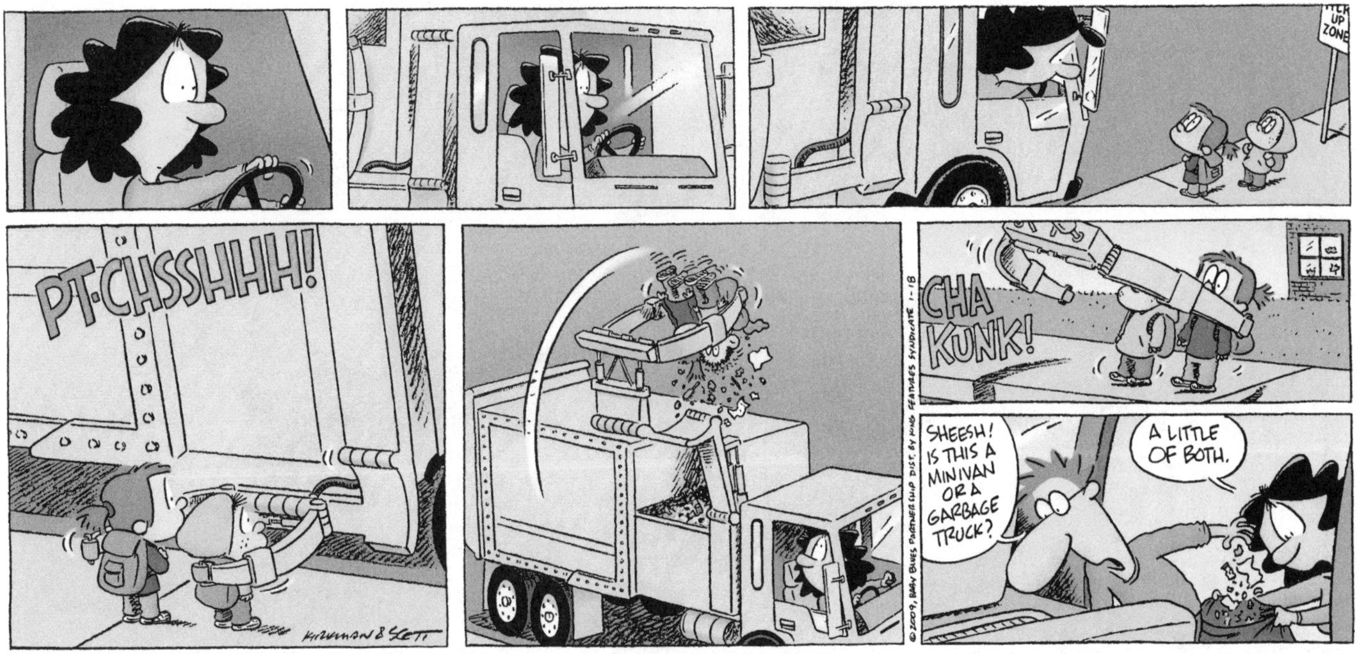
UP ZONE
PT-CHSSHHH!
KIRKMAN & SCOTT
CHA KUNK!
© 2009, BABY BLUES PARTNERSHIP DIST. BY KING FEATURES SYNDICATE 1-18
SHEESH! IS THIS A MINIVAN OR A GARBAGE TRUCK?
A LITTLE OF BOTH.

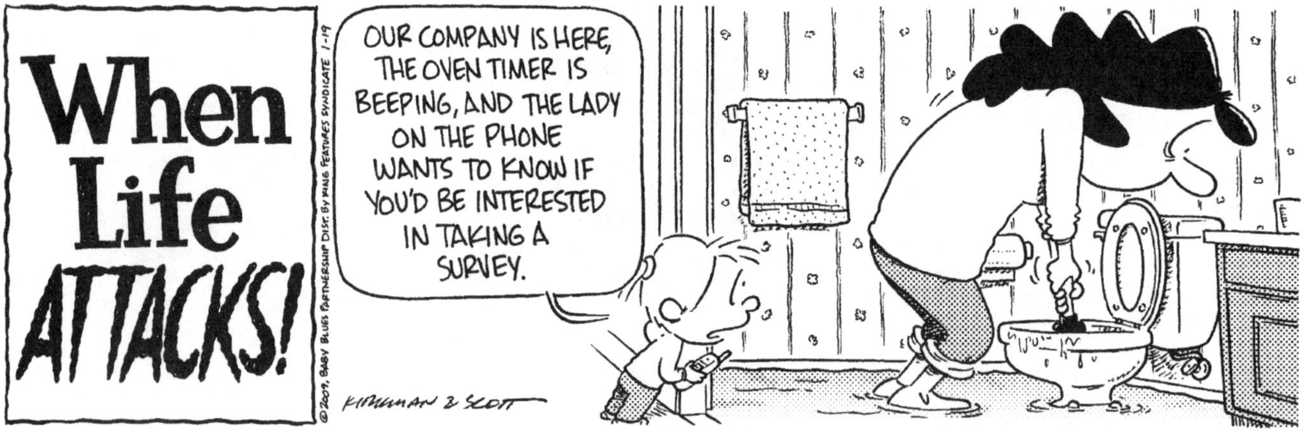
When Life ATTACKS!
© 2009, Baby Blues Partnership Dist. by King Features Syndicate 1-19
OUR COMPANY IS HERE, THE OVEN TIMER IS BEEPING, AND THE LADY ON THE PHONE WANTS TO KNOW IF YOU'D BE INTERESTED IN TAKING A SURVEY.
KIRKMAN & SCOTT

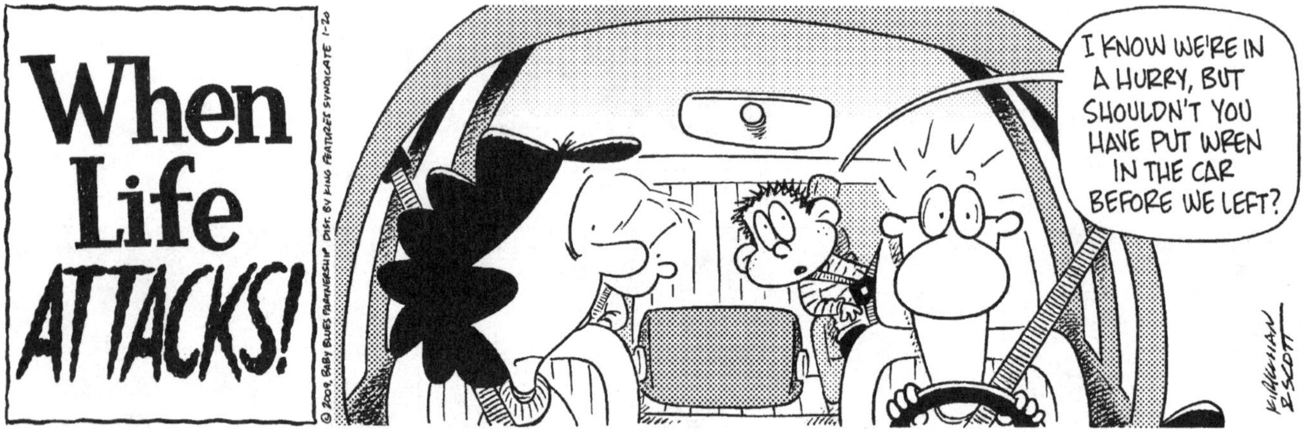
When Life ATTACKS!
© 2009, Baby Blues Partnership Dist. by King Features Syndicate 1-20
I KNOW WE'RE IN A HURRY, BUT SHOULDN'T YOU HAVE PUT WREN IN THE CAR BEFORE WE LEFT?
KIRKMAN & SCOTT

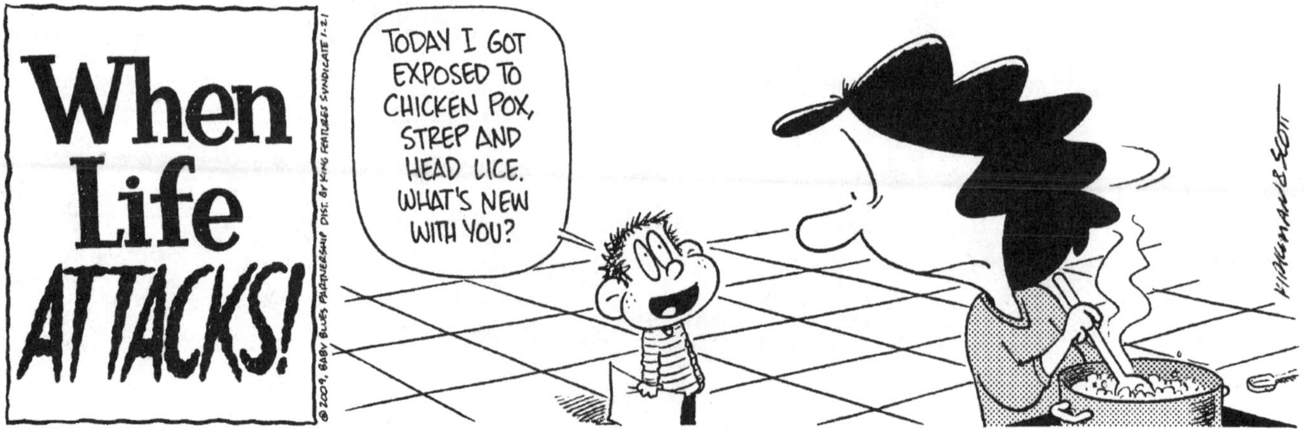
When Life ATTACKS!
© 2009, Baby Blues Partnership Dist. by King Features Syndicate 1-21
TODAY I GOT EXPOSED TO CHICKEN POX, STREP AND HEAD LICE. WHAT'S NEW WITH YOU?
KIRKMAN & SCOTT

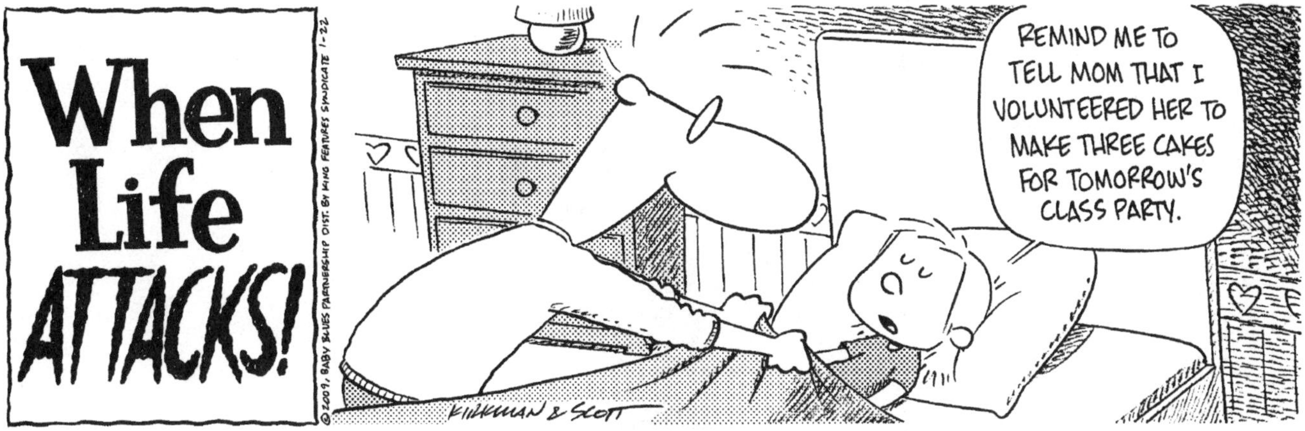
When Life ATTACKS!
©2009, BABY BLUES PARTNERSHIP DIST. BY KING FEATURES SYNDICATE 1-22
REMIND ME TO TELL MOM THAT I VOLUNTEERED HER TO MAKE THREE CAKES FOR TOMORROW'S CLASS PARTY.
KIRKMAN & SCOTT

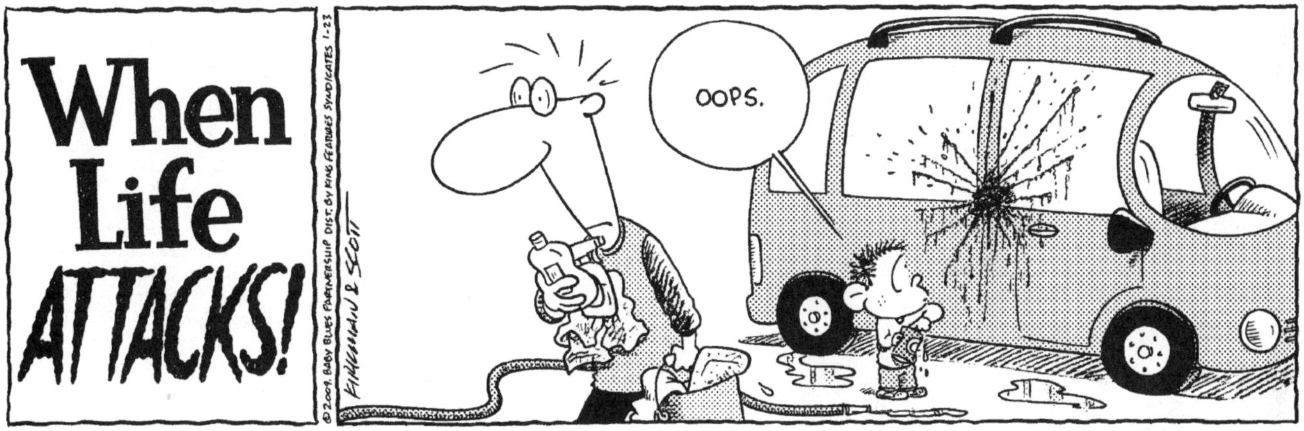
When Life ATTACKS!
©2009, BABY BLUES PARTNERSHIP DIST. BY KING FEATURES SYNDICATES 1-23
OOPS.
KIRKMAN & SCOTT

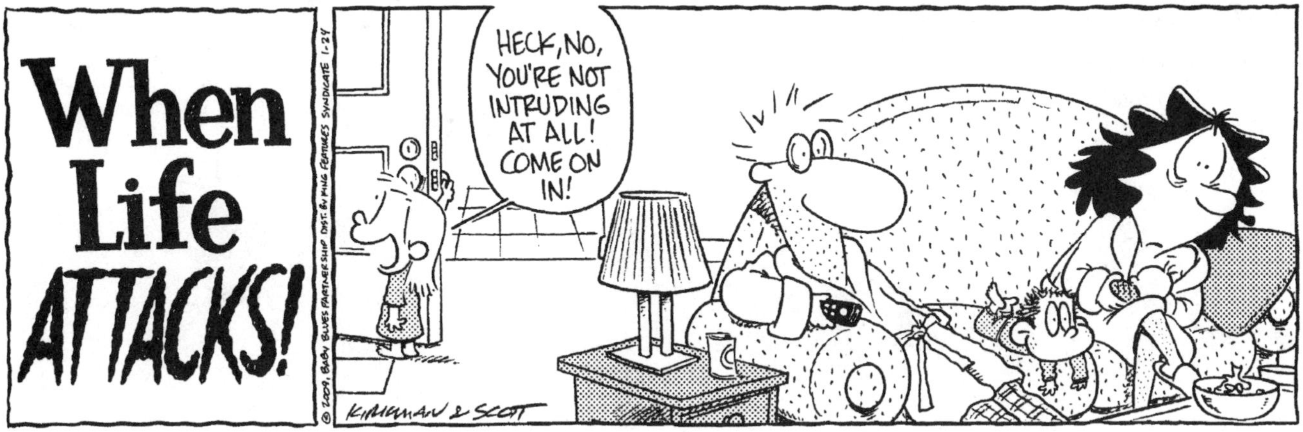
When Life ATTACKS!
©2009, BABY BLUES PARTNERSHIP DIST. BY KING FEATURES SYNDICATE 1-24
HECK, NO, YOU'RE NOT INTRUDING AT ALL! COME ON IN!
KIRKMAN & SCOTT

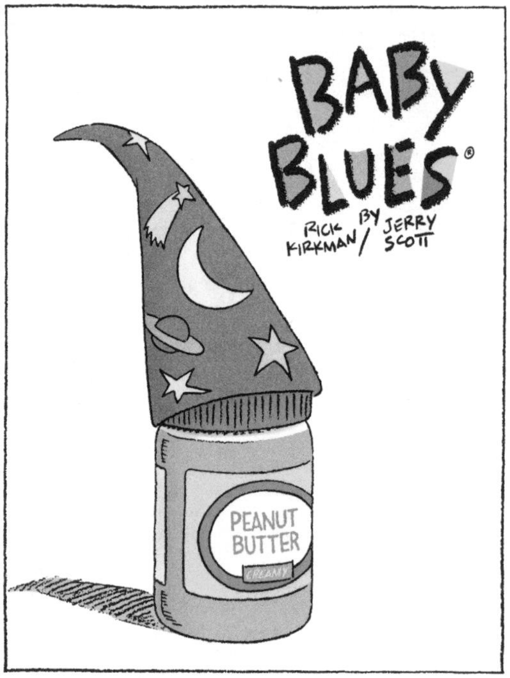
BABY BLUES®
BY RICK KIRKMAN / JERRY SCOTT
PEANUT BUTTER
CREAMY

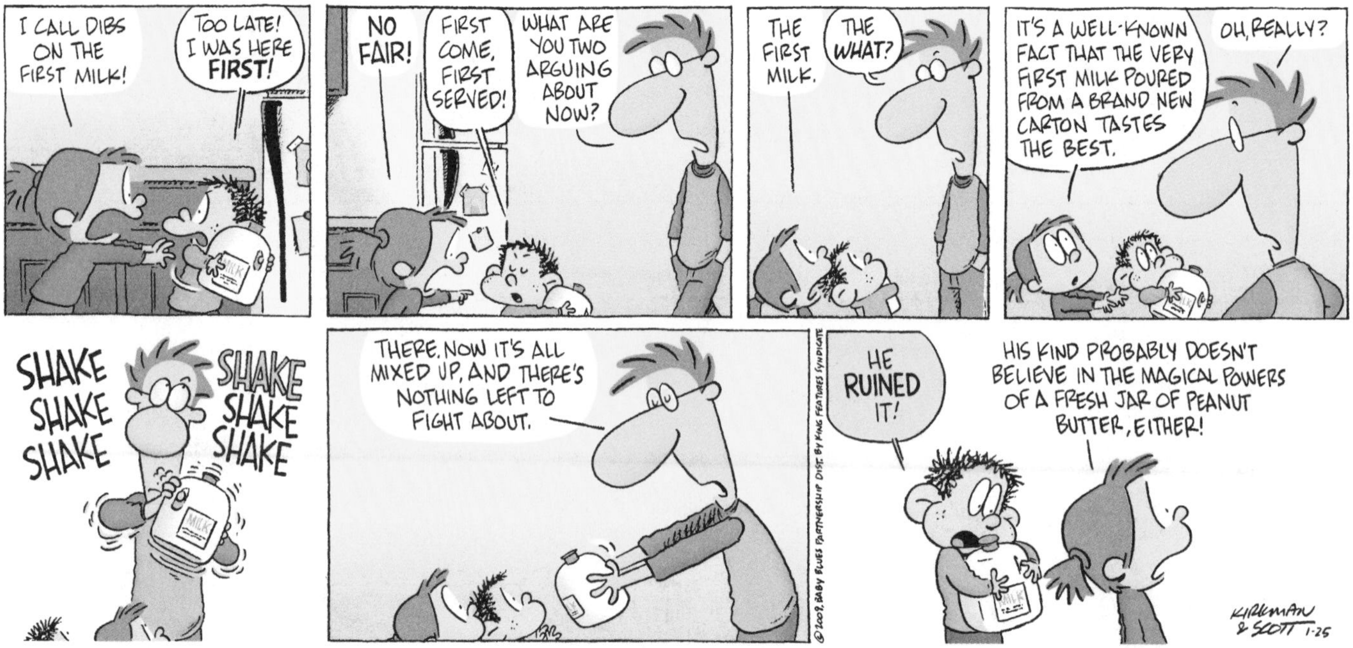
I CALL DIBS ON THE FIRST MILK!
TOO LATE! I WAS HERE **FIRST!**
MILK
NO FAIR!
FIRST COME, FIRST SERVED!
WHAT ARE YOU TWO ARGUING ABOUT NOW?
THE FIRST MILK.
THE **WHAT?**
IT'S A WELL-KNOWN FACT THAT THE VERY FIRST MILK POURED FROM A BRAND NEW CARTON TASTES THE BEST.
OH, REALLY?
SHAKE SHAKE SHAKE
SHAKE SHAKE SHAKE
MILK
THERE. NOW IT'S ALL MIXED UP, AND THERE'S NOTHING LEFT TO FIGHT ABOUT.
© 2009, BABY BLUES PARTNERSHIP DIST. BY KING FEATURES SYNDICATE
HE **RUINED** IT!
HIS KIND PROBABLY DOESN'T BELIEVE IN THE MAGICAL POWERS OF A FRESH JAR OF PEANUT BUTTER, EITHER!
MILK
KIRKMAN & SCOTT 1-25

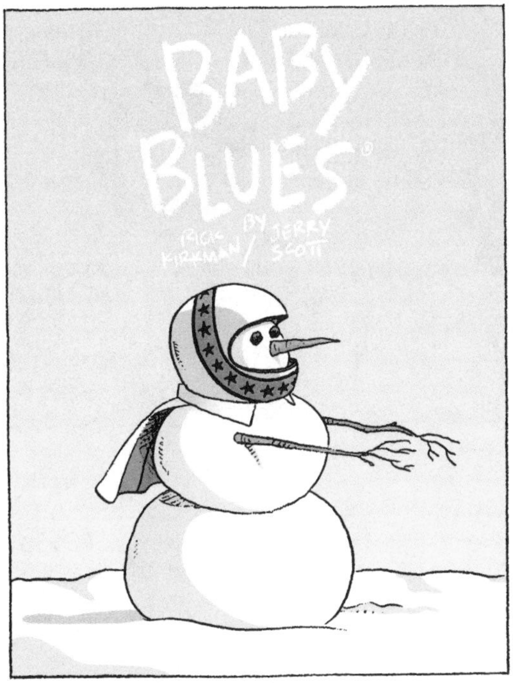
BABY BLUES®
BY RICK KIRKMAN / JERRY SCOTT

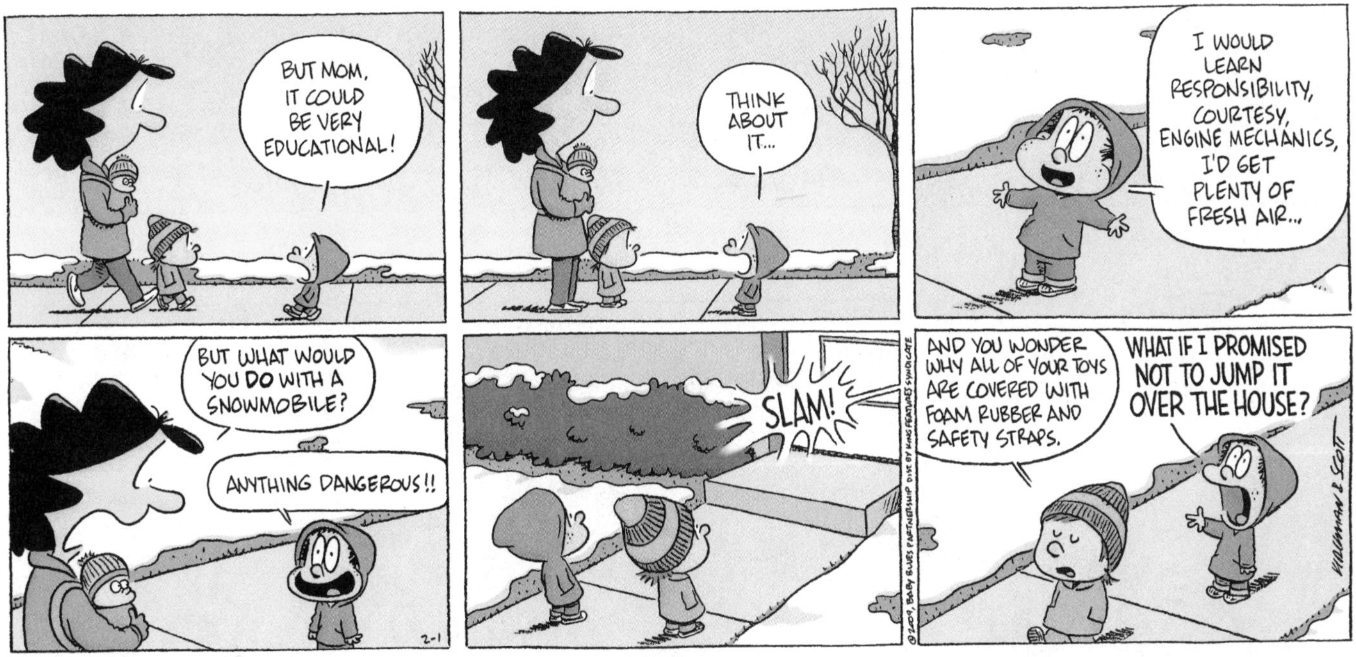
BUT MOM, IT COULD BE VERY EDUCATIONAL!
THINK ABOUT IT...
I WOULD LEARN RESPONSIBILITY, COURTESY, ENGINE MECHANICS, I'D GET PLENTY OF FRESH AIR...
BUT WHAT WOULD YOU **DO** WITH A SNOWMOBILE?
ANYTHING DANGEROUS!!
2-1
SLAM!
©2009, BABY BLUES PARTNERSHIP DIST. BY KING FEATURES SYNDICATE
AND YOU WONDER WHY ALL OF YOUR TOYS ARE COVERED WITH FOAM RUBBER AND SAFETY STRAPS.
WHAT IF I PROMISED NOT TO JUMP IT OVER THE HOUSE?
KIRKMAN & SCOTT

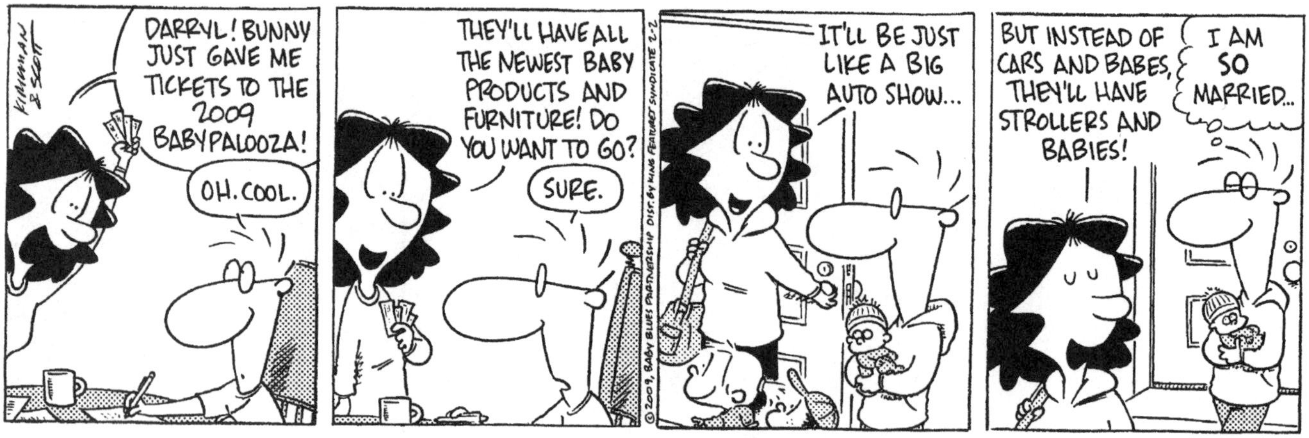
DARRYL! BUNNY JUST GAVE ME TICKETS TO THE 2009 BABYPALOOZA!
OH. COOL.
THEY'LL HAVE ALL THE NEWEST BABY PRODUCTS AND FURNITURE! DO YOU WANT TO GO?
SURE.
IT'LL BE JUST LIKE A BIG AUTO SHOW...
BUT INSTEAD OF CARS AND BABES, THEY'LL HAVE STROLLERS AND BABIES!
I AM SO MARRIED...

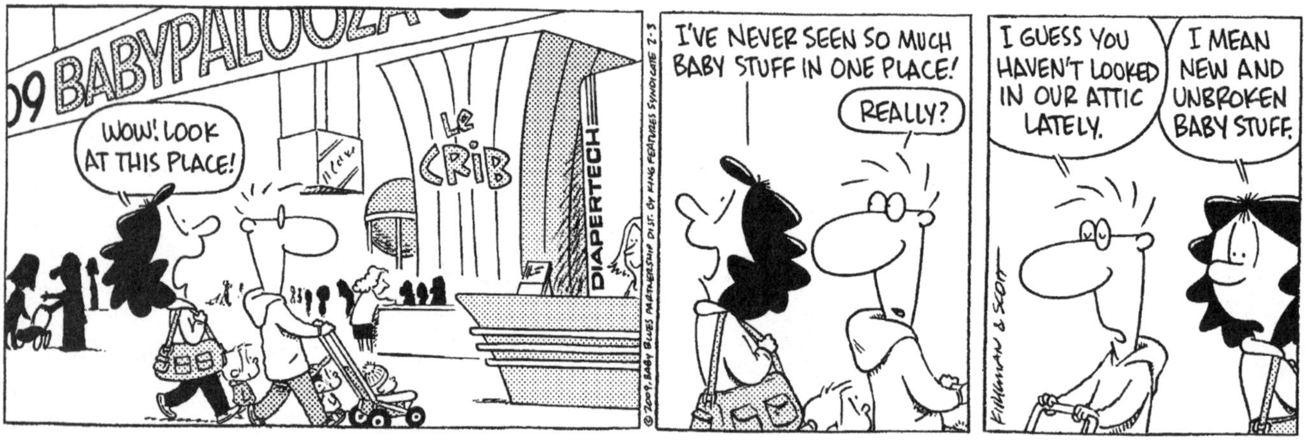
09 BABYPALOOZA
WOW! LOOK AT THIS PLACE!
LE CRIB
DIAPERTECH
I'VE NEVER SEEN SO MUCH BABY STUFF IN ONE PLACE!
REALLY?
I GUESS YOU HAVEN'T LOOKED IN OUR ATTIC LATELY.
I MEAN NEW AND UNBROKEN BABY STUFF.

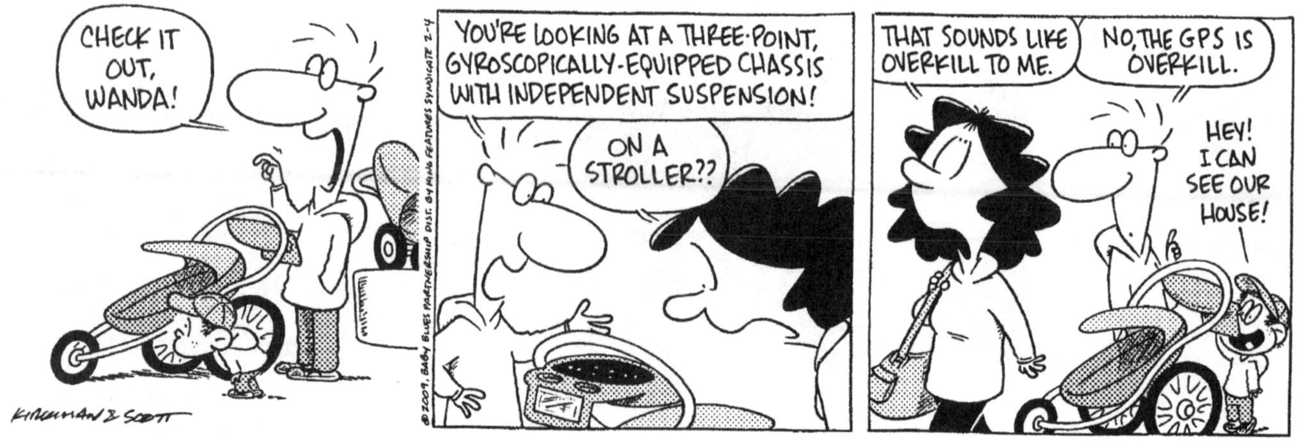
CHECK IT OUT, WANDA!
YOU'RE LOOKING AT A THREE-POINT, GYROSCOPICALLY-EQUIPPED CHASSIS WITH INDEPENDENT SUSPENSION!
ON A STROLLER??
THAT SOUNDS LIKE OVERKILL TO ME.
NO, THE GPS IS OVERKILL.
HEY! I CAN SEE OUR HOUSE!

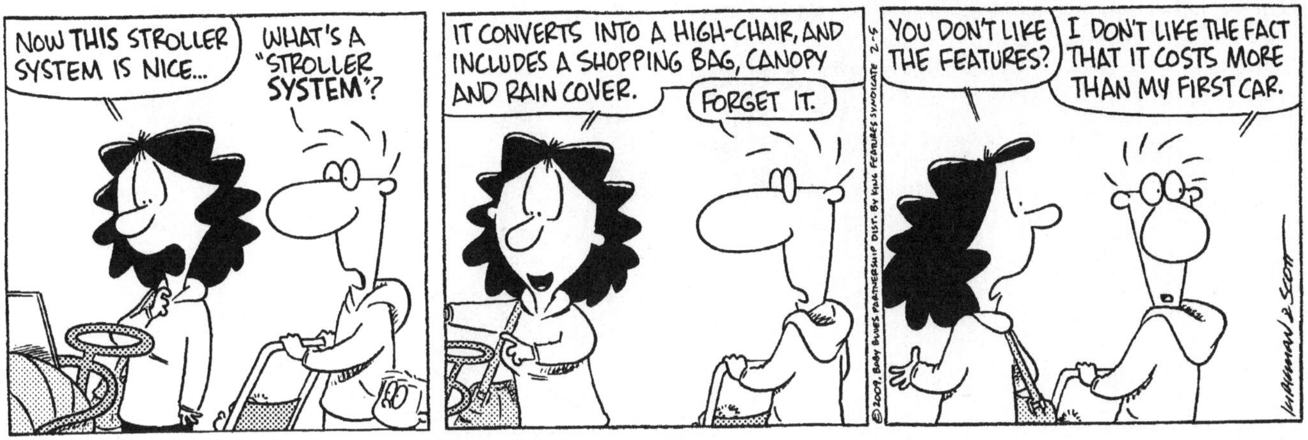
NOW THIS STROLLER SYSTEM IS NICE...
WHAT'S A "STROLLER SYSTEM"?
IT CONVERTS INTO A HIGH-CHAIR, AND INCLUDES A SHOPPING BAG, CANOPY AND RAIN COVER.
FORGET IT.
YOU DON'T LIKE THE FEATURES?
I DON'T LIKE THE FACT THAT IT COSTS MORE THAN MY FIRST CAR.
KIRKMAN & SCOTT

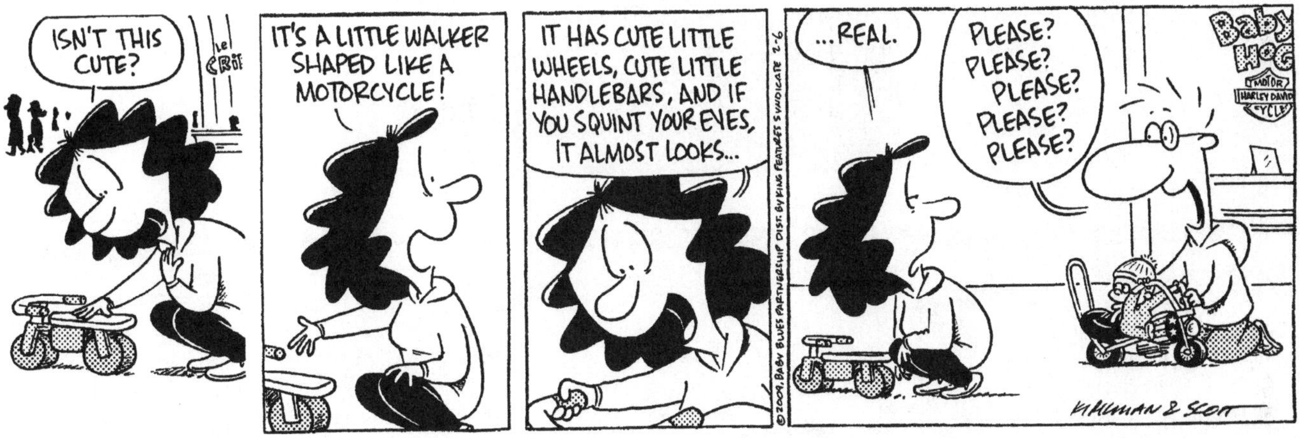
ISN'T THIS CUTE?
IT'S A LITTLE WALKER SHAPED LIKE A MOTORCYCLE!
IT HAS CUTE LITTLE WHEELS, CUTE LITTLE HANDLEBARS, AND IF YOU SQUINT YOUR EYES, IT ALMOST LOOKS...
...REAL.
PLEASE? PLEASE? PLEASE? PLEASE? PLEASE?
Baby HOG
KIRKMAN & SCOTT

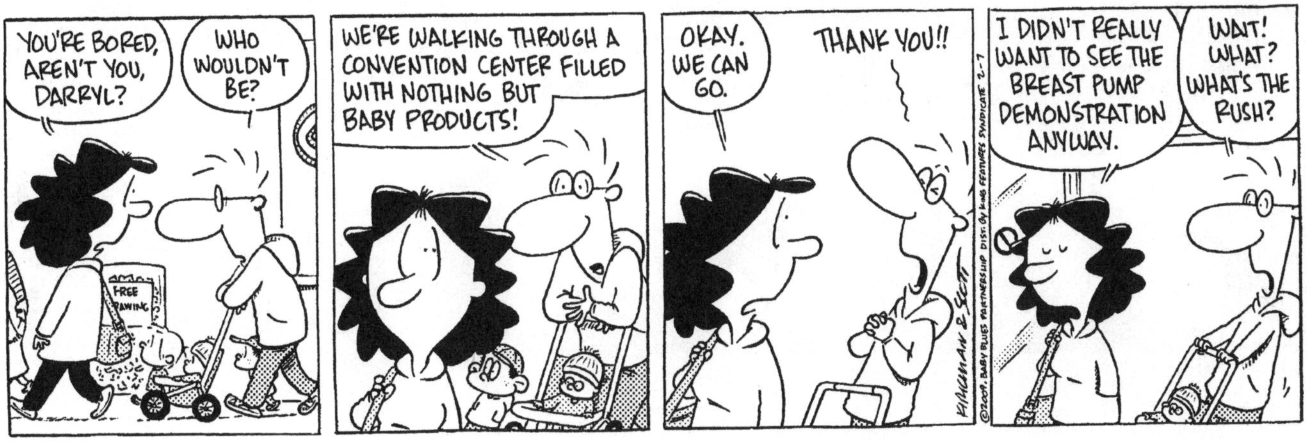
YOU'RE BORED, AREN'T YOU, DARRYL?
WHO WOULDN'T BE?
FREE DRAWING
WE'RE WALKING THROUGH A CONVENTION CENTER FILLED WITH NOTHING BUT BABY PRODUCTS!
OKAY. WE CAN GO.
THANK YOU!!
I DIDN'T REALLY WANT TO SEE THE BREAST PUMP DEMONSTRATION ANYWAY.
WAIT! WHAT? WHAT'S THE RUSH?
KIRKMAN & SCOTT

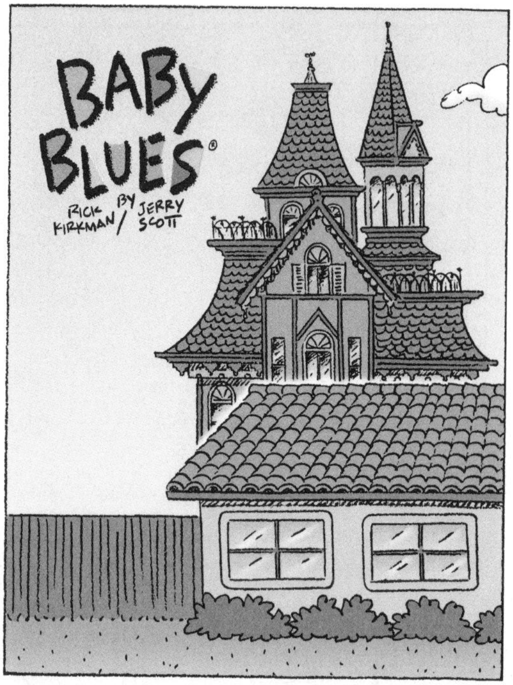

BABY BLUES®
BY RICK KIRKMAN / JERRY SCOTT

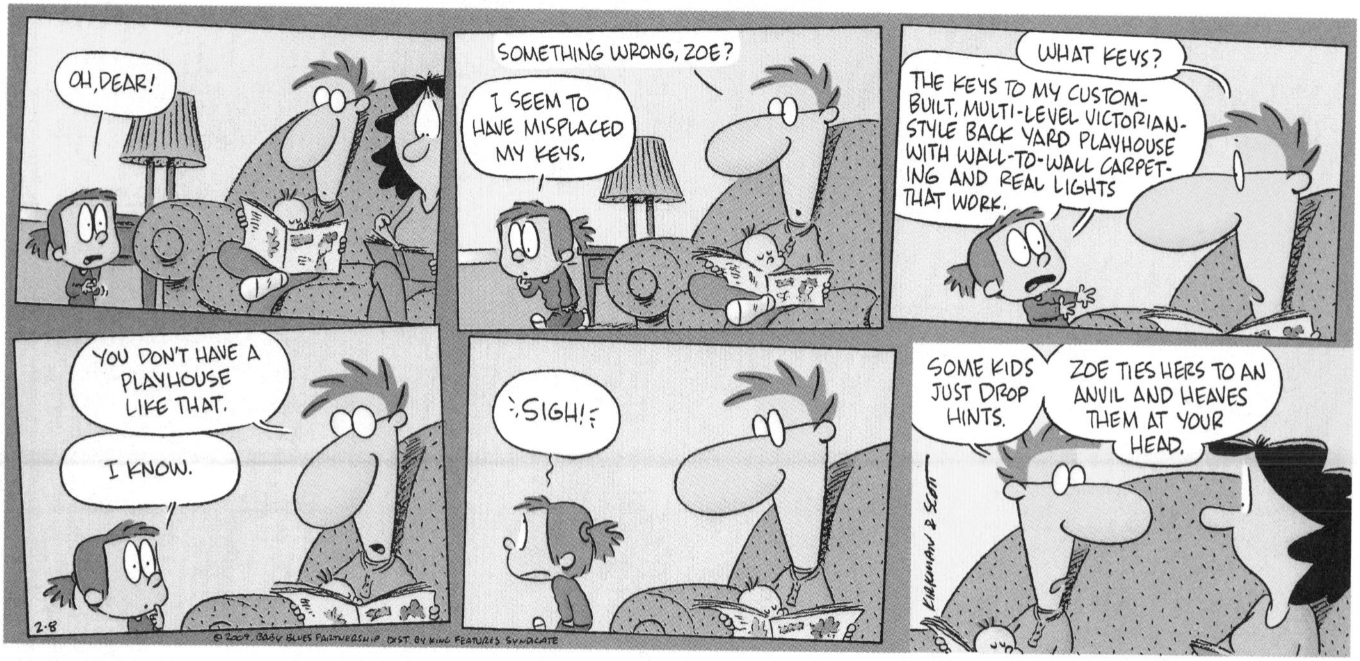

OH, DEAR!
SOMETHING WRONG, ZOE?
I SEEM TO HAVE MISPLACED MY KEYS.
WHAT KEYS?
THE KEYS TO MY CUSTOM-BUILT, MULTI-LEVEL VICTORIAN-STYLE BACK YARD PLAYHOUSE WITH WALL-TO-WALL CARPETING AND REAL LIGHTS THAT WORK.
YOU DON'T HAVE A PLAYHOUSE LIKE THAT.
I KNOW.
SIGH!
SOME KIDS JUST DROP HINTS.
ZOE TIES HERS TO AN ANVIL AND HEAVES THEM AT YOUR HEAD.
KIRKMAN & SCOTT
2-8
© 2009, BABY BLUES PARTNERSHIP DIST. BY KING FEATURES SYNDICATE

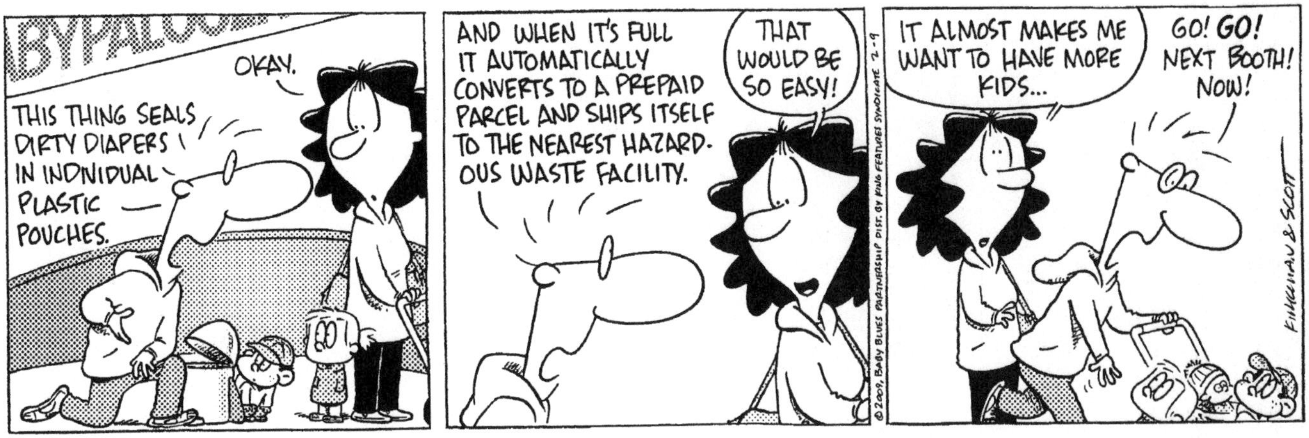
THIS THING SEALS DIRTY DIAPERS IN INDIVIDUAL PLASTIC POUCHES.
OKAY.
AND WHEN IT'S FULL IT AUTOMATICALLY CONVERTS TO A PREPAID PARCEL AND SHIPS ITSELF TO THE NEAREST HAZARD-OUS WASTE FACILITY.
THAT WOULD BE SO EASY!
© 2009, BABY BLUES PARTNERSHIP DIST. BY KING FEATURES SYNDICATE 2-9
IT ALMOST MAKES ME WANT TO HAVE MORE KIDS...
GO! **GO!** NEXT BOOTH! NOW!
KIRKMAN & SCOTT

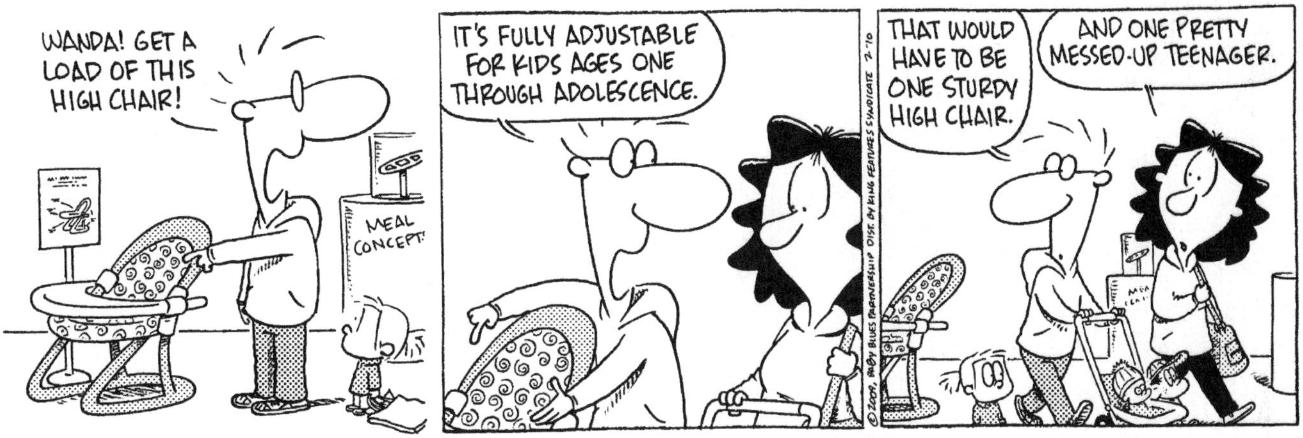
WANDA! GET A LOAD OF THIS HIGH CHAIR!
MEAL CONCEPT
IT'S FULLY ADJUSTABLE FOR KIDS AGES ONE THROUGH ADOLESCENCE.
© 2009, BABY BLUES PARTNERSHIP DIST. BY KING FEATURES SYNDICATE 2-10
THAT WOULD HAVE TO BE ONE STURDY HIGH CHAIR.
AND ONE PRETTY MESSED-UP TEENAGER.

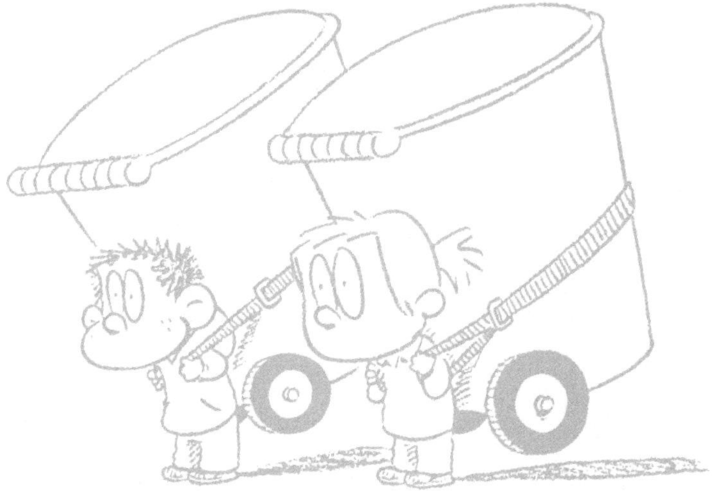

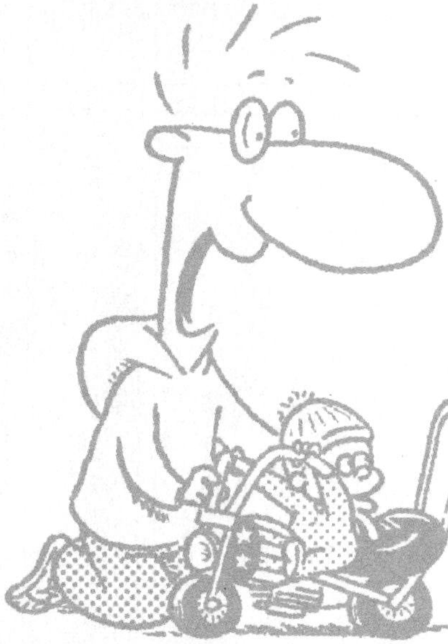

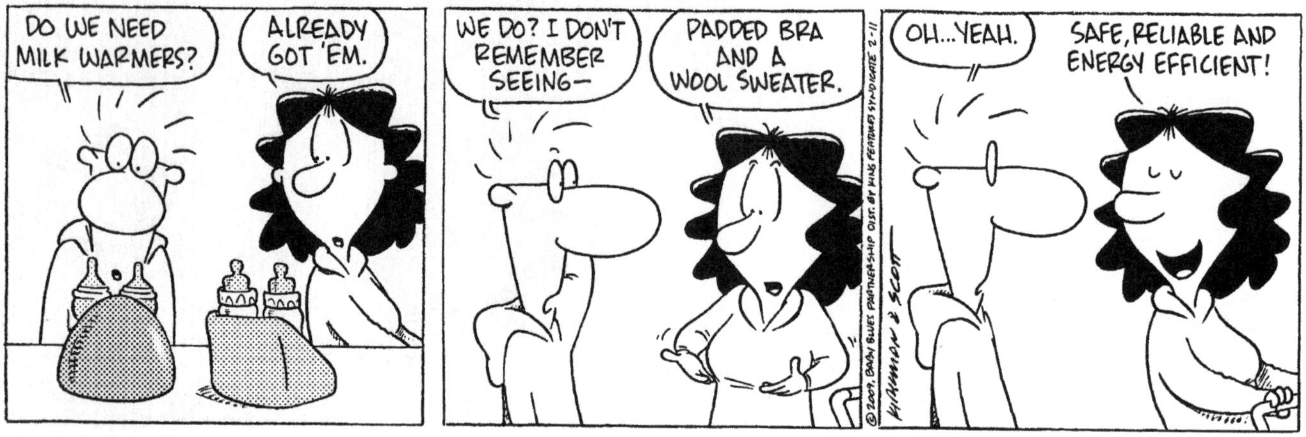
DO WE NEED MILK WARMERS?
ALREADY GOT 'EM.
WE DO? I DON'T REMEMBER SEEING—
PADDED BRA AND A WOOL SWEATER.
© 2009, BABY BLUES PARTNERSHIP DIST. BY KING FEATURES SYNDICATE 2-11
KIRKMAN & SCOTT
OH...YEAH.
SAFE, RELIABLE AND ENERGY EFFICIENT!

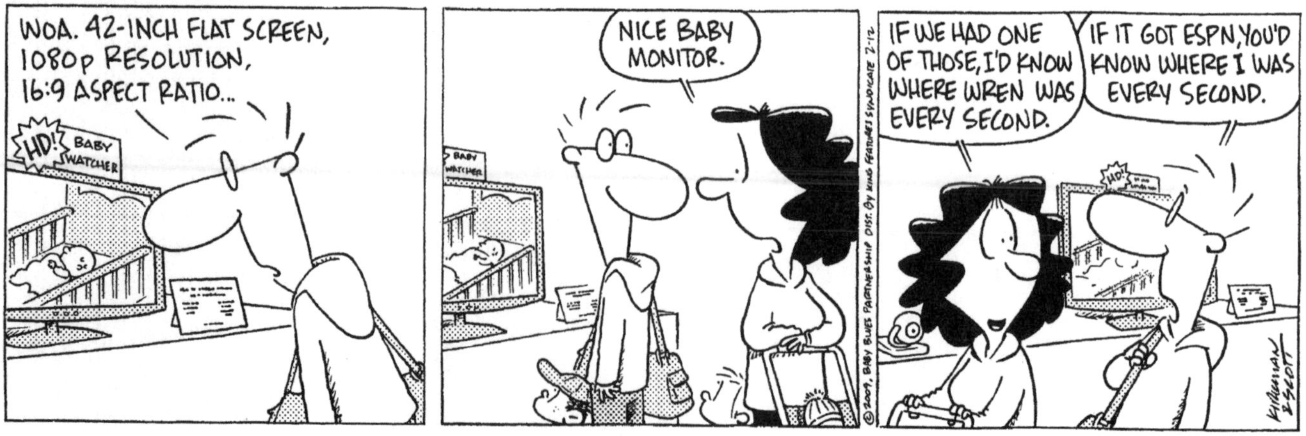
WOA. 42-INCH FLAT SCREEN, 1080p RESOLUTION, 16:9 ASPECT RATIO...
HD!
BABY WATCHER
NICE BABY MONITOR.
© 2009, BABY BLUES PARTNERSHIP DIST. BY KING FEATURES SYNDICATE 2-12
IF WE HAD ONE OF THOSE, I'D KNOW WHERE WREN WAS EVERY SECOND.
IF IT GOT ESPN, YOU'D KNOW WHERE I WAS EVERY SECOND.
KIRKMAN & SCOTT

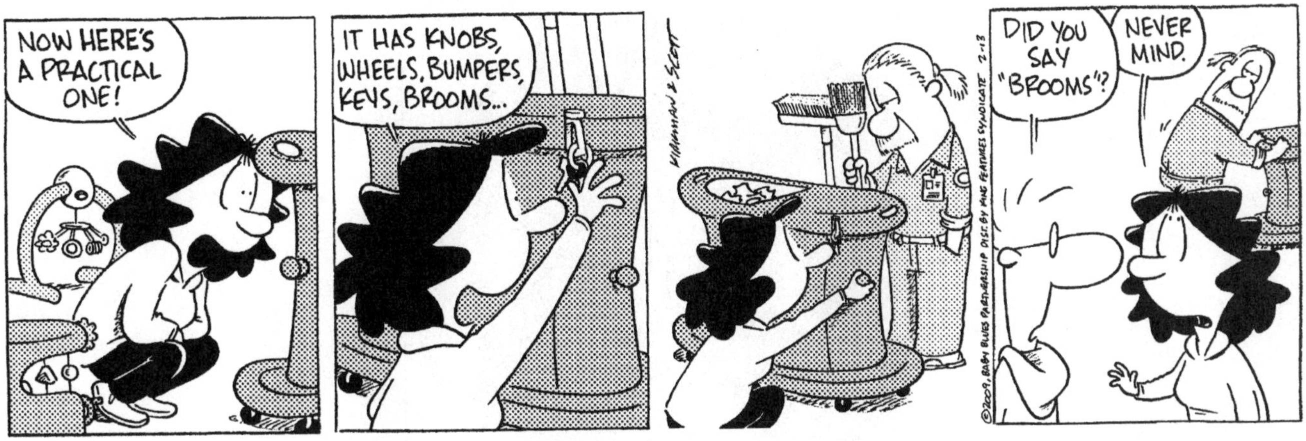
NOW HERE'S A PRACTICAL ONE!
IT HAS KNOBS, WHEELS, BUMPERS, KEYS, BROOMS...
KIRKMAN & SCOTT
©2009, BABY BLUES PARTNERSHIP DIST. BY KING FEATURES SYNDICATE 2-13
DID YOU SAY "BROOMS"?
NEVER MIND.

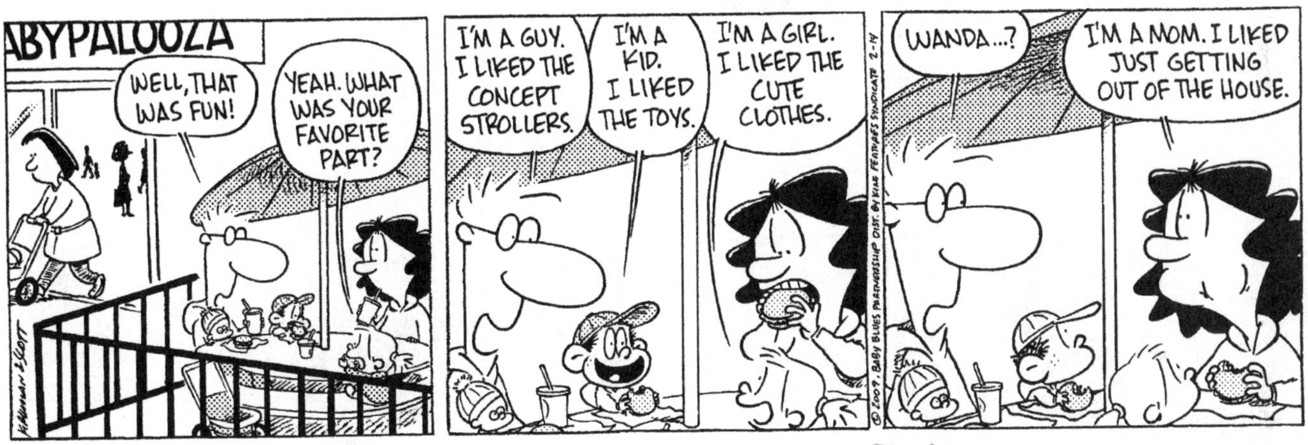
ABYPALOOZA
WELL, THAT WAS FUN!
YEAH. WHAT WAS YOUR FAVORITE PART?
KIRKMAN & SCOTT
I'M A GUY. I LIKED THE CONCEPT STROLLERS.
I'M A KID. I LIKED THE TOYS.
I'M A GIRL. I LIKED THE CUTE CLOTHES.
© 2009, BABY BLUES PARTNERSHIP DIST. BY KING FEATURES SYNDICATE 2-14
WANDA...?
I'M A MOM. I LIKED JUST GETTING OUT OF THE HOUSE.

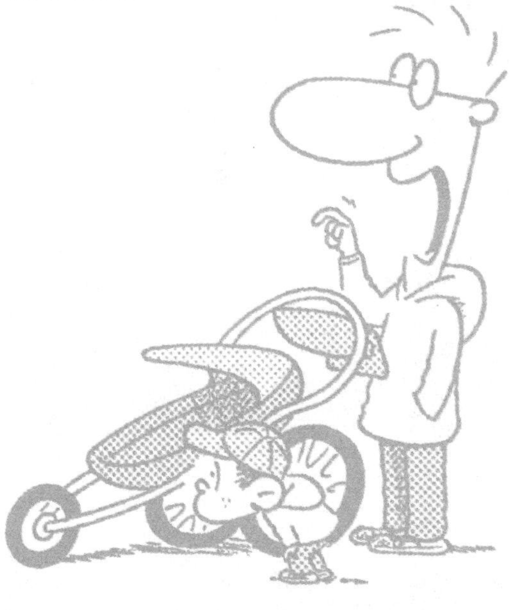

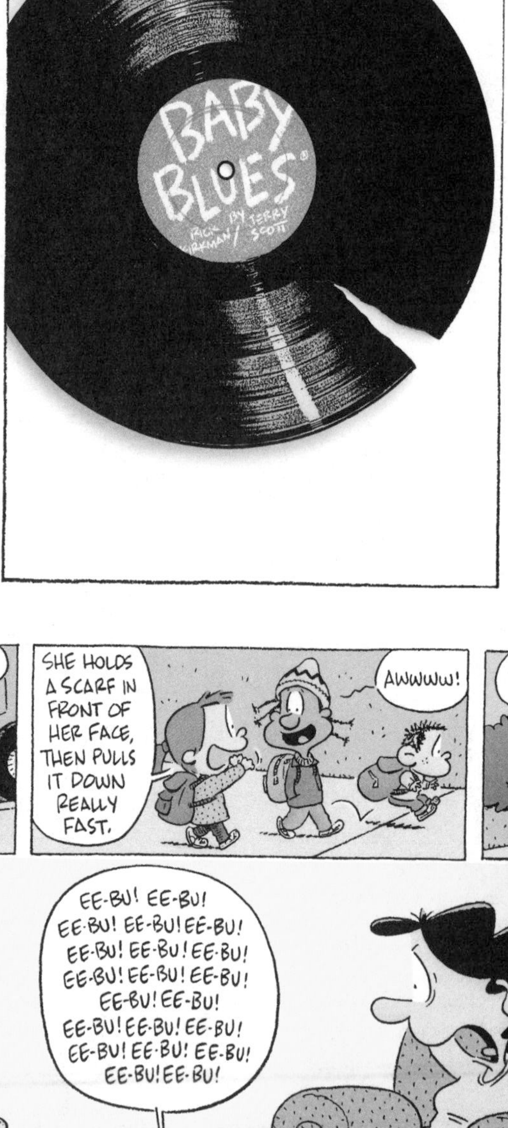
BABY BLUES®
BY RICK KIRKMAN / TERRY SCOTT

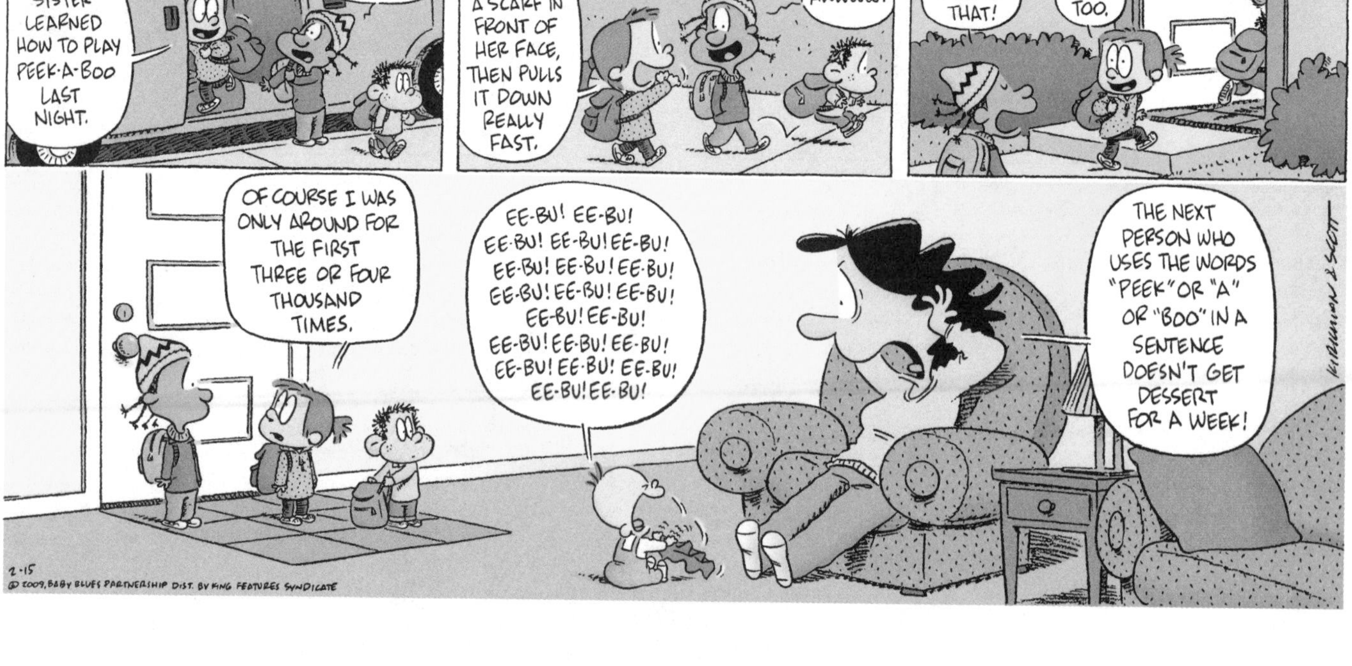
MY BABY SISTER LEARNED HOW TO PLAY PEEK-A-BOO LAST NIGHT.
AWWWW!
SHE HOLDS A SCARF IN FRONT OF HER FACE, THEN PULLS IT DOWN REALLY FAST.
AWWWW!
I **LOVE** THAT!
ME, TOO.
OF COURSE I WAS ONLY AROUND FOR THE FIRST THREE OR FOUR THOUSAND TIMES.
EE-BU! EE-BU!
THE NEXT PERSON WHO USES THE WORDS "PEEK" OR "A" OR "BOO" IN A SENTENCE DOESN'T GET DESSERT FOR A WEEK!
KIRKMAN & SCOTT
2-15
© 2009, BABY BLUES PARTNERSHIP DIST. BY KING FEATURES SYNDICATE

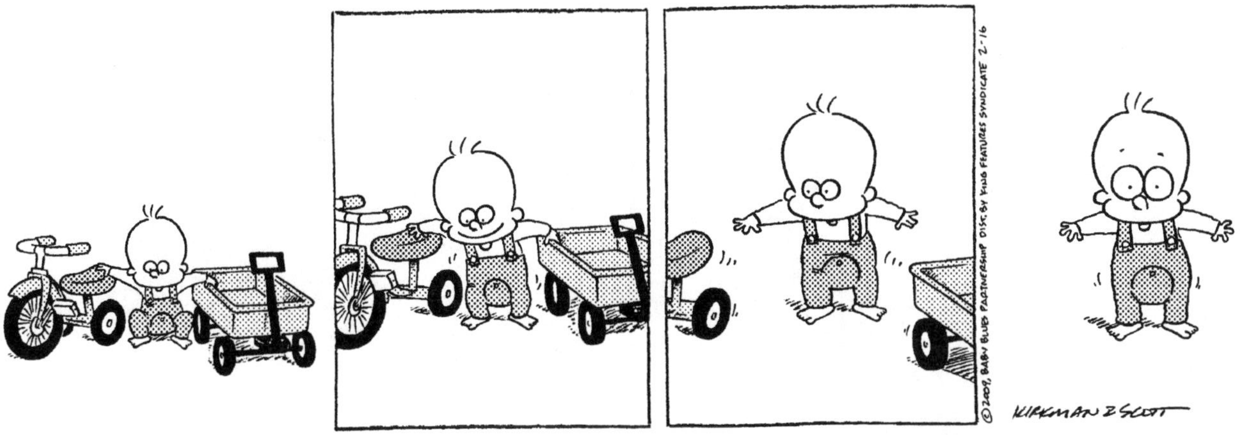
©2009, BABY BLUES PARTNERSHIP DIST. BY KING FEATURES SYNDICATE 2-16
KIRKMAN & SCOTT

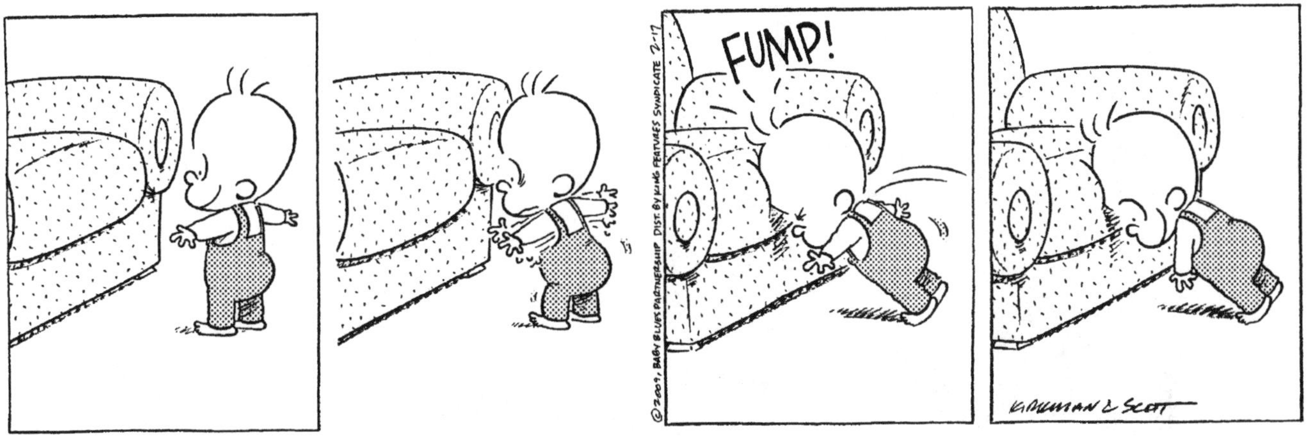
©2009, BABY BLUES PARTNERSHIP DIST. BY KING FEATURES SYNDICATE 2-17
FUMP!
KIRKMAN & SCOTT

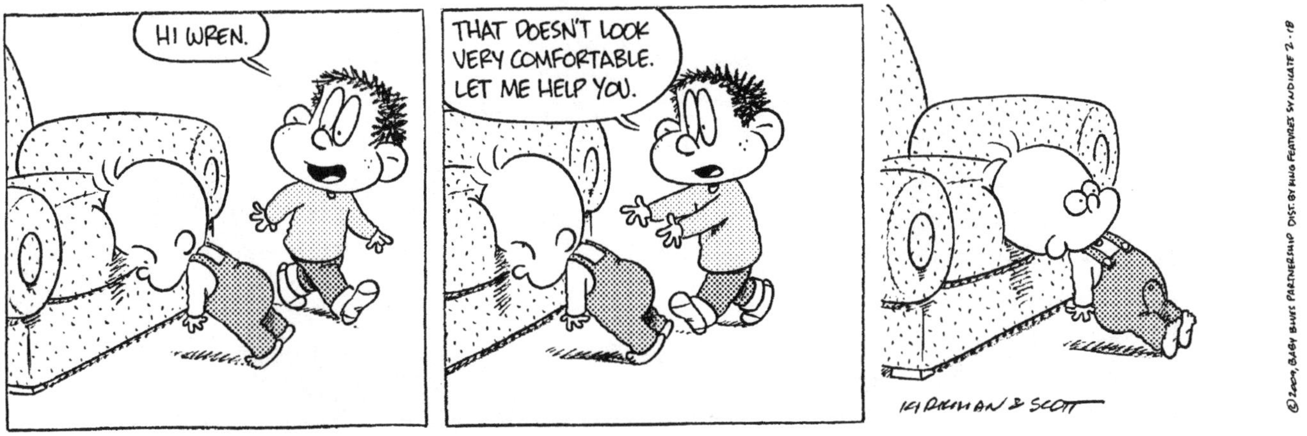
HI WREN.
THAT DOESN'T LOOK VERY COMFORTABLE. LET ME HELP YOU.
KIRKMAN & SCOTT
©2009, BABY BLUES PARTNERSHIP DIST. BY KING FEATURES SYNDICATE 2-18

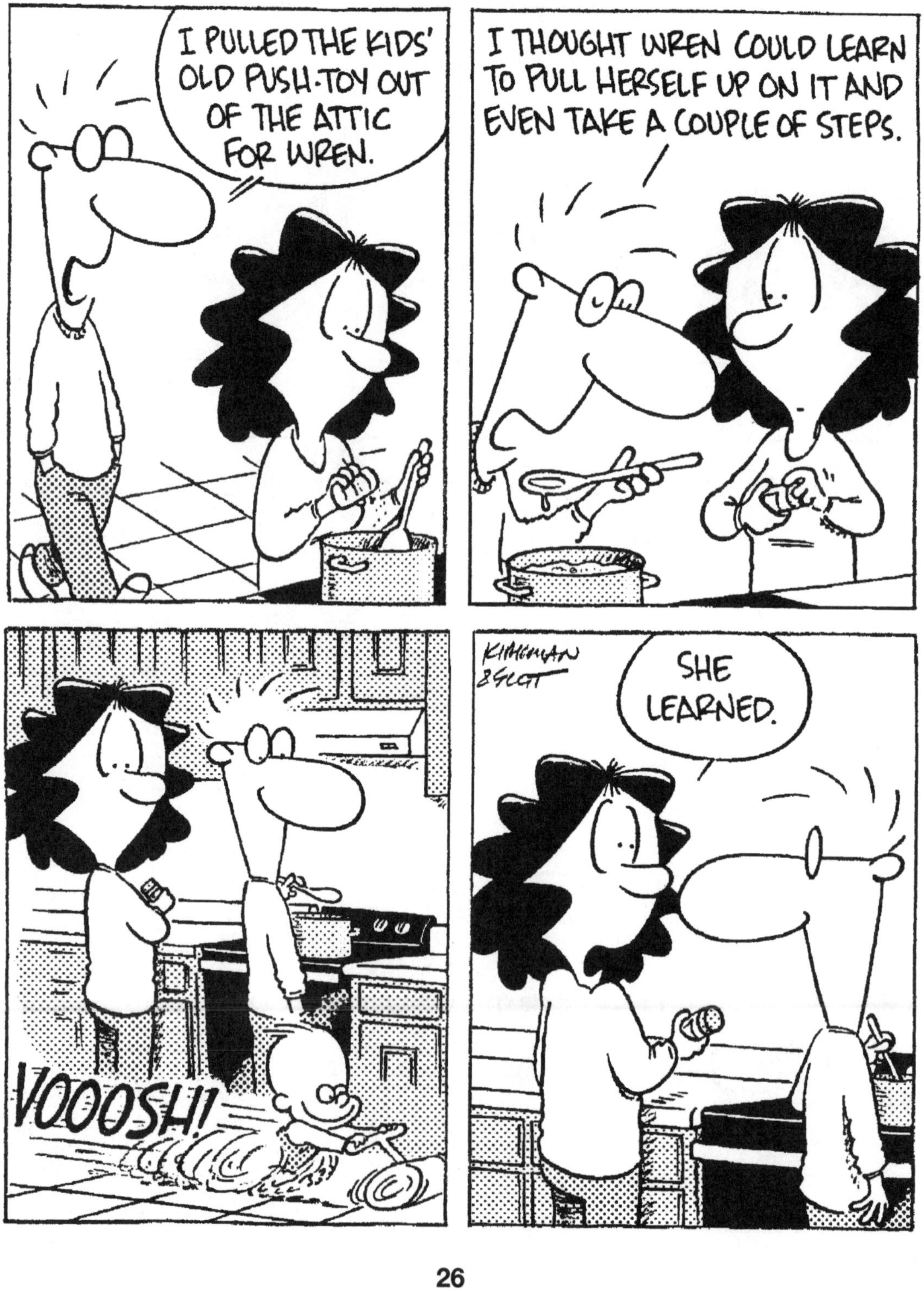
I PULLED THE KIDS' OLD PUSH-TOY OUT OF THE ATTIC FOR WREN.
I THOUGHT WREN COULD LEARN TO PULL HERSELF UP ON IT AND EVEN TAKE A COUPLE OF STEPS.
VOOOSH!
SHE LEARNED.

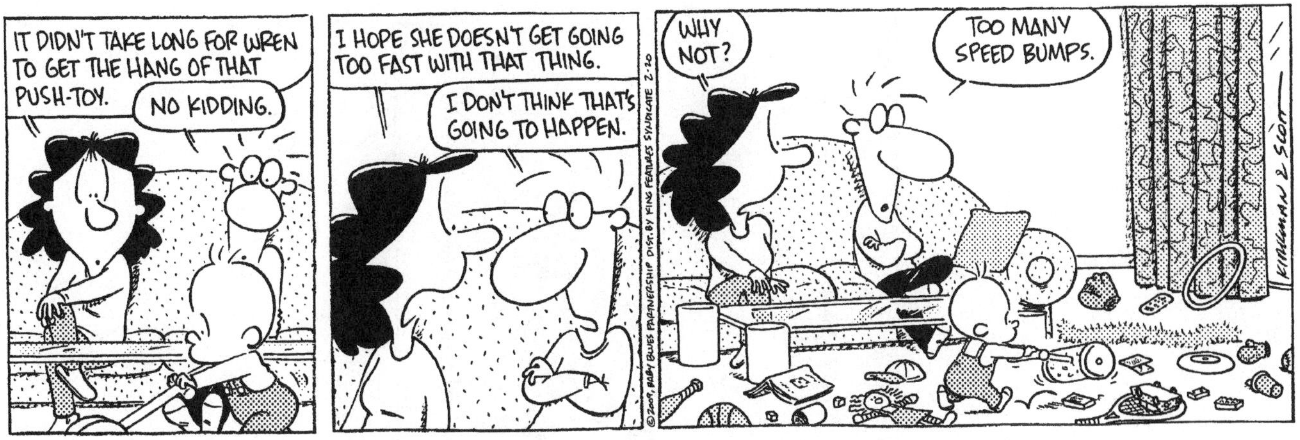
IT DIDN'T TAKE LONG FOR WREN TO GET THE HANG OF THAT PUSH-TOY.
NO KIDDING.
I HOPE SHE DOESN'T GET GOING TOO FAST WITH THAT THING.
I DON'T THINK THAT'S GOING TO HAPPEN.
©2009, BABY BLUES PARTNERSHIP DIST. BY KING FEATURES SYNDICATE 2-20
WHY NOT?
TOO MANY SPEED BUMPS.
KIRKMAN & SCOTT

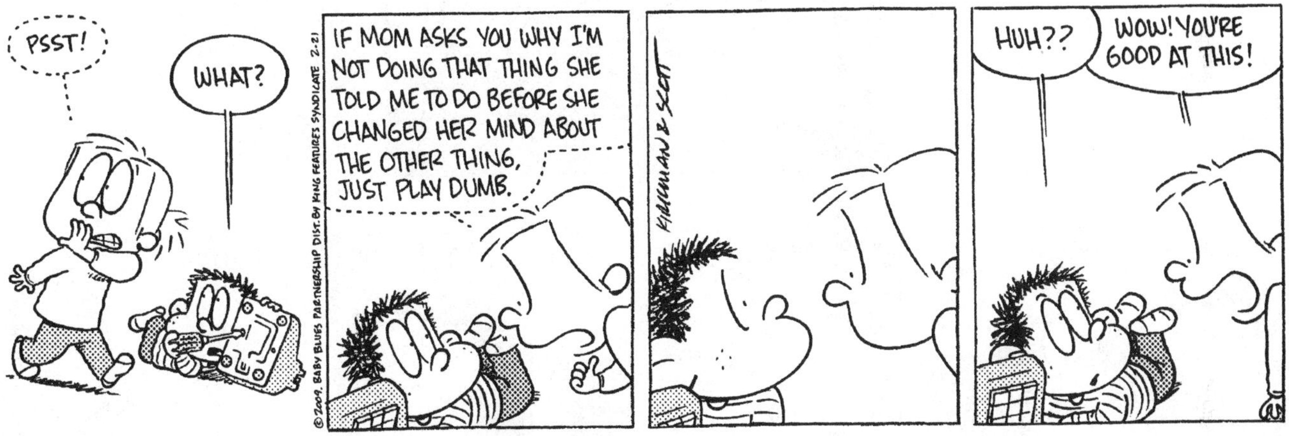
PSST!
WHAT?
©2009, BABY BLUES PARTNERSHIP DIST. BY KING FEATURES SYNDICATE 2-21
IF MOM ASKS YOU WHY I'M NOT DOING THAT THING SHE TOLD ME TO DO BEFORE SHE CHANGED HER MIND ABOUT THE OTHER THING, JUST PLAY DUMB.
KIRKMAN & SCOTT
HUH??
WOW! YOU'RE GOOD AT THIS!

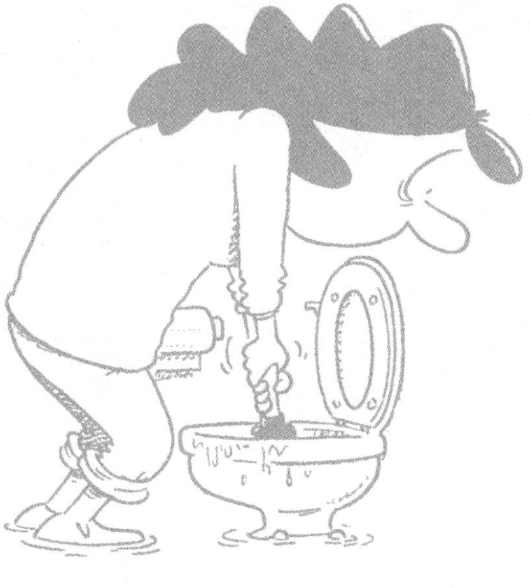

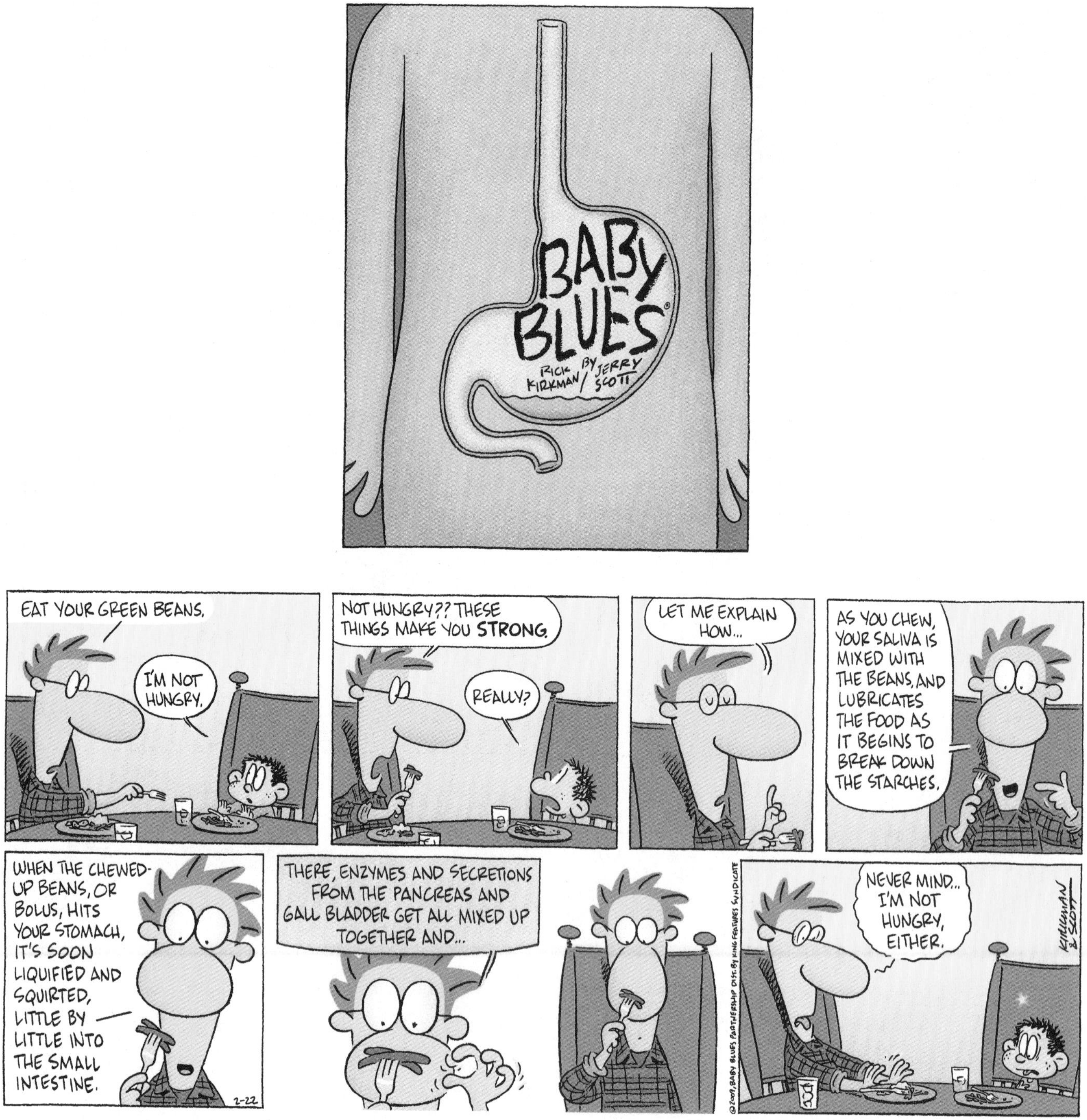
BABY BLUES®
BY RICK KIRKMAN / JERRY SCOTT
EAT YOUR GREEN BEANS.
I'M NOT HUNGRY.
NOT HUNGRY?? THESE THINGS MAKE YOU STRONG.
REALLY?
LET ME EXPLAIN HOW...
AS YOU CHEW, YOUR SALIVA IS MIXED WITH THE BEANS, AND LUBRICATES THE FOOD AS IT BEGINS TO BREAK DOWN THE STARCHES.
WHEN THE CHEWED-UP BEANS, OR BOLUS, HITS YOUR STOMACH, IT'S SOON LIQUIFIED AND SQUIRTED, LITTLE BY LITTLE INTO THE SMALL INTESTINE.
2-22
THERE, ENZYMES AND SECRETIONS FROM THE PANCREAS AND GALL BLADDER GET ALL MIXED UP TOGETHER AND...
©2009, BABY BLUES PARTNERSHIP DIST. BY KING FEATURES SYNDICATE
NEVER MIND... I'M NOT HUNGRY, EITHER.
KIRKMAN & SCOTT

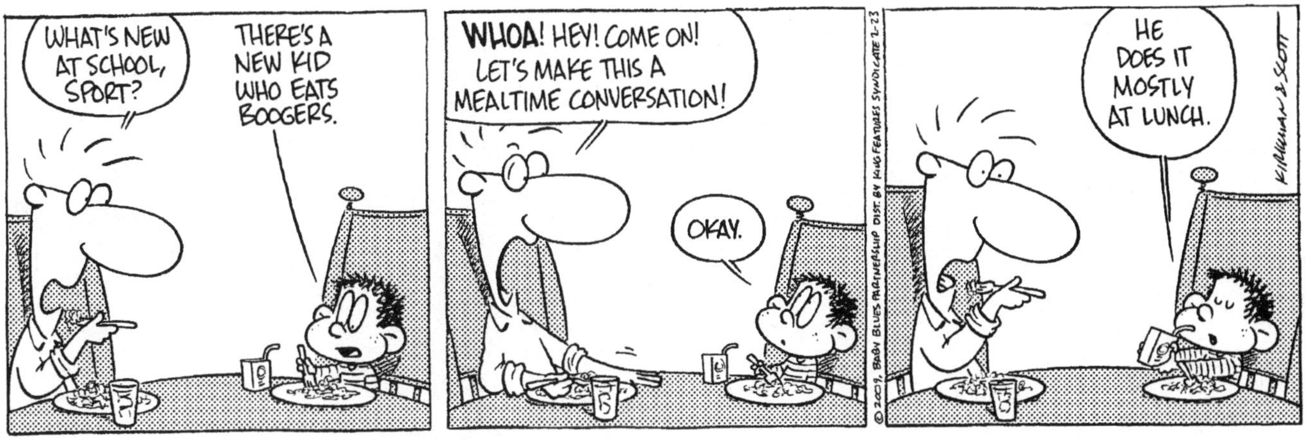
WHAT'S NEW AT SCHOOL, SPORT?
THERE'S A NEW KID WHO EATS BOOGERS.
WHOA! HEY! COME ON! LET'S MAKE THIS A MEALTIME CONVERSATION!
OKAY.
HE DOES IT MOSTLY AT LUNCH.
© 2009, BABY BLUES PARTNERSHIP DIST. BY KING FEATURES SYNDICATE 2-23
KIRKMAN & SCOTT

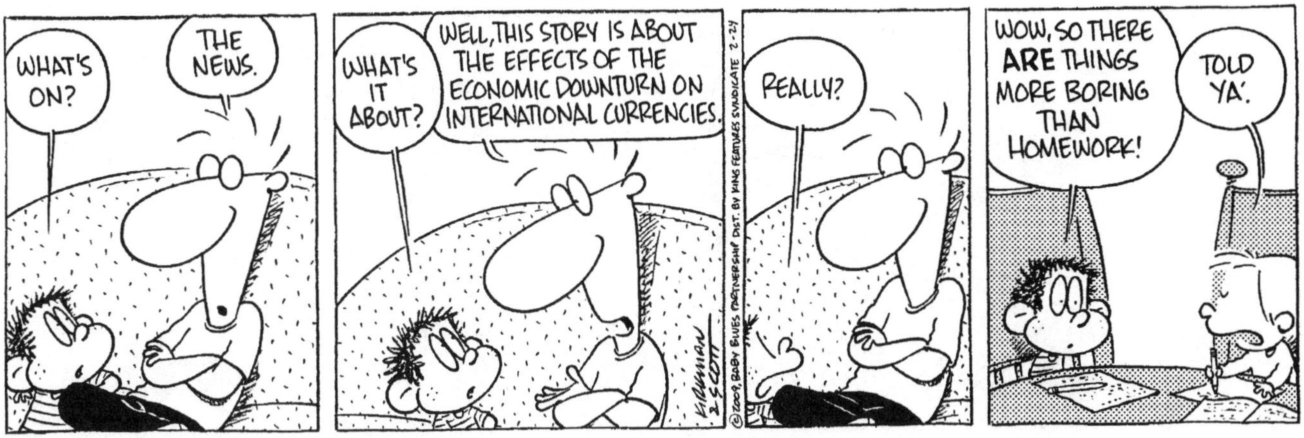
WHAT'S ON?
THE NEWS.
WHAT'S IT ABOUT?
WELL, THIS STORY IS ABOUT THE EFFECTS OF THE ECONOMIC DOWNTURN ON INTERNATIONAL CURRENCIES.
KIRKMAN & SCOTT
© 2009, BABY BLUES PARTNERSHIP DIST. BY KING FEATURES SYNDICATE 2-24
REALLY?
WOW, SO THERE **ARE** THINGS MORE BORING THAN HOMEWORK!
TOLD YA'.

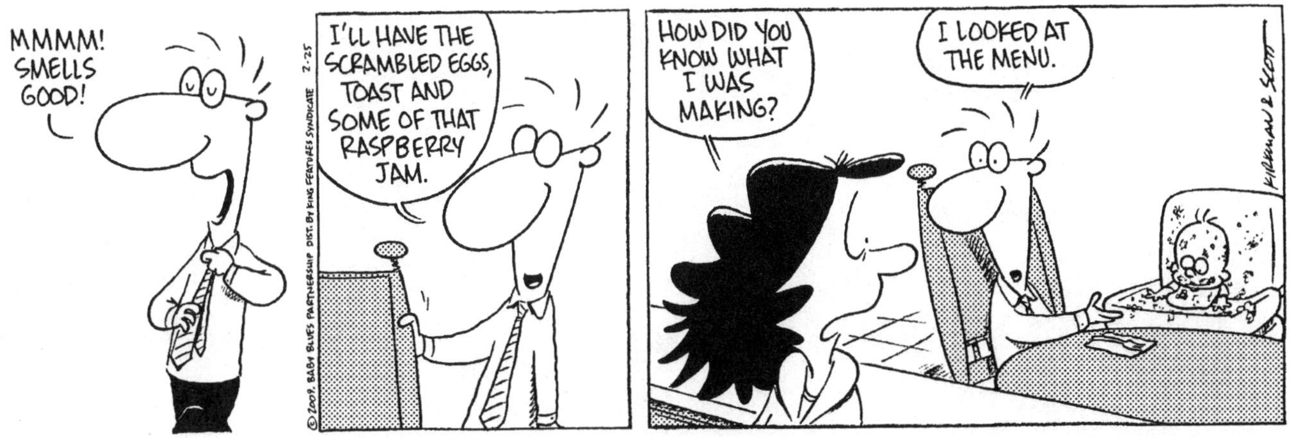
MMMM! SMELLS GOOD!
© 2009, BABY BLUES PARTNERSHIP DIST. BY KING FEATURES SYNDICATE 2-25
I'LL HAVE THE SCRAMBLED EGGS, TOAST AND SOME OF THAT RASPBERRY JAM.
HOW DID YOU KNOW WHAT I WAS MAKING?
I LOOKED AT THE MENU.
KIRKMAN & SCOTT

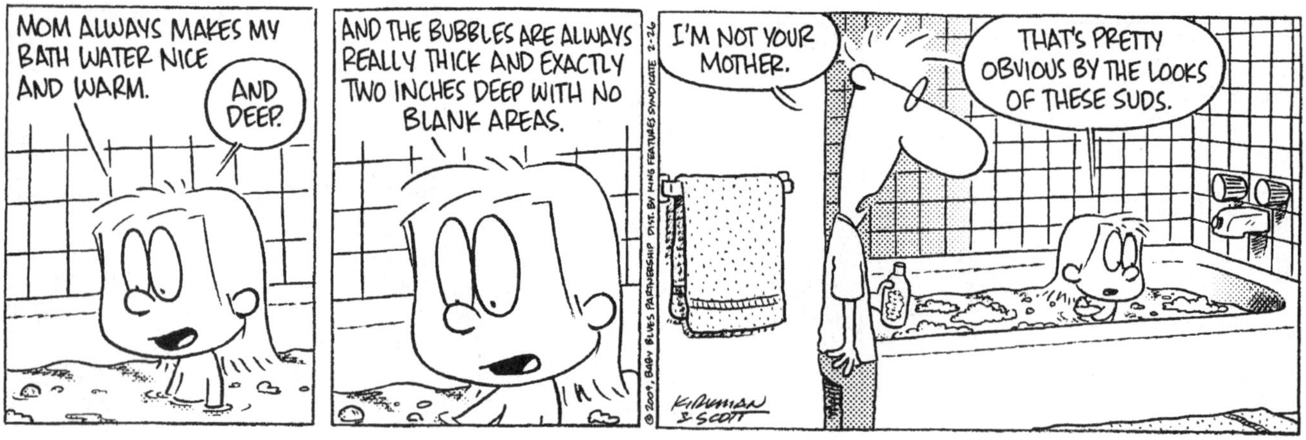
MOM ALWAYS MAKES MY BATH WATER NICE AND WARM.
AND DEEP.
AND THE BUBBLES ARE ALWAYS REALLY THICK AND EXACTLY TWO INCHES DEEP WITH NO BLANK AREAS.
© 2009, BABY BLUES PARTNERSHIP DIST. BY KING FEATURES SYNDICATE 2-26
I'M NOT YOUR MOTHER.
THAT'S PRETTY OBVIOUS BY THE LOOKS OF THESE SUDS.
KIRKMAN & SCOTT

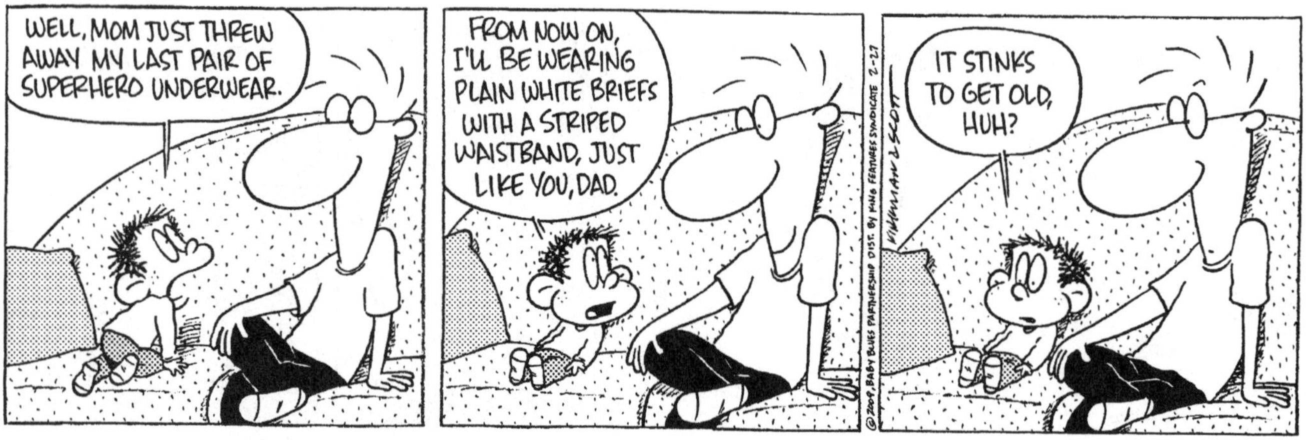
WELL, MOM JUST THREW AWAY MY LAST PAIR OF SUPERHERO UNDERWEAR.
FROM NOW ON, I'LL BE WEARING PLAIN WHITE BRIEFS WITH A STRIPED WAISTBAND, JUST LIKE YOU, DAD.
© 2009, BABY BLUES PARTNERSHIP DIST. BY KING FEATURES SYNDICATE 2-27
KIRKMAN & SCOTT
IT STINKS TO GET OLD, HUH?

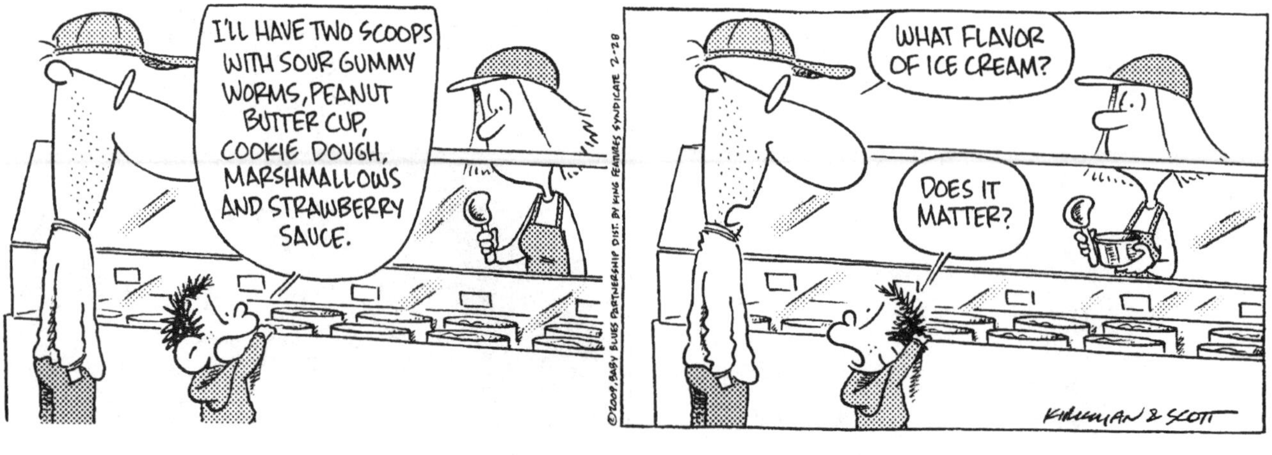
I'LL HAVE TWO SCOOPS WITH SOUR GUMMY WORMS, PEANUT BUTTER CUP, COOKIE DOUGH, MARSHMALLOWS AND STRAWBERRY SAUCE.
© 2009, BABY BLUES PARTNERSHIP DIST. BY KING FEATURES SYNDICATE 2-28
WHAT FLAVOR OF ICE CREAM?
DOES IT MATTER?
KIRKMAN & SCOTT

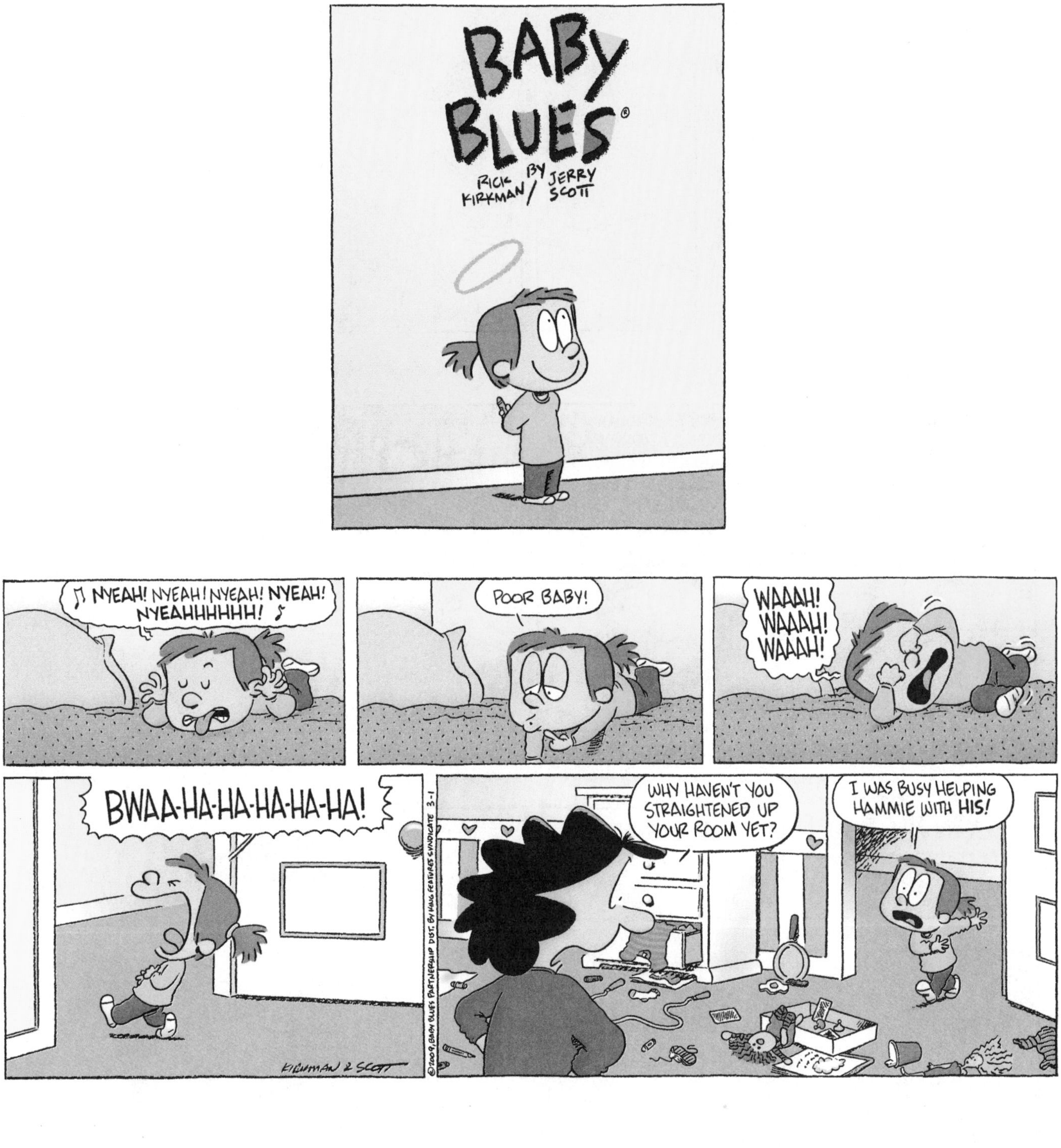
BABY BLUES®
BY RICK KIRKMAN / JERRY SCOTT
NYEAH! NYEAH! NYEAH! NYEAH! NYEAHHHHHH!
POOR BABY!
WAAAH! WAAAH! WAAAH!
BWAA-HA-HA-HA-HA-HA!
©2009, BABY BLUES PARTNERSHIP DIST. BY KING FEATURES SYNDICATE 3-1
KIRKMAN & SCOTT
WHY HAVEN'T YOU STRAIGHTENED UP YOUR ROOM YET?
I WAS BUSY HELPING HAMMIE WITH HIS!

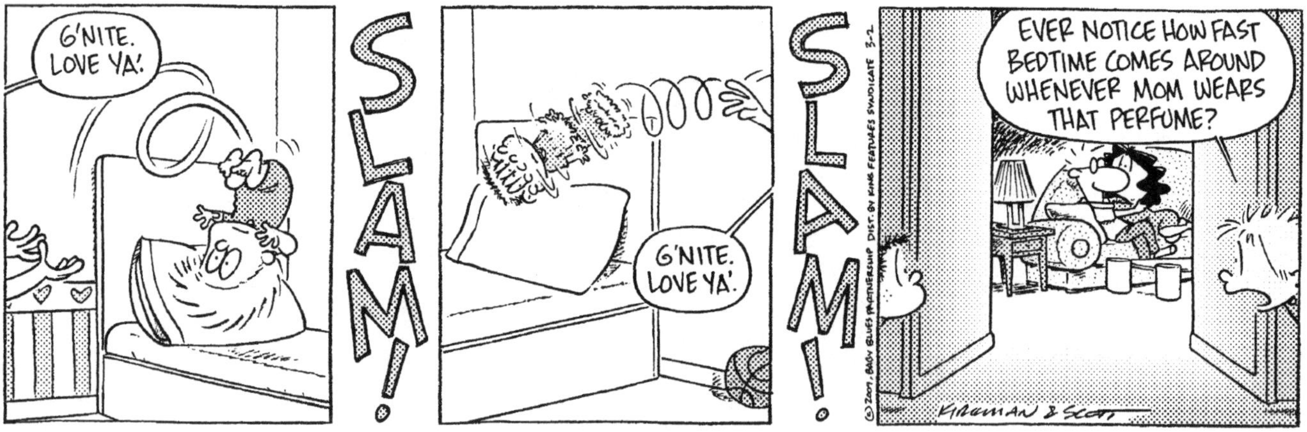
G'NITE. LOVE YA'.
SLAM!
G'NITE. LOVE YA'.
SLAM!
EVER NOTICE HOW FAST BEDTIME COMES AROUND WHENEVER MOM WEARS THAT PERFUME?
KIRKMAN & SCOTT

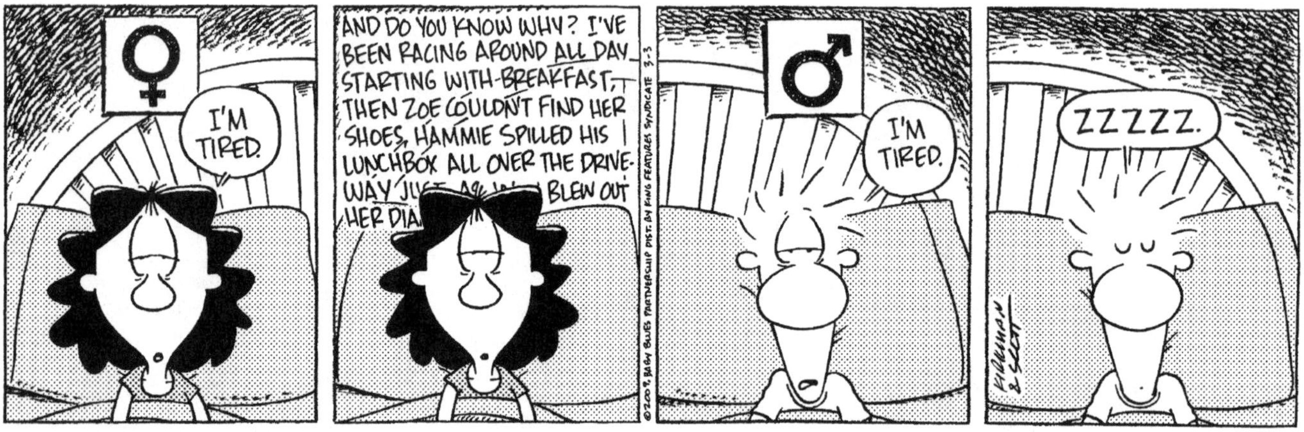
I'M TIRED.
AND DO YOU KNOW WHY? I'VE BEEN RACING AROUND ALL DAY STARTING WITH BREAKFAST, THEN ZOE COULDN'T FIND HER SHOES, HAMMIE SPILLED HIS LUNCHBOX ALL OVER THE DRIVEWAY
BLEW OUT
I'M TIRED.
ZZZZZ.
KIRKMAN & SCOTT

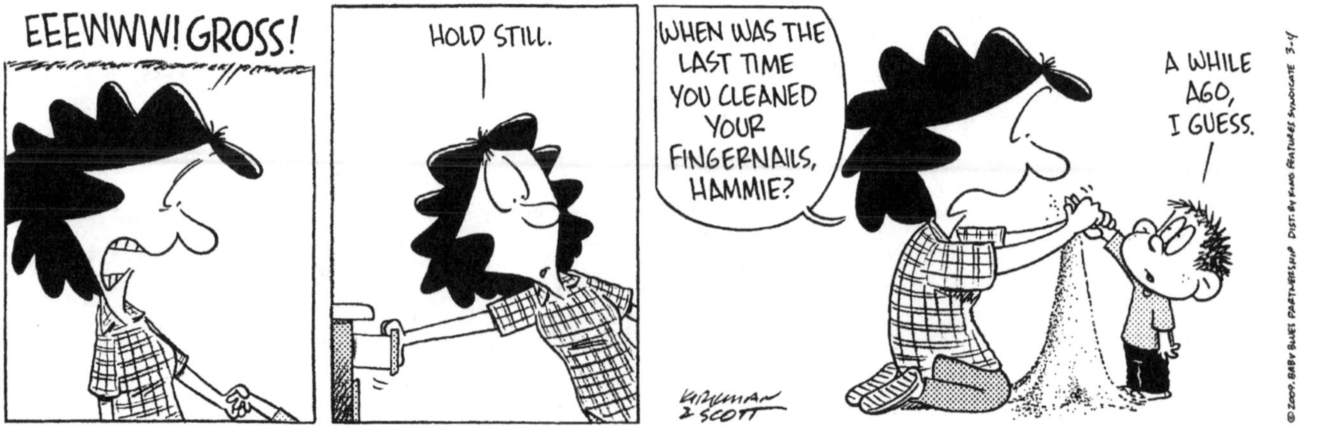
EEEWWW! GROSS!
HOLD STILL.
WHEN WAS THE LAST TIME YOU CLEANED YOUR FINGERNAILS, HAMMIE?
A WHILE AGO, I GUESS.
KIRKMAN & SCOTT

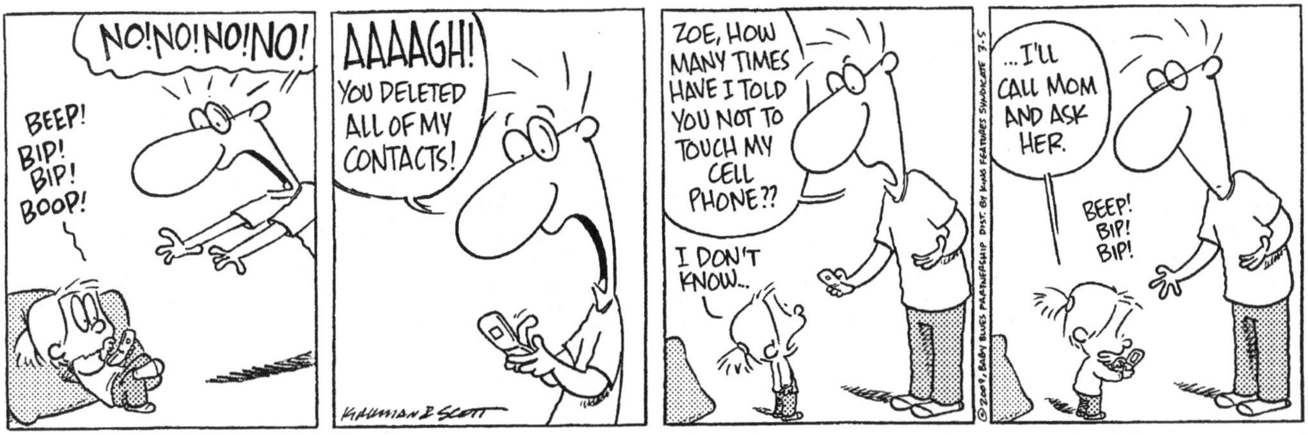
BEEP! BIP! BIP! BOOP!
NO!NO!NO!NO!
AAAAGH! YOU DELETED ALL OF MY CONTACTS!
KIRKMAN & SCOTT
ZOE, HOW MANY TIMES HAVE I TOLD YOU NOT TO TOUCH MY CELL PHONE??
I DON'T KNOW...
©2009, BABY BLUES PARTNERSHIP DIST. BY KING FEATURES SYNDICATE 3-5
...I'LL CALL MOM AND ASK HER.
BEEP! BIP! BIP!

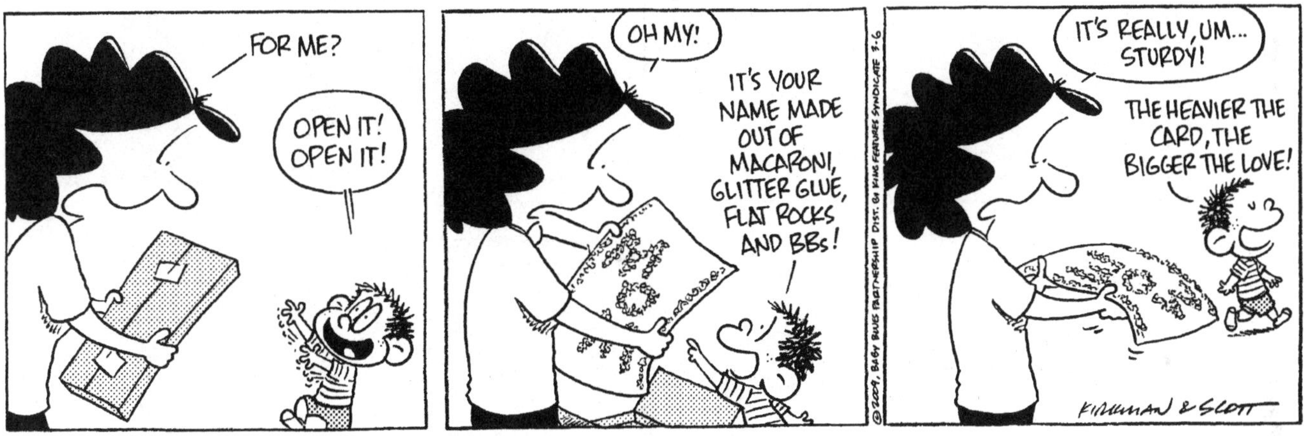
FOR ME?
OPEN IT! OPEN IT!
OH MY!
IT'S YOUR NAME MADE OUT OF MACARONI, GLITTER GLUE, FLAT ROCKS AND BBs!
©2009, BABY BLUES PARTNERSHIP DIST. BY KING FEATURES SYNDICATE 3-6
IT'S REALLY, UM... STURDY!
THE HEAVIER THE CARD, THE BIGGER THE LOVE!
KIRKMAN & SCOTT

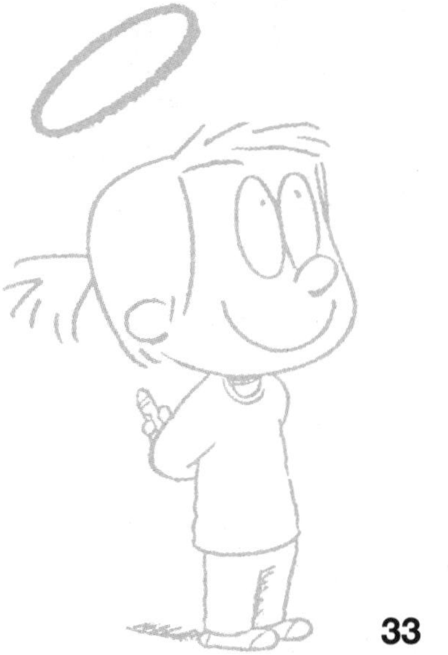

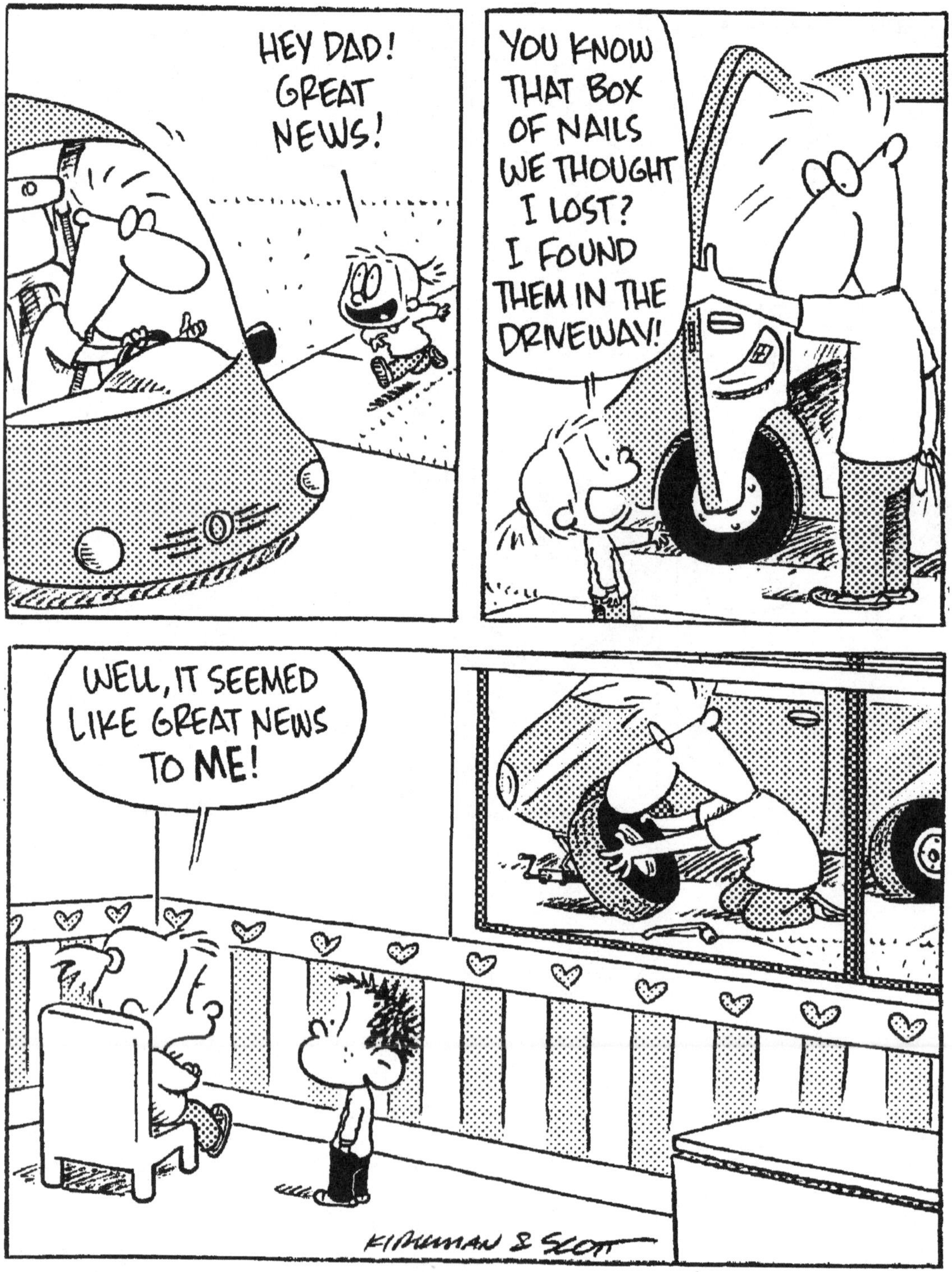
HEY DAD! GREAT NEWS!
YOU KNOW THAT BOX OF NAILS WE THOUGHT I LOST? I FOUND THEM IN THE DRIVEWAY!
WELL, IT SEEMED LIKE GREAT NEWS TO ME!
KIRKMAN & SCOTT

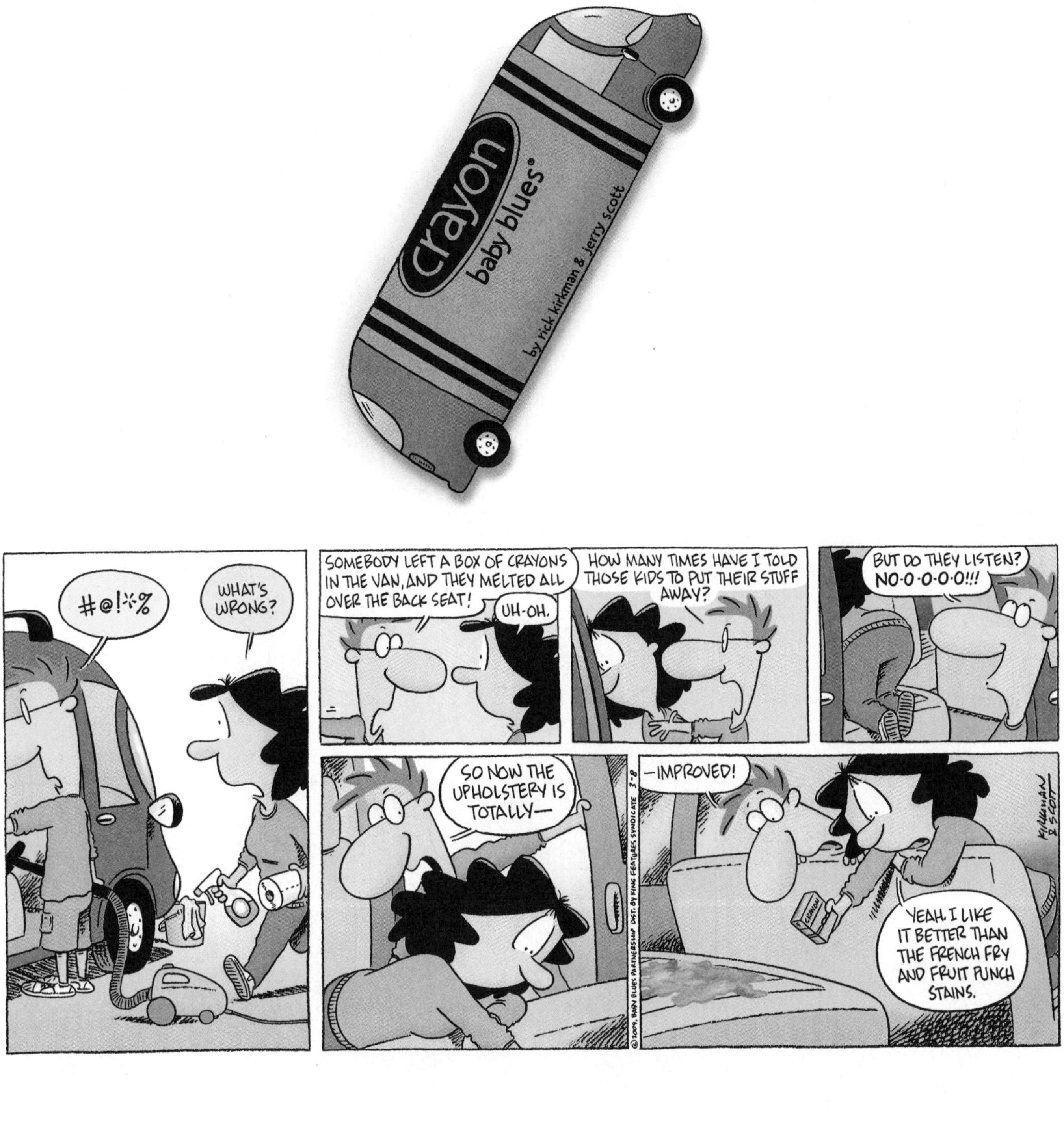
crayon
baby blues®
by rick kirkman & jerry scott
#@!*%
WHAT'S WRONG?
SOMEBODY LEFT A BOX OF CRAYONS IN THE VAN, AND THEY MELTED ALL OVER THE BACK SEAT!
UH-OH.
HOW MANY TIMES HAVE I TOLD THOSE KIDS TO PUT THEIR STUFF AWAY?
BUT DO THEY LISTEN? NO-O-O-O-O!!!
SO NOW THE UPHOLSTERY IS TOTALLY—
©2009, BABY BLUES PARTNERSHIP DIST. BY KING FEATURES SYNDICATE 3-8
—IMPROVED!
YEAH. I LIKE IT BETTER THAN THE FRENCH FRY AND FRUIT PUNCH STAINS.
CRAYON
KIRKMAN & SCOTT

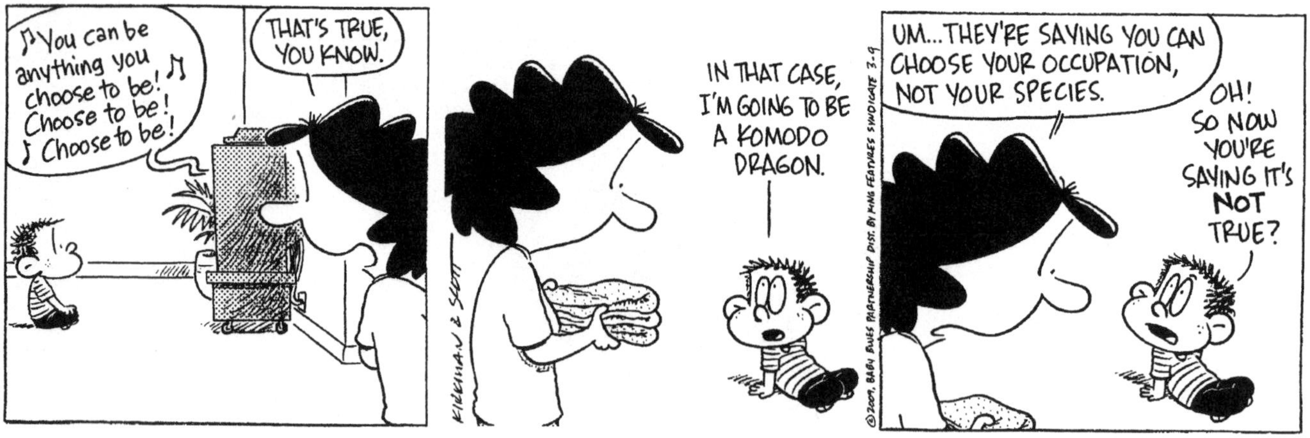
♪You can be anything you choose to be! ♫ Choose to be! ♪ Choose to be!
THAT'S TRUE, YOU KNOW.
KIRKMAN & SCOTT
IN THAT CASE, I'M GOING TO BE A KOMODO DRAGON.
©2009, BABY BLUES PARTNERSHIP DIST. BY KING FEATURES SYNDICATE 3-9
UM...THEY'RE SAYING YOU CAN CHOOSE YOUR OCCUPATION, NOT YOUR SPECIES.
OH! SO NOW YOU'RE SAYING IT'S **NOT** TRUE?

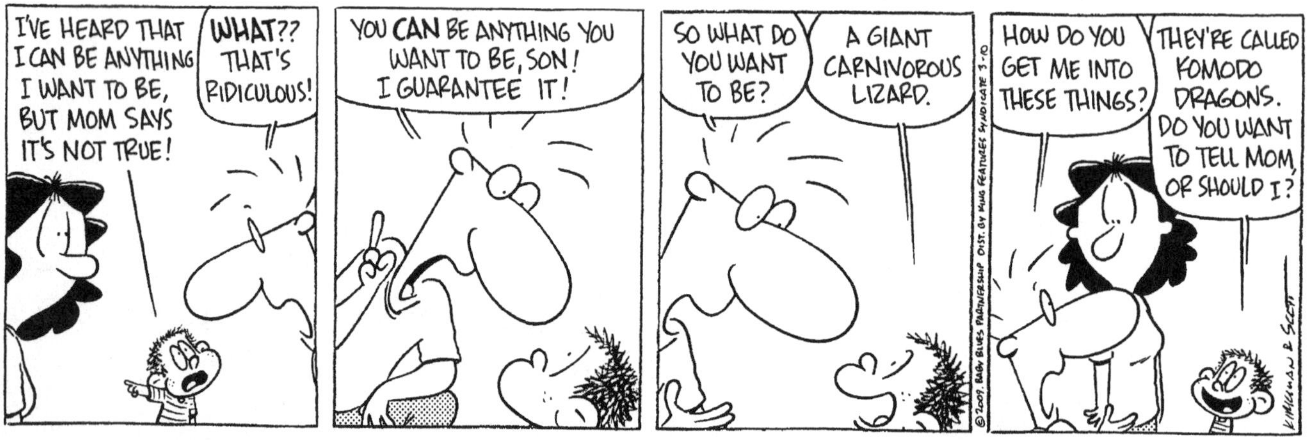
I'VE HEARD THAT I CAN BE ANYTHING I WANT TO BE, BUT MOM SAYS IT'S NOT TRUE!
WHAT?? THAT'S RIDICULOUS!
YOU **CAN** BE ANYTHING YOU WANT TO BE, SON! I GUARANTEE IT!
SO WHAT DO YOU WANT TO BE?
A GIANT CARNIVOROUS LIZARD.
©2009, BABY BLUES PARTNERSHIP DIST. BY KING FEATURES SYNDICATE 3-10
HOW DO YOU GET ME INTO THESE THINGS?
THEY'RE CALLED KOMODO DRAGONS. DO YOU WANT TO TELL MOM, OR SHOULD I?
KIRKMAN & SCOTT

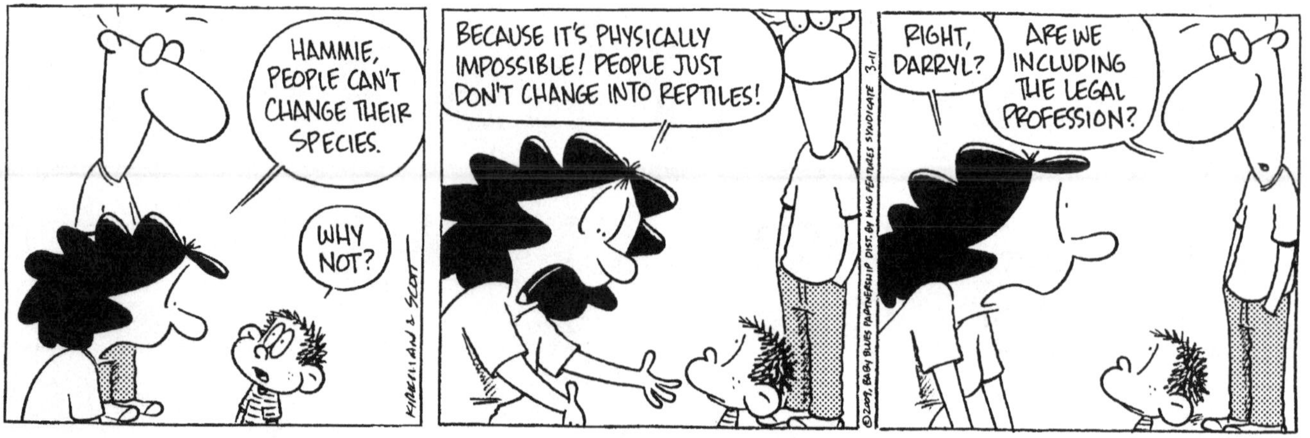
HAMMIE, PEOPLE CAN'T CHANGE THEIR SPECIES.
WHY NOT?
KIRKMAN & SCOTT
BECAUSE IT'S PHYSICALLY IMPOSSIBLE! PEOPLE JUST DON'T CHANGE INTO REPTILES!
©2009, BABY BLUES PARTNERSHIP DIST. BY KING FEATURES SYNDICATE 3-11
RIGHT, DARRYL?
ARE WE INCLUDING THE LEGAL PROFESSION?

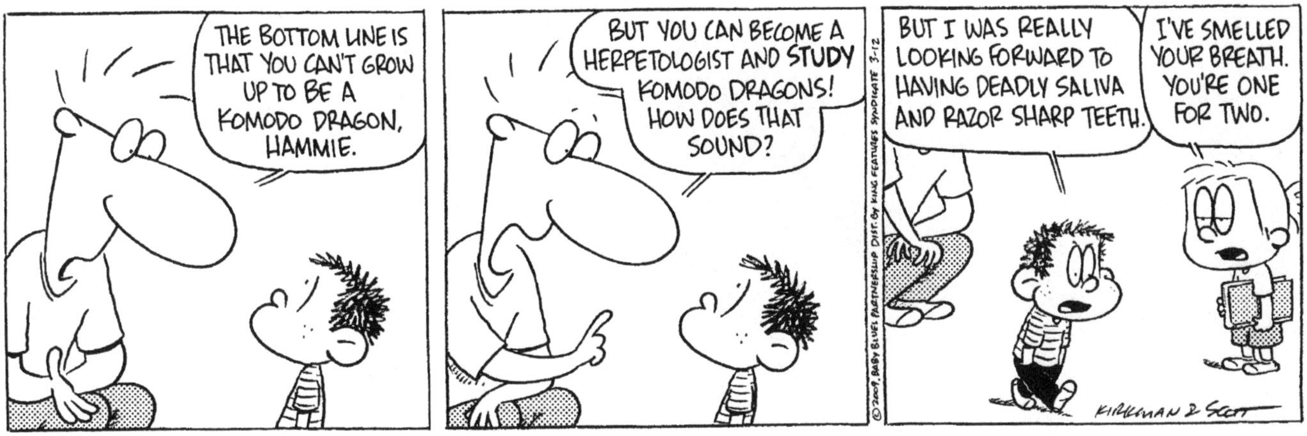
THE BOTTOM LINE IS THAT YOU CAN'T GROW UP TO BE A KOMODO DRAGON, HAMMIE.
BUT YOU CAN BECOME A HERPETOLOGIST AND STUDY KOMODO DRAGONS! HOW DOES THAT SOUND?
©2009, BABY BLUES PARTNERSHIP DIST. BY KING FEATURES SYNDICATE 3-12
BUT I WAS REALLY LOOKING FORWARD TO HAVING DEADLY SALIVA AND RAZOR SHARP TEETH.
I'VE SMELLED YOUR BREATH. YOU'RE ONE FOR TWO.
KIRKMAN & SCOTT

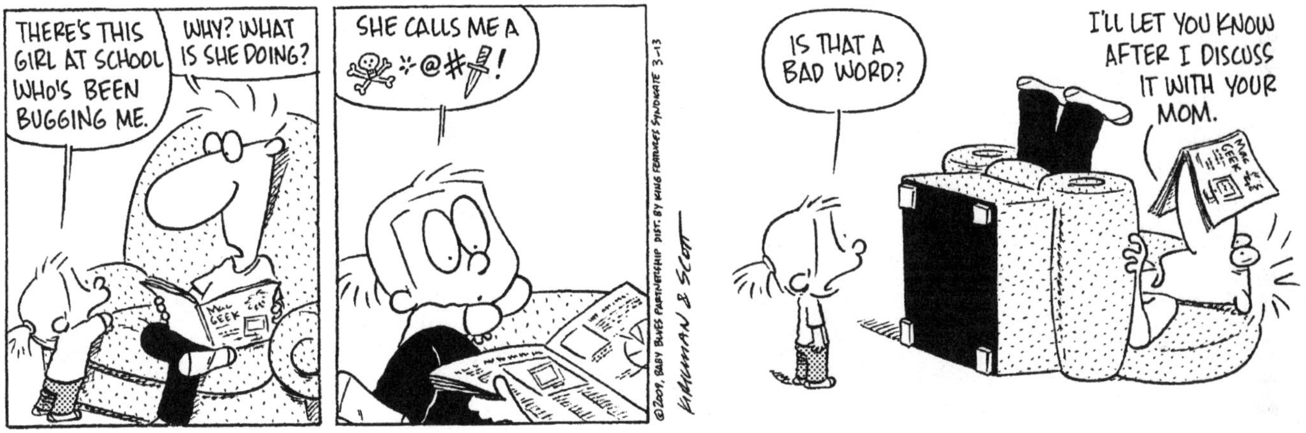
THERE'S THIS GIRL AT SCHOOL WHO'S BEEN BUGGING ME.
WHY? WHAT IS SHE DOING?
SHE CALLS ME A @#!
©2009, BABY BLUES PARTNERSHIP DIST. BY KING FEATURES SYNDICATE 3-13
KIRKMAN & SCOTT
IS THAT A BAD WORD?
I'LL LET YOU KNOW AFTER I DISCUSS IT WITH YOUR MOM.

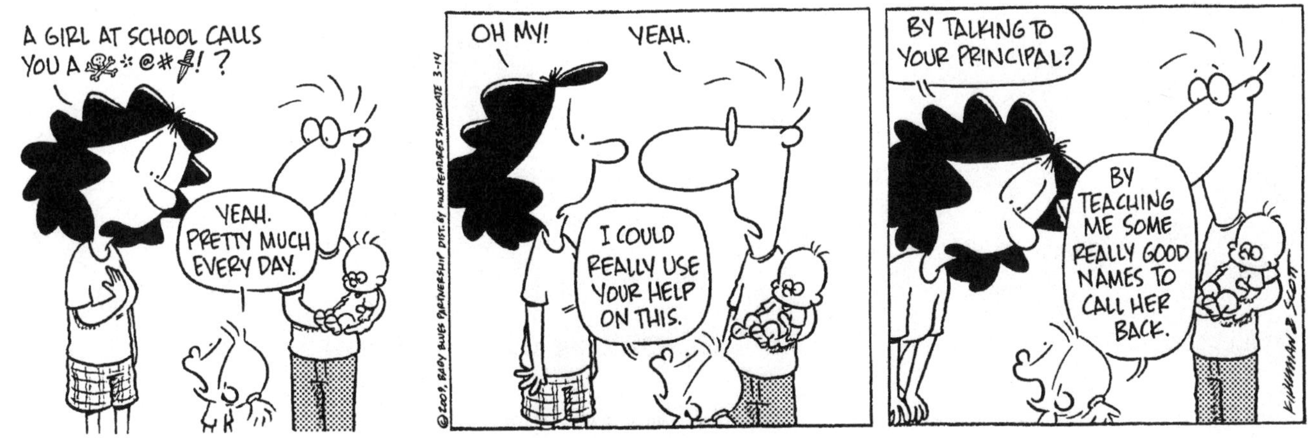
A GIRL AT SCHOOL CALLS YOU A @#!?
YEAH. PRETTY MUCH EVERY DAY.
©2009, BABY BLUES PARTNERSHIP DIST. BY KING FEATURES SYNDICATE 3-14
OH MY!
YEAH.
I COULD REALLY USE YOUR HELP ON THIS.
BY TALKING TO YOUR PRINCIPAL?
BY TEACHING ME SOME REALLY GOOD NAMES TO CALL HER BACK.
KIRKMAN & SCOTT

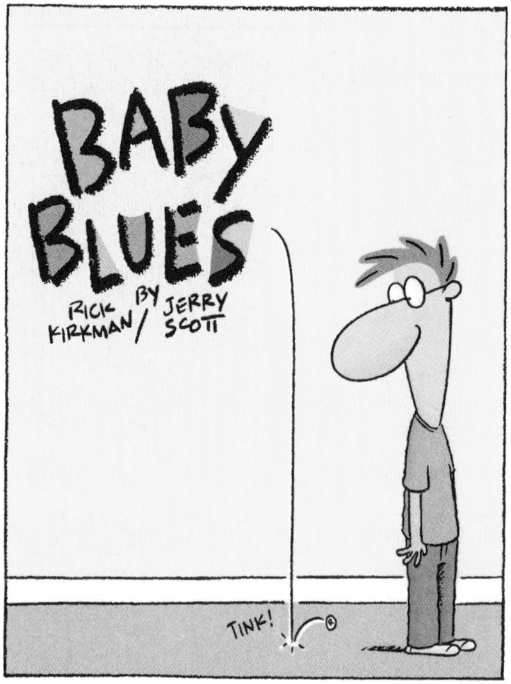
BABY BLUES
BY RICK KIRKMAN / JERRY SCOTT
TINK!

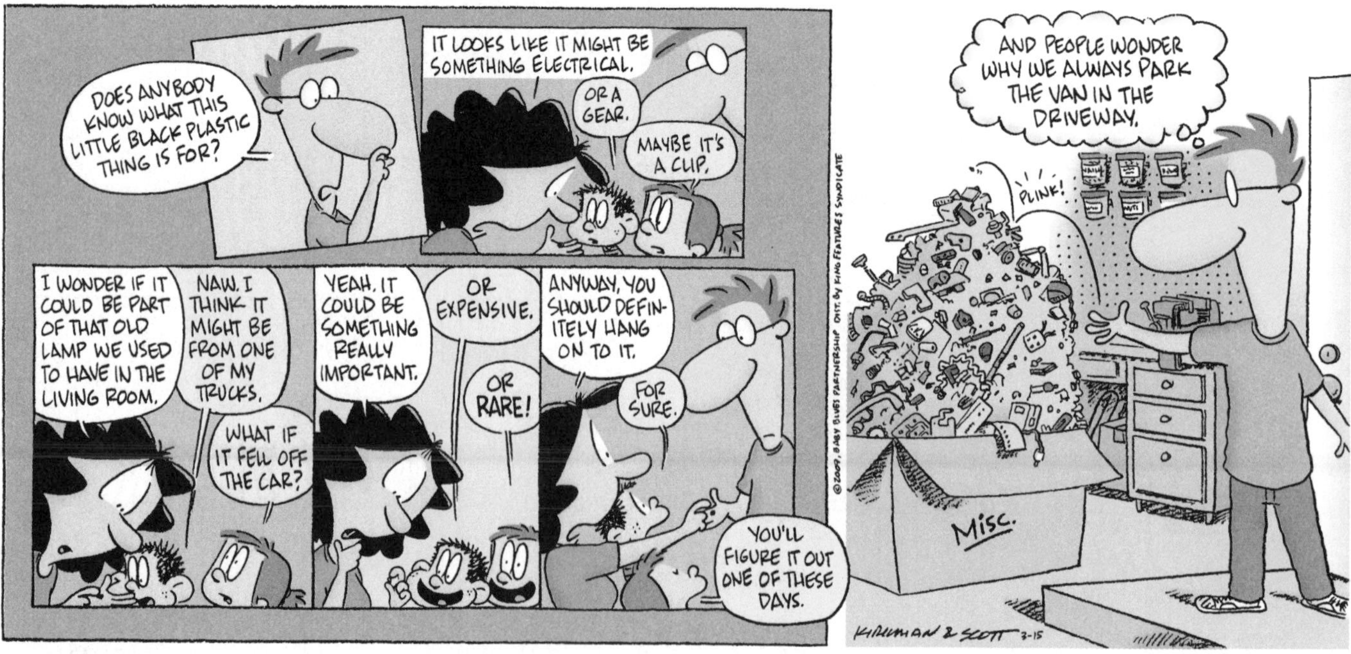
DOES ANYBODY KNOW WHAT THIS LITTLE BLACK PLASTIC THING IS FOR?
IT LOOKS LIKE IT MIGHT BE SOMETHING ELECTRICAL.
OR A GEAR.
MAYBE IT'S A CLIP.
I WONDER IF IT COULD BE PART OF THAT OLD LAMP WE USED TO HAVE IN THE LIVING ROOM.
NAW. I THINK IT MIGHT BE FROM ONE OF MY TRUCKS.
WHAT IF IT FELL OFF THE CAR?
YEAH. IT COULD BE SOMETHING REALLY IMPORTANT.
OR EXPENSIVE.
OR RARE!
ANYWAY, YOU SHOULD DEFINITELY HANG ON TO IT.
FOR SURE.
YOU'LL FIGURE IT OUT ONE OF THESE DAYS.
AND PEOPLE WONDER WHY WE ALWAYS PARK THE VAN IN THE DRIVEWAY.
PLINK!
MISC.
KIRKMAN & SCOTT 3-15

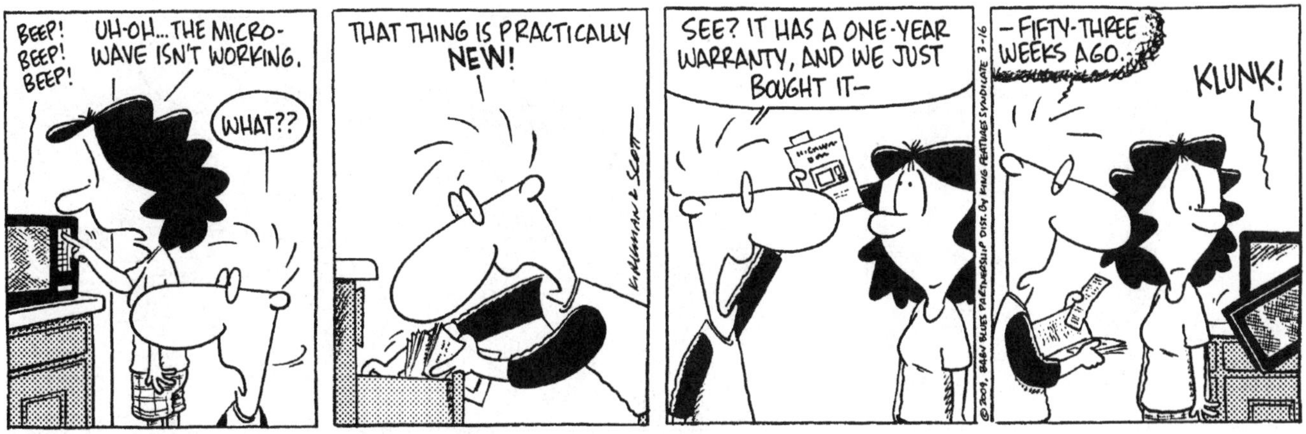
BEEP! BEEP! BEEP!
UH-OH...THE MICRO-WAVE ISN'T WORKING.
WHAT??
THAT THING IS PRACTICALLY NEW!
KIRKMAN & SCOTT
SEE? IT HAS A ONE-YEAR WARRANTY, AND WE JUST BOUGHT IT—
© 2009, BABY BLUES PARTNERSHIP DIST. BY KING FEATURES SYNDICATE 3-16
—FIFTY-THREE WEEKS AGO.
KLUNK!

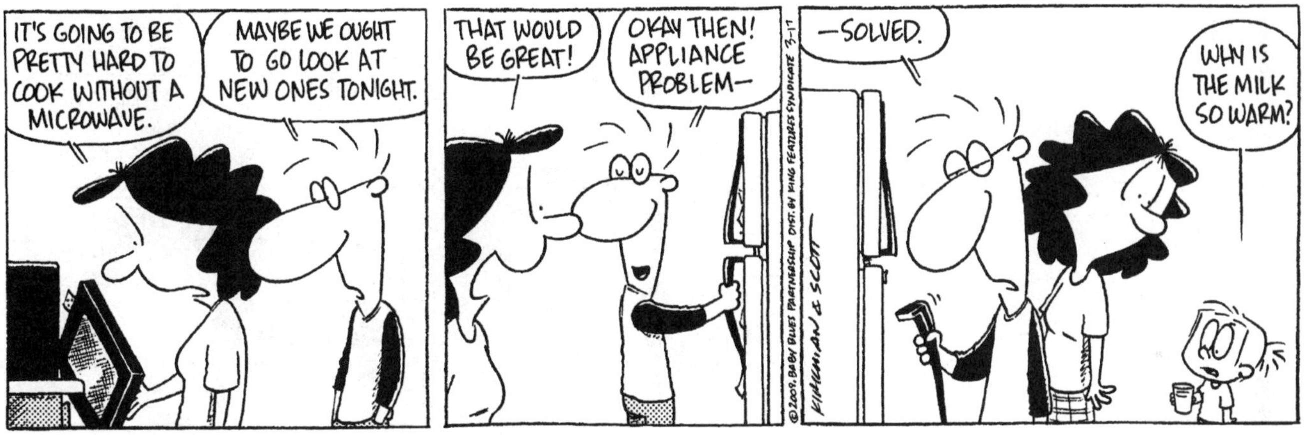
IT'S GOING TO BE PRETTY HARD TO COOK WITHOUT A MICROWAVE.
MAYBE WE OUGHT TO GO LOOK AT NEW ONES TONIGHT.
THAT WOULD BE GREAT!
OKAY THEN! APPLIANCE PROBLEM—
© 2009, BABY BLUES PARTNERSHIP DIST. BY KING FEATURES SYNDICATE 3-17
KIRKMAN & SCOTT
—SOLVED.
WHY IS THE MILK SO WARM?

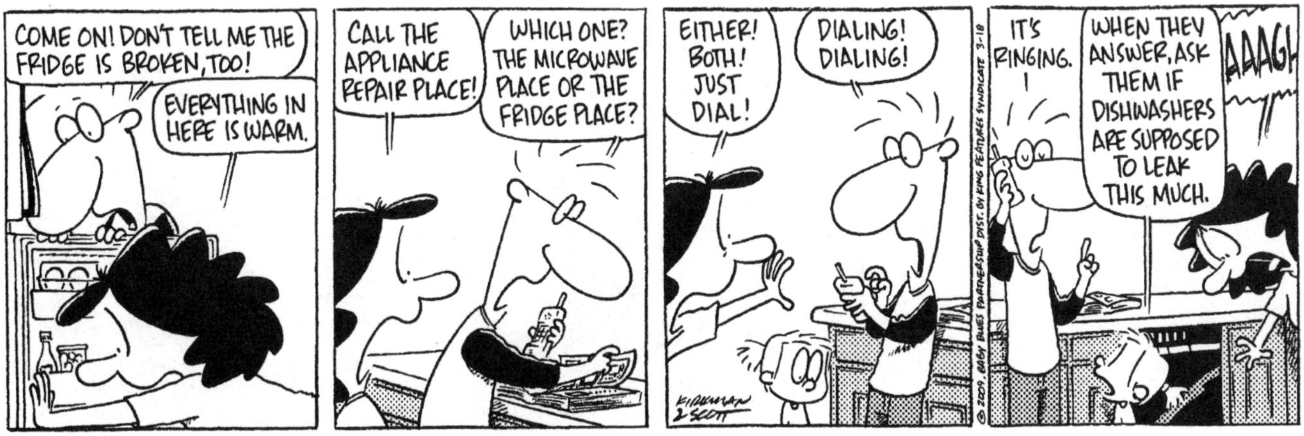
COME ON! DON'T TELL ME THE FRIDGE IS BROKEN, TOO!
EVERYTHING IN HERE IS WARM.
CALL THE APPLIANCE REPAIR PLACE!
WHICH ONE? THE MICROWAVE PLACE OR THE FRIDGE PLACE?
EITHER! BOTH! JUST DIAL!
DIALING! DIALING!
KIRKMAN & SCOTT
© 2009, BABY BLUES PARTNERSHIP DIST. BY KING FEATURES SYNDICATE 3-18
IT'S RINGING.
WHEN THEY ANSWER, ASK THEM IF DISHWASHERS ARE SUPPOSED TO LEAK THIS MUCH.
AAAGH

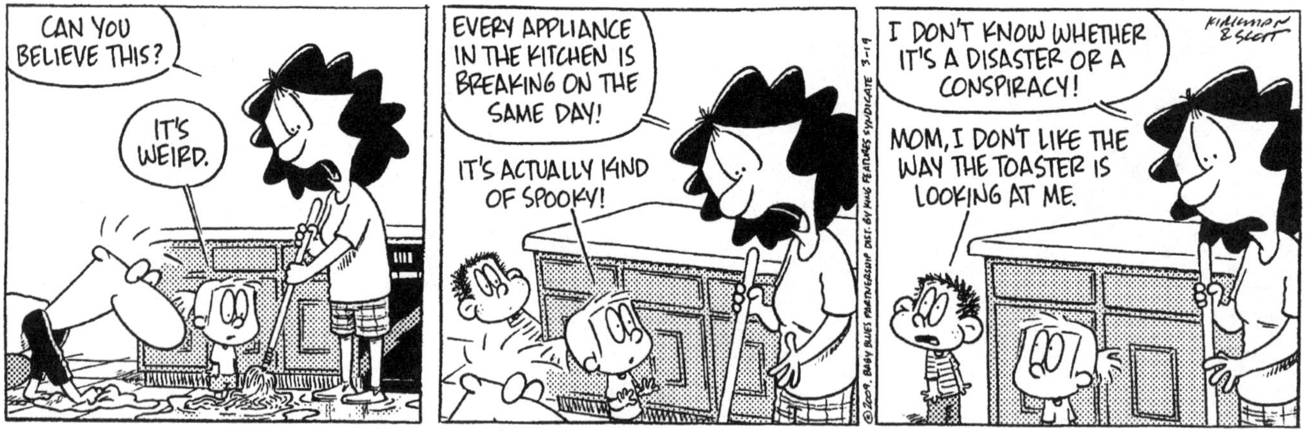
CAN YOU BELIEVE THIS?
IT'S WEIRD.
EVERY APPLIANCE IN THE KITCHEN IS BREAKING ON THE SAME DAY!
IT'S ACTUALLY KIND OF SPOOKY!
©2009, BABY BLUES PARTNERSHIP DIST. BY KING FEATURES SYNDICATE 3-19
I DON'T KNOW WHETHER IT'S A DISASTER OR A CONSPIRACY!
MOM, I DON'T LIKE THE WAY THE TOASTER IS LOOKING AT ME.
KIRKMAN & SCOTT

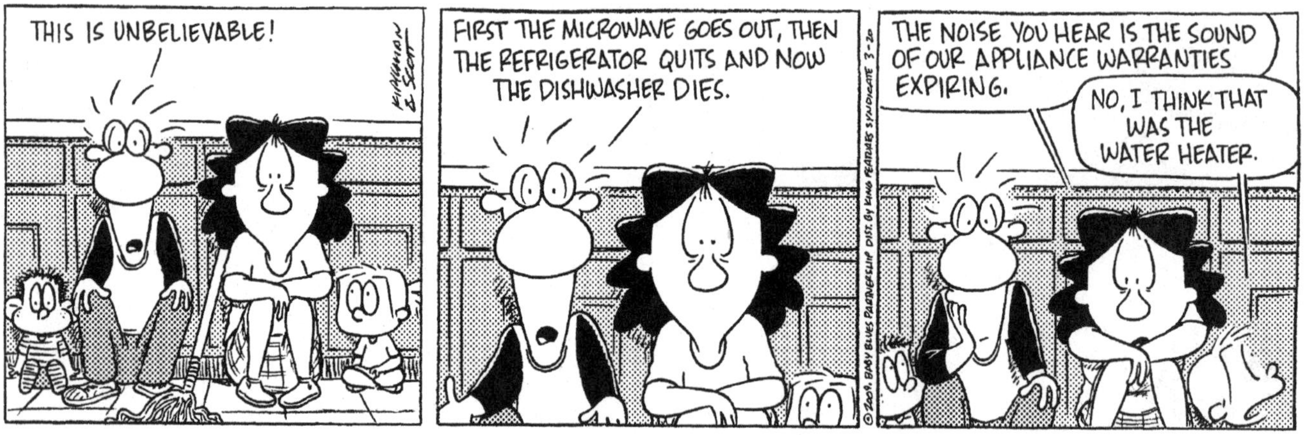
THIS IS UNBELIEVABLE!
KIRKMAN & SCOTT
FIRST THE MICROWAVE GOES OUT, THEN THE REFRIGERATOR QUITS AND NOW THE DISHWASHER DIES.
©2009, BABY BLUES PARTNERSHIP DIST. BY KING FEATURES SYNDICATE 3-20
THE NOISE YOU HEAR IS THE SOUND OF OUR APPLIANCE WARRANTIES EXPIRING.
NO, I THINK THAT WAS THE WATER HEATER.

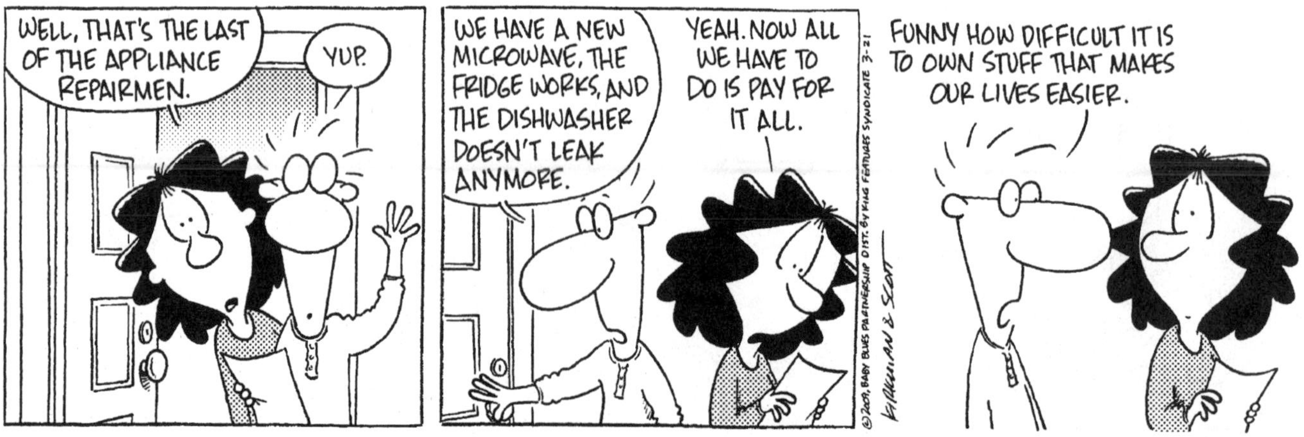
WELL, THAT'S THE LAST OF THE APPLIANCE REPAIRMEN.
YUP.
WE HAVE A NEW MICROWAVE, THE FRIDGE WORKS, AND THE DISHWASHER DOESN'T LEAK ANYMORE.
YEAH. NOW ALL WE HAVE TO DO IS PAY FOR IT ALL.
©2009, BABY BLUES PARTNERSHIP DIST. BY KING FEATURES SYNDICATE 3-21
KIRKMAN & SCOTT
FUNNY HOW DIFFICULT IT IS TO OWN STUFF THAT MAKES OUR LIVES EASIER.

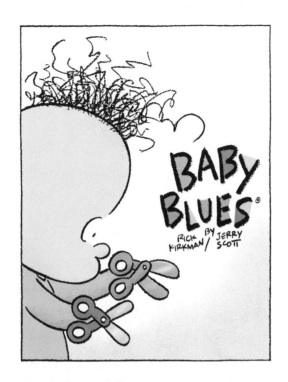

BABY BLUES®
BY RICK KIRKMAN / JERRY SCOTT

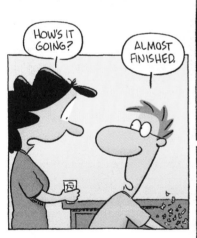

HOW'S IT GOING?
ALMOST FINISHED.
I HAVE ALL THE TAX FORMS TOGETHER, AND I'M JUST PUTTING SOME OLD RECEIPTS THROUGH THE SHREDDER.
GOOD.
JUST BE SURE SHE DOESN'T PUT ANY OF IT IN HER MOUTH.
© 2009, BABY BLUES PARTNERSHIP DIST. BY KING FEATURES SYNDICATE 3-22
KIRKMAN & SCOTT

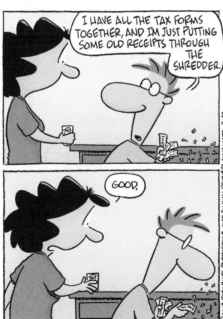

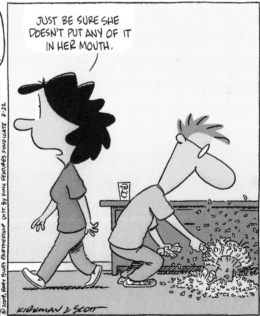

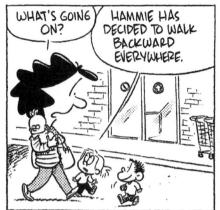

WHAT'S GOING ON?
HAMMIE HAS DECIDED TO WALK BACKWARD EVERYWHERE.
I CAN SEE THAT, BUT WHY?
KIRKMAN & SCOTT
© 2009, BABY BLUES PARTNERSHIP DIST. BY KING FEATURES SYNDICATE 3-23
GO WITH IT. IT'S LESS ANNOYING THAN WHEN HE TALKS BACKWARDS.
.HAƎY, HO

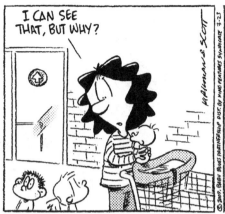

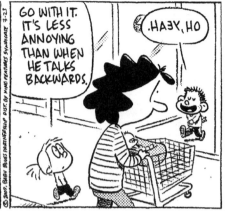

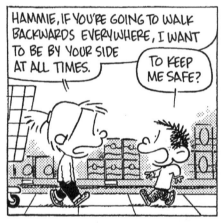

HAMMIE, IF YOU'RE GOING TO WALK BACKWARDS EVERYWHERE, I WANT TO BE BY YOUR SIDE AT ALL TIMES.
TO KEEP ME SAFE?
CONK!
HA! HA! HA! HA! HA! HA!
© 2009, BABY BLUES PARTNERSHIP DIST. BY KING FEATURES SYNDICATE 3-24
SOMETHING LIKE THAT.
KIRKMAN & SCOTT

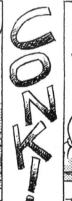

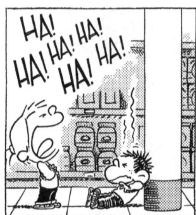

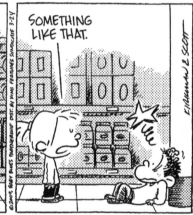

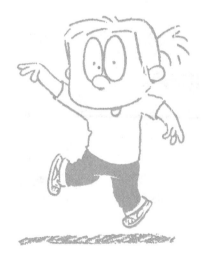

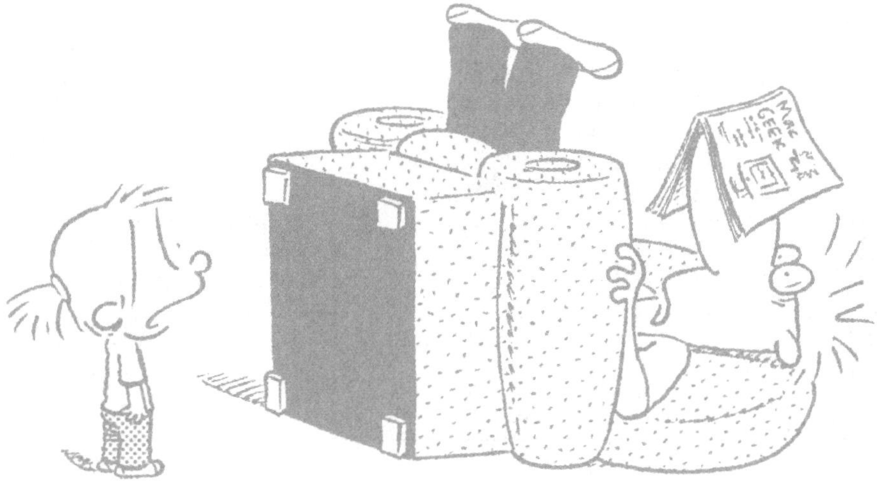
MAC GEEK

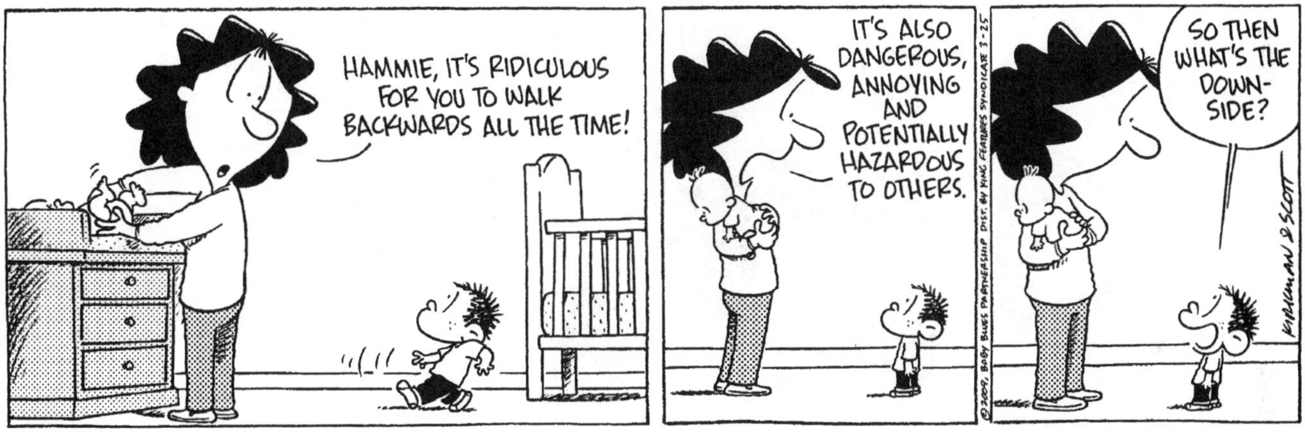
HAMMIE, IT'S RIDICULOUS FOR YOU TO WALK BACKWARDS ALL THE TIME!
IT'S ALSO DANGEROUS, ANNOYING AND POTENTIALLY HAZARDOUS TO OTHERS.
© 2009, BABY BLUES PARTNERSHIP DIST. BY KING FEATURES SYNDICATE 3-25
SO THEN WHAT'S THE DOWN-SIDE?
KIRKMAN & SCOTT

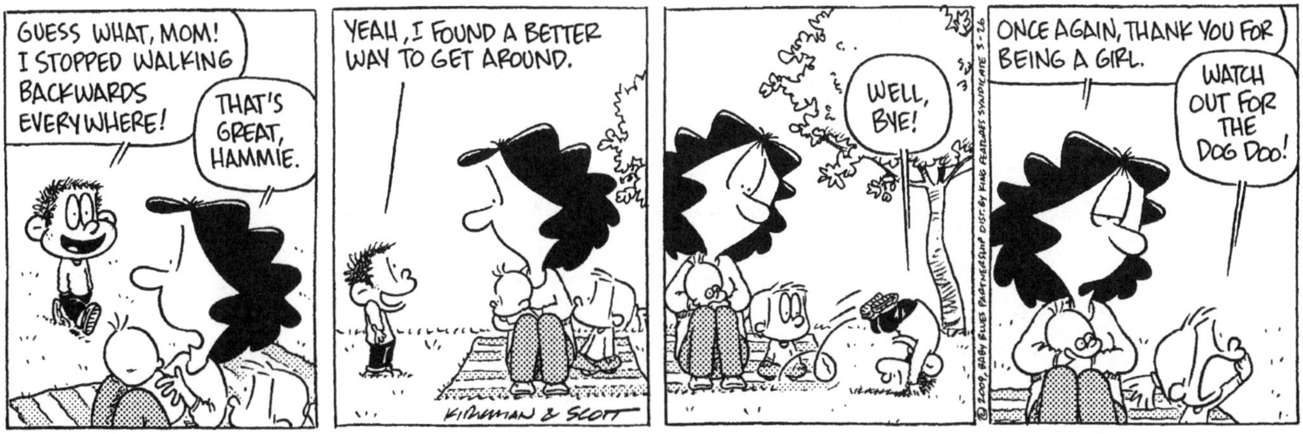
GUESS WHAT, MOM! I STOPPED WALKING BACKWARDS EVERYWHERE!
THAT'S GREAT, HAMMIE.
YEAH, I FOUND A BETTER WAY TO GET AROUND.
KIRKMAN & SCOTT
WELL, BYE!
© 2009, BABY BLUES PARTNERSHIP DIST. BY KING FEATURES SYNDICATE 3-26
ONCE AGAIN, THANK YOU FOR BEING A GIRL.
WATCH OUT FOR THE DOG DOO!

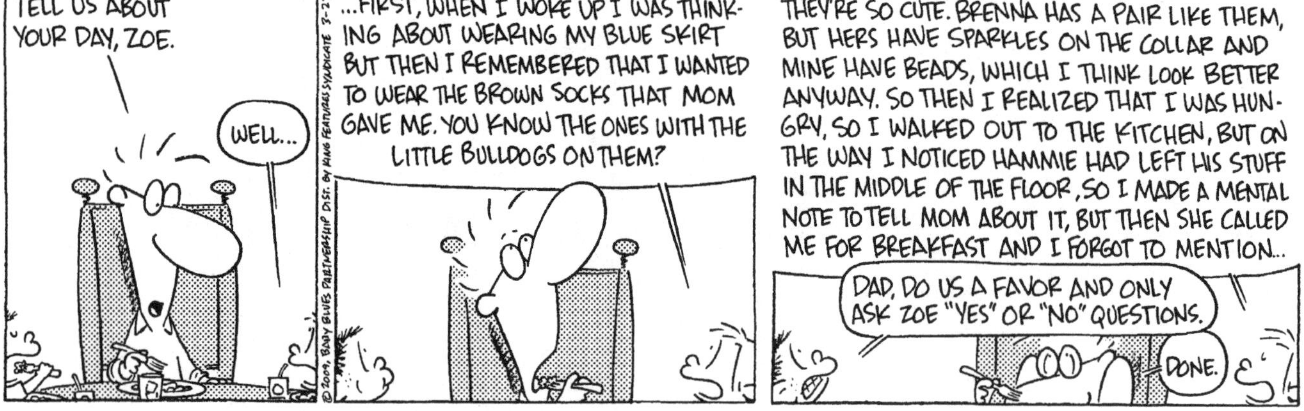
TELL US ABOUT YOUR DAY, ZOE.
WELL...
©2009, BABY BLUES PARTNERSHIP DIST. BY KING FEATURES SYNDICATE 3-27
...FIRST, WHEN I WOKE UP I WAS THINKING ABOUT WEARING MY BLUE SKIRT BUT THEN I REMEMBERED THAT I WANTED TO WEAR THE BROWN SOCKS THAT MOM GAVE ME. YOU KNOW THE ONES WITH THE LITTLE BULLDOGS ON THEM?
THEY'RE SO CUTE. BRENNA HAS A PAIR LIKE THEM, BUT HERS HAVE SPARKLES ON THE COLLAR AND MINE HAVE BEADS, WHICH I THINK LOOK BETTER ANYWAY. SO THEN I REALIZED THAT I WAS HUNGRY, SO I WALKED OUT TO THE KITCHEN, BUT ON THE WAY I NOTICED HAMMIE HAD LEFT HIS STUFF IN THE MIDDLE OF THE FLOOR, SO I MADE A MENTAL NOTE TO TELL MOM ABOUT IT, BUT THEN SHE CALLED ME FOR BREAKFAST AND I FORGOT TO MENTION...
DAD, DO US A FAVOR AND ONLY ASK ZOE "YES" OR "NO" QUESTIONS.
DONE.

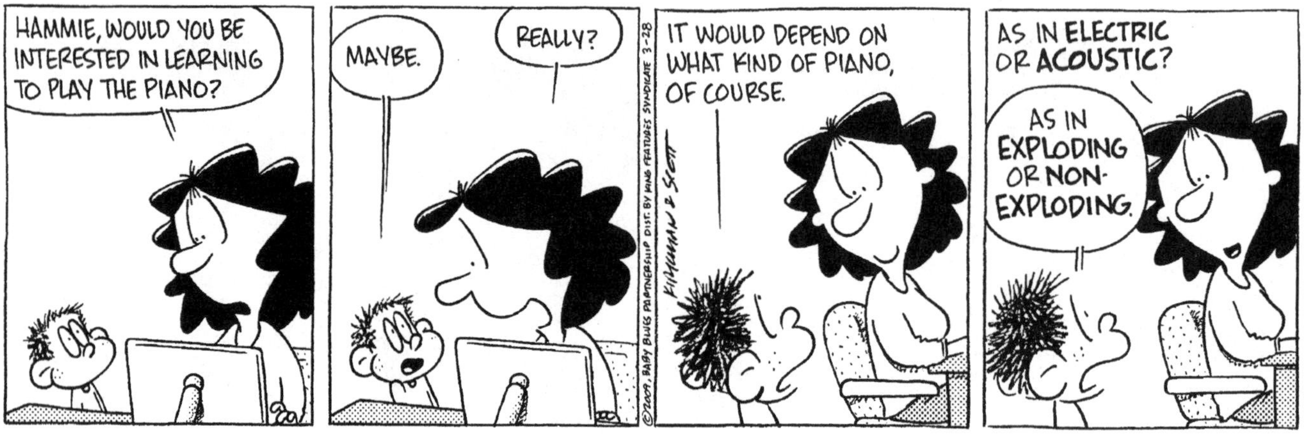
HAMMIE, WOULD YOU BE INTERESTED IN LEARNING TO PLAY THE PIANO?
MAYBE.
REALLY?
©2009, BABY BLUES PARTNERSHIP DIST. BY KING FEATURES SYNDICATE 3-28
KIRKMAN & SCOTT
IT WOULD DEPEND ON WHAT KIND OF PIANO, OF COURSE.
AS IN ELECTRIC OR ACOUSTIC?
AS IN EXPLODING OR NON-EXPLODING.

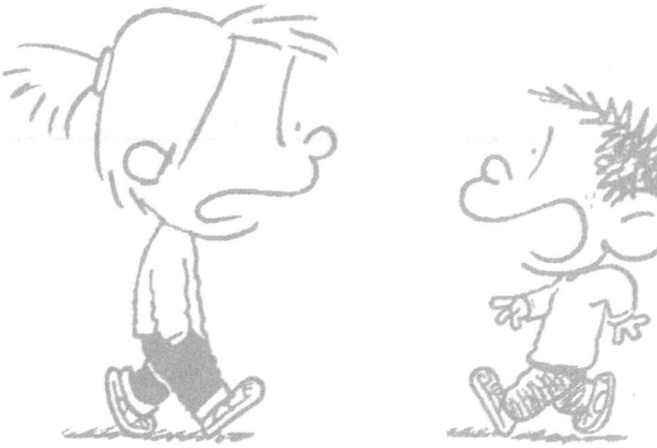

BABY BLUES®

RICK KIRKMAN BY JERRY SCOTT

MOM, SHOULD I WEAR THE BROWN LOAFERS OR THE BLUE SNEAKERS?

EITHER PAIR, IT'S UP TO YOU.

BUT I DON'T KNOW WHICH TO PICK!

THEY BOTH LOOK NICE.

BUT WHICH ONES WOULD LOOK NICER?

I MEAN, IF YOU WERE ME AND YOU WERE WEARING THIS OUTFIT, WHICH SHOES WOULD YOU CHOOSE?

OKAY, OKAY...

...IF I WERE YOU, I'D PROBABLY CHOOSE THE, UM... BLUE SNEAKERS.

WHY DO YOU ALWAYS HAVE TO BE SO CONTROLLING?

45

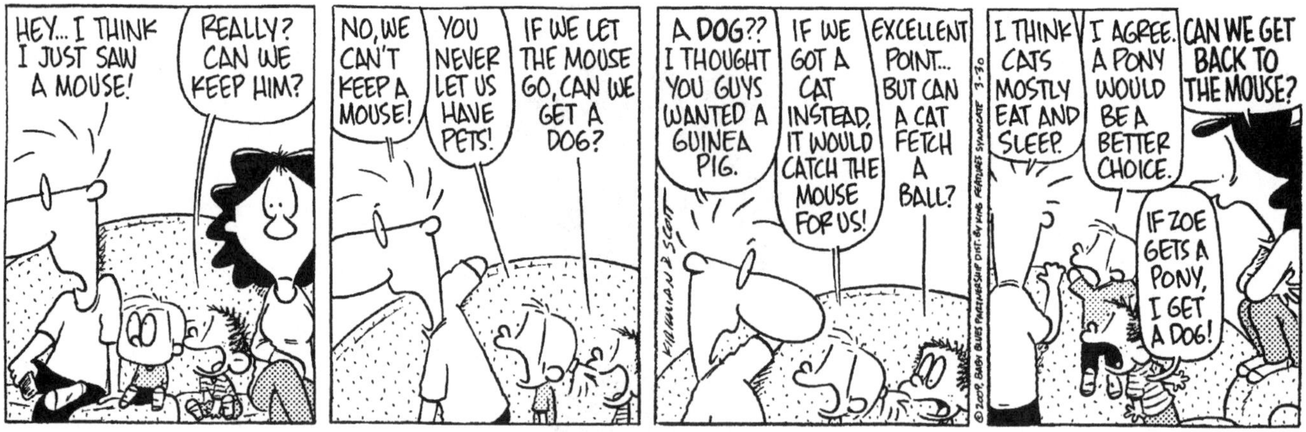
HEY... I THINK I JUST SAW A MOUSE!
REALLY? CAN WE KEEP HIM?
NO, WE CAN'T KEEP A MOUSE!
YOU NEVER LET US HAVE PETS!
IF WE LET THE MOUSE GO, CAN WE GET A DOG?
KIRKMAN & SCOTT
A DOG?? I THOUGHT YOU GUYS WANTED A GUINEA PIG.
IF WE GOT A CAT INSTEAD, IT WOULD CATCH THE MOUSE FOR US!
EXCELLENT POINT... BUT CAN A CAT FETCH A BALL?
© 2009, BABY BLUES PARTNERSHIP DIST. BY KING FEATURES SYNDICATE 3-30
I THINK CATS MOSTLY EAT AND SLEEP.
I AGREE. A PONY WOULD BE A BETTER CHOICE.
IF ZOE GETS A PONY, I GET A DOG!
CAN WE GET BACK TO THE MOUSE?

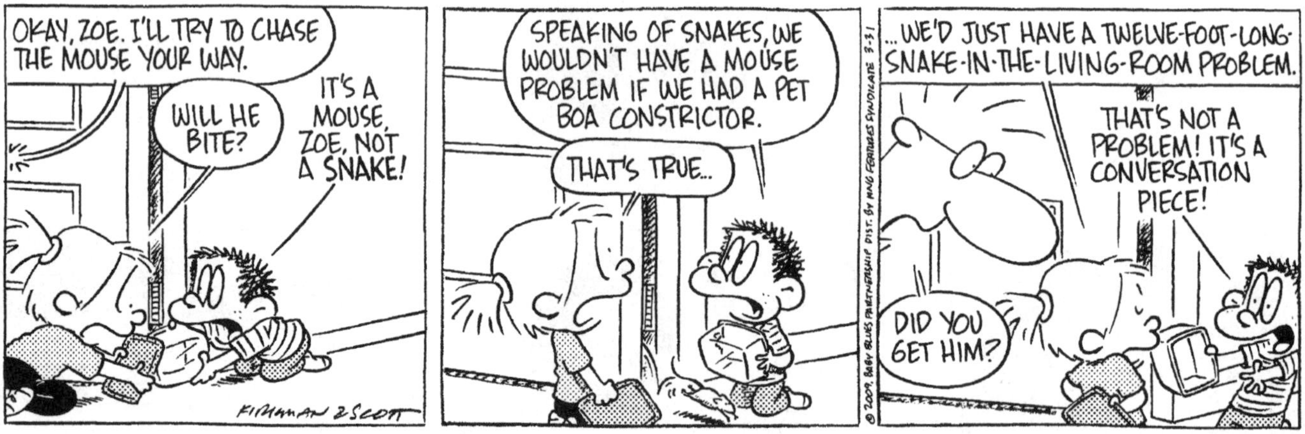
OKAY, ZOE. I'LL TRY TO CHASE THE MOUSE YOUR WAY.
WILL HE BITE?
IT'S A MOUSE, ZOE, NOT A SNAKE!
KIRKMAN & SCOTT
SPEAKING OF SNAKES, WE WOULDN'T HAVE A MOUSE PROBLEM IF WE HAD A PET BOA CONSTRICTOR.
THAT'S TRUE...
© 2009, BABY BLUES PARTNERSHIP DIST. BY KING FEATURES SYNDICATE 3-31
...WE'D JUST HAVE A TWELVE-FOOT-LONG-SNAKE-IN-THE-LIVING-ROOM PROBLEM.
THAT'S NOT A PROBLEM! IT'S A CONVERSATION PIECE!
DID YOU GET HIM?

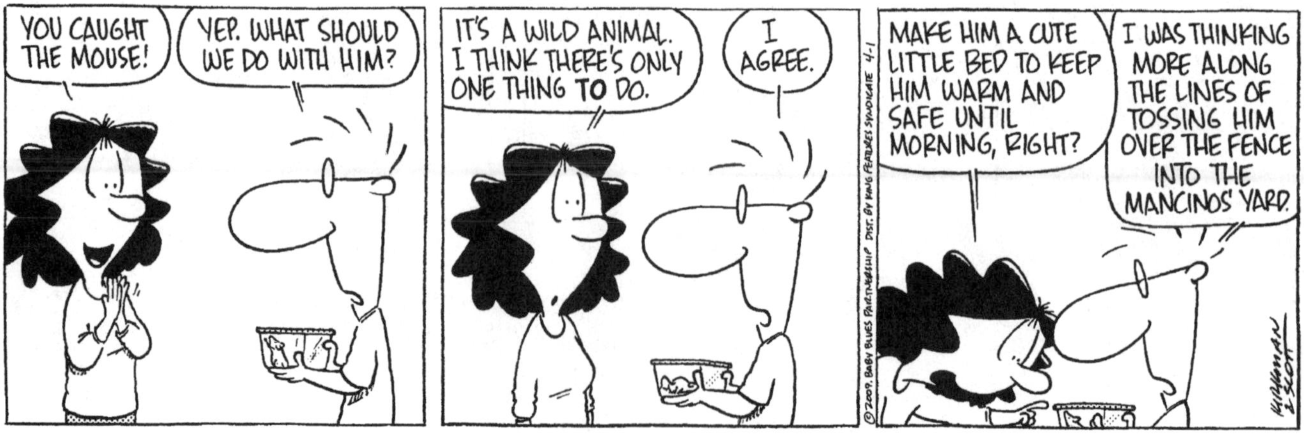
YOU CAUGHT THE MOUSE!
YEP. WHAT SHOULD WE DO WITH HIM?
IT'S A WILD ANIMAL. I THINK THERE'S ONLY ONE THING TO DO.
I AGREE.
© 2009, BABY BLUES PARTNERSHIP DIST. BY KING FEATURES SYNDICATE 4-1
MAKE HIM A CUTE LITTLE BED TO KEEP HIM WARM AND SAFE UNTIL MORNING, RIGHT?
I WAS THINKING MORE ALONG THE LINES OF TOSSING HIM OVER THE FENCE INTO THE MANCINOS' YARD.
KIRKMAN & SCOTT

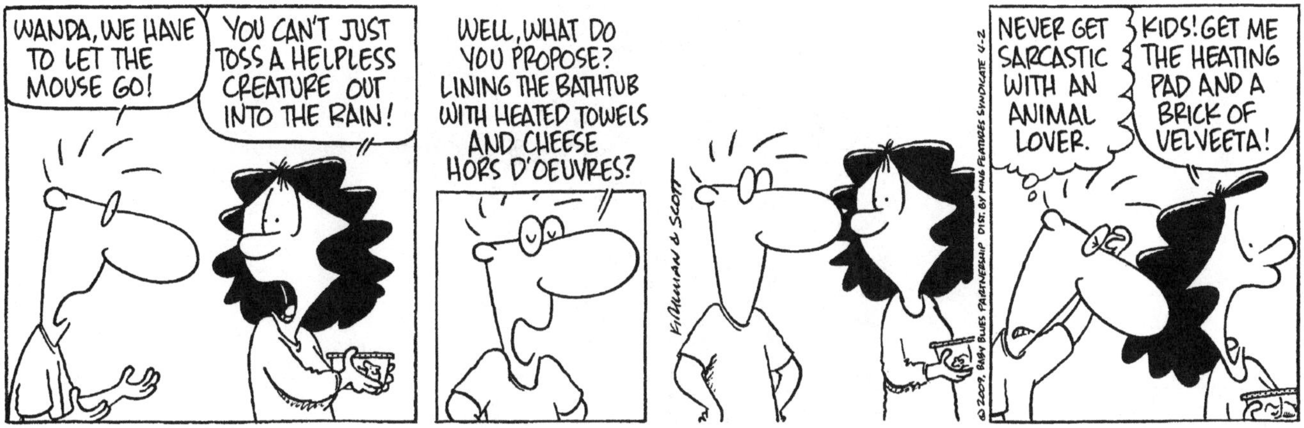
WANDA, WE HAVE TO LET THE MOUSE GO!
YOU CAN'T JUST TOSS A HELPLESS CREATURE OUT INTO THE RAIN!
WELL, WHAT DO YOU PROPOSE? LINING THE BATHTUB WITH HEATED TOWELS AND CHEESE HORS D'OEUVRES?
KIRKMAN & SCOTT
NEVER GET SARCASTIC WITH AN ANIMAL LOVER.
KIDS! GET ME THE HEATING PAD AND A BRICK OF VELVEETA!
© 2009, BABY BLUES PARTNERSHIP DIST. BY KING FEATURES SYNDICATE 4-2

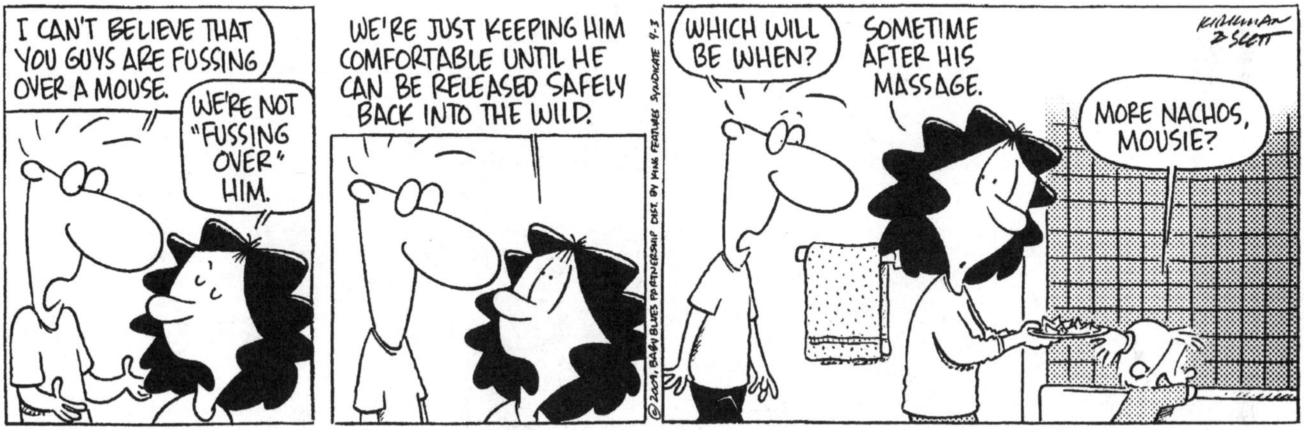
I CAN'T BELIEVE THAT YOU GUYS ARE FUSSING OVER A MOUSE.
WE'RE NOT "FUSSING OVER" HIM.
WE'RE JUST KEEPING HIM COMFORTABLE UNTIL HE CAN BE RELEASED SAFELY BACK INTO THE WILD.
© 2009, BABY BLUES PARTNERSHIP DIST. BY KING FEATURES SYNDICATE 4-3
WHICH WILL BE WHEN?
SOMETIME AFTER HIS MASSAGE.
KIRKMAN & SCOTT
MORE NACHOS, MOUSIE?

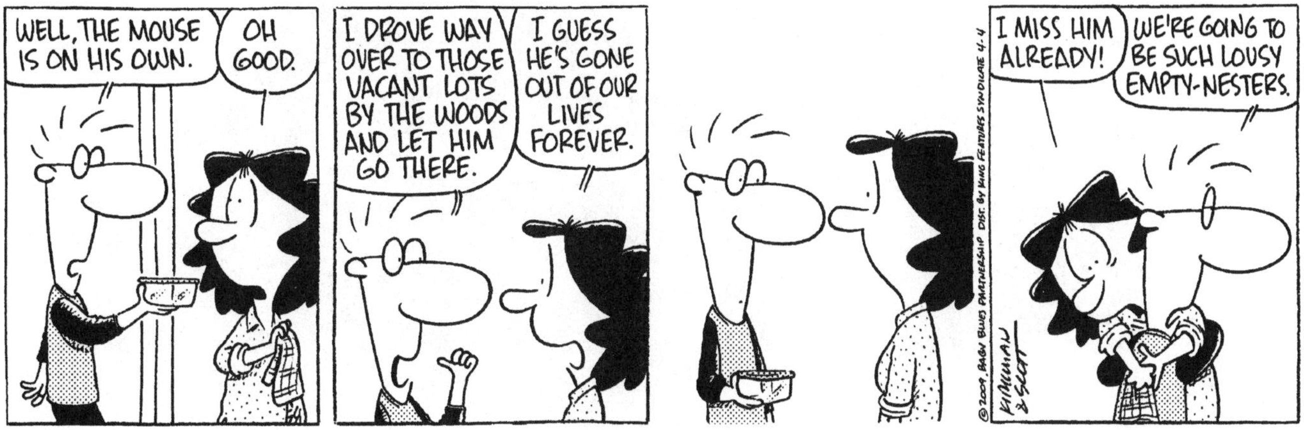
WELL, THE MOUSE IS ON HIS OWN.
OH GOOD.
I DROVE WAY OVER TO THOSE VACANT LOTS BY THE WOODS AND LET HIM GO THERE.
I GUESS HE'S GONE OUT OF OUR LIVES FOREVER.
© 2009, BABY BLUES PARTNERSHIP DIST. BY KING FEATURES SYNDICATE 4-4
KIRKMAN & SCOTT
I MISS HIM ALREADY!
WE'RE GOING TO BE SUCH LOUSY EMPTY-NESTERS.

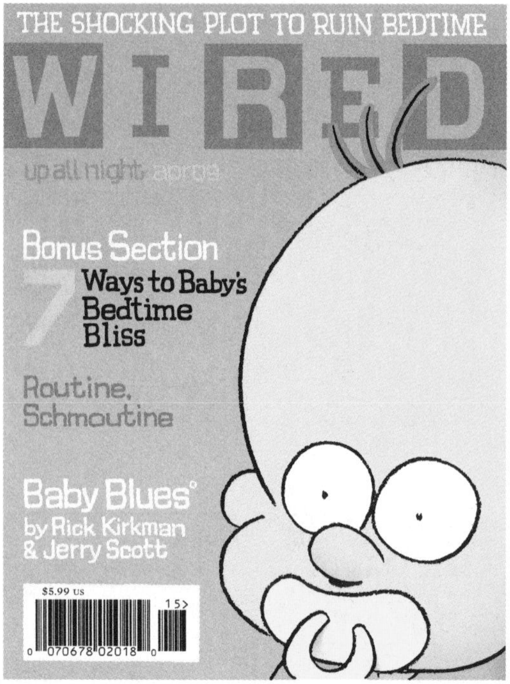
THE SHOCKING PLOT TO RUIN BEDTIME
WIRED
up all night
Bonus Section
7 Ways to Baby's Bedtime Bliss
Routine, Schmoutine
Baby Blues°
by Rick Kirkman & Jerry Scott
$5.99 US

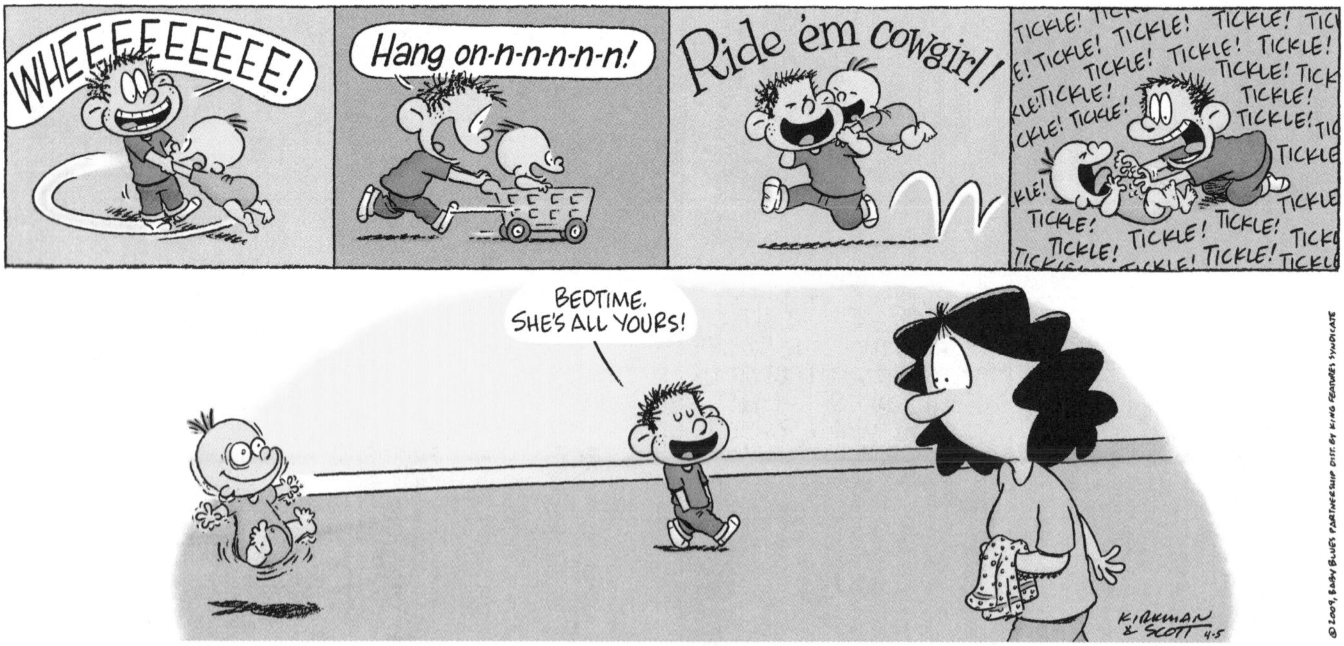
WHEEEEEEEEE!
Hang on-n-n-n-n-n!
Ride 'em cowgirl!
TICKLE! TICKLE! TICKLE! TICKLE!
BEDTIME. SHE'S ALL YOURS!
KIRKMAN & SCOTT 4-5
© 2009, Baby Blues Partnership Dist. by King Features Syndicate

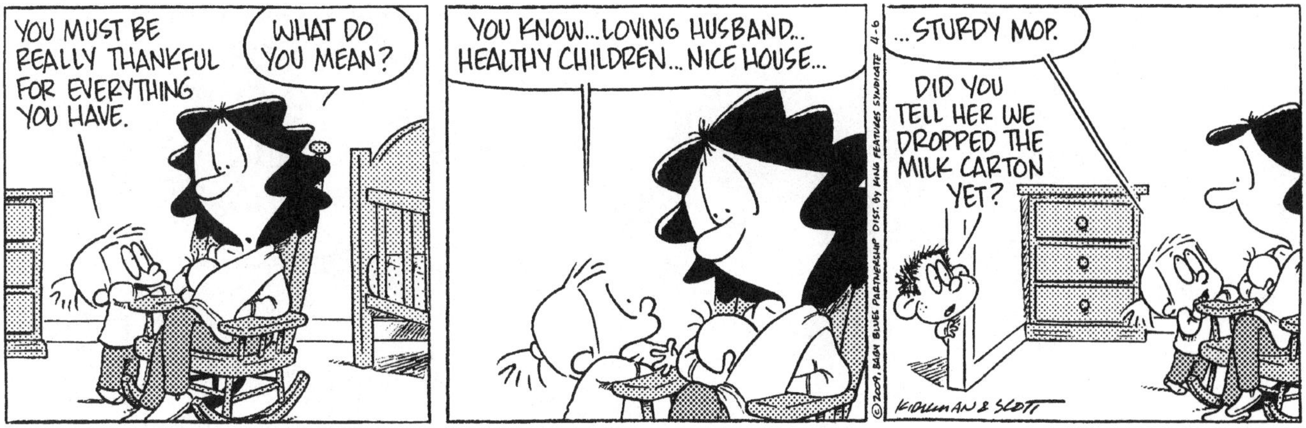
YOU MUST BE REALLY THANKFUL FOR EVERYTHING YOU HAVE.
WHAT DO YOU MEAN?
YOU KNOW...LOVING HUSBAND... HEALTHY CHILDREN...NICE HOUSE...
©2009, BABY BLUES PARTNERSHIP DIST. BY KING FEATURES SYNDICATE 4-6
...STURDY MOP.
DID YOU TELL HER WE DROPPED THE MILK CARTON YET?
KIRKMAN & SCOTT

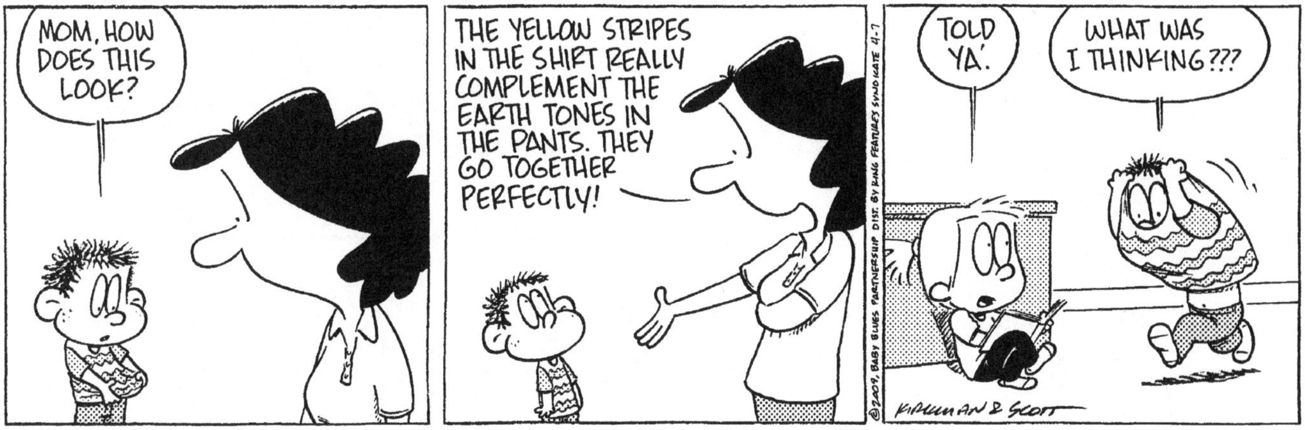
MOM, HOW DOES THIS LOOK?
THE YELLOW STRIPES IN THE SHIRT REALLY COMPLEMENT THE EARTH TONES IN THE PANTS. THEY GO TOGETHER PERFECTLY!
©2009, BABY BLUES PARTNERSHIP DIST. BY KING FEATURES SYNDICATE 4-7
TOLD YA'.
WHAT WAS I THINKING???
KIRKMAN & SCOTT

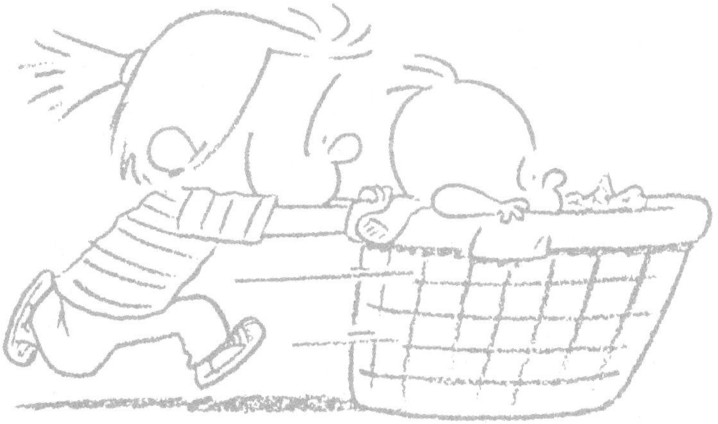

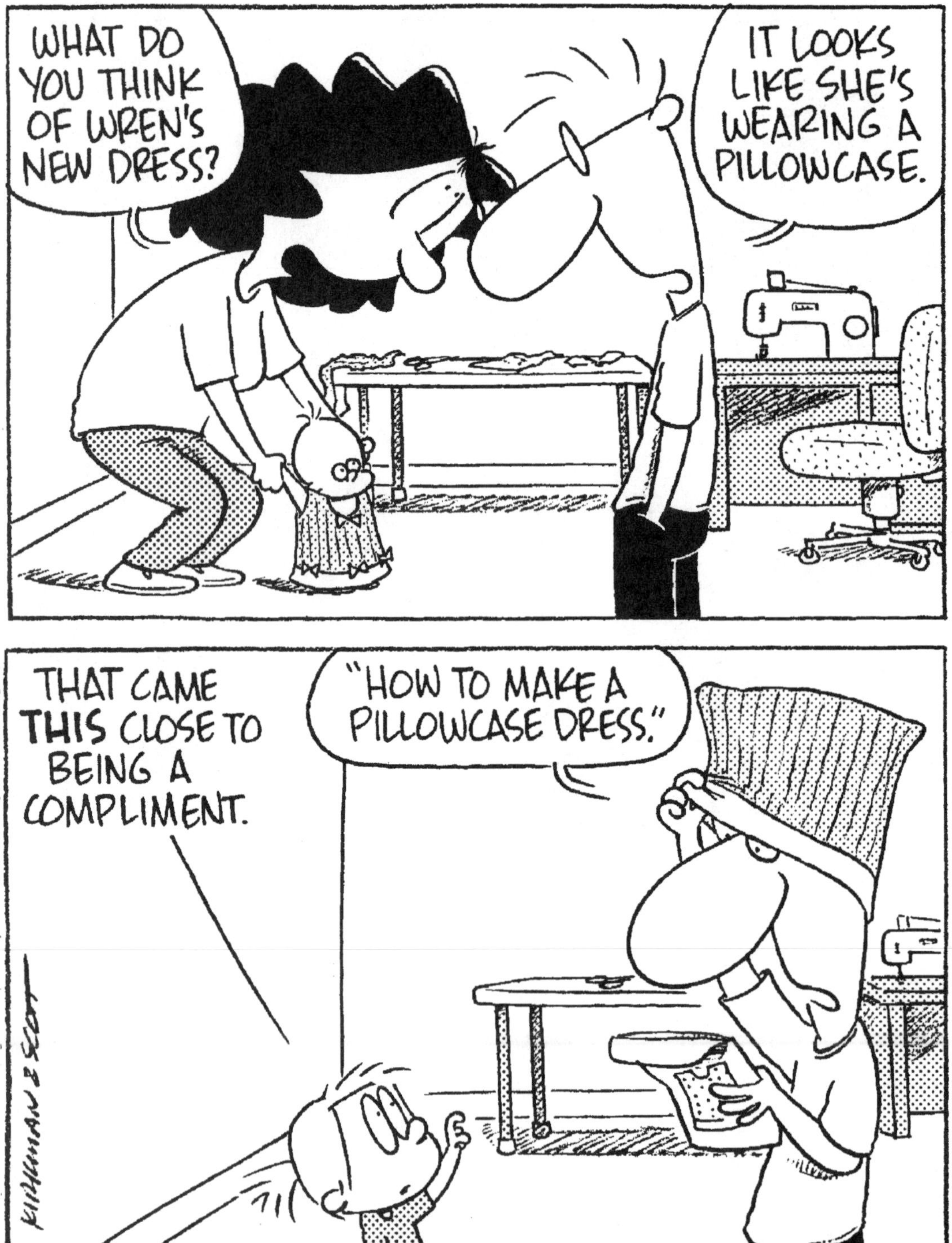
WHAT DO YOU THINK OF WREN'S NEW DRESS?
IT LOOKS LIKE SHE'S WEARING A PILLOWCASE.
THAT CAME THIS CLOSE TO BEING A COMPLIMENT.
"HOW TO MAKE A PILLOWCASE DRESS."
KIRKMAN & SCOTT

MOM SAID YOU HAVE TO PICK UP YOUR STUFF.

LOOK AT THIS MESS! IT'S A NIGHTMARE! THIS ISN'T A LIVING ROOM... IT'S A LANDFILL!

YOU PICK UP YOUR STUFF, TOO, ZOE.

THAT WOMAN HAS ISSUES.

HI ZOE. IT'S DAD. IS MOM THERE? IS SHE HERE?? SHE'S ALWAYS HERE!

SHE HAS THREE KIDS. WHERE ELSE WOULD SHE BE?

THEY AREN'T CALLED STAY-AT-HOME-MOMS BECAUSE THEY'RE ALWAYS JETTING OFF TO PARIS, YOU KNOW!

THIS IS A SETUP, ISN'T IT?

IF I WERE YOU, I'D BE PLANNING A ROMANTIC GETAWAY.

If I were you I'd be planning a romantic getaway

She has 3 kids. Where else would she be?

ALWAYS here

They a stay-at becau

FIND THE MATCHING SOCK... SHIRT FOLDING CONTEST... WIPE THE COUNTER... TRASH CAN RACE...

KIRKMAN & SCOTT

...AND THERE ARE A LOT MORE FUN IDEAS WHERE THOSE CAME FROM!

ON SECOND THOUGHT, I THINK WE'LL PLAY BY OURSELVES.

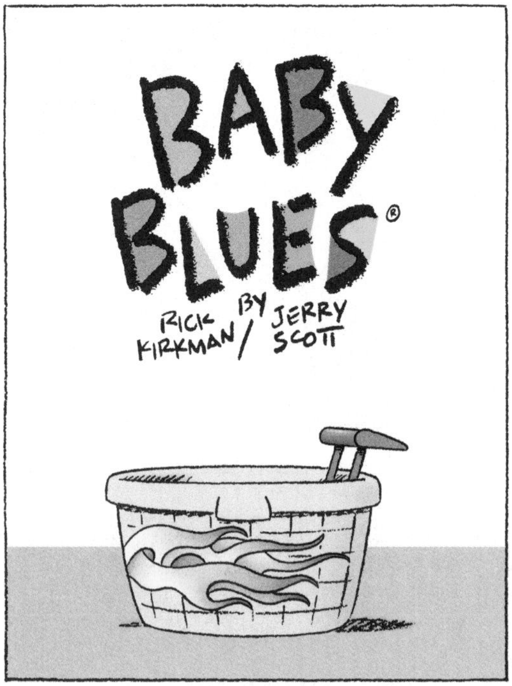
BABY BLUES®
BY RICK KIRKMAN / JERRY SCOTT

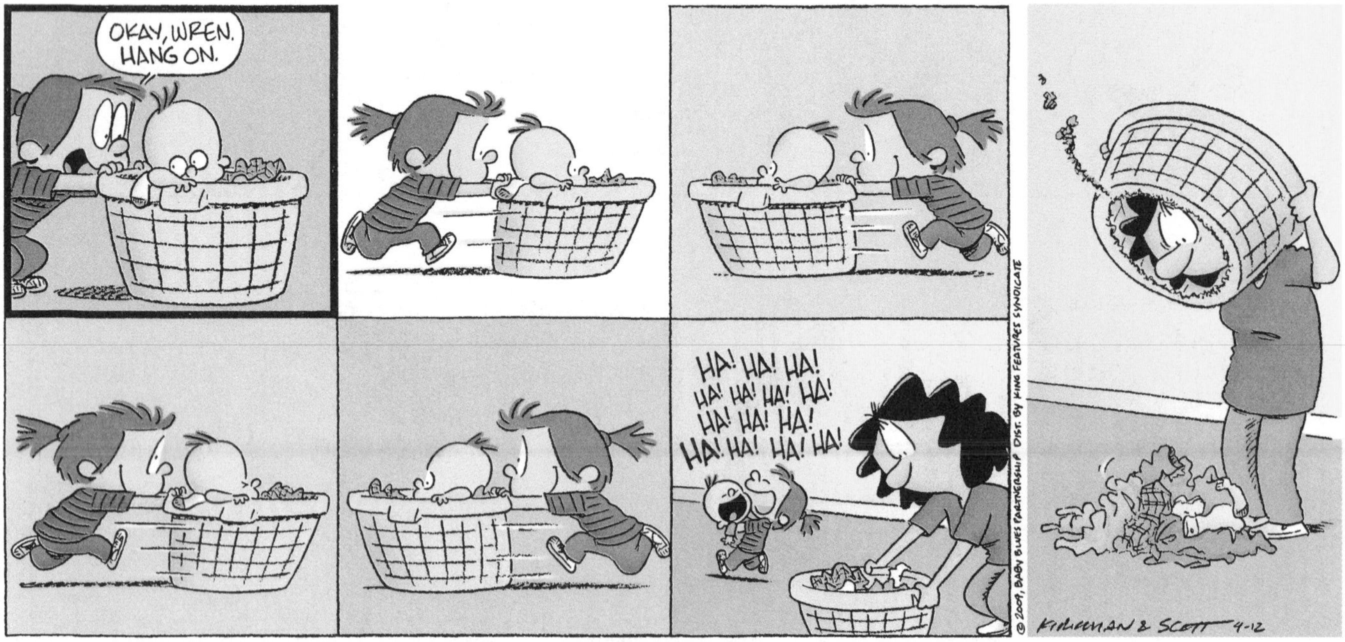
OKAY, WREN. HANG ON.
HA! HA! HA! HA! HA! HA! HA! HA! HA! HA! HA! HA! HA! HA! HA!
© 2009, BABY BLUES PARTNERSHIP DIST. BY KING FEATURES SYNDICATE
KIRKMAN & SCOTT 4-12

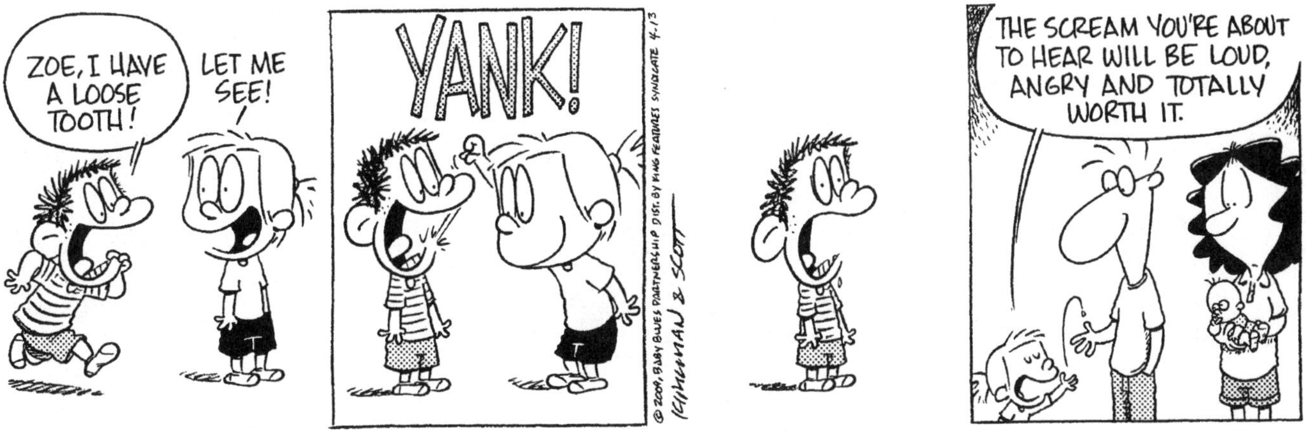
ZOE, I HAVE A LOOSE TOOTH!
LET ME SEE!
YANK!
© 2009, BABY BLUES PARTNERSHIP DIST. BY KING FEATURES SYNDICATE 4.13
KIRKMAN & SCOTT
THE SCREAM YOU'RE ABOUT TO HEAR WILL BE LOUD, ANGRY AND TOTALLY WORTH IT.

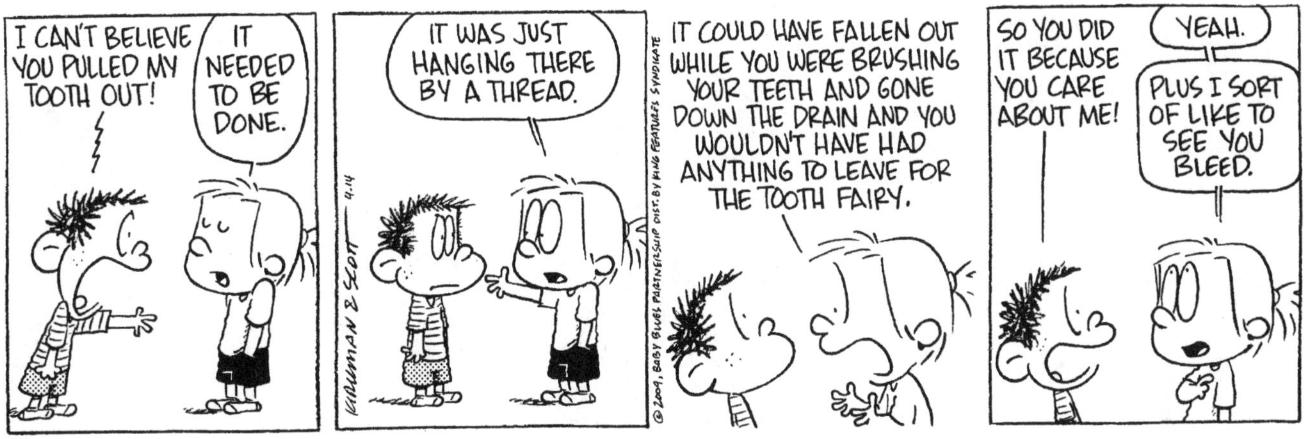
I CAN'T BELIEVE YOU PULLED MY TOOTH OUT!
IT NEEDED TO BE DONE.
IT WAS JUST HANGING THERE BY A THREAD.
KIRKMAN & SCOTT 4.14
© 2009, BABY BLUES PARTNERSHIP DIST. BY KING FEATURES SYNDICATE
IT COULD HAVE FALLEN OUT WHILE YOU WERE BRUSHING YOUR TEETH AND GONE DOWN THE DRAIN AND YOU WOULDN'T HAVE HAD ANYTHING TO LEAVE FOR THE TOOTH FAIRY.
SO YOU DID IT BECAUSE YOU CARE ABOUT ME!
YEAH.
PLUS I SORT OF LIKE TO SEE YOU BLEED.

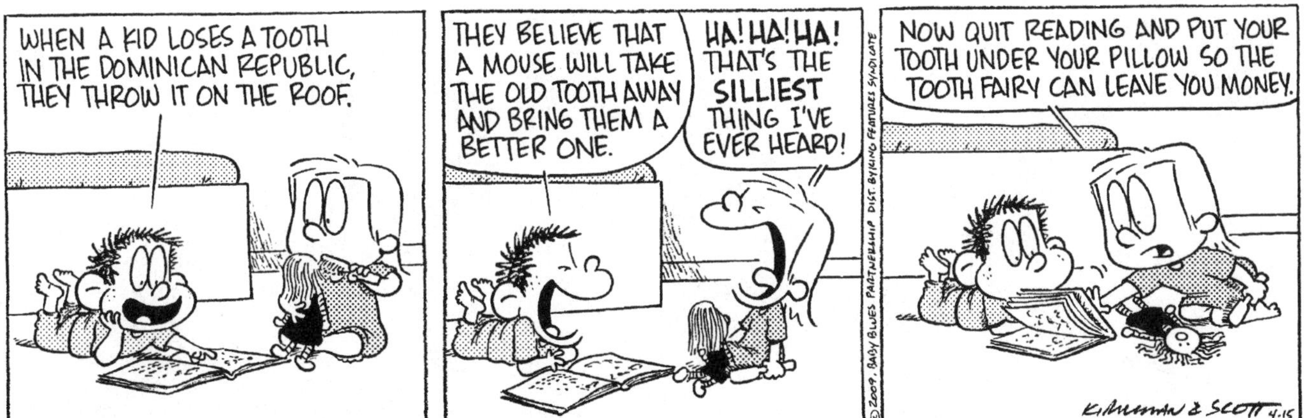
WHEN A KID LOSES A TOOTH IN THE DOMINICAN REPUBLIC, THEY THROW IT ON THE ROOF.
THEY BELIEVE THAT A MOUSE WILL TAKE THE OLD TOOTH AWAY AND BRING THEM A BETTER ONE.
HA! HA! HA! THAT'S THE SILLIEST THING I'VE EVER HEARD!
© 2009, BABY BLUES PARTNERSHIP DIST. BY KING FEATURES SYNDICATE
NOW QUIT READING AND PUT YOUR TOOTH UNDER YOUR PILLOW SO THE TOOTH FAIRY CAN LEAVE YOU MONEY.
KIRKMAN & SCOTT 4.15

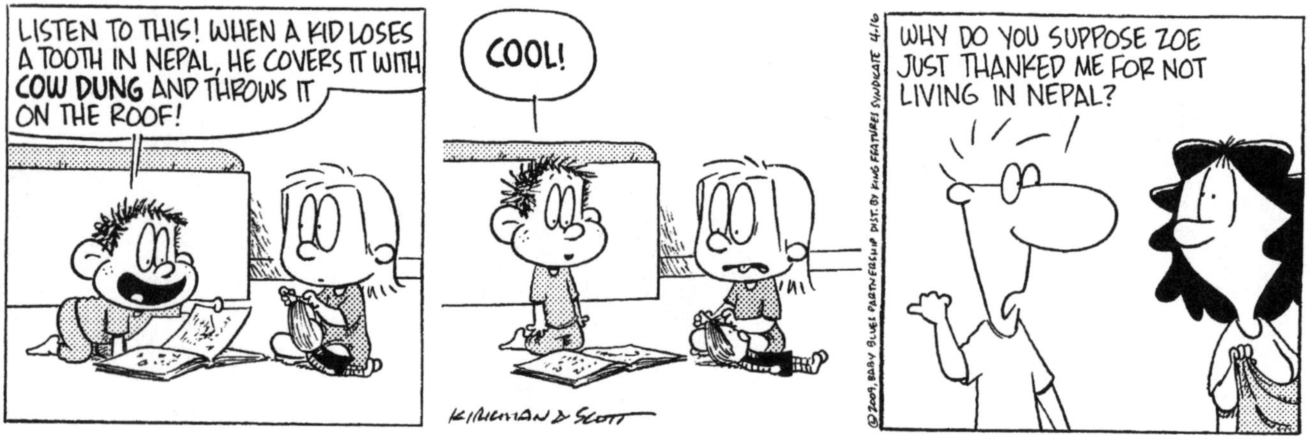
LISTEN TO THIS! WHEN A KID LOSES A TOOTH IN NEPAL, HE COVERS IT WITH **COW DUNG** AND THROWS IT ON THE ROOF!
COOL!
KIRKMAN & SCOTT
WHY DO YOU SUPPOSE ZOE JUST THANKED ME FOR NOT LIVING IN NEPAL?
© 2009, BABY BLUES PARTNERSHIP DIST. BY KING FEATURES SYNDICATE 4.16

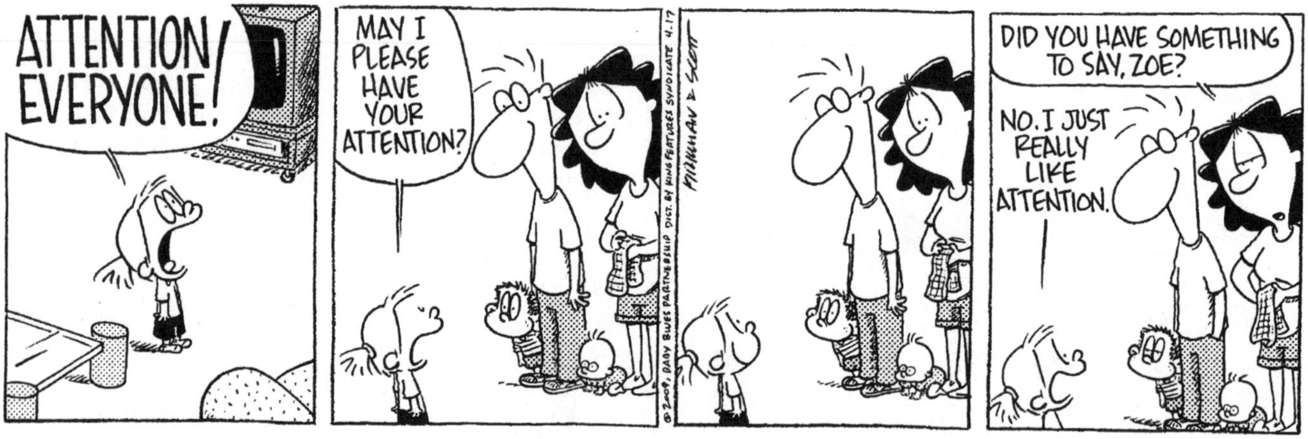
ATTENTION EVERYONE!
MAY I PLEASE HAVE YOUR ATTENTION?
© 2009, BABY BLUES PARTNERSHIP DIST. BY KING FEATURES SYNDICATE 4.17
KIRKMAN & SCOTT
DID YOU HAVE SOMETHING TO SAY, ZOE?
NO. I JUST REALLY LIKE ATTENTION.

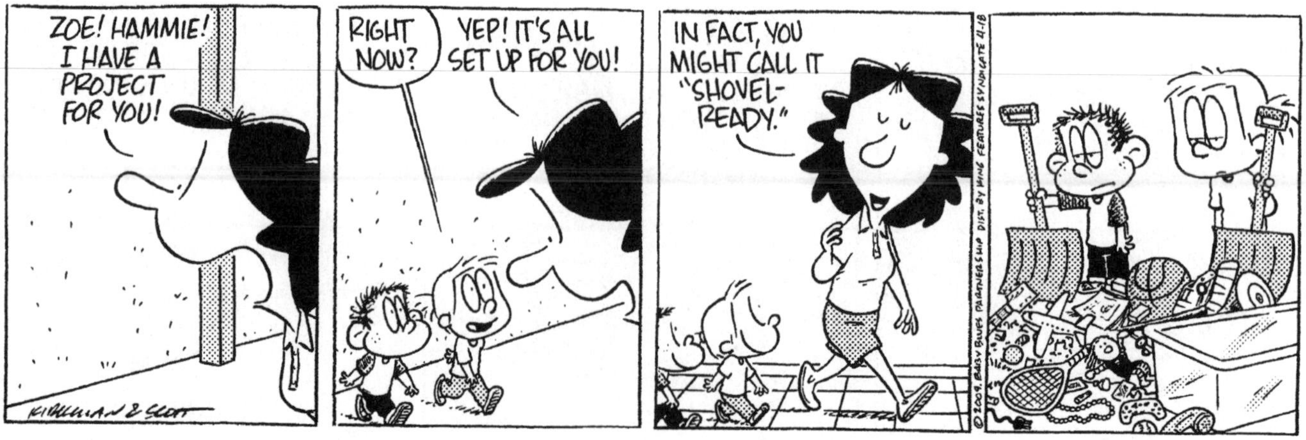
ZOE! HAMMIE! I HAVE A PROJECT FOR YOU!
KIRKMAN & SCOTT
RIGHT NOW?
YEP! IT'S ALL SET UP FOR YOU!
IN FACT, YOU MIGHT CALL IT "SHOVEL-READY."
© 2009, BABY BLUES PARTNERSHIP DIST. BY KING FEATURES SYNDICATE 4.18

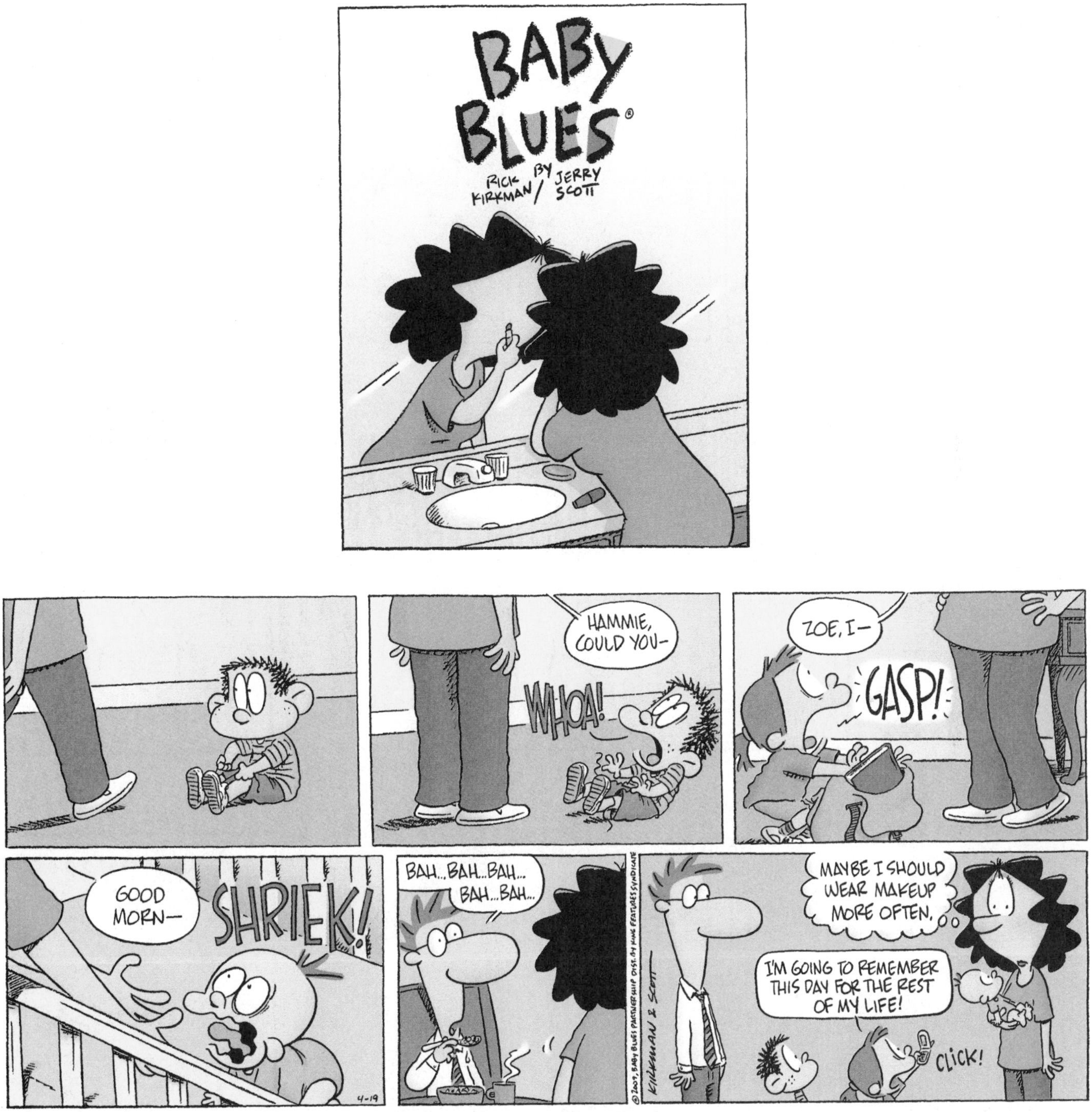
BABY BLUES®
BY RICK KIRKMAN / JERRY SCOTT
HAMMIE, COULD YOU—
WHOA!
ZOE, I—
GASP!
GOOD MORN—
SHRIEK!
4-19
BAH... BAH... BAH...
BAH... BAH...
©2009, BABY BLUES PARTNERSHIP DIST. BY KING FEATURES SYNDICATE
KIRKMAN & SCOTT
MAYBE I SHOULD WEAR MAKEUP MORE OFTEN.
I'M GOING TO REMEMBER THIS DAY FOR THE REST OF MY LIFE!
CLICK!

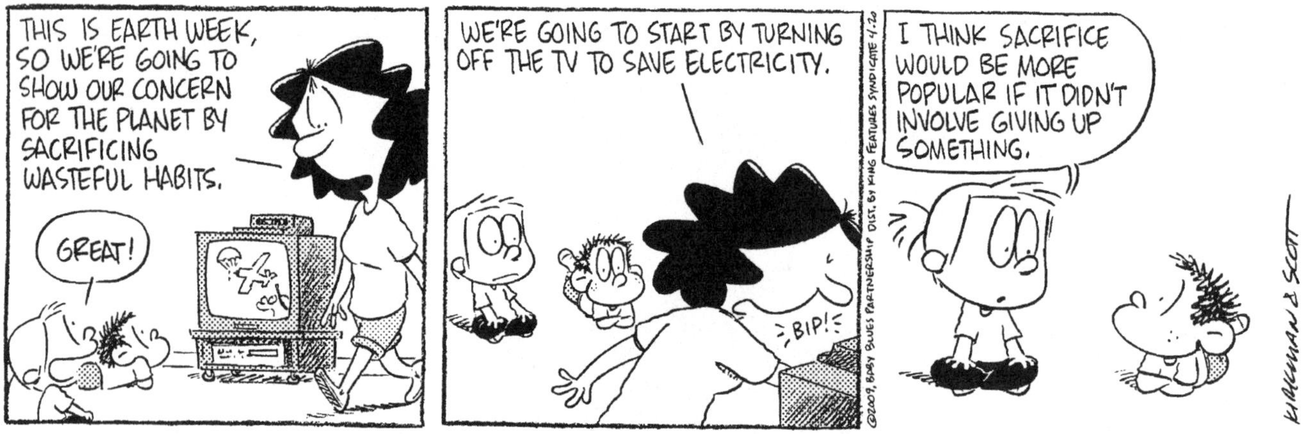
THIS IS EARTH WEEK, SO WE'RE GOING TO SHOW OUR CONCERN FOR THE PLANET BY SACRIFICING WASTEFUL HABITS.
GREAT!
WE'RE GOING TO START BY TURNING OFF THE TV TO SAVE ELECTRICITY.
BIP!
I THINK SACRIFICE WOULD BE MORE POPULAR IF IT DIDN'T INVOLVE GIVING UP SOMETHING.
©2009, BABY BLUES PARTNERSHIP DIST. BY KING FEATURES SYNDICATE 4-20
KIRKMAN & SCOTT

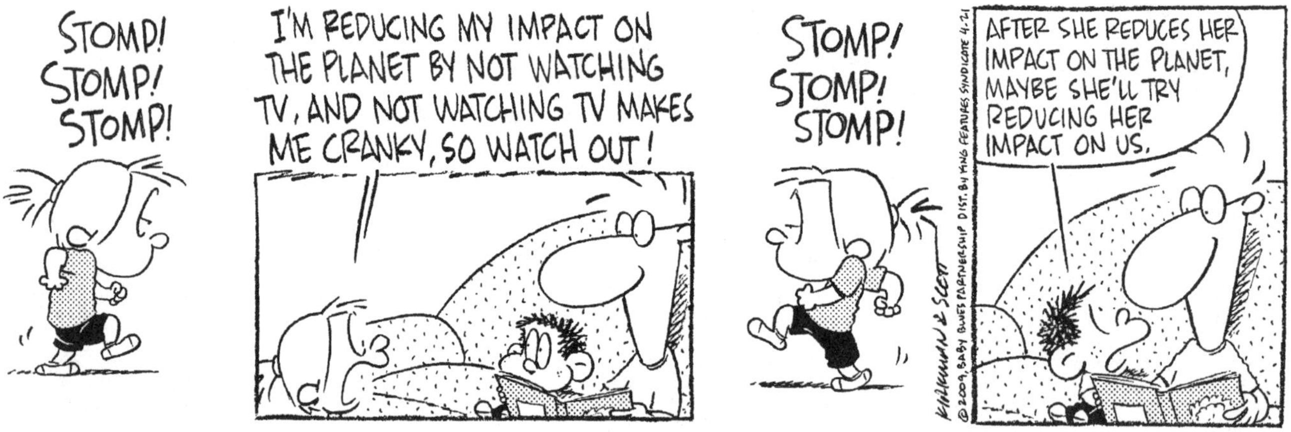
STOMP! STOMP! STOMP!
I'M REDUCING MY IMPACT ON THE PLANET BY NOT WATCHING TV, AND NOT WATCHING TV MAKES ME CRANKY, SO WATCH OUT!
STOMP! STOMP! STOMP!
KIRKMAN & SCOTT
©2009, BABY BLUES PARTNERSHIP DIST. BY KING FEATURES SYNDICATE 4-21
AFTER SHE REDUCES HER IMPACT ON THE PLANET, MAYBE SHE'LL TRY REDUCING HER IMPACT ON US.

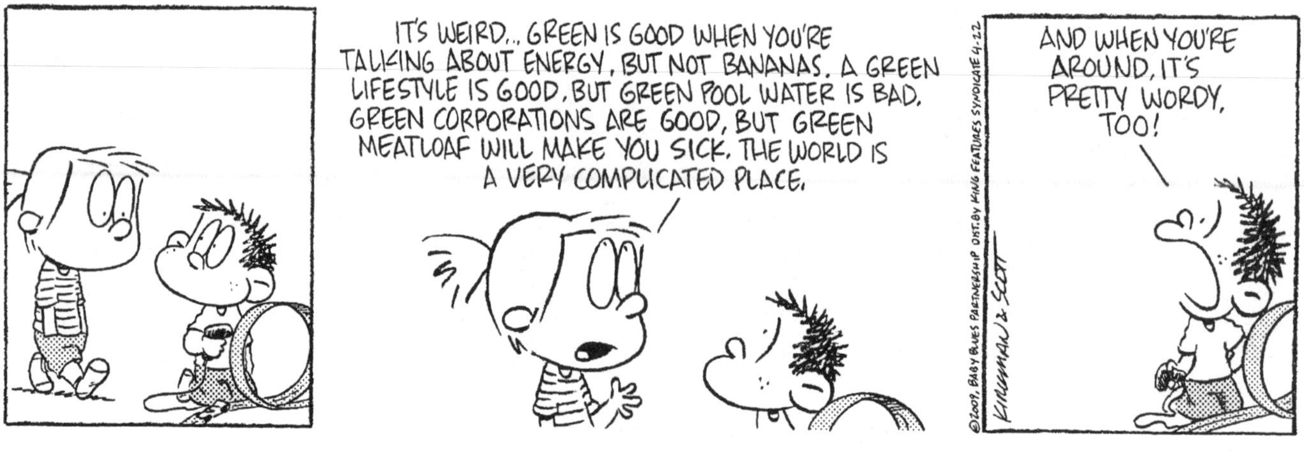
IT'S WEIRD... GREEN IS GOOD WHEN YOU'RE TALKING ABOUT ENERGY, BUT NOT BANANAS. A GREEN LIFESTYLE IS GOOD, BUT GREEN POOL WATER IS BAD. GREEN CORPORATIONS ARE GOOD, BUT GREEN MEATLOAF WILL MAKE YOU SICK. THE WORLD IS A VERY COMPLICATED PLACE.
©2009, BABY BLUES PARTNERSHIP DIST. BY KING FEATURES SYNDICATE 4-22
KIRKMAN & SCOTT
AND WHEN YOU'RE AROUND, IT'S PRETTY WORDY, TOO!

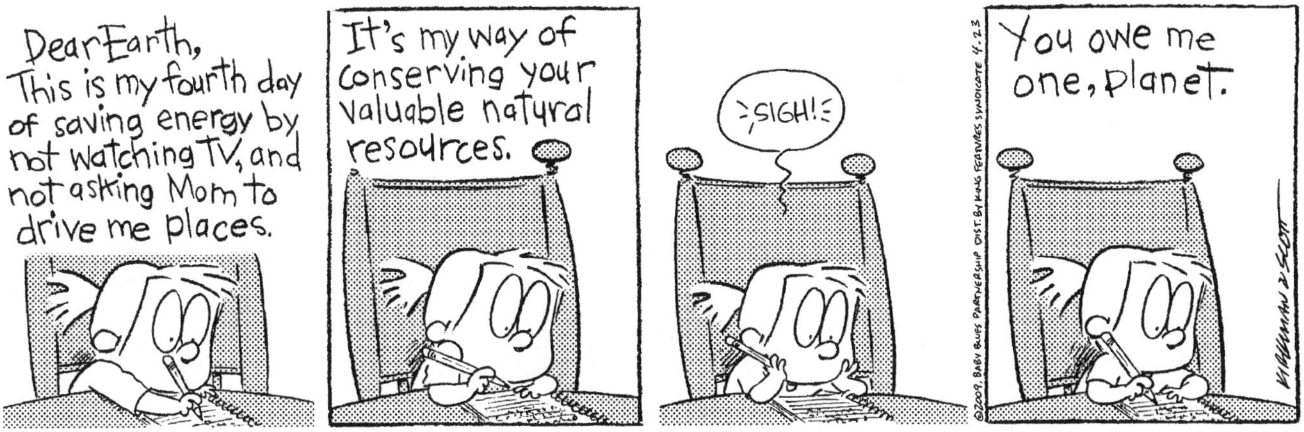
Dear Earth,
This is my fourth day of saving energy by not watching TV, and not asking Mom to drive me places.
It's my way of conserving your valuable natural resources.
SIGH!
You owe me one, planet.
©2009, Baby Blues Partnership Dist. By King Features Syndicate 4-23
Kirkman & Scott

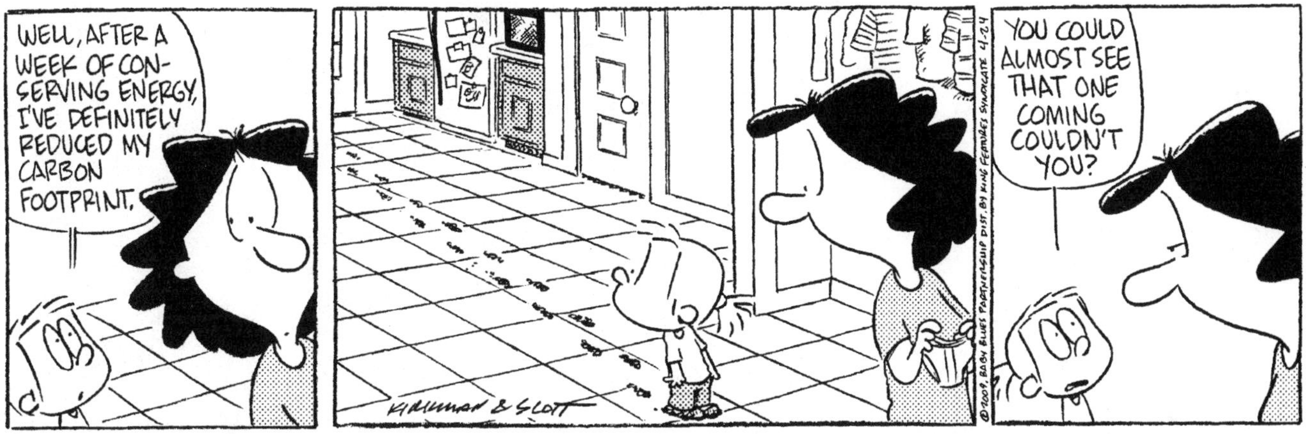
WELL, AFTER A WEEK OF CONSERVING ENERGY, I'VE DEFINITELY REDUCED MY CARBON FOOTPRINT.
KIRKMAN & SCOTT
©2009, Baby Blues Partnership Dist. By King Features Syndicate 4-24
YOU COULD ALMOST SEE THAT ONE COMING COULDN'T YOU?

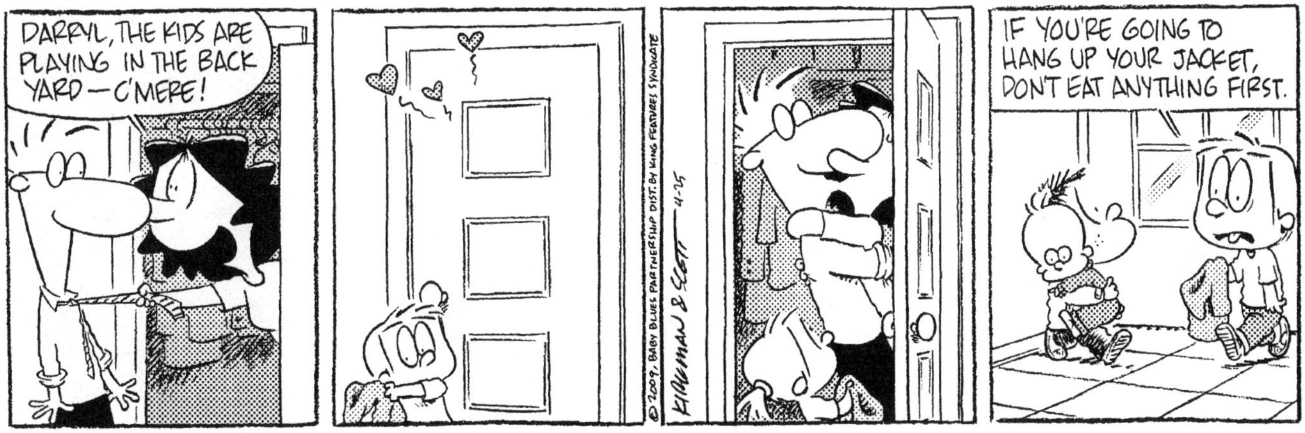
DARRYL, THE KIDS ARE PLAYING IN THE BACK YARD—C'MERE!
©2009, Baby Blues Partnership Dist. By King Features Syndicate
Kirkman & Scott 4-25
IF YOU'RE GOING TO HANG UP YOUR JACKET, DON'T EAT ANYTHING FIRST.

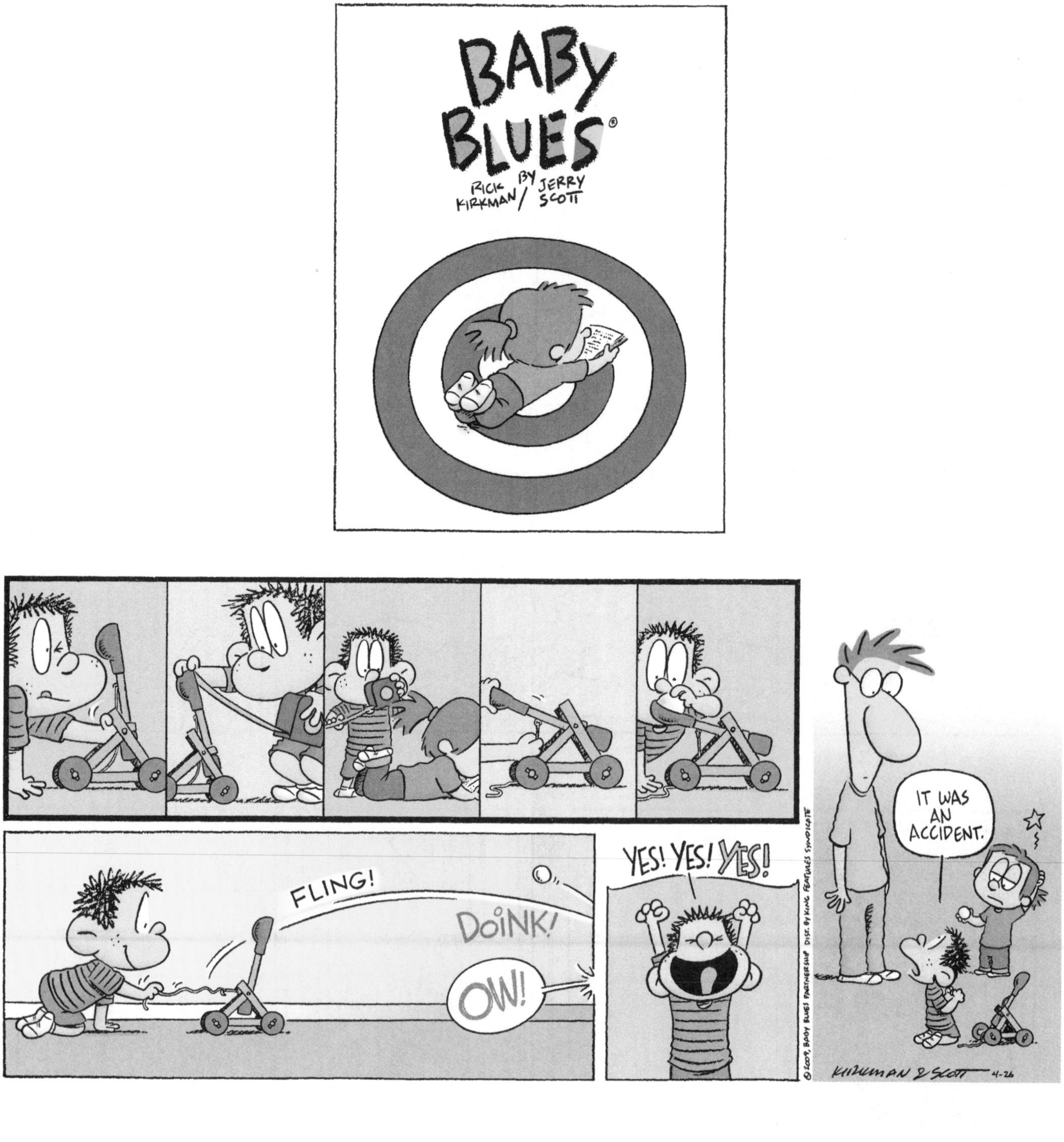
BABY BLUES®
BY RICK KIRKMAN / JERRY SCOTT
FLING!
DOINK!
OW!
YES! YES! YES!
IT WAS AN ACCIDENT.
©2009, BABY BLUES PARTNERSHIP DIST. BY KING FEATURES SYNDICATE
KIRKMAN & SCOTT 4-26

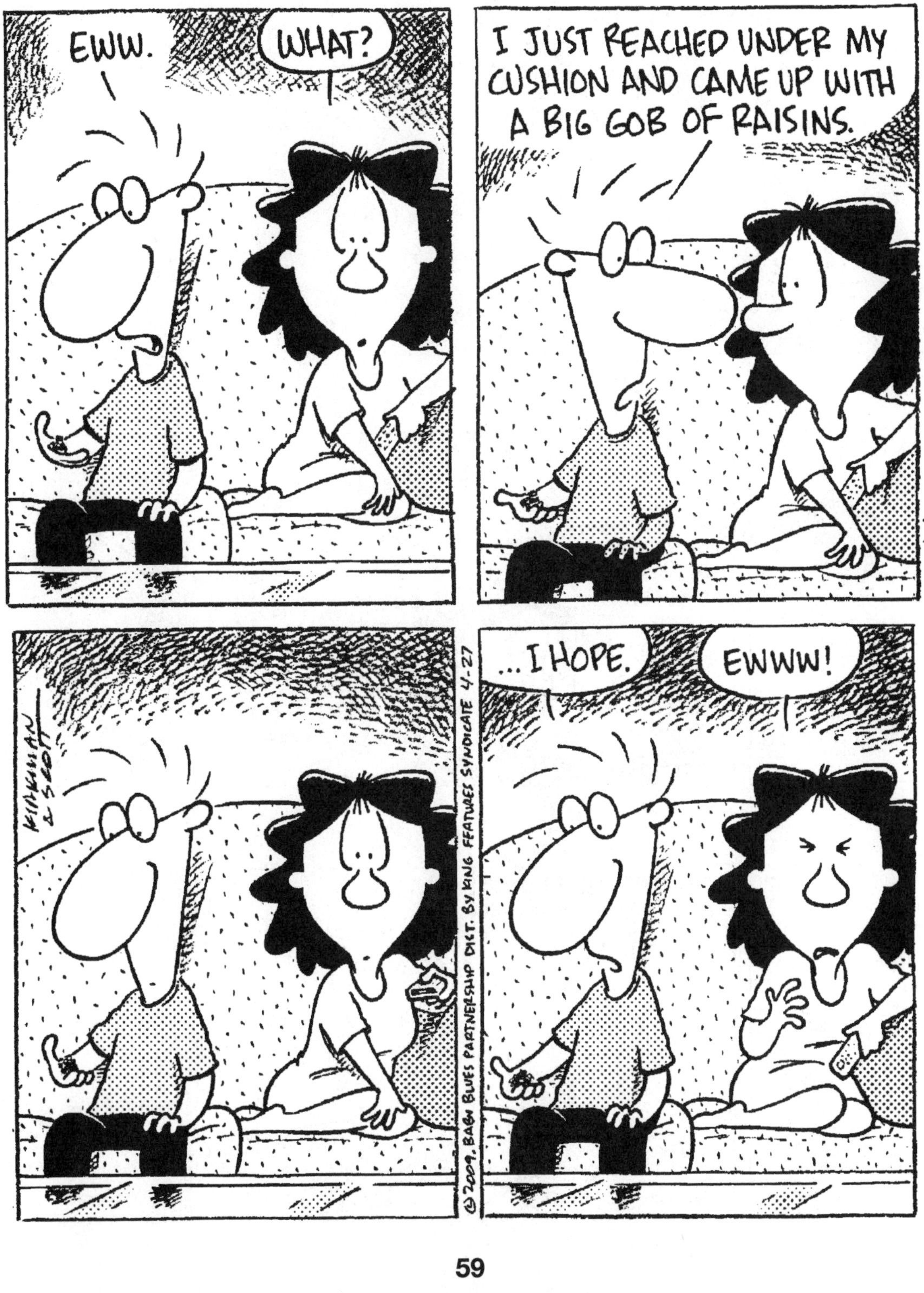
EWW.
WHAT?
I JUST REACHED UNDER MY CUSHION AND CAME UP WITH A BIG GOB OF RAISINS.
KIRKMAN & SCOTT
© 2009, BAGN BLUES PARTNERSHIP DIST. BY KING FEATURES SYNDICATE 4-27
...I HOPE.
EWWW!

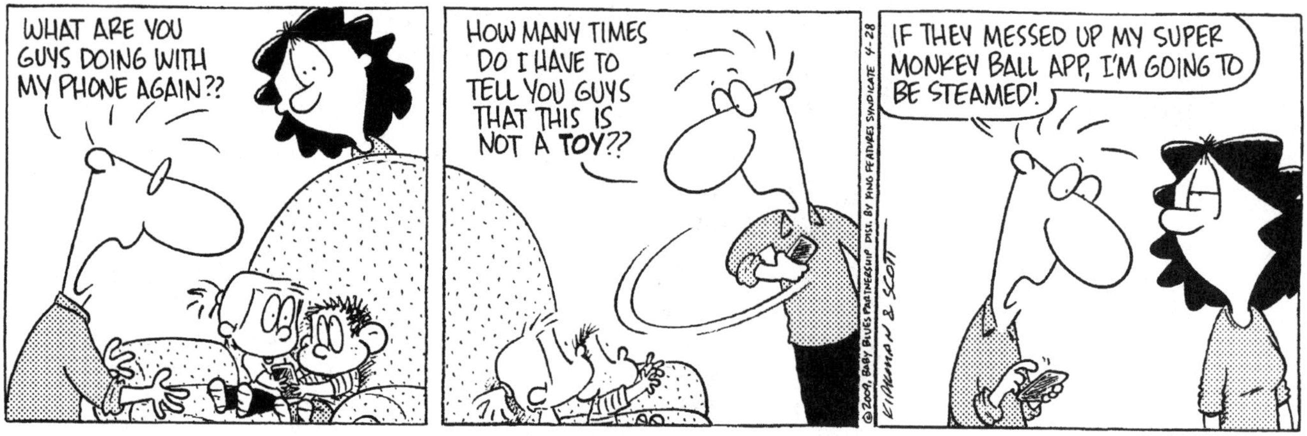
WHAT ARE YOU GUYS DOING WITH MY PHONE AGAIN??
HOW MANY TIMES DO I HAVE TO TELL YOU GUYS THAT THIS IS NOT A **TOY**??
© 2009, BABY BLUES PARTNERSHIP DIST. BY KING FEATURES SYNDICATE 4-28
KIRKMAN & SCOTT
IF THEY MESSED UP MY SUPER MONKEY BALL APP, I'M GOING TO BE STEAMED!

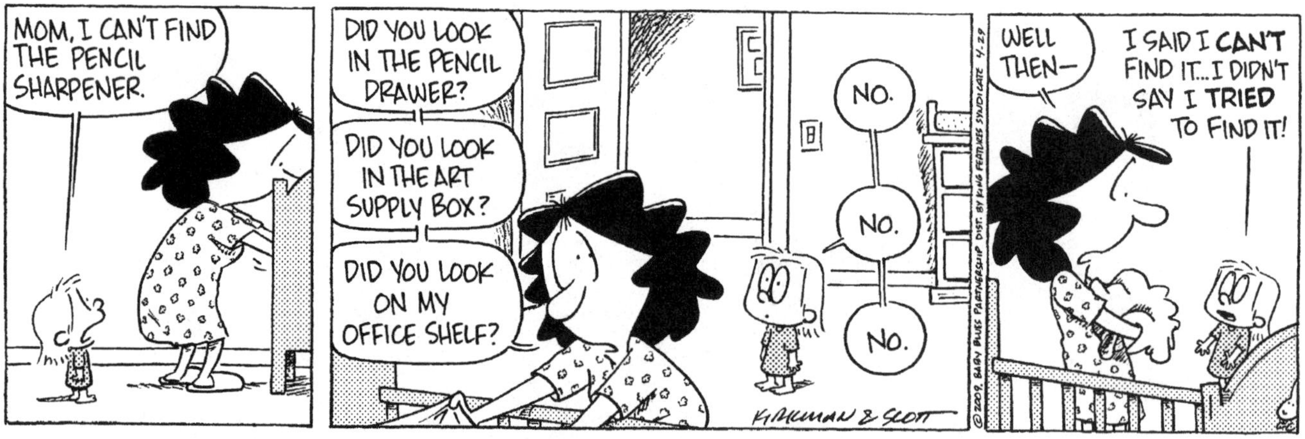
MOM, I CAN'T FIND THE PENCIL SHARPENER.
DID YOU LOOK IN THE PENCIL DRAWER?
DID YOU LOOK IN THE ART SUPPLY BOX?
DID YOU LOOK ON MY OFFICE SHELF?
NO.
NO.
NO.
KIRKMAN & SCOTT
© 2009, BABY BLUES PARTNERSHIP DIST. BY KING FEATURES SYNDICATE 4-29
WELL THEN—
I SAID I **CAN'T** FIND IT... I DIDN'T SAY I **TRIED** TO FIND IT!

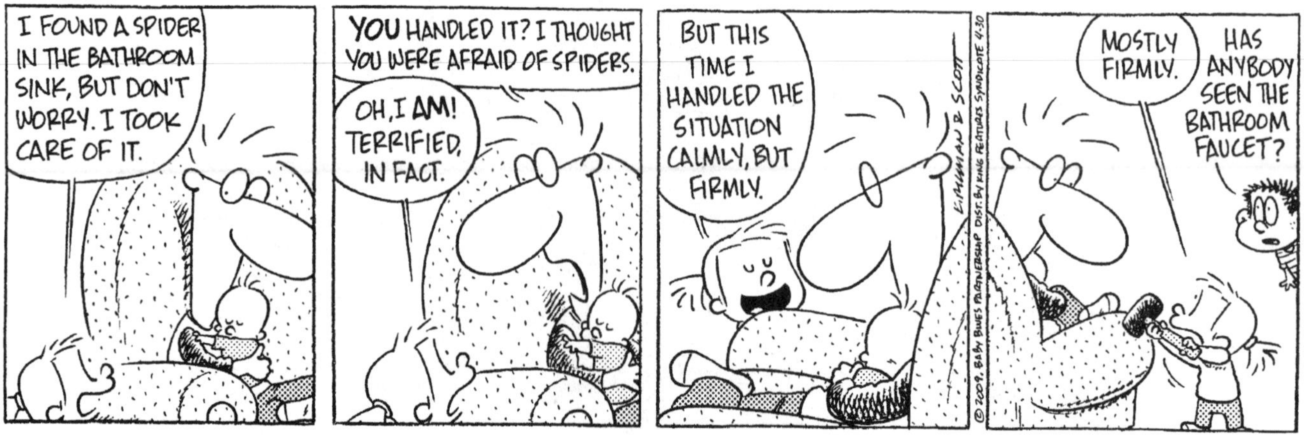
I FOUND A SPIDER IN THE BATHROOM SINK, BUT DON'T WORRY. I TOOK CARE OF IT.
YOU HANDLED IT? I THOUGHT YOU WERE AFRAID OF SPIDERS.
OH, I **AM**! TERRIFIED, IN FACT.
BUT THIS TIME I HANDLED THE SITUATION CALMLY, BUT FIRMLY.
KIRKMAN & SCOTT
© 2009, BABY BLUES PARTNERSHIP DIST. BY KING FEATURES SYNDICATE 4-30
MOSTLY FIRMLY.
HAS ANYBODY SEEN THE BATHROOM FAUCET?

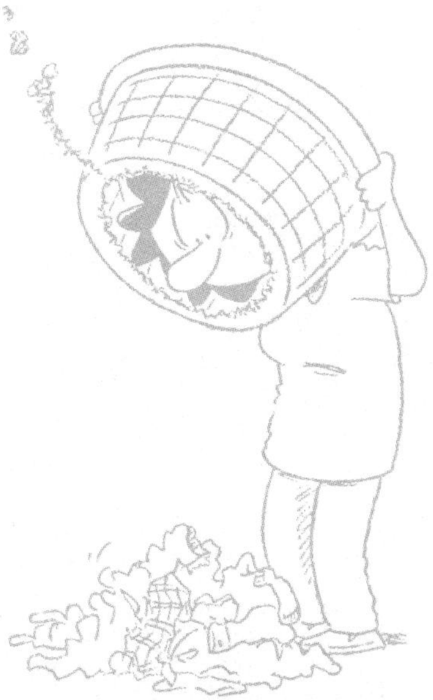

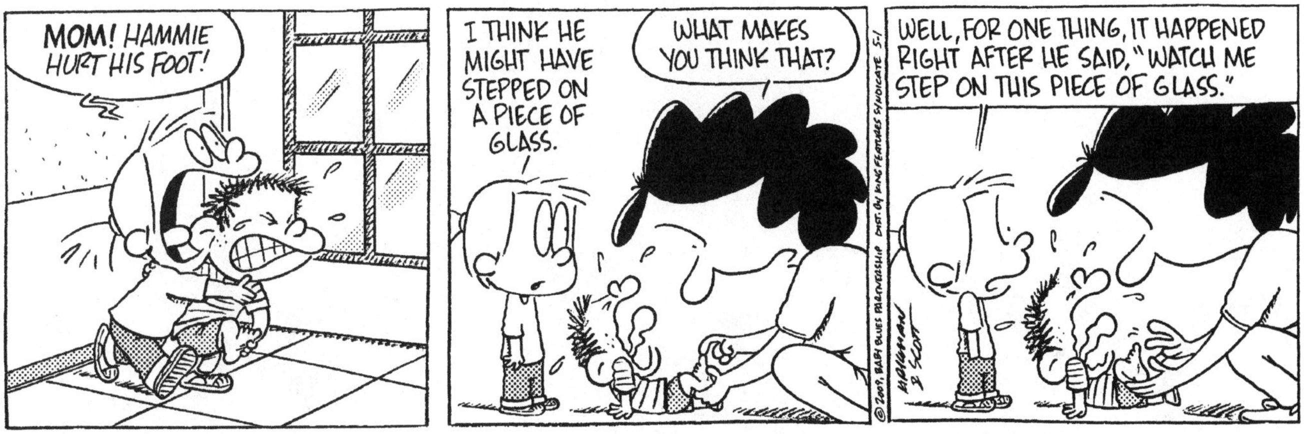
MOM! HAMMIE HURT HIS FOOT!
I THINK HE MIGHT HAVE STEPPED ON A PIECE OF GLASS.
WHAT MAKES YOU THINK THAT?
WELL, FOR ONE THING, IT HAPPENED RIGHT AFTER HE SAID, "WATCH ME STEP ON THIS PIECE OF GLASS."
© 2009, BABY BLUES PARTNERSHIP DIST. BY KING FEATURES SYNDICATE 5-1
KIRKMAN & SCOTT

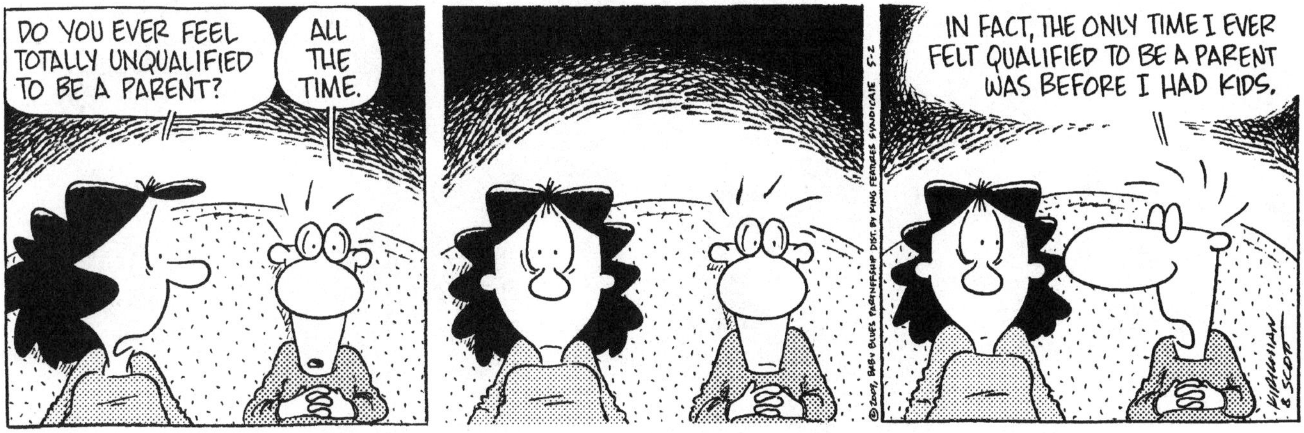
DO YOU EVER FEEL TOTALLY UNQUALIFIED TO BE A PARENT?
ALL THE TIME.
IN FACT, THE ONLY TIME I EVER FELT QUALIFIED TO BE A PARENT WAS BEFORE I HAD KIDS.
© 2009, BABY BLUES PARTNERSHIP DIST. BY KING FEATURES SYNDICATE 5-2
KIRKMAN & SCOTT

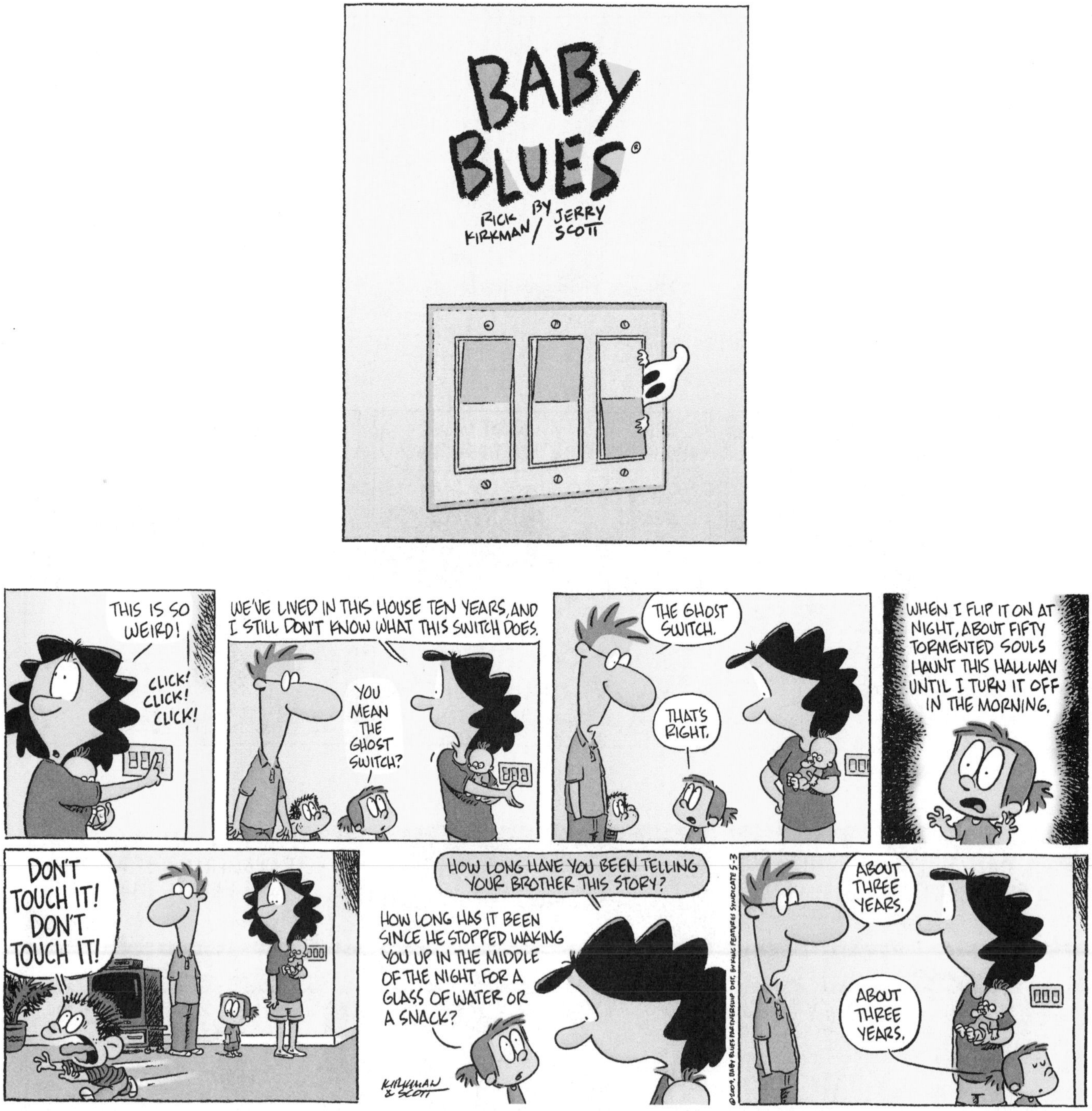
BABY BLUES®
BY RICK KIRKMAN / JERRY SCOTT
THIS IS SO WEIRD!
CLICK! CLICK! CLICK!
WE'VE LIVED IN THIS HOUSE TEN YEARS, AND I STILL DON'T KNOW WHAT THIS SWITCH DOES.
YOU MEAN THE GHOST SWITCH?
THE GHOST SWITCH.
THAT'S RIGHT.
WHEN I FLIP IT ON AT NIGHT, ABOUT FIFTY TORMENTED SOULS HAUNT THIS HALLWAY UNTIL I TURN IT OFF IN THE MORNING.
DON'T TOUCH IT! DON'T TOUCH IT!
HOW LONG HAVE YOU BEEN TELLING YOUR BROTHER THIS STORY?
HOW LONG HAS IT BEEN SINCE HE STOPPED WAKING YOU UP IN THE MIDDLE OF THE NIGHT FOR A GLASS OF WATER OR A SNACK?
KIRKMAN & SCOTT
©2009, BABY BLUES PARTNERSHIP DIST. BY KING FEATURES SYNDICATE 5-3
ABOUT THREE YEARS.
ABOUT THREE YEARS.

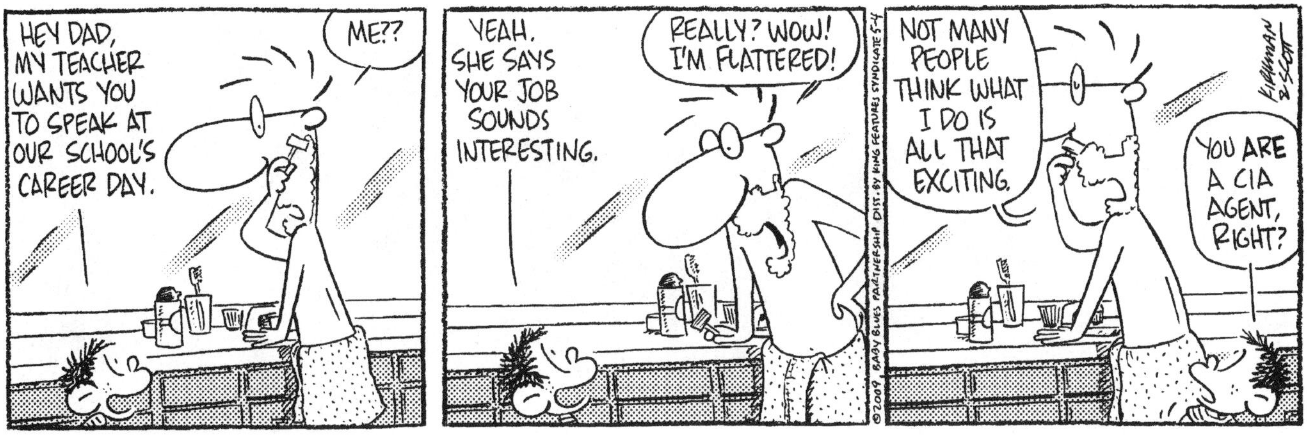
HEY DAD, MY TEACHER WANTS YOU TO SPEAK AT OUR SCHOOL'S CAREER DAY.
ME??
YEAH. SHE SAYS YOUR JOB SOUNDS INTERESTING.
REALLY? WOW! I'M FLATTERED!
© 2009 BABY BLUES PARTNERSHIP DIST. BY KING FEATURES SYNDICATE 5-4
NOT MANY PEOPLE THINK WHAT I DO IS ALL THAT EXCITING.
YOU **ARE** A CIA AGENT, RIGHT?
KIRKMAN & SCOTT

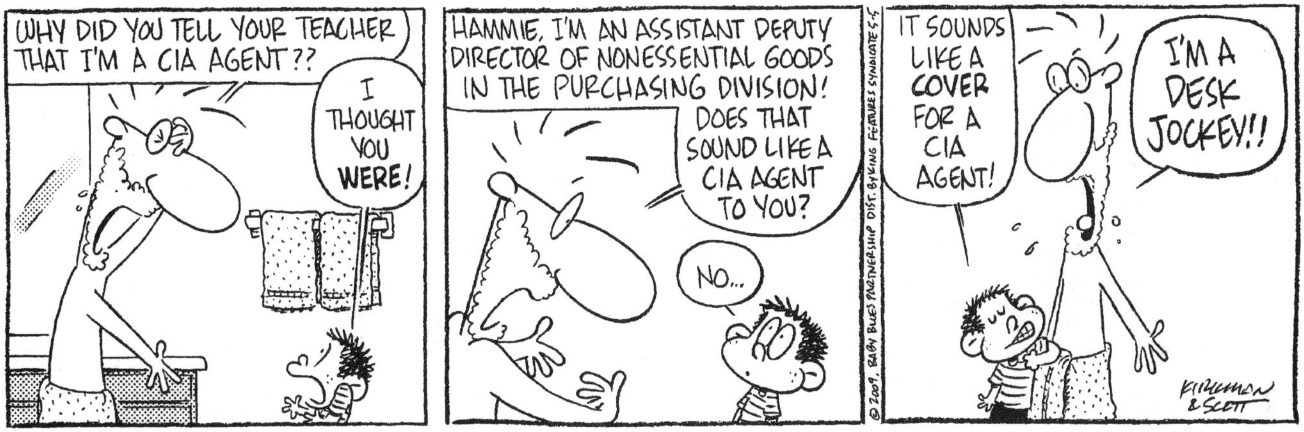
WHY DID YOU TELL YOUR TEACHER THAT I'M A CIA AGENT??
I THOUGHT YOU **WERE**!
HAMMIE, I'M AN ASSISTANT DEPUTY DIRECTOR OF NONESSENTIAL GOODS IN THE PURCHASING DIVISION!
DOES THAT SOUND LIKE A CIA AGENT TO YOU?
NO...
© 2009 BABY BLUES PARTNERSHIP DIST. BY KING FEATURES SYNDICATE 5-5
IT SOUNDS LIKE A **COVER** FOR A CIA AGENT!
I'M A DESK JOCKEY!!
KIRKMAN & SCOTT

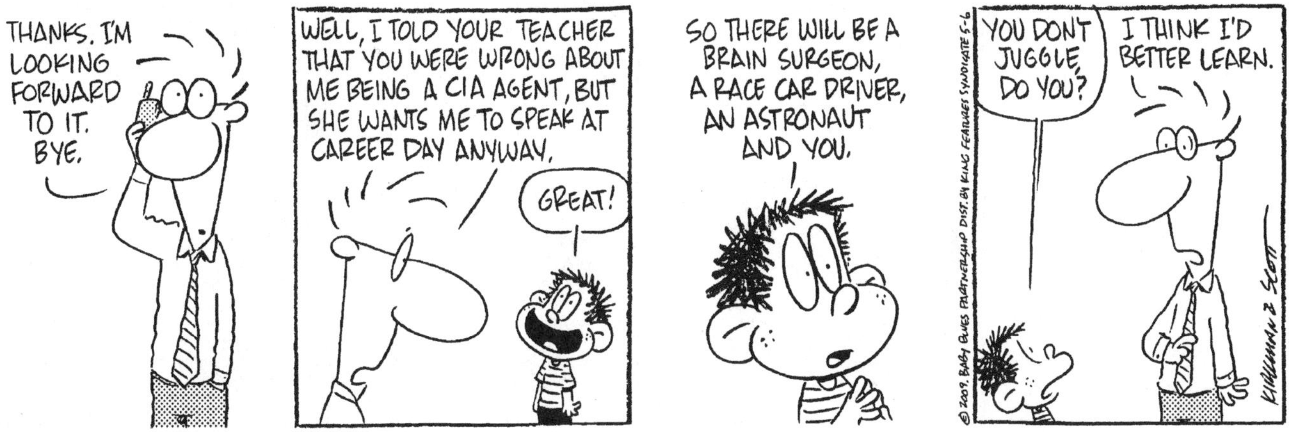
THANKS. I'M LOOKING FORWARD TO IT. BYE.
WELL, I TOLD YOUR TEACHER THAT YOU WERE WRONG ABOUT ME BEING A CIA AGENT, BUT SHE WANTS ME TO SPEAK AT CAREER DAY ANYWAY.
GREAT!
SO THERE WILL BE A BRAIN SURGEON, A RACE CAR DRIVER, AN ASTRONAUT AND YOU.
© 2009 BABY BLUES PARTNERSHIP DIST. BY KING FEATURES SYNDICATE 5-6
YOU DON'T JUGGLE, DO YOU?
I THINK I'D BETTER LEARN.
KIRKMAN & SCOTT

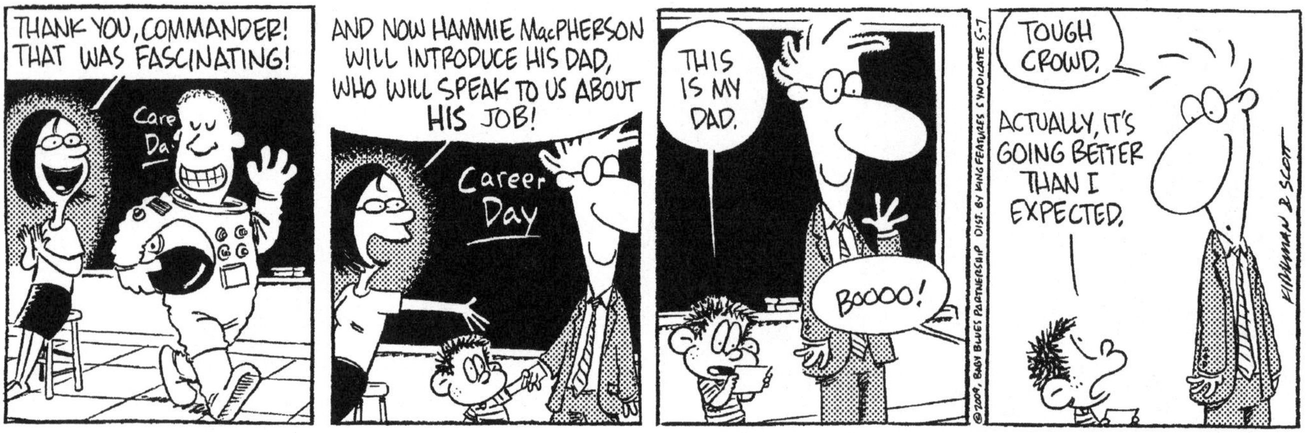
THANK YOU, COMMANDER! THAT WAS FASCINATING!
Career Day
AND NOW HAMMIE MacPHERSON WILL INTRODUCE HIS DAD, WHO WILL SPEAK TO US ABOUT HIS JOB!
Career Day
© 2009, BABY BLUES PARTNERSHIP DIST. BY KING FEATURES SYNDICATE 5-7
THIS IS MY DAD.
BOOOO!
TOUGH CROWD.
ACTUALLY, IT'S GOING BETTER THAN I EXPECTED.
KIRKMAN & SCOTT

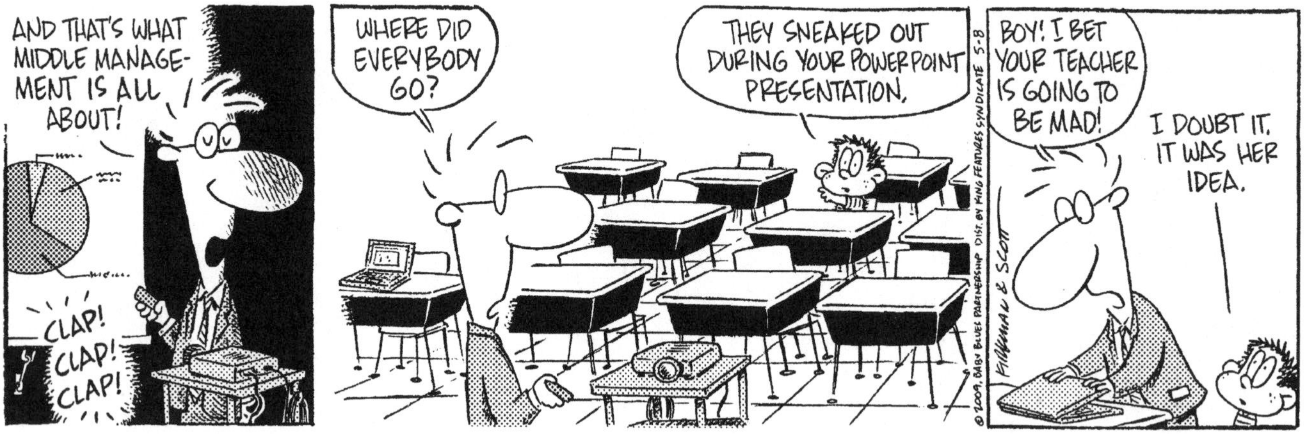
AND THAT'S WHAT MIDDLE MANAGEMENT IS ALL ABOUT!
CLAP! CLAP! CLAP!
WHERE DID EVERYBODY GO?
THEY SNEAKED OUT DURING YOUR POWERPOINT PRESENTATION.
© 2009, BABY BLUES PARTNERSHIP DIST. BY KING FEATURES SYNDICATE 5-8
KIRKMAN & SCOTT
BOY! I BET YOUR TEACHER IS GOING TO BE MAD!
I DOUBT IT. IT WAS HER IDEA.

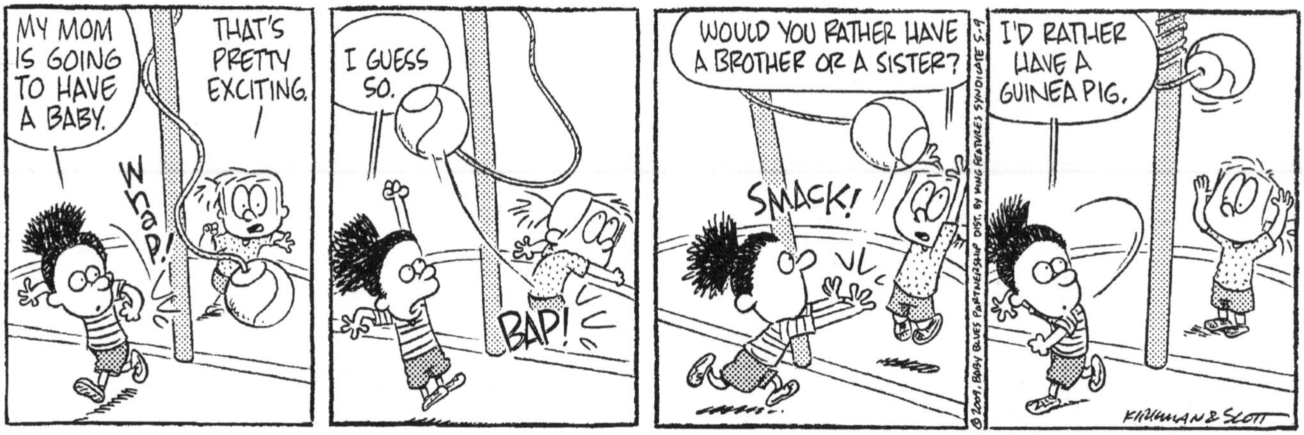
MY MOM IS GOING TO HAVE A BABY.
THAT'S PRETTY EXCITING.
WHAP!
I GUESS SO.
BAP!
WOULD YOU RATHER HAVE A BROTHER OR A SISTER?
SMACK!
© 2009, BABY BLUES PARTNERSHIP DIST. BY KING FEATURES SYNDICATE 5-9
I'D RATHER HAVE A GUINEA PIG.
KIRKMAN & SCOTT

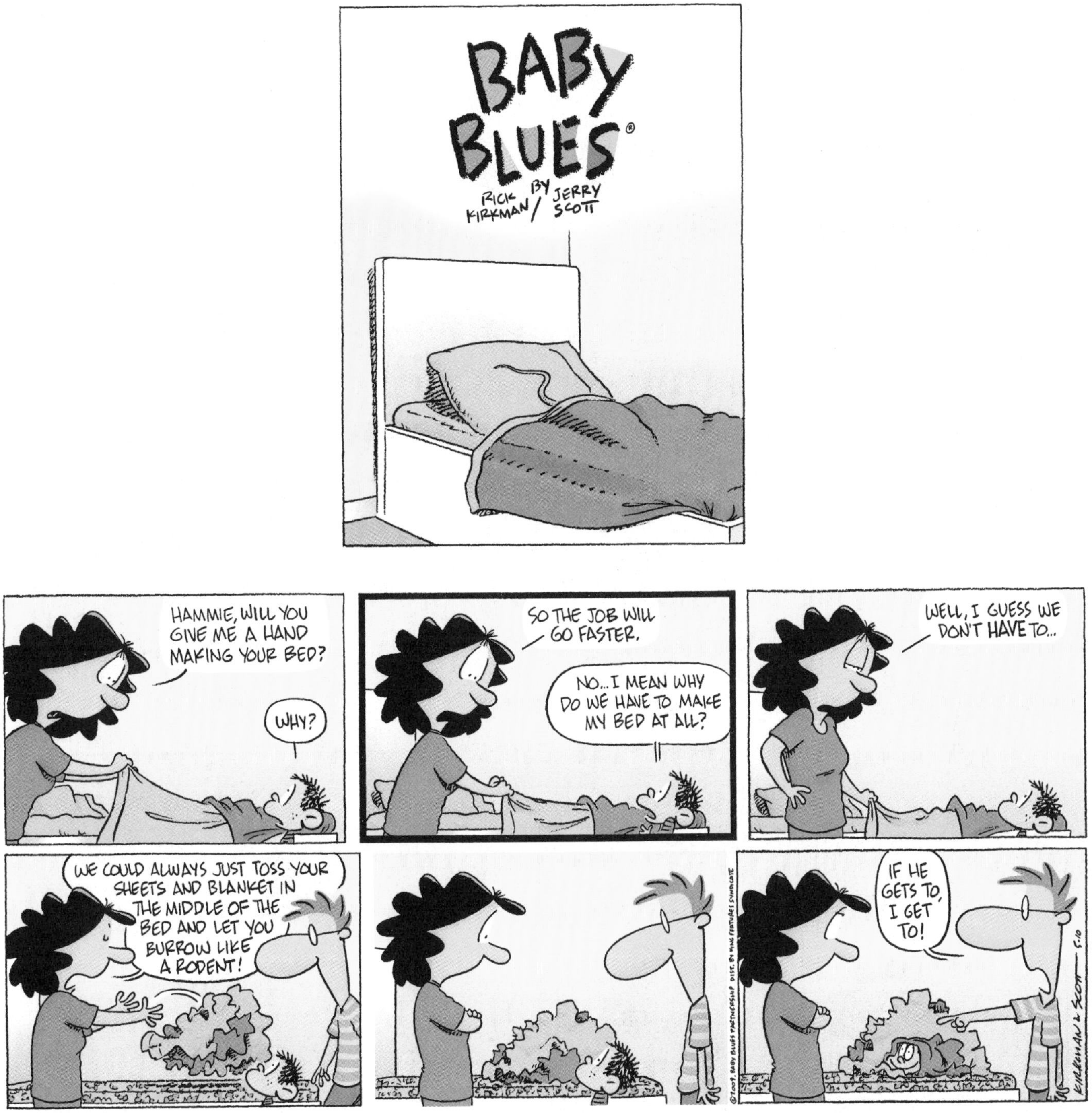
BABY BLUES®
BY RICK KIRKMAN / JERRY SCOTT
HAMMIE, WILL YOU GIVE ME A HAND MAKING YOUR BED?
WHY?
SO THE JOB WILL GO FASTER.
NO... I MEAN WHY DO WE HAVE TO MAKE MY BED AT ALL?
WELL, I GUESS WE DON'T HAVE TO...
WE COULD ALWAYS JUST TOSS YOUR SHEETS AND BLANKET IN THE MIDDLE OF THE BED AND LET YOU BURROW LIKE A RODENT!
©2009, BABY BLUES PARTNERSHIP DIST. BY KING FEATURES SYNDICATE
IF HE GETS TO, I GET TO!
KIRKMAN & SCOTT
5-10

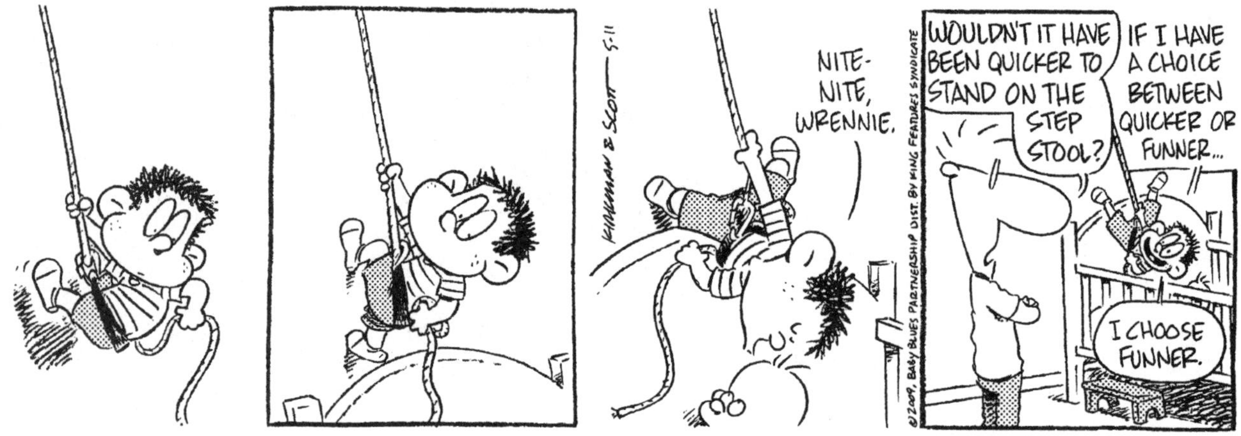
KIRKMAN & SCOTT 5-11
NITE-NITE, WRENNIE.
©2009, BABY BLUES PARTNERSHIP DIST. BY KING FEATURES SYNDICATE
WOULDN'T IT HAVE BEEN QUICKER TO STAND ON THE STEP STOOL?
IF I HAVE A CHOICE BETWEEN QUICKER OR FUNNER...
I CHOOSE FUNNER.

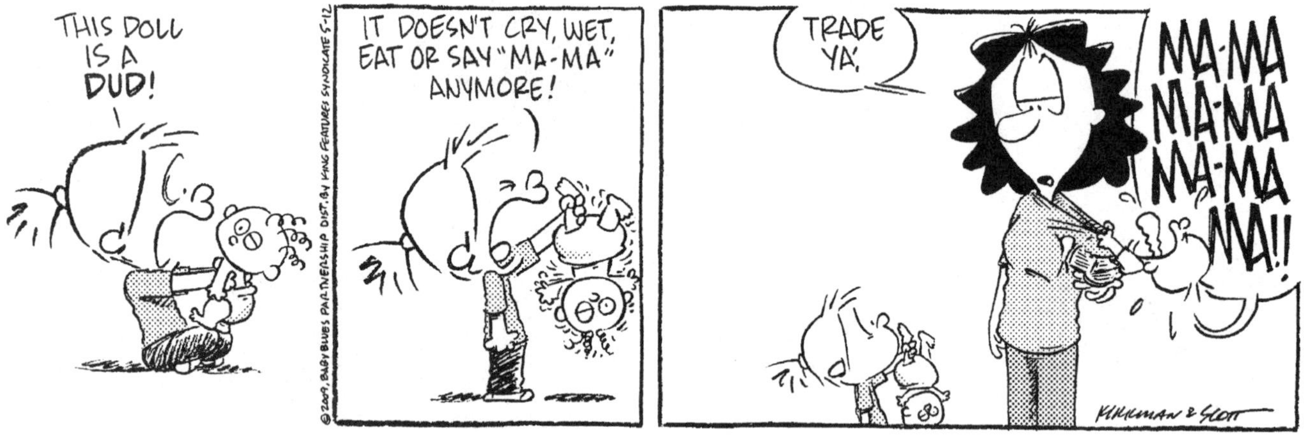
THIS DOLL IS A DUD!
©2009, BABY BLUES PARTNERSHIP DIST. BY KING FEATURES SYNDICATE 5-12
IT DOESN'T CRY, WET, EAT OR SAY "MA-MA" ANYMORE!
TRADE YA'.
MA-MA MA-MA MA-MA MA!!
KIRKMAN & SCOTT

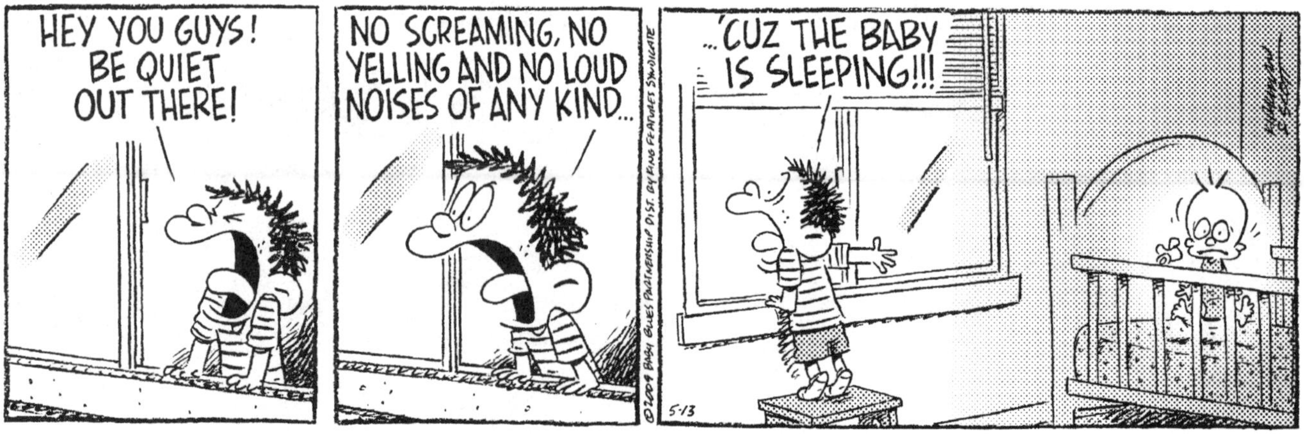
HEY YOU GUYS! BE QUIET OUT THERE!
NO SCREAMING, NO YELLING AND NO LOUD NOISES OF ANY KIND...
©2009 BABY BLUES PARTNERSHIP DIST. BY KING FEATURES SYNDICATE
...'CUZ THE BABY IS SLEEPING!!!
5-13

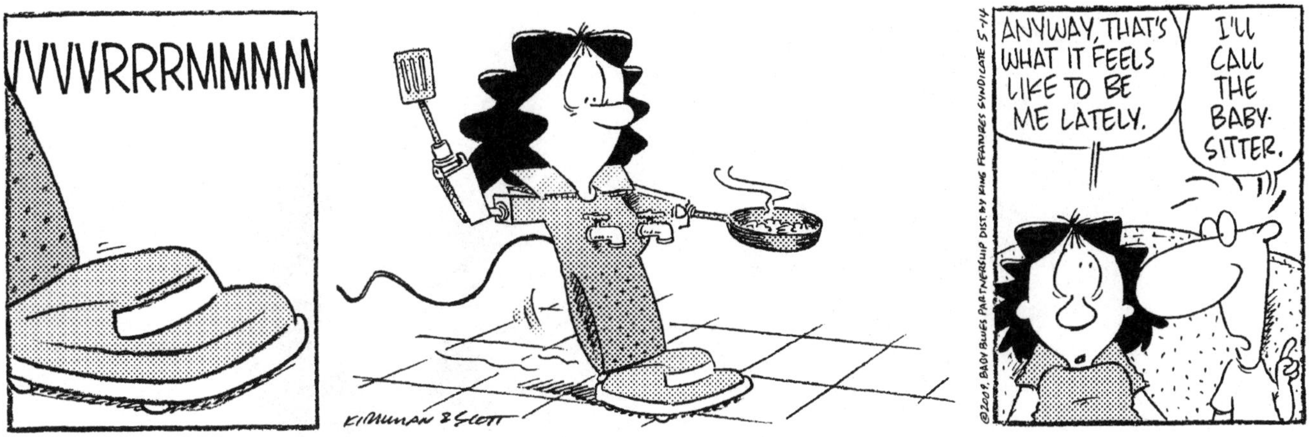
VVVVRRRRMMMMN
ANYWAY, THAT'S WHAT IT FEELS LIKE TO BE ME LATELY.
I'LL CALL THE BABY-SITTER.

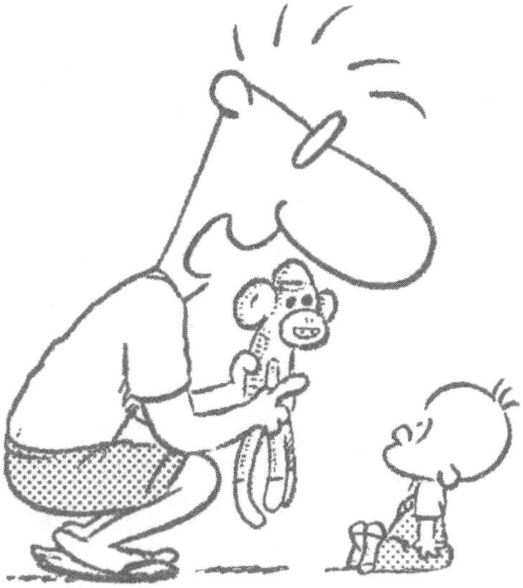

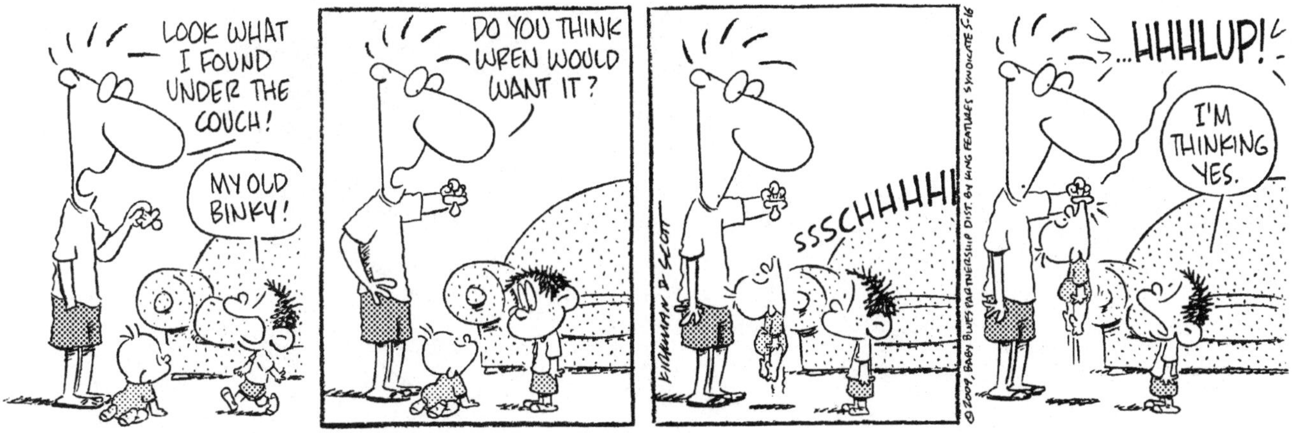
LOOK WHAT I FOUND UNDER THE COUCH!
MY OLD BINKY!
DO YOU THINK WREN WOULD WANT IT?
SSSCHHHHH
...HHHLUP!
I'M THINKING YES.

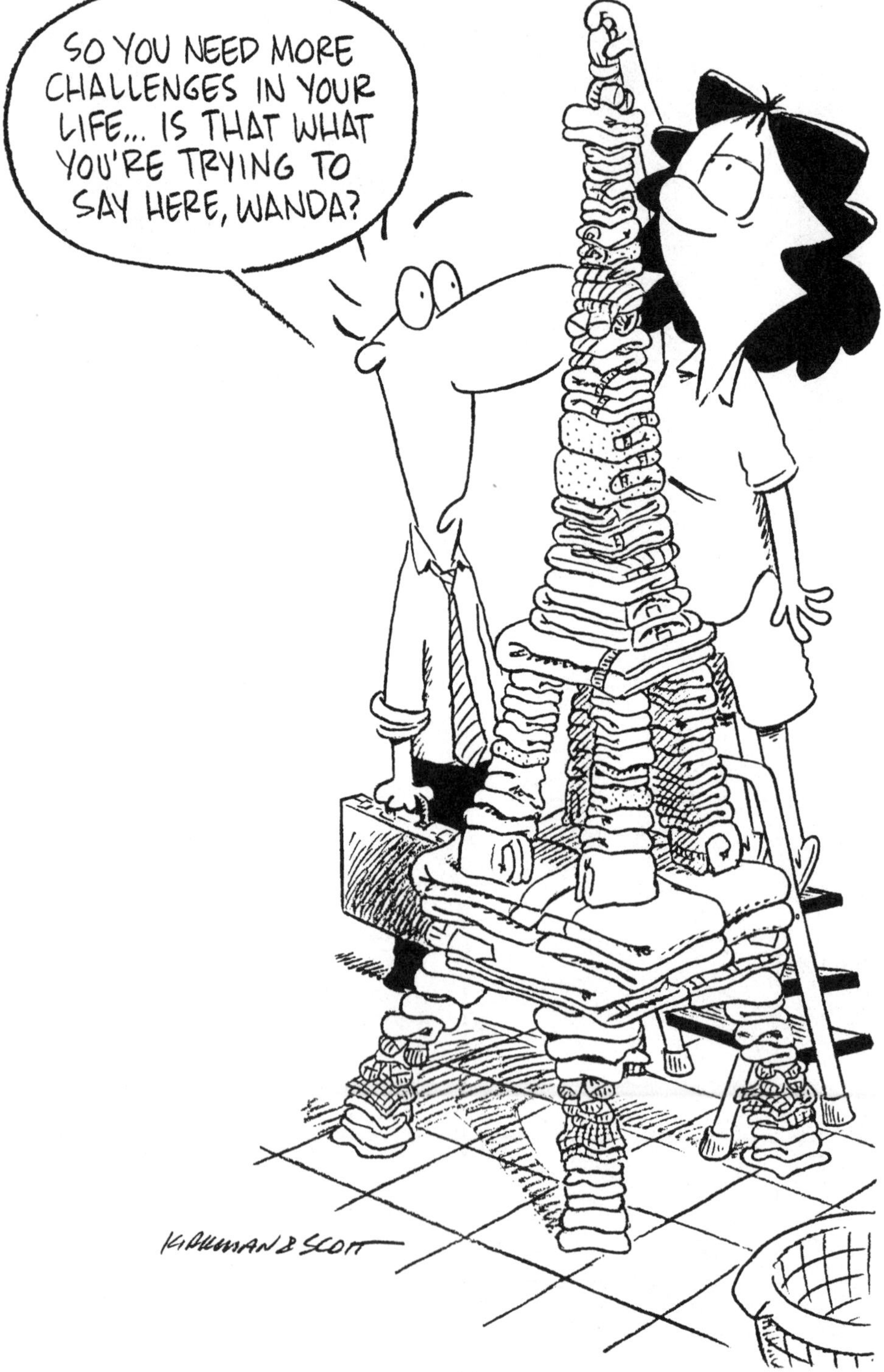
SO YOU NEED MORE CHALLENGES IN YOUR LIFE... IS THAT WHAT YOU'RE TRYING TO SAY HERE, WANDA?
KIRKMAN & SCOTT

BABY BLUES®
BY RICK KIRKMAN / JERRY SCOTT
IN

...A-A-A-AND THAT SHOULD DO IT!
YAY! YOU FIXED IT!
LONG DIVISION?
HOW DID YOU GUESS?
SNIFF! SNIFF! UH-OH...
OKAY... NOW I THINK I GET IT.
CAN YOU...?
SURE.
POP!
THERE YOU GO.
THANKS.
I GET A LOT ACCOMPLISHED WHEN I WORK AT HOME...
...EXCEPT WORK.
5-17
KIRKMAN & SCOTT
©2009, BABY BLUES PARTNERSHIP DIST. BY KING FEATURES SYNDICATE

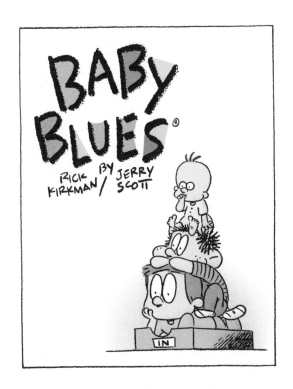

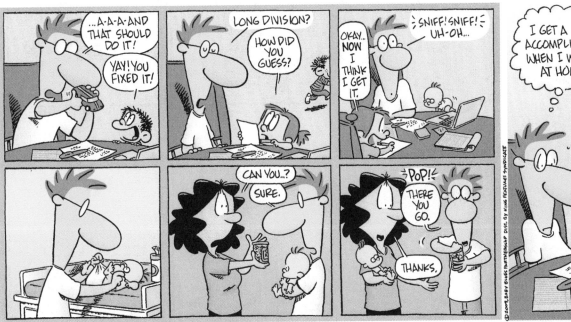

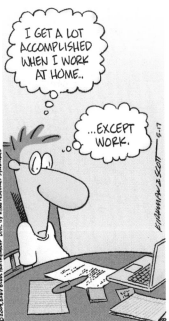

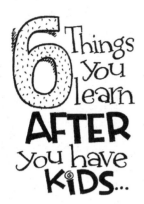

6 Things you learn **AFTER** you have **KIDS...**

YOU WANT SOME DESSERT NOW?
SURE.
KIRKMAN & SCOTT
© 2009, BABY BLUES PARTNERSHIP DIST. BY KING FEATURES SYNDICATE 5-18

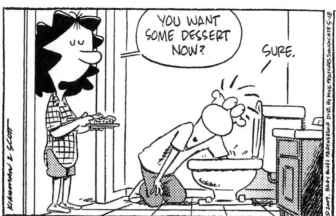

1.

Things you thought were really gross now barely qualify as yucky.

6 Things you learn **AFTER** you have **KIDS...**

KIRKMAN & SCOTT
© 2009, BABY BLUES PARTNERSHIP DIST. BY KING FEATURES SYNDICATE 5-19

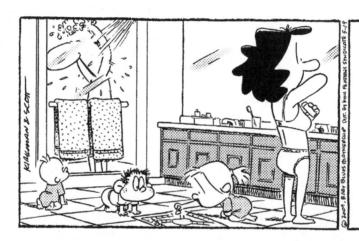

2.

The definition of privacy gets a lot looser.

6 Things you learn **AFTER** you have **KIDS...**

KIRKMAN & SCOTT
© 2009, BABY BLUES PARTNERSHIP DIST. BY KING FEATURES SYNDICATE 5-20

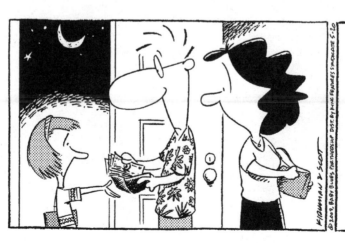

3.

Free time is anything but that.

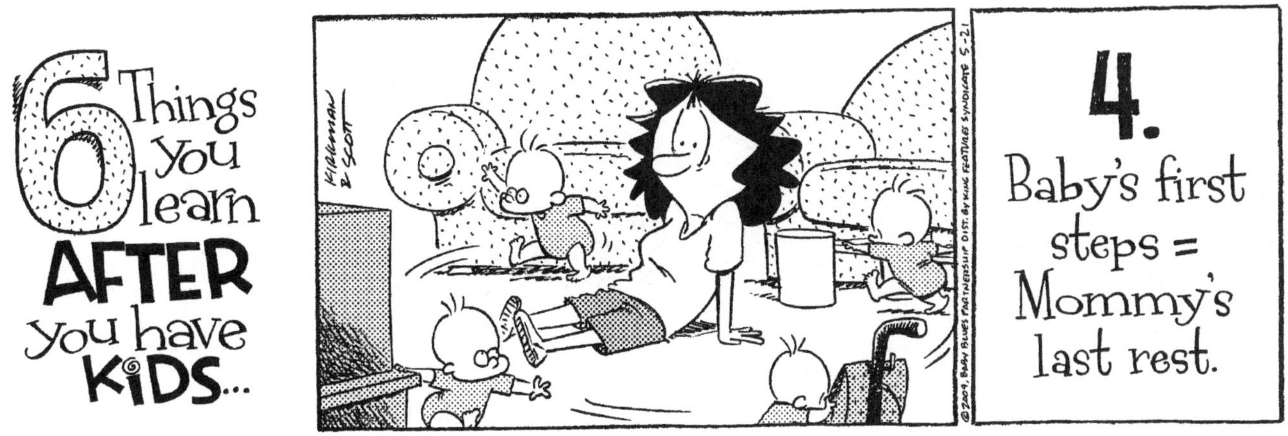
6 Things you learn AFTER you have KIDS...
KIRKMAN & SCOTT
©2009, BABY BLUES PARTNERSHIP DIST. BY KING FEATURES SYNDICATE 5-21
4.
Baby's first steps = Mommy's last rest.

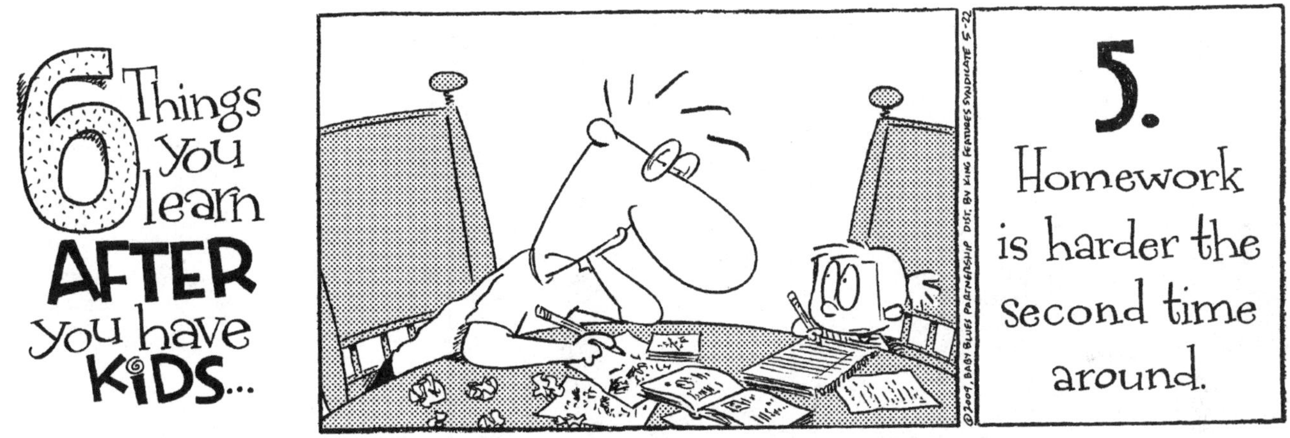
6 Things you learn AFTER you have KIDS...
©2009, BABY BLUES PARTNERSHIP DIST. BY KING FEATURES SYNDICATE 5-22
5.
Homework is harder the second time around.

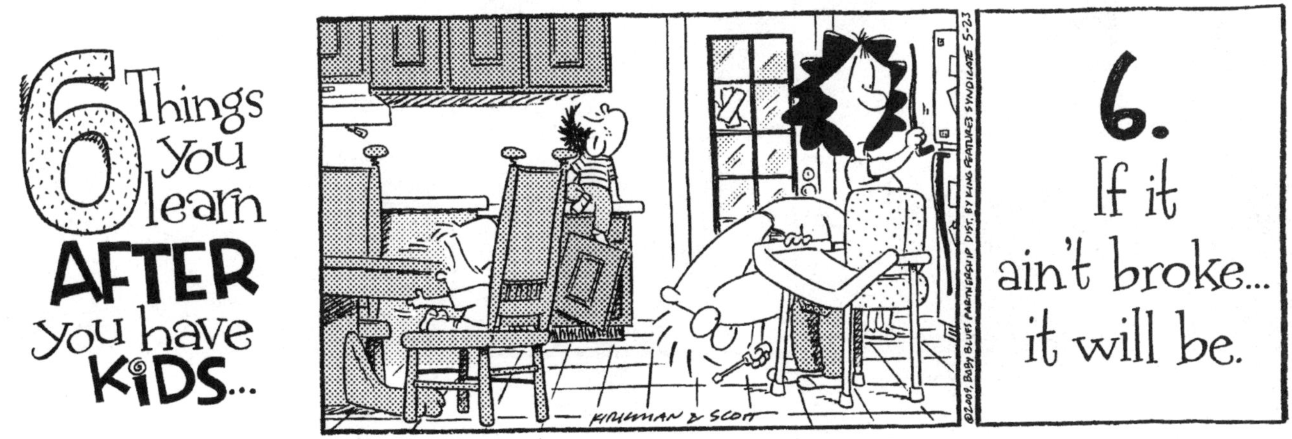
6 Things you learn AFTER you have KIDS...
©2009, BABY BLUES PARTNERSHIP DIST. BY KING FEATURES SYNDICATE 5-23
KIRKMAN & SCOTT
6.
If it ain't broke... it will be.

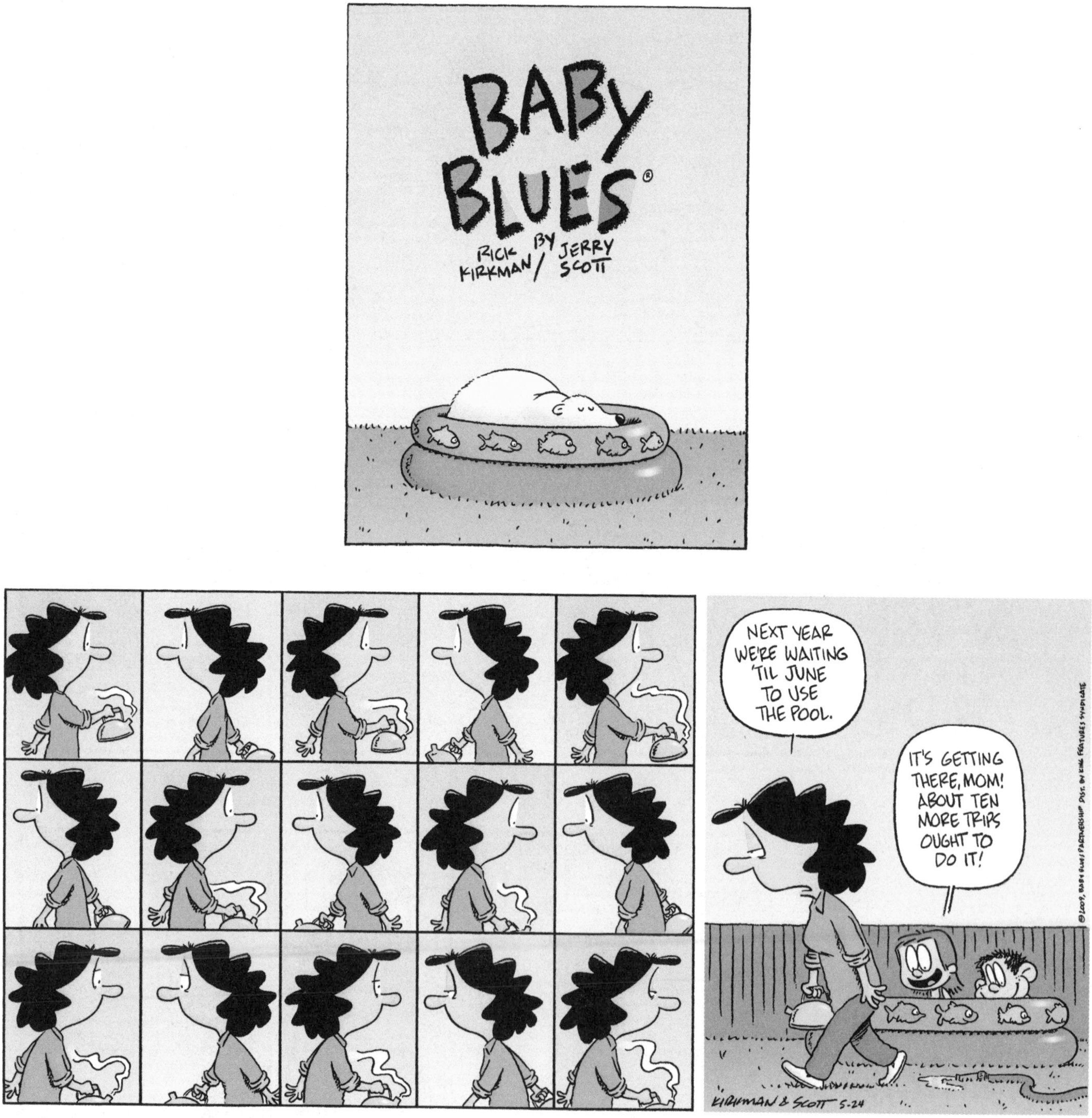
BABY BLUES®
BY RICK KIRKMAN / JERRY SCOTT
NEXT YEAR WE'RE WAITING 'TIL JUNE TO USE THE POOL.
IT'S GETTING THERE, MOM! ABOUT TEN MORE TRIPS OUGHT TO DO IT!
KIRKMAN & SCOTT 5-24
©2009, BABY BLUES PARTNERSHIP DIST. BY KING FEATURES SYNDICATE

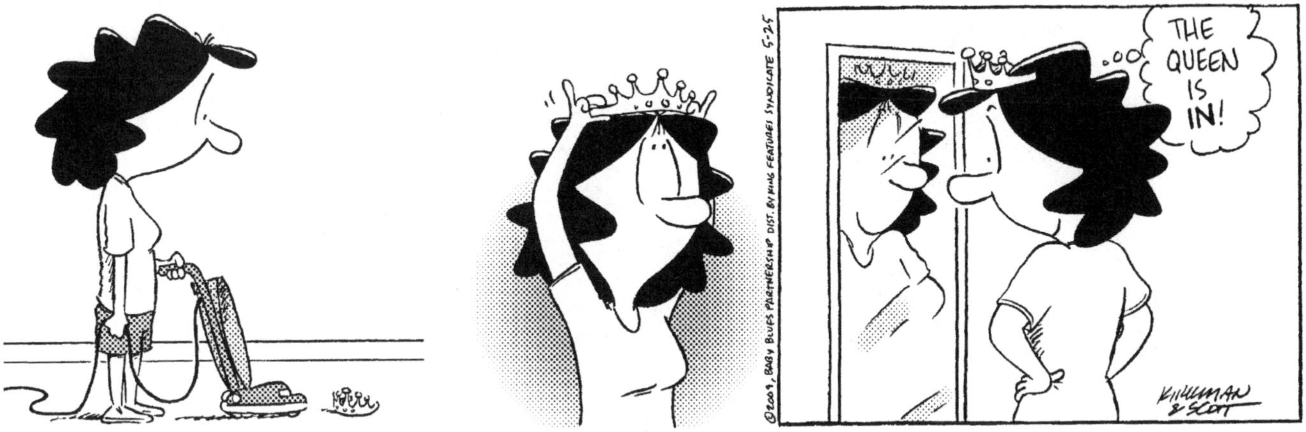
©2009, BABY BLUES PARTNERSHIP DIST. BY KING FEATURES SYNDICATE 5-25
THE QUEEN IS IN!
KIRKMAN & SCOTT

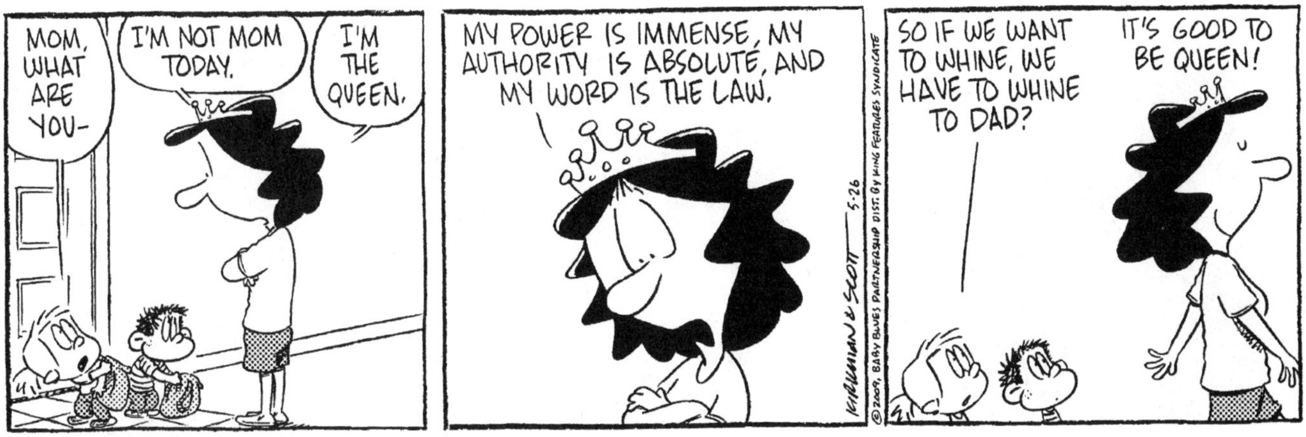
MOM, WHAT ARE YOU-
I'M NOT MOM TODAY.
I'M THE QUEEN.
MY POWER IS IMMENSE, MY AUTHORITY IS ABSOLUTE, AND MY WORD IS THE LAW.
KIRKMAN & SCOTT 5-26
©2009, BABY BLUES PARTNERSHIP DIST. BY KING FEATURES SYNDICATE
SO IF WE WANT TO WHINE, WE HAVE TO WHINE TO DAD?
IT'S GOOD TO BE QUEEN!

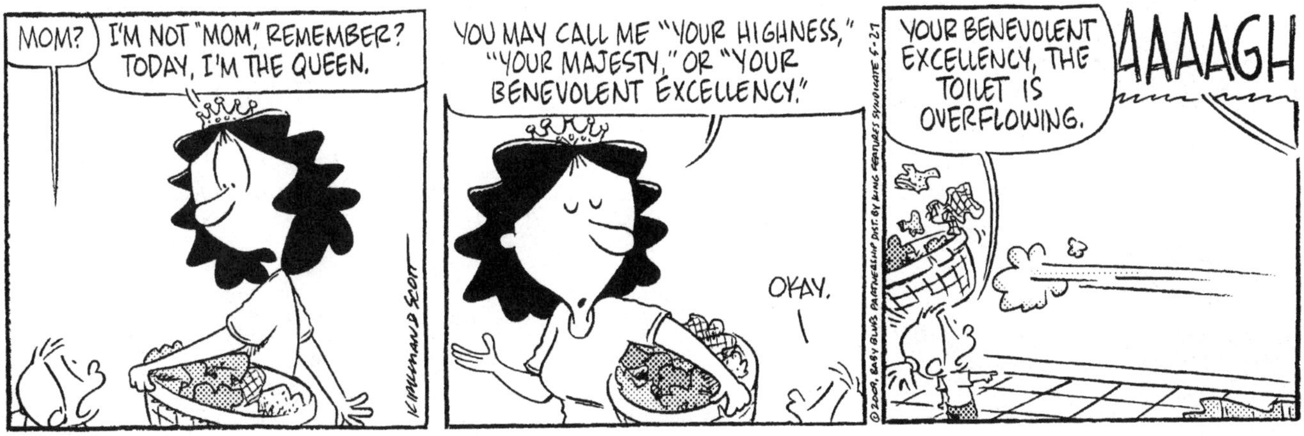
MOM?
I'M NOT "MOM," REMEMBER? TODAY, I'M THE QUEEN.
KIRKMAN & SCOTT
YOU MAY CALL ME "YOUR HIGHNESS," "YOUR MAJESTY," OR "YOUR BENEVOLENT EXCELLENCY."
OKAY.
©2009, BABY BLUES PARTNERSHIP DIST. BY KING FEATURES SYNDICATE 5-27
YOUR BENEVOLENT EXCELLENCY, THE TOILET IS OVERFLOWING.
AAAAGH

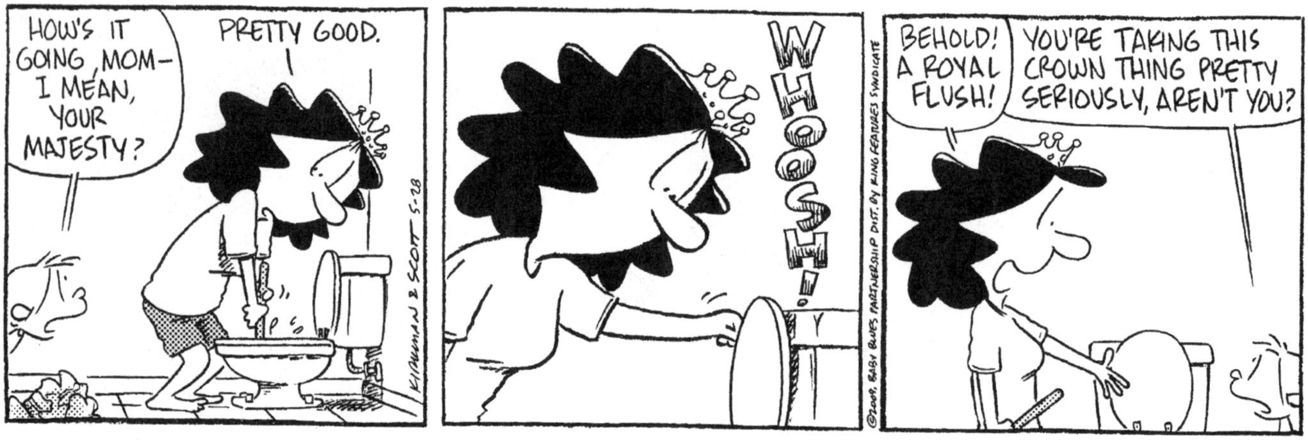
HOW'S IT GOING, MOM— I MEAN, YOUR MAJESTY?
PRETTY GOOD.
KIRKMAN & SCOTT 5-28
WHOOSH!
©2009, BABY BLUES PARTNERSHIP DIST. BY KING FEATURES SYNDICATE
BEHOLD! A ROYAL FLUSH!
YOU'RE TAKING THIS CROWN THING PRETTY SERIOUSLY, AREN'T YOU?

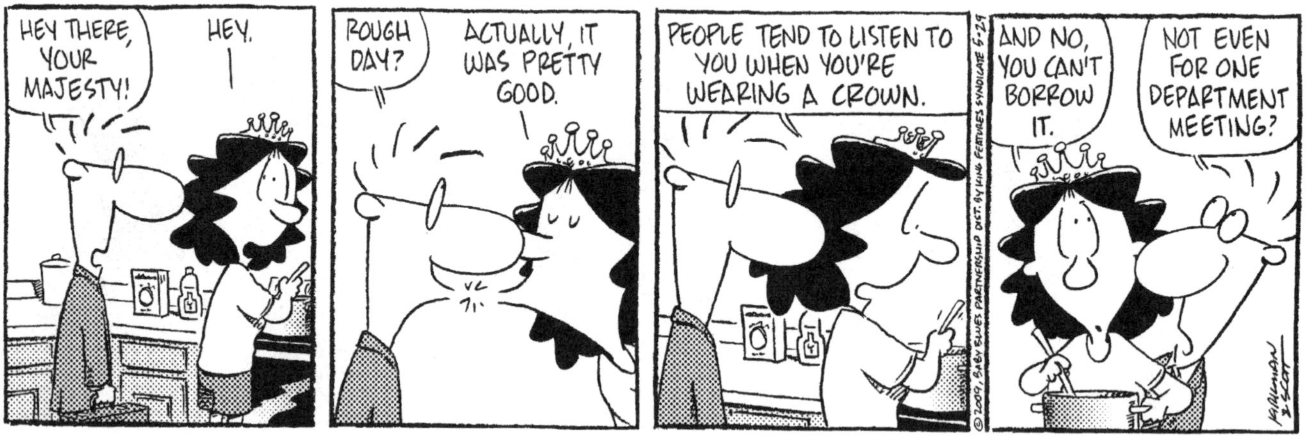
HEY THERE, YOUR MAJESTY!
HEY.
ROUGH DAY?
ACTUALLY, IT WAS PRETTY GOOD.
PEOPLE TEND TO LISTEN TO YOU WHEN YOU'RE WEARING A CROWN.
©2009, BABY BLUES PARTNERSHIP DIST. BY KING FEATURES SYNDICATE 5-29
AND NO, YOU CAN'T BORROW IT.
NOT EVEN FOR ONE DEPARTMENT MEETING?
KIRKMAN & SCOTT

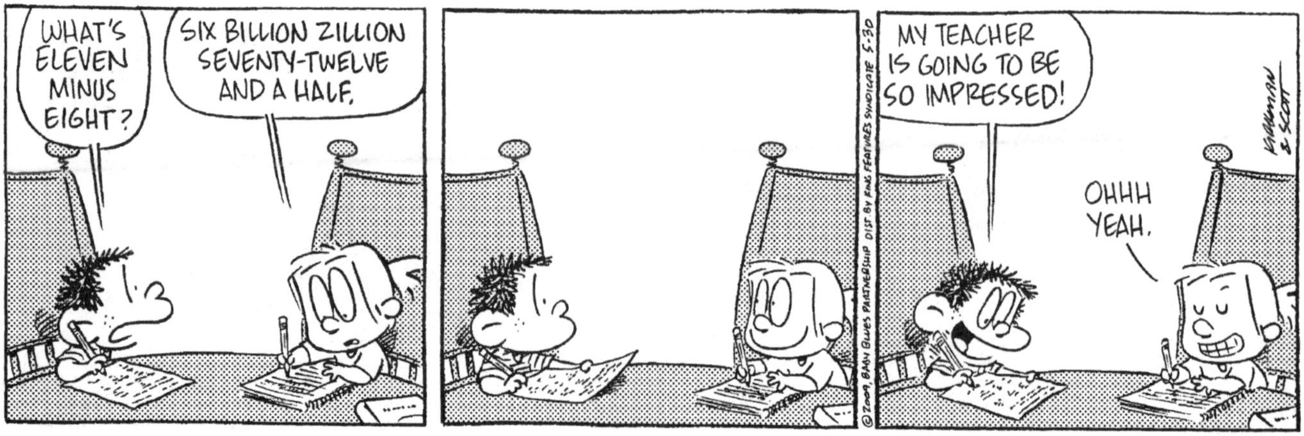
WHAT'S ELEVEN MINUS EIGHT?
SIX BILLION ZILLION SEVENTY-TWELVE AND A HALF.
©2009, BABY BLUES PARTNERSHIP DIST. BY KING FEATURES SYNDICATE 5-30
MY TEACHER IS GOING TO BE SO IMPRESSED!
OHHH YEAH.
KIRKMAN & SCOTT

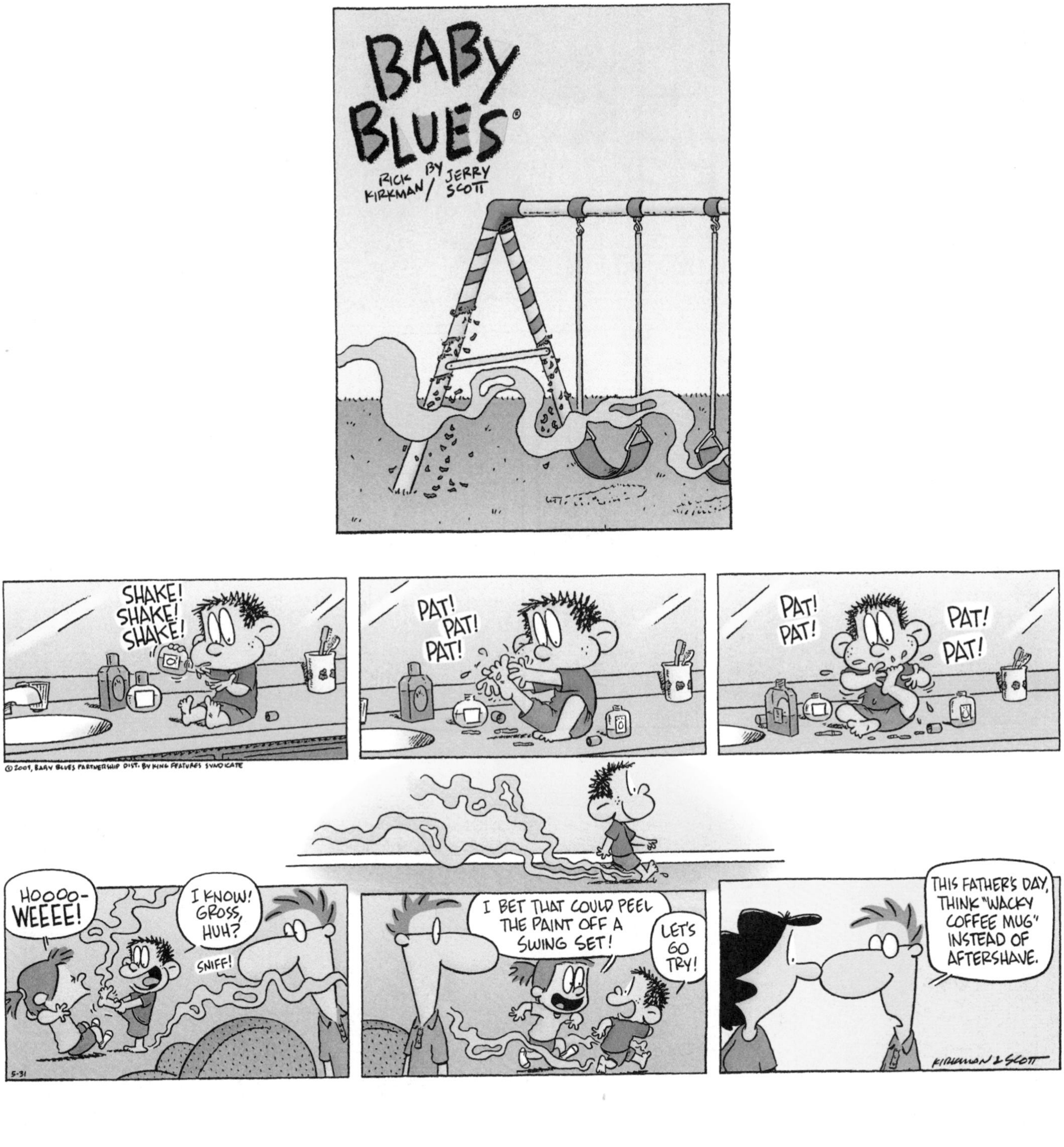
BABY BLUES®
RICK KIRKMAN / BY JERRY SCOTT
SHAKE! SHAKE! SHAKE!
PAT! PAT! PAT!
PAT! PAT!
PAT! PAT!
© 2009, BABY BLUES PARTNERSHIP DIST. BY KING FEATURES SYNDICATE
HOOOO-WEEEE!
I KNOW! GROSS, HUH?
SNIFF!
5-31
I BET THAT COULD PEEL THE PAINT OFF A SWING SET!
LET'S GO TRY!
THIS FATHER'S DAY, THINK "WACKY COFFEE MUG" INSTEAD OF AFTERSHAVE.
KIRKMAN & SCOTT

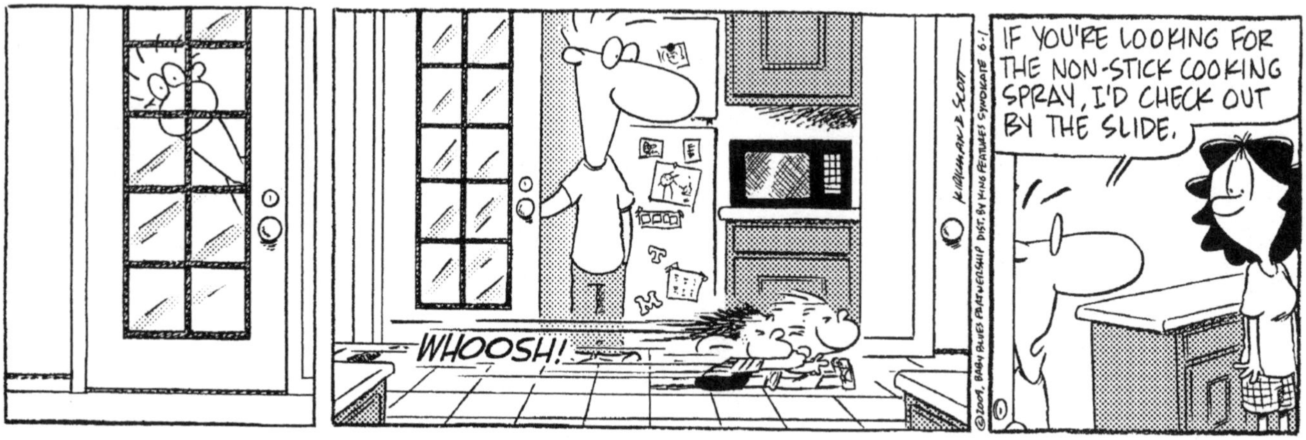
WHOOSH!
IF YOU'RE LOOKING FOR THE NON-STICK COOKING SPRAY, I'D CHECK OUT BY THE SLIDE.

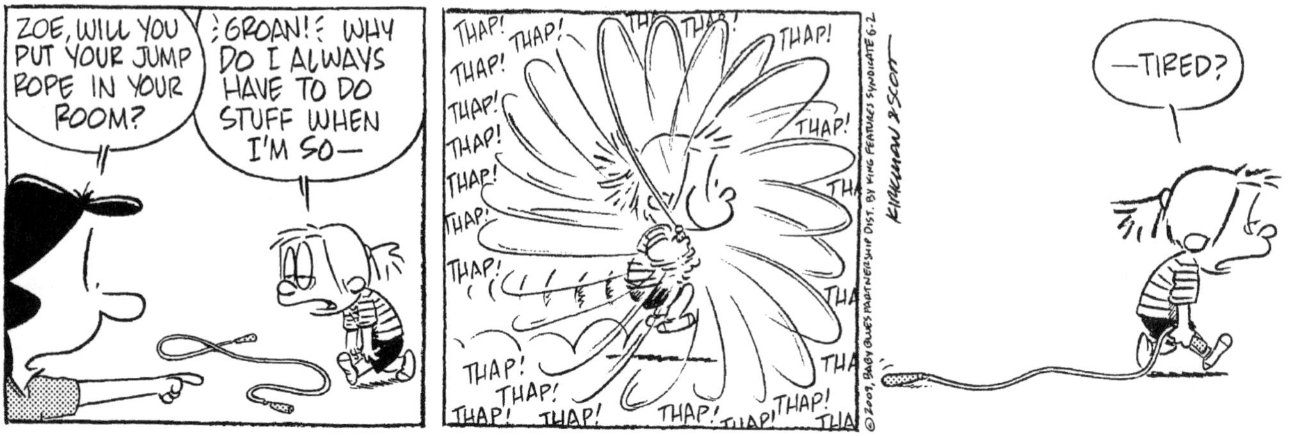
ZOE, WILL YOU PUT YOUR JUMP ROPE IN YOUR ROOM?
:GROAN!: WHY DO I ALWAYS HAVE TO DO STUFF WHEN I'M SO—
THAP! THAP! THAP! THAP! THAP! THAP! THAP! THAP! THAP! THAP! THAP! THAP! THAP! THAP! THAP! THAP!
—TIRED?

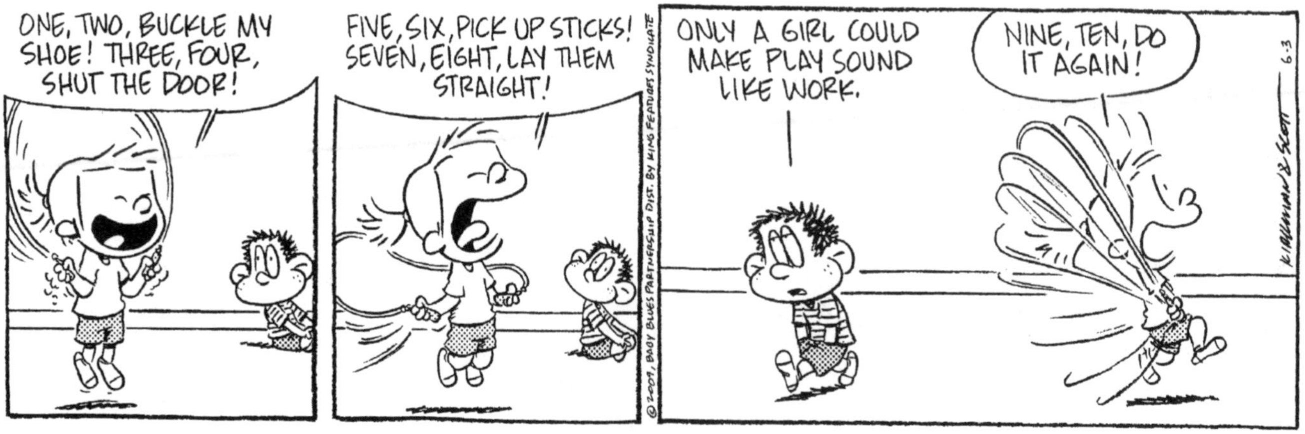
ONE, TWO, BUCKLE MY SHOE! THREE, FOUR, SHUT THE DOOR!
FIVE, SIX, PICK UP STICKS! SEVEN, EIGHT, LAY THEM STRAIGHT!
ONLY A GIRL COULD MAKE PLAY SOUND LIKE WORK.
NINE, TEN, DO IT AGAIN!

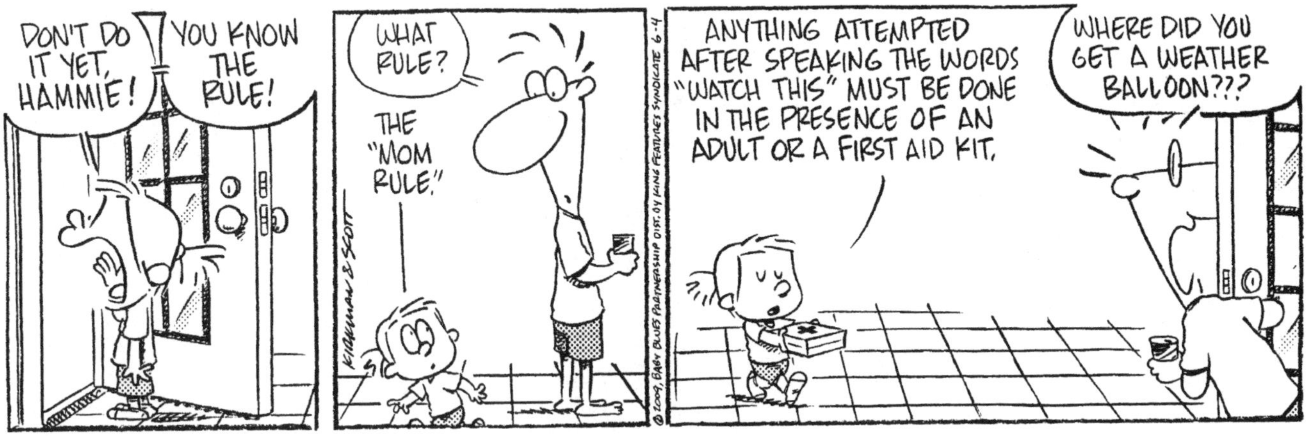
DON'T DO IT YET, HAMMIE!
YOU KNOW THE RULE!
WHAT RULE?
THE "MOM RULE."
KIRKMAN & SCOTT
© 2009, BABY BLUES PARTNERSHIP DIST. BY KING FEATURES SYNDICATE 6-4
ANYTHING ATTEMPTED AFTER SPEAKING THE WORDS "WATCH THIS" MUST BE DONE IN THE PRESENCE OF AN ADULT OR A FIRST AID KIT.
WHERE DID YOU GET A WEATHER BALLOON???

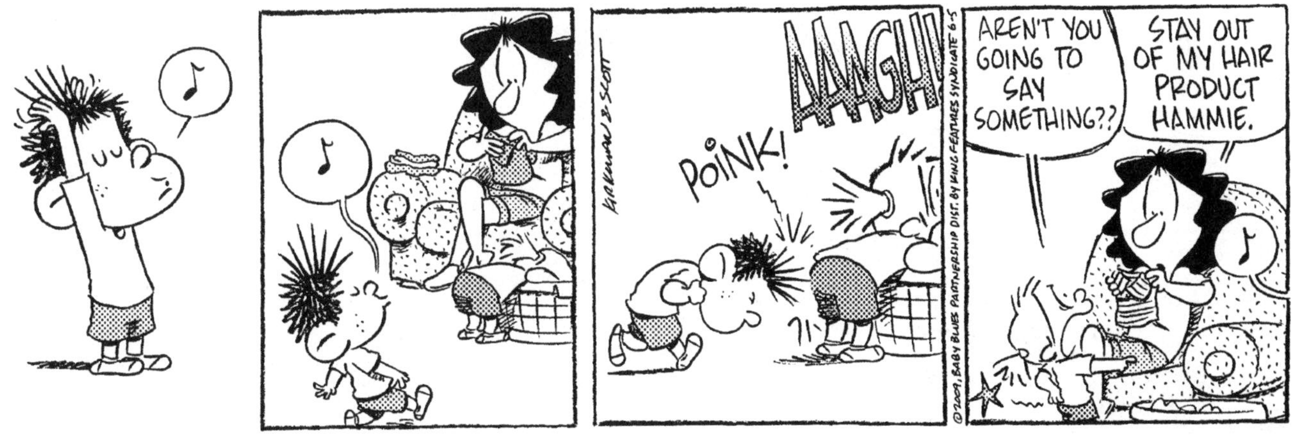
KIRKMAN & SCOTT
AAAGH!
POINK!
© 2009, BABY BLUES PARTNERSHIP DIST. BY KING FEATURES SYNDICATE 6-5
AREN'T YOU GOING TO SAY SOMETHING??
STAY OUT OF MY HAIR PRODUCT HAMMIE.

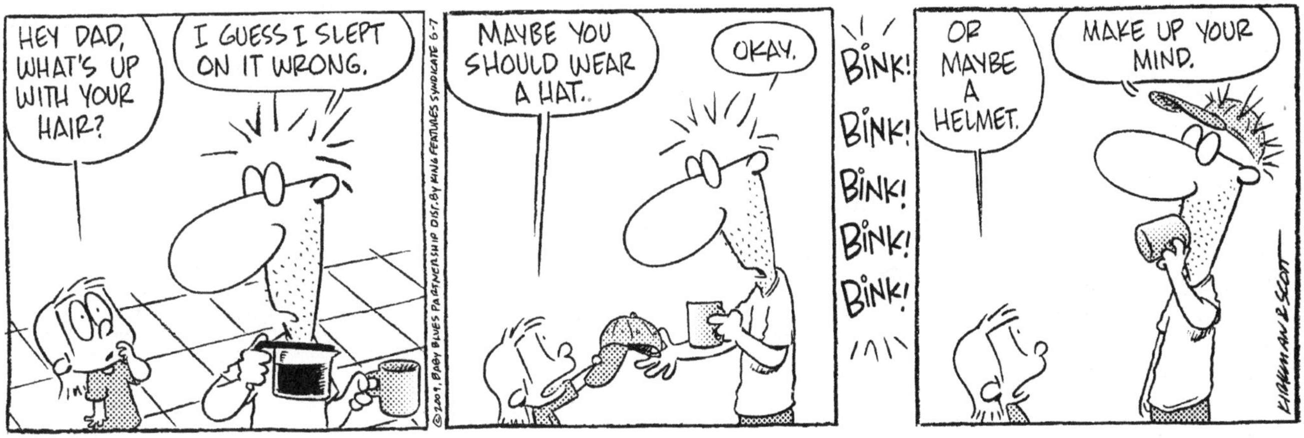
HEY DAD, WHAT'S UP WITH YOUR HAIR?
I GUESS I SLEPT ON IT WRONG.
© 2009, BABY BLUES PARTNERSHIP DIST. BY KING FEATURES SYNDICATE 6-7
MAYBE YOU SHOULD WEAR A HAT.
OKAY.
BINK! BINK! BINK! BINK! BINK!
OR MAYBE A HELMET.
MAKE UP YOUR MIND.
KIRKMAN & SCOTT

BABY BLUES®
BY RICK KIRKMAN / JERRY SCOTT

WHAT DO YOU THINK?
WHAT IS IT?
IT'S A TURTLE! SEE? A HEAD, FOUR LEGS AND A TAIL!
HMMM.
SO THAT'S THE HEAD?
NO. THAT'S A LEG.
SO THAT'S THE HEAD.
NO. THAT'S ANOTHER LEG.
AND THAT'S A LEG, AND THAT'S A LEG, TOO!
ARE YOU SURE?
YES, I'M— OH, NEVER MIND! JUST FORGET I EVER MADE IT!
BAM! BAM! BAM! BAM! BAM!
OKAY! OKAY! OKAY!
KIRKMAN & SCOTT 6-7
©2009 BABY BLUES PARTNERSHIP DIST. BY KING FEATURES SYNDICATE
HEY, NICE TURTLE.
AAAAUGHH!

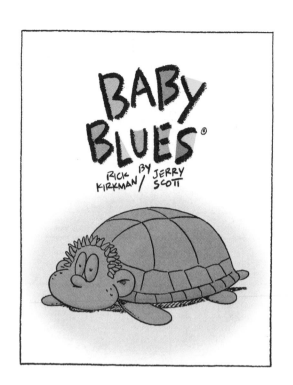

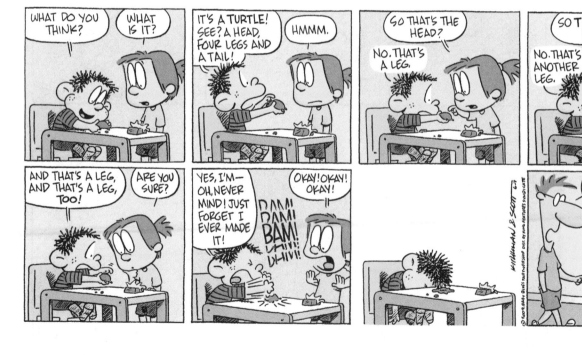

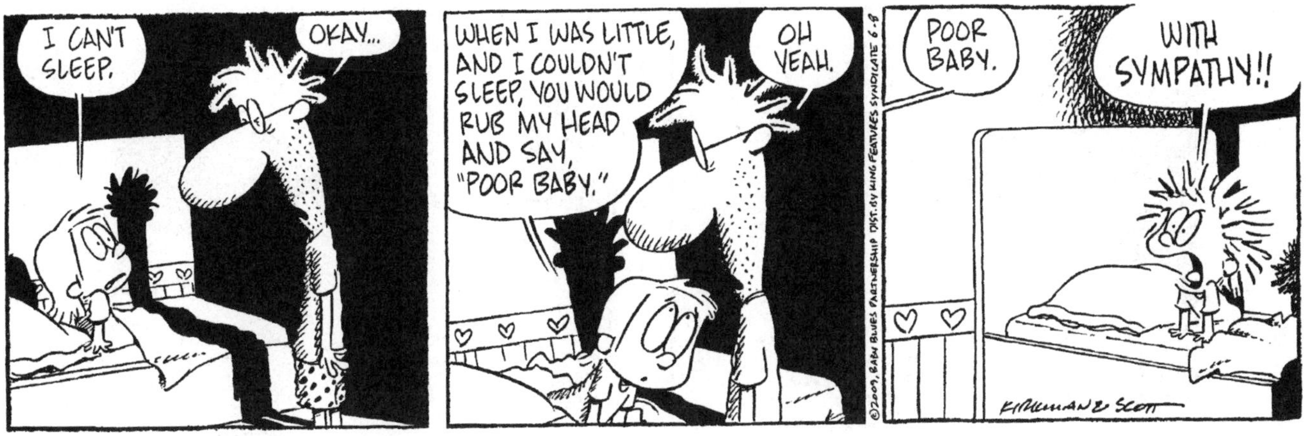
I CAN'T SLEEP.
OKAY...
WHEN I WAS LITTLE, AND I COULDN'T SLEEP, YOU WOULD RUB MY HEAD AND SAY, "POOR BABY."
OH YEAH.
©2009, BABY BLUES PARTNERSHIP DIST. BY KING FEATURES SYNDICATE 6-8
POOR BABY.
WITH SYMPATHY!!
KIRKMAN & SCOTT

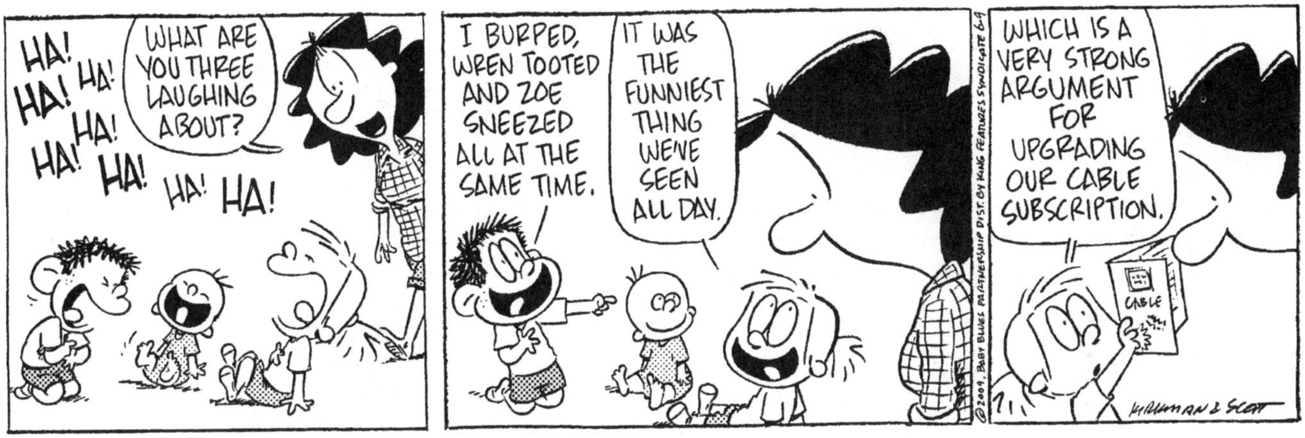
HA! HA! HA! HA! HA! HA! HA! HA!
WHAT ARE YOU THREE LAUGHING ABOUT?
I BURPED, WREN TOOTED AND ZOE SNEEZED ALL AT THE SAME TIME.
IT WAS THE FUNNIEST THING WE'VE SEEN ALL DAY.
©2009, BABY BLUES PARTNERSHIP DIST. BY KING FEATURES SYNDICATE 6-9
WHICH IS A VERY STRONG ARGUMENT FOR UPGRADING OUR CABLE SUBSCRIPTION.
CABLE
KIRKMAN & SCOTT

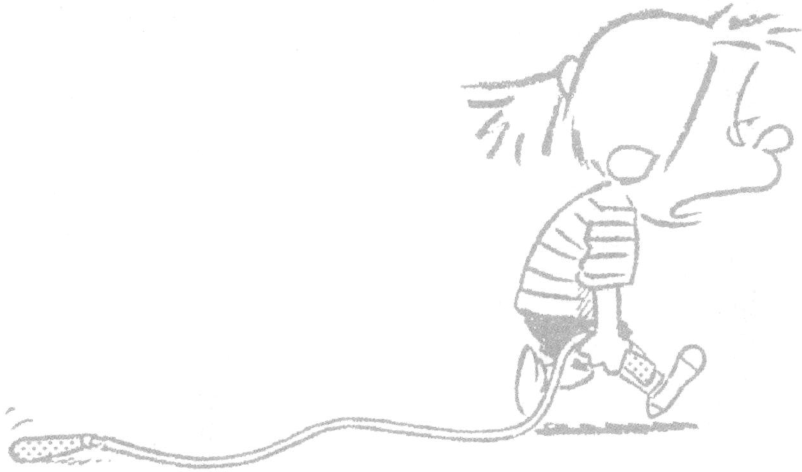

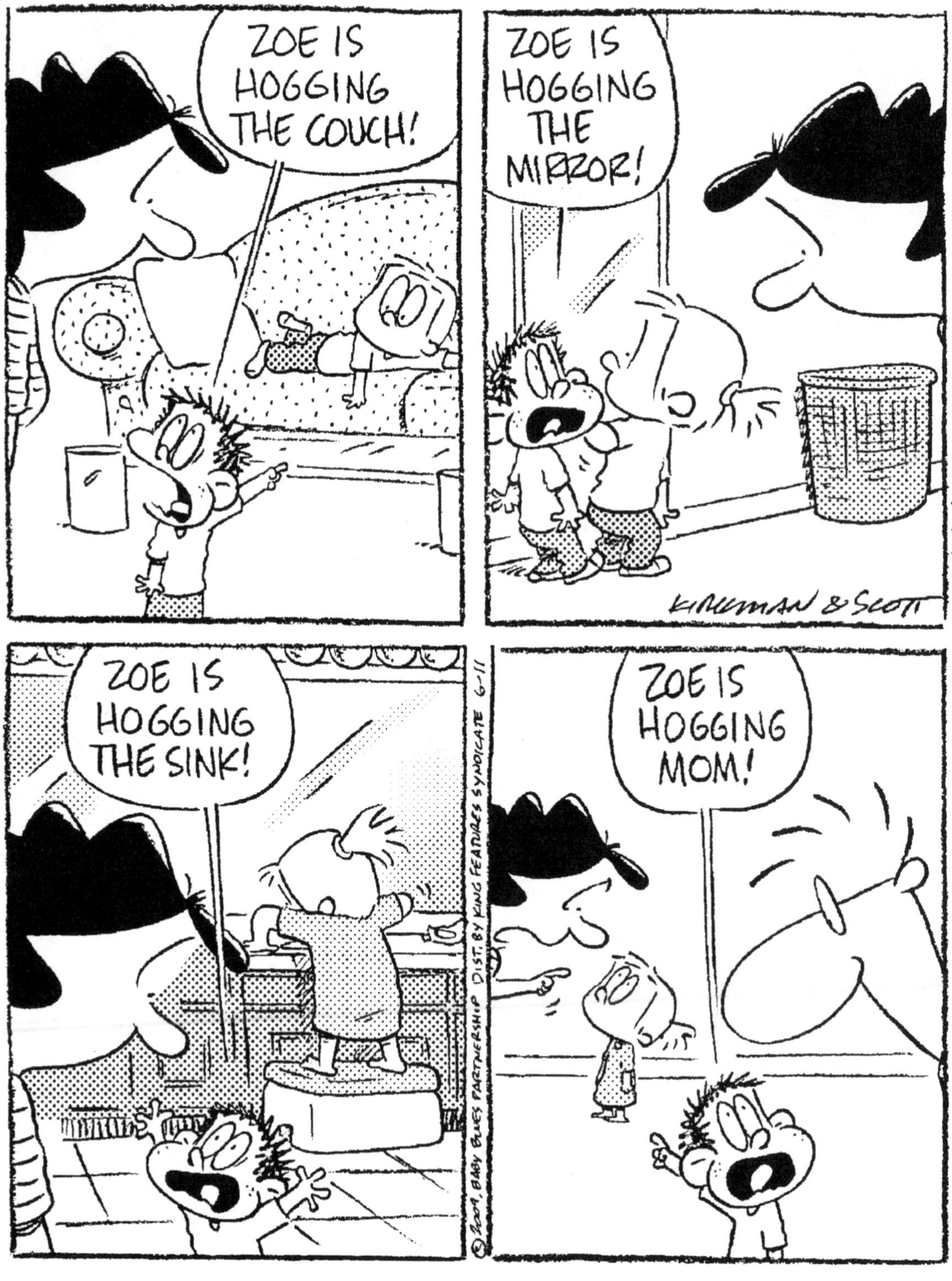
ZOE IS HOGGING THE COUCH!
ZOE IS HOGGING THE MIRROR!
KIRKMAN & SCOTT
ZOE IS HOGGING THE SINK!
© 2009, BABY BLUES PARTNERSHIP DIST. BY KING FEATURES SYNDICATE 6-11
ZOE IS HOGGING MOM!

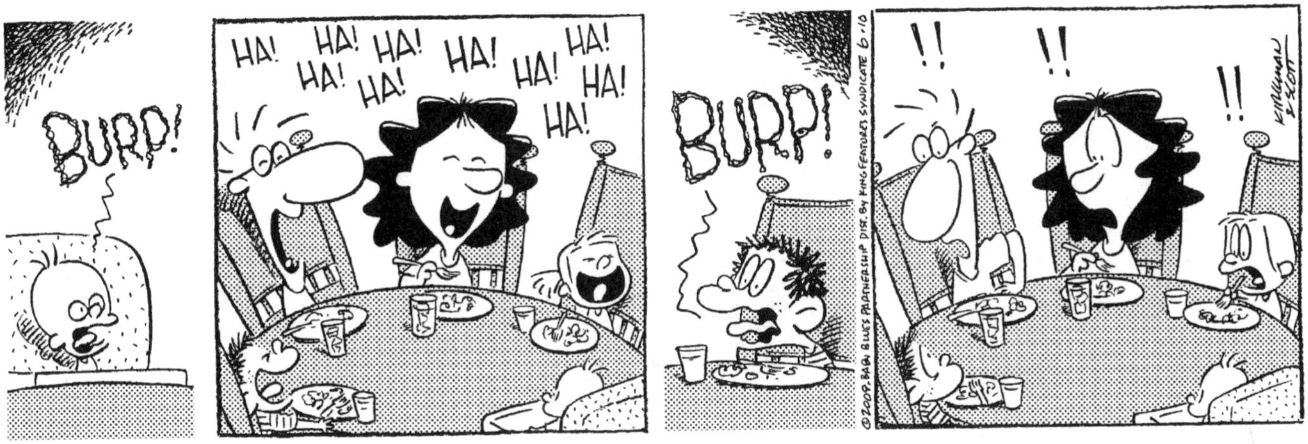
BURP!
HA! HA! HA! HA! HA! HA! HA! HA! HA! HA!
BURP!
©2009, Baby Blues Partnership Dist. by King Features Syndicate 6-10
!! !! !!
Kirkman & Scott

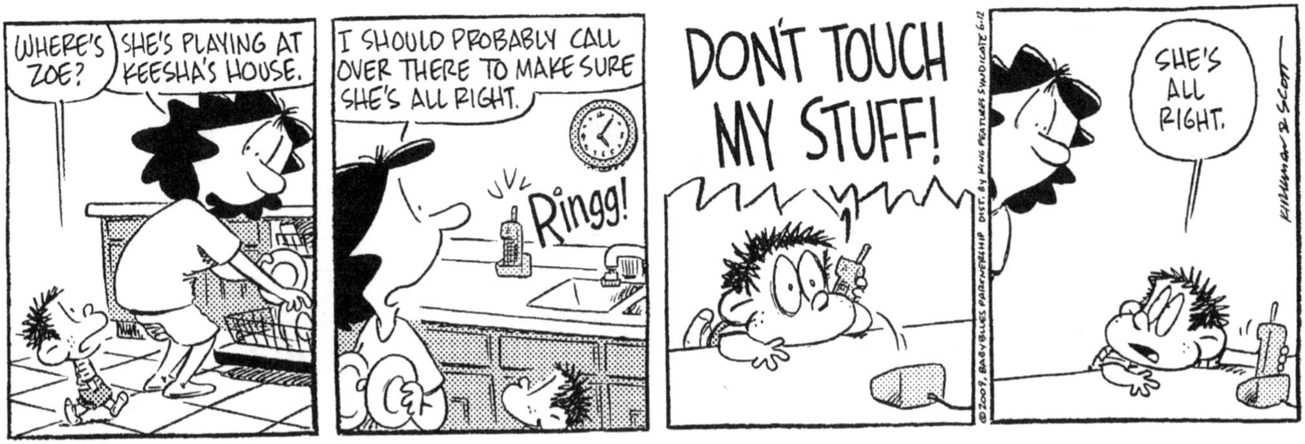
WHERE'S ZOE?
SHE'S PLAYING AT KEESHA'S HOUSE.
I SHOULD PROBABLY CALL OVER THERE TO MAKE SURE SHE'S ALL RIGHT.
Ringg!
DON'T TOUCH MY STUFF!
©2009, Baby Blues Partnership Dist. by King Features Syndicate 6-12
SHE'S ALL RIGHT.
Kirkman & Scott

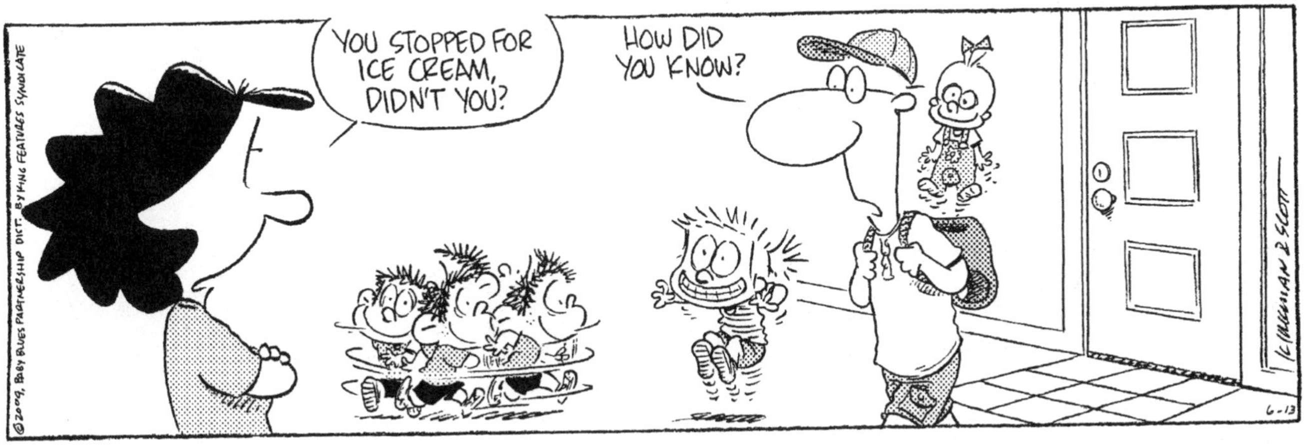
©2009, Baby Blues Partnership Dist. by King Features Syndicate
YOU STOPPED FOR ICE CREAM, DIDN'T YOU?
HOW DID YOU KNOW?
Kirkman & Scott
6-13

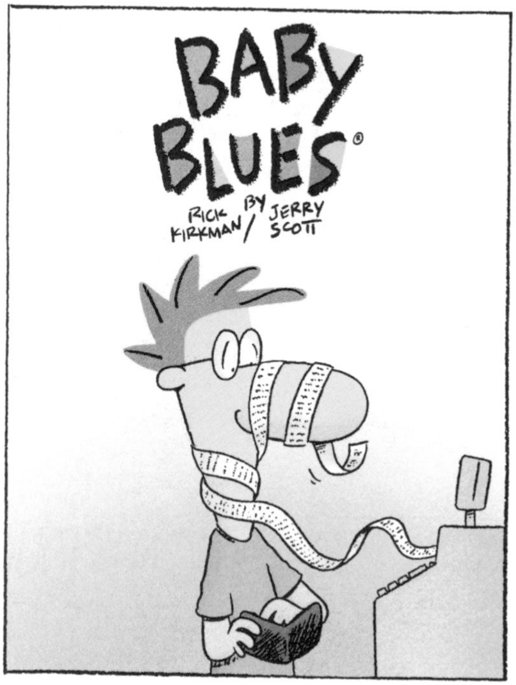
BABY BLUES®
RICK KIRKMAN / BY JERRY SCOTT

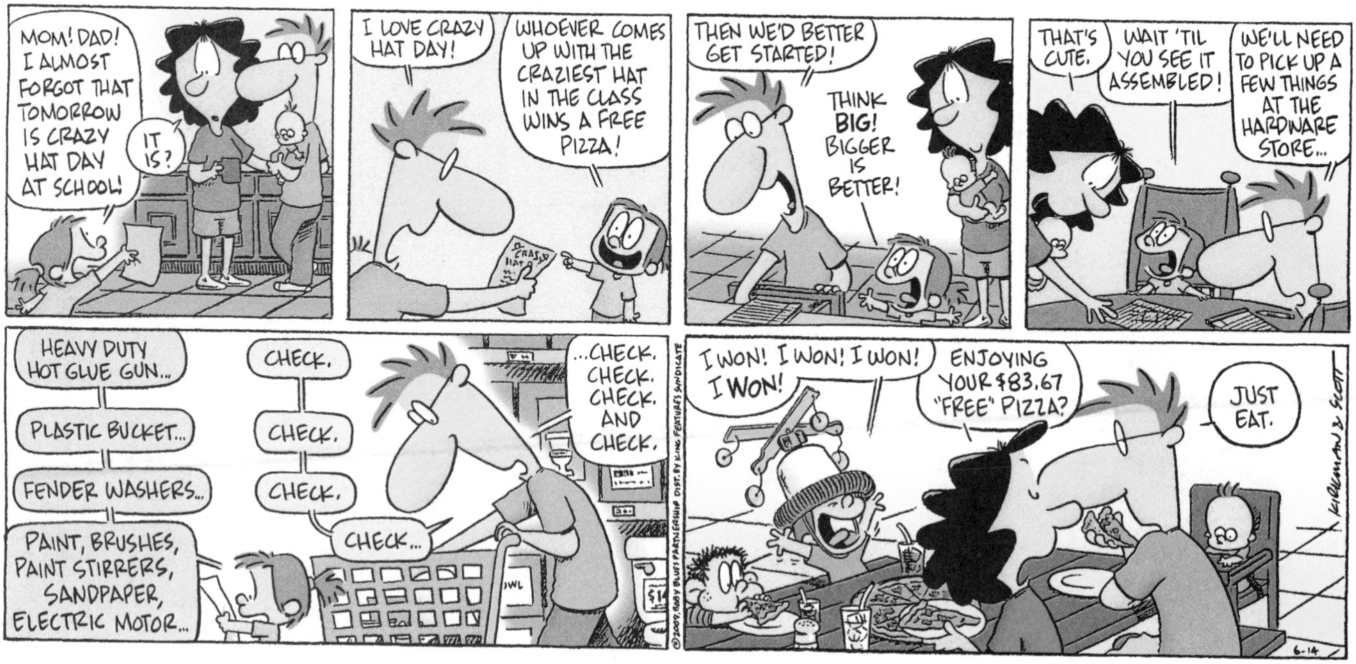
MOM! DAD! I ALMOST FORGOT THAT TOMORROW IS CRAZY HAT DAY AT SCHOOL!
IT IS?
I LOVE CRAZY HAT DAY!
WHOEVER COMES UP WITH THE CRAZIEST HAT IN THE CLASS WINS A FREE PIZZA!
THEN WE'D BETTER GET STARTED!
THINK BIG! BIGGER IS BETTER!
THAT'S CUTE.
WAIT 'TIL YOU SEE IT ASSEMBLED!
WE'LL NEED TO PICK UP A FEW THINGS AT THE HARDWARE STORE...
HEAVY DUTY HOT GLUE GUN...
CHECK.
PLASTIC BUCKET...
CHECK.
FENDER WASHERS...
CHECK.
PAINT, BRUSHES, PAINT STIRRERS, SANDPAPER, ELECTRIC MOTOR...
CHECK...
...CHECK. CHECK. CHECK. AND CHECK.
©2009, BABY BLUES PARTNERSHIP DIST. BY KING FEATURES SYNDICATE
I WON! I WON! I WON! I WON!
ENJOYING YOUR $83.67 "FREE" PIZZA?
JUST EAT.
KIRKMAN & SCOTT
6-14

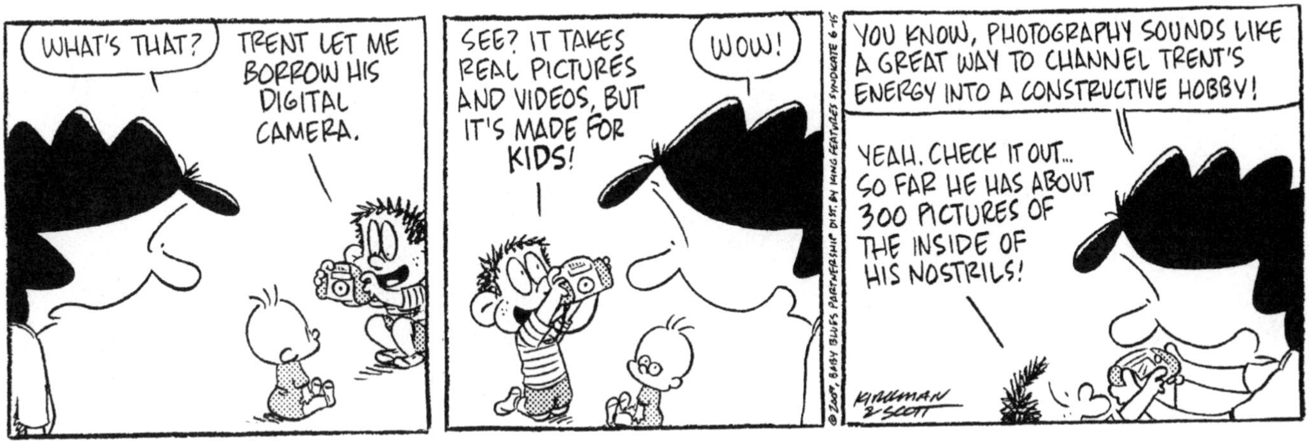
WHAT'S THAT?
TRENT LET ME BORROW HIS DIGITAL CAMERA.
SEE? IT TAKES REAL PICTURES AND VIDEOS, BUT IT'S MADE FOR KIDS!
WOW!
YOU KNOW, PHOTOGRAPHY SOUNDS LIKE A GREAT WAY TO CHANNEL TRENT'S ENERGY INTO A CONSTRUCTIVE HOBBY!
YEAH. CHECK IT OUT... SO FAR HE HAS ABOUT 300 PICTURES OF THE INSIDE OF HIS NOSTRILS!
© 2009, BABY BLUES PARTNERSHIP DIST. BY KING FEATURES SYNDICATE 6-15
KIRKMAN & SCOTT

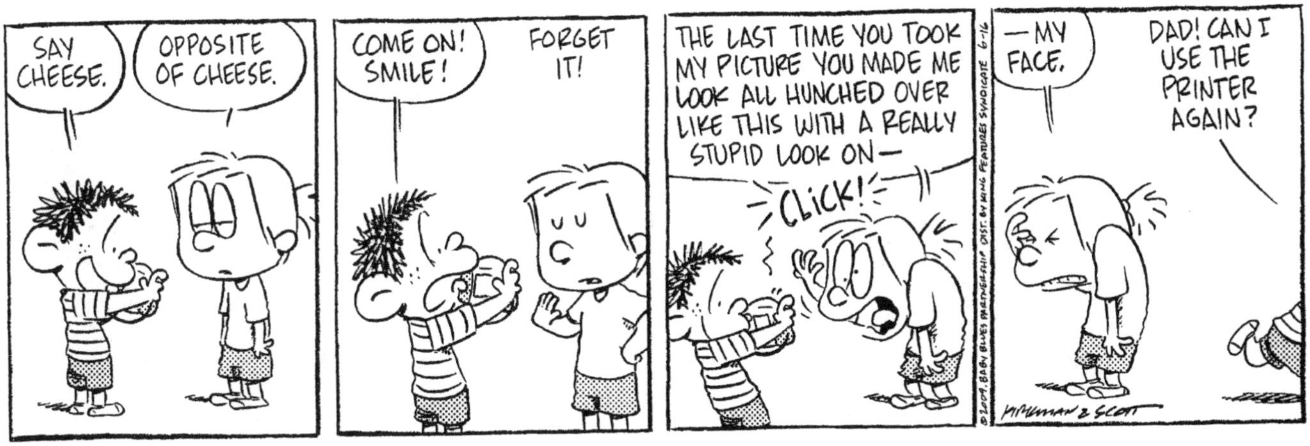
SAY CHEESE.
OPPOSITE OF CHEESE.
COME ON! SMILE!
FORGET IT!
THE LAST TIME YOU TOOK MY PICTURE YOU MADE ME LOOK ALL HUNCHED OVER LIKE THIS WITH A REALLY STUPID LOOK ON—
CLICK!
—MY FACE.
DAD! CAN I USE THE PRINTER AGAIN?
© 2009, BABY BLUES PARTNERSHIP DIST. BY KING FEATURES SYNDICATE 6-16
KIRKMAN & SCOTT

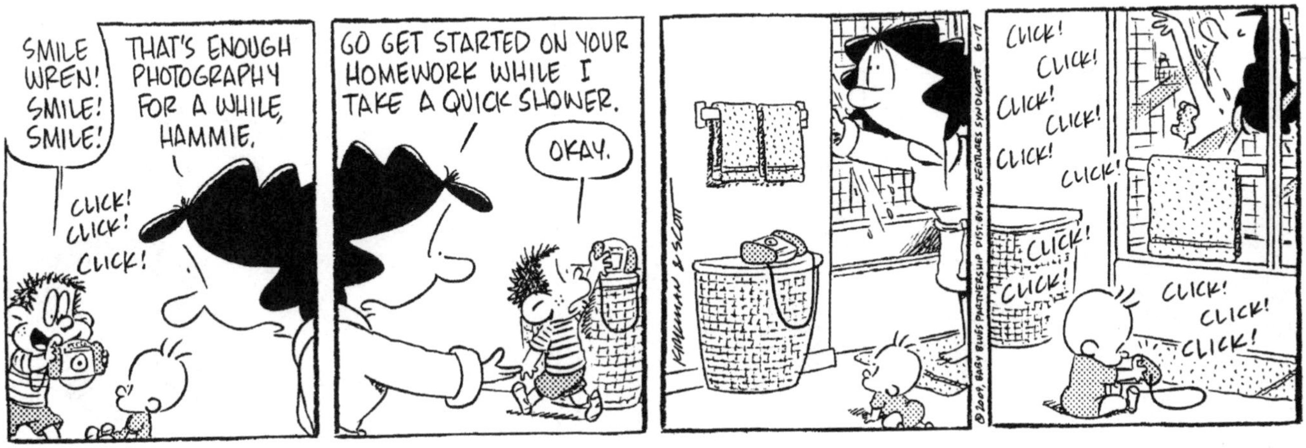
SMILE WREN! SMILE! SMILE!
CLICK! CLICK! CLICK!
THAT'S ENOUGH PHOTOGRAPHY FOR A WHILE, HAMMIE.
GO GET STARTED ON YOUR HOMEWORK WHILE I TAKE A QUICK SHOWER.
OKAY.
KIRKMAN & SCOTT
© 2009, BABY BLUES PARTNERSHIP DIST. BY KING FEATURES SYNDICATE 6-17
CLICK! CLICK! CLICK! CLICK! CLICK! CLICK! CLICK! CLICK!
CLICK! CLICK! CLICK!

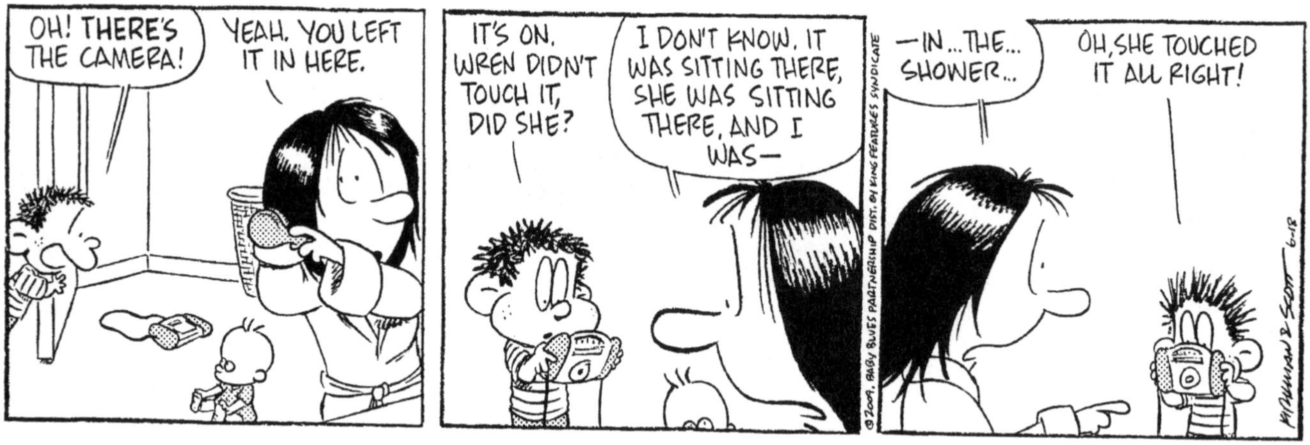
OH! THERE'S THE CAMERA!
YEAH. YOU LEFT IT IN HERE.
IT'S ON. WREN DIDN'T TOUCH IT, DID SHE?
I DON'T KNOW. IT WAS SITTING THERE, SHE WAS SITTING THERE, AND I WAS—
©2009, BABY BLUES PARTNERSHIP DIST. BY KING FEATURES SYNDICATE
—IN...THE... SHOWER...
OH, SHE TOUCHED IT ALL RIGHT!
KIRKMAN & SCOTT 6-18

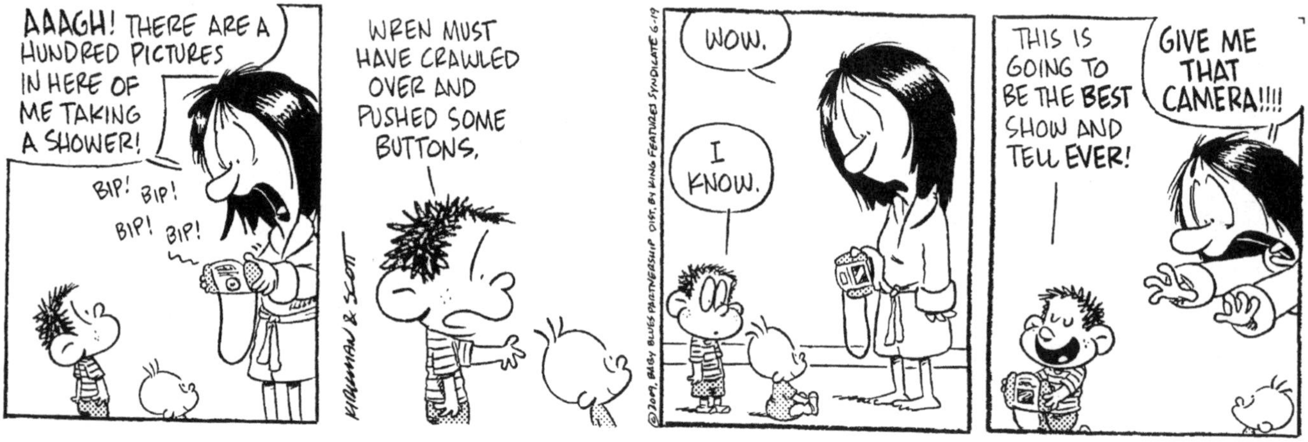
AAAGH! THERE ARE A HUNDRED PICTURES IN HERE OF ME TAKING A SHOWER!
BIP! BIP! BIP! BIP!
KIRKMAN & SCOTT
WREN MUST HAVE CRAWLED OVER AND PUSHED SOME BUTTONS.
©2009, BABY BLUES PARTNERSHIP DIST. BY KING FEATURES SYNDICATE 6-19
WOW.
I KNOW.
THIS IS GOING TO BE THE BEST SHOW AND TELL EVER!
GIVE ME THAT CAMERA!!!!

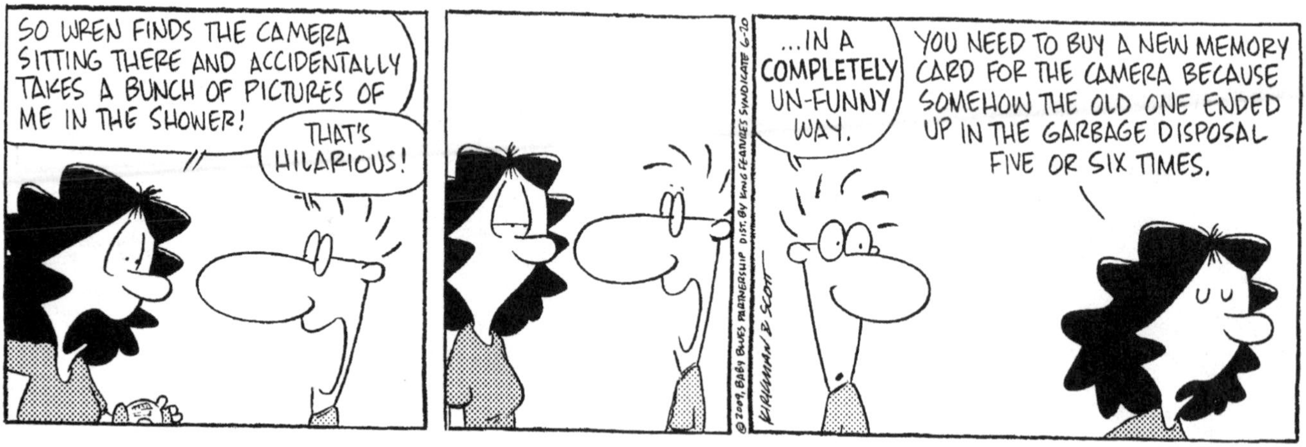
SO WREN FINDS THE CAMERA SITTING THERE AND ACCIDENTALLY TAKES A BUNCH OF PICTURES OF ME IN THE SHOWER!
THAT'S HILARIOUS!
©2009, BABY BLUES PARTNERSHIP DIST. BY KING FEATURES SYNDICATE 6-20
KIRKMAN & SCOTT
...IN A COMPLETELY UN-FUNNY WAY.
YOU NEED TO BUY A NEW MEMORY CARD FOR THE CAMERA BECAUSE SOMEHOW THE OLD ONE ENDED UP IN THE GARBAGE DISPOSAL FIVE OR SIX TIMES.

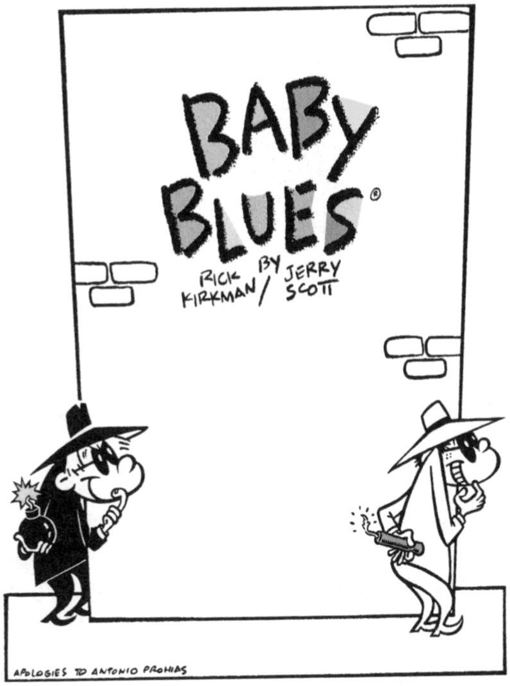
BABY BLUES®
BY RICK KIRKMAN / JERRY SCOTT
APOLOGIES TO ANTONIO PROHIAS

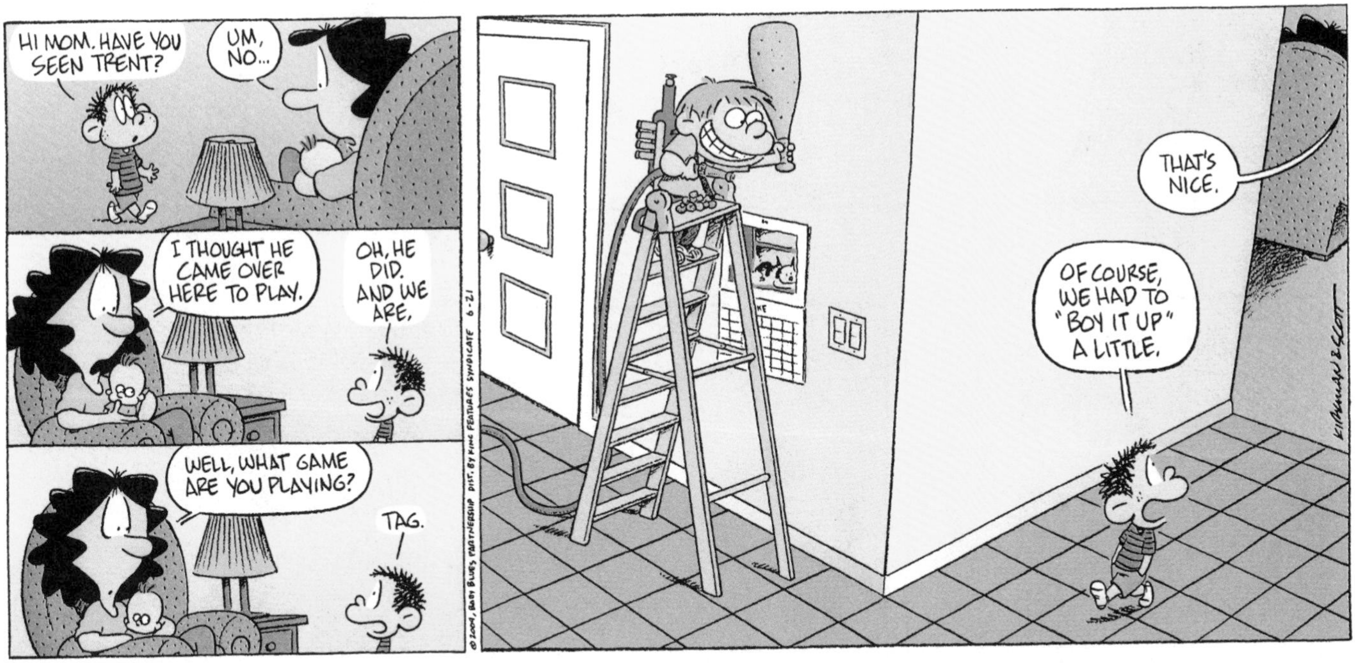
HI MOM. HAVE YOU SEEN TRENT?
UM, NO...
I THOUGHT HE CAME OVER HERE TO PLAY.
OH, HE DID. AND WE ARE.
WELL, WHAT GAME ARE YOU PLAYING?
TAG.
THAT'S NICE.
OF COURSE, WE HAD TO "BOY IT UP" A LITTLE.

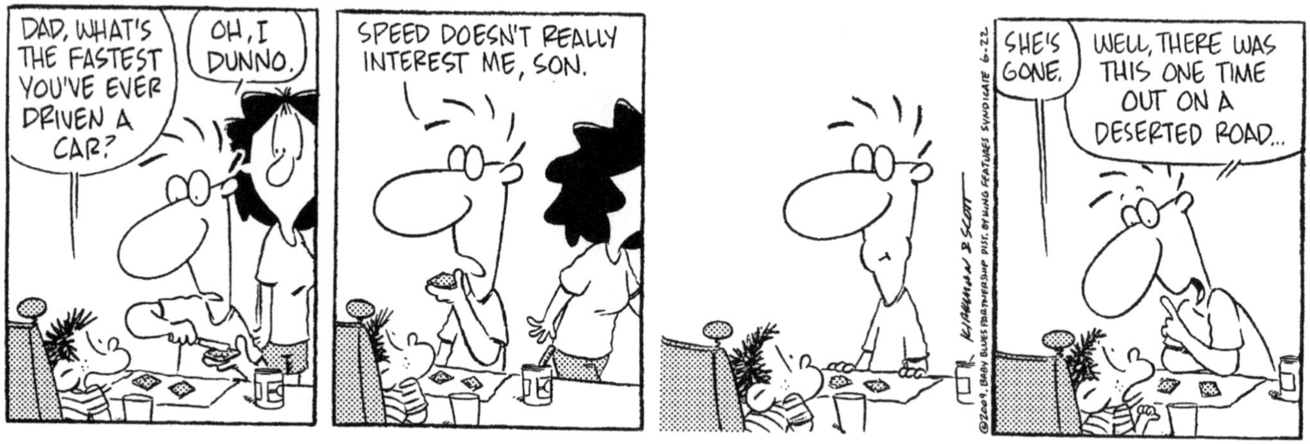
DAD, WHAT'S THE FASTEST YOU'VE EVER DRIVEN A CAR?
OH, I DUNNO.
SPEED DOESN'T REALLY INTEREST ME, SON.
KIRKMAN & SCOTT
©2009, BABY BLUES PARTNERSHIP DIST. BY KING FEATURES SYNDICATE 6-22
SHE'S GONE.
WELL, THERE WAS THIS ONE TIME OUT ON A DESERTED ROAD...

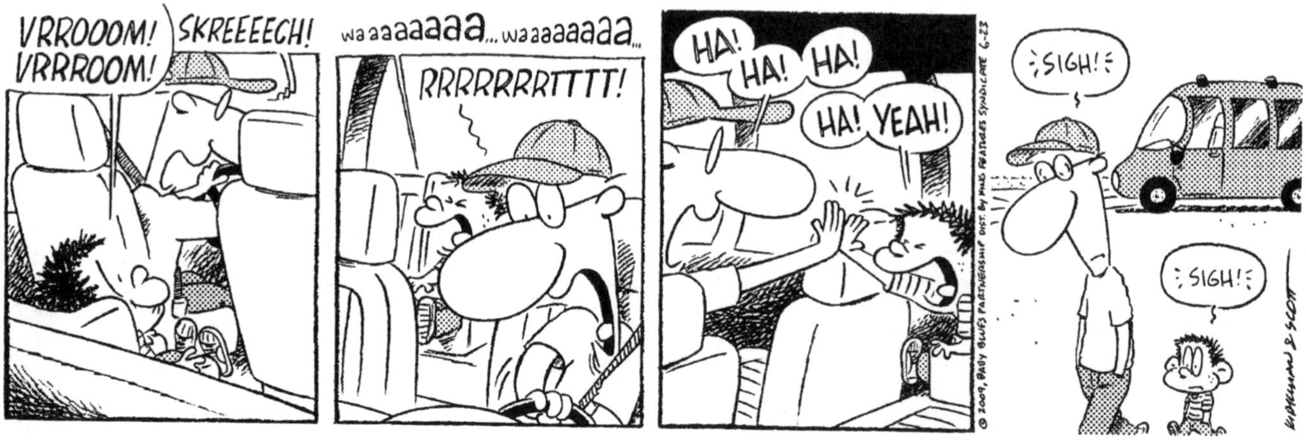
VRROOOM! VRRROOM!
SKREEEEECH!
waaaaaaaa... waaaaaaaaa...
RRRRRRRRTTTTT!
HA!
HA!
HA!
HA! YEAH!
©2009, BABY BLUES PARTNERSHIP DIST. BY KING FEATURES SYNDICATE 6-23
SIGH!
SIGH!
KIRKMAN & SCOTT

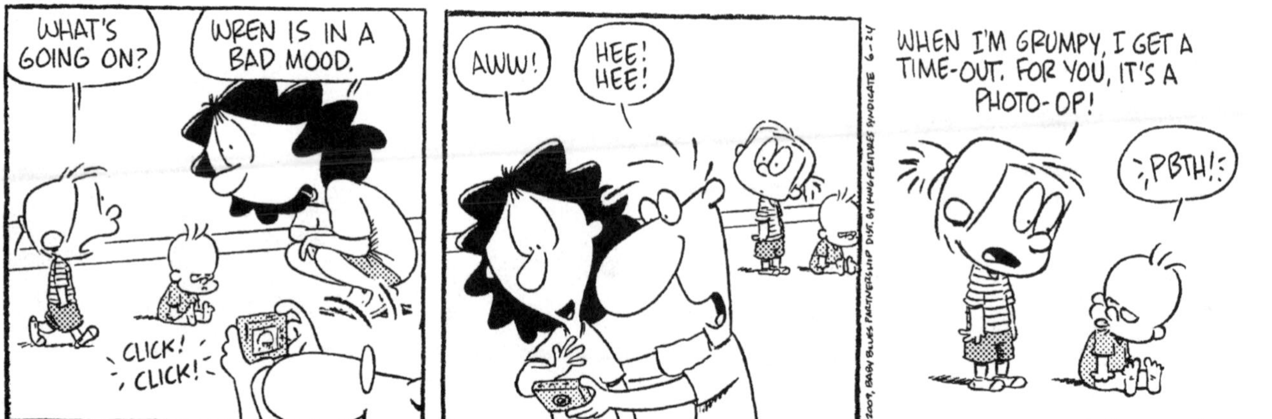
WHAT'S GOING ON?
WREN IS IN A BAD MOOD.
CLICK! CLICK!
AWW!
HEE! HEE!
©2009, BABY BLUES PARTNERSHIP DIST. BY KING FEATURES SYNDICATE 6-24
WHEN I'M GRUMPY, I GET A TIME-OUT. FOR YOU, IT'S A PHOTO-OP!
PBTH!
KIRKMAN & SCOTT

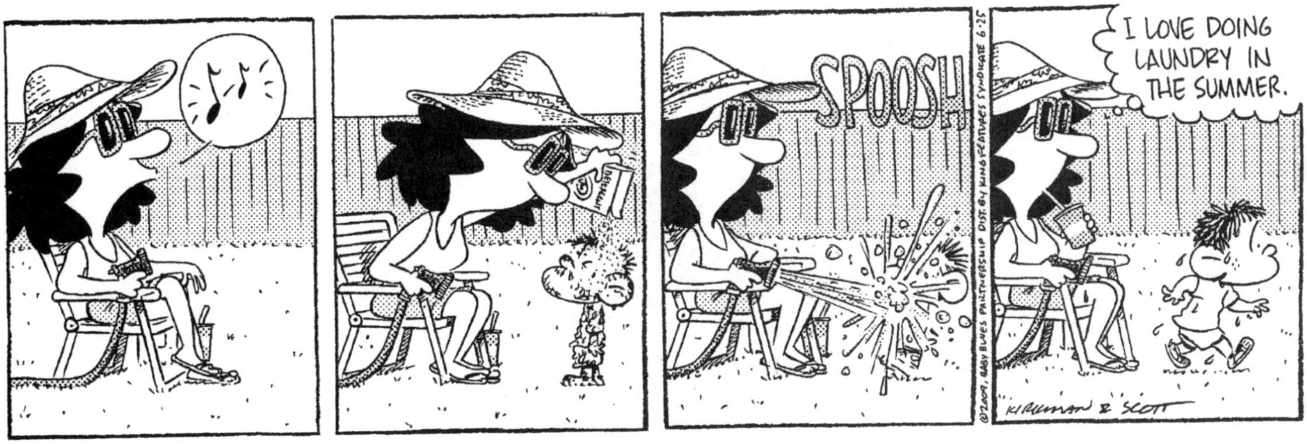
SPOOSH
I LOVE DOING LAUNDRY IN THE SUMMER.
©2009, BABY BLUES PARTNERSHIP DIST. BY KING FEATURES SYNDICATE 6-25
KIRKMAN & SCOTT

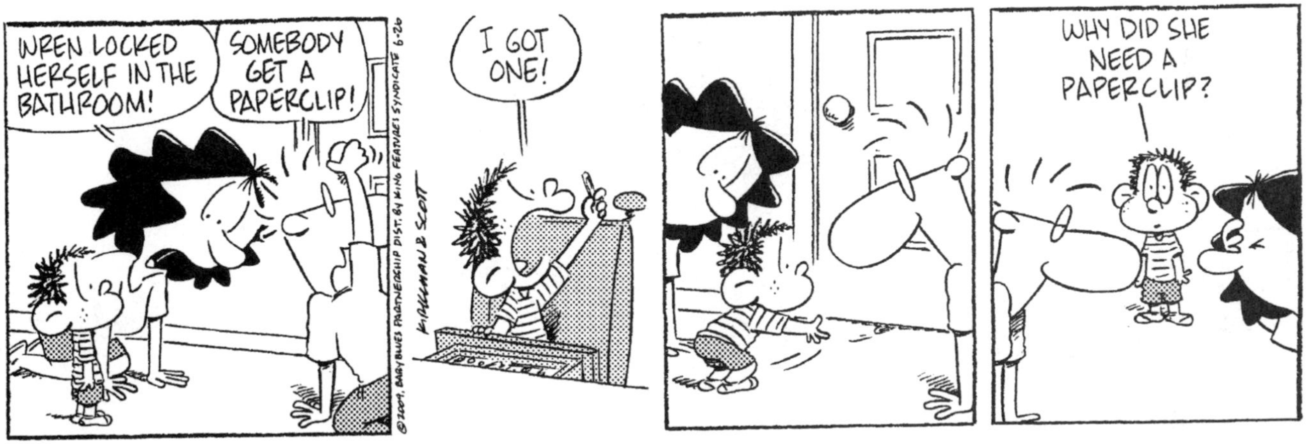
WREN LOCKED HERSELF IN THE BATHROOM!
SOMEBODY GET A PAPERCLIP!
©2009, BABY BLUES PARTNERSHIP DIST. BY KING FEATURES SYNDICATE 6-26
KIRKMAN & SCOTT
I GOT ONE!
WHY DID SHE NEED A PAPERCLIP?

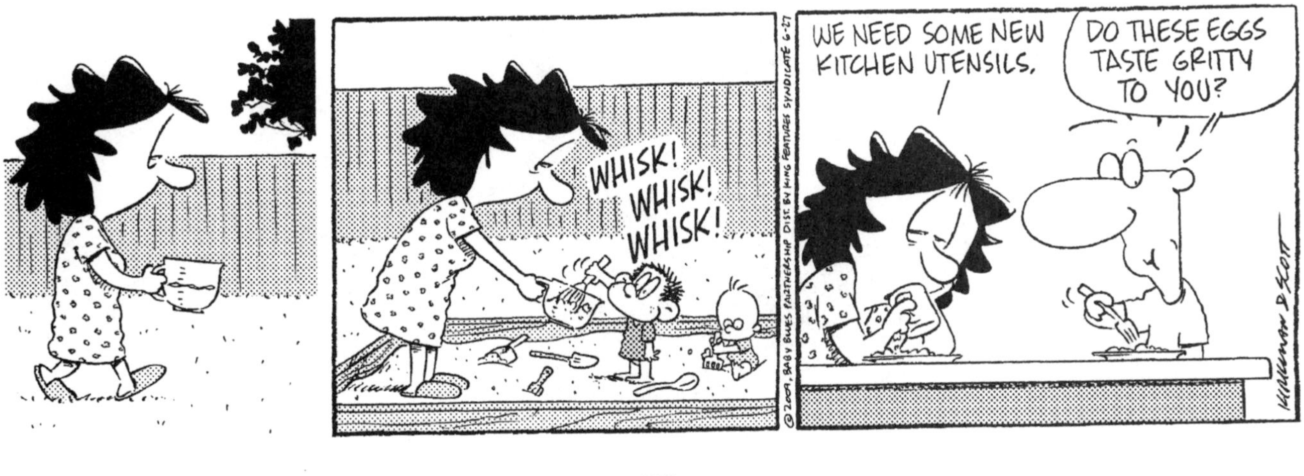
WHISK! WHISK! WHISK!
©2009, BABY BLUES PARTNERSHIP DIST. BY KING FEATURES SYNDICATE 6-27
WE NEED SOME NEW KITCHEN UTENSILS.
DO THESE EGGS TASTE GRITTY TO YOU?
KIRKMAN & SCOTT

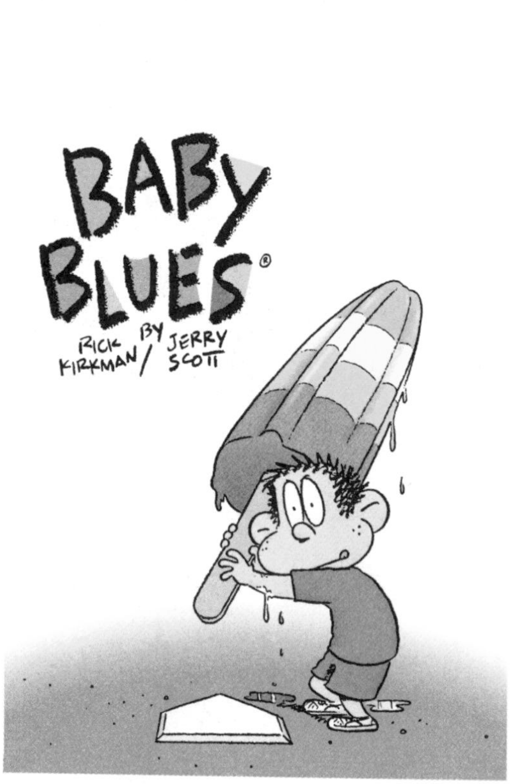
BABY BLUES®
BY RICK KIRKMAN / JERRY SCOTT

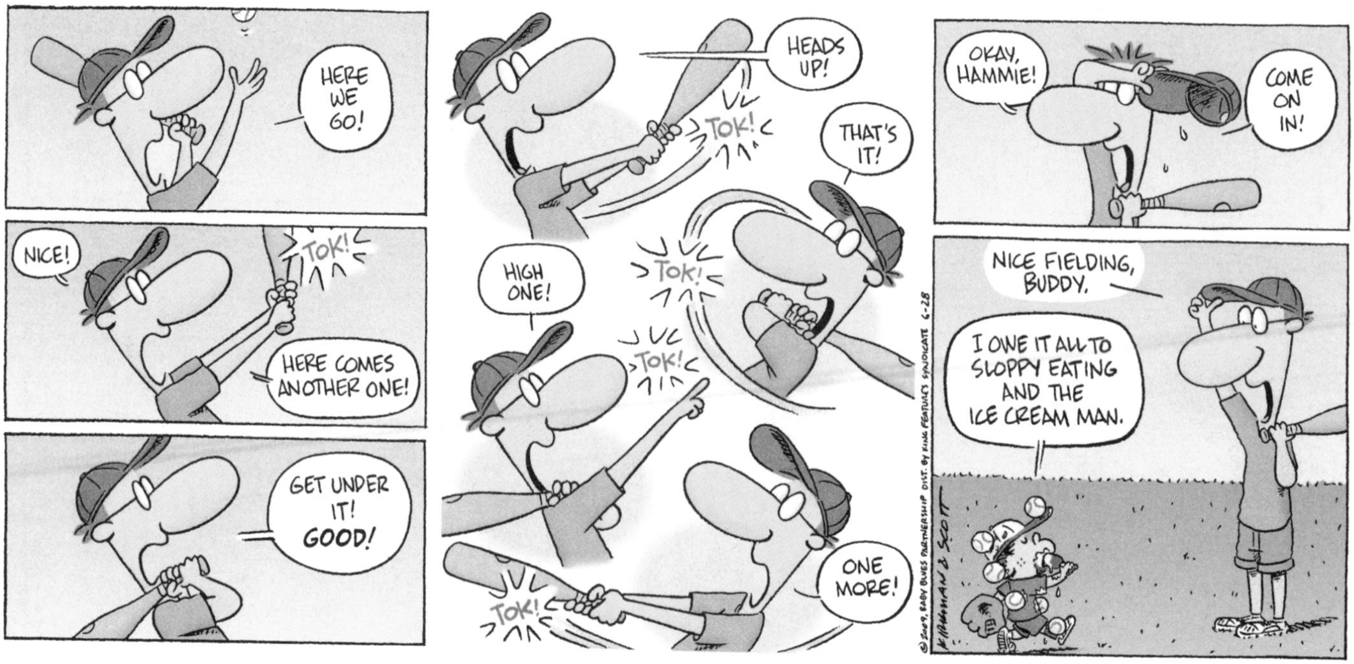
HERE WE GO!
NICE!
TOK!
HERE COMES ANOTHER ONE!
GET UNDER IT! GOOD!
HEADS UP!
TOK!
THAT'S IT!
TOK!
HIGH ONE!
TOK!
ONE MORE!
TOK!
OKAY, HAMMIE!
COME ON IN!
NICE FIELDING, BUDDY.
I OWE IT ALL TO SLOPPY EATING AND THE ICE CREAM MAN.
KIRKMAN & SCOTT
© 2009, BABY BLUES PARTNERSHIP DIST. BY KING FEATURES SYNDICATE 6-28

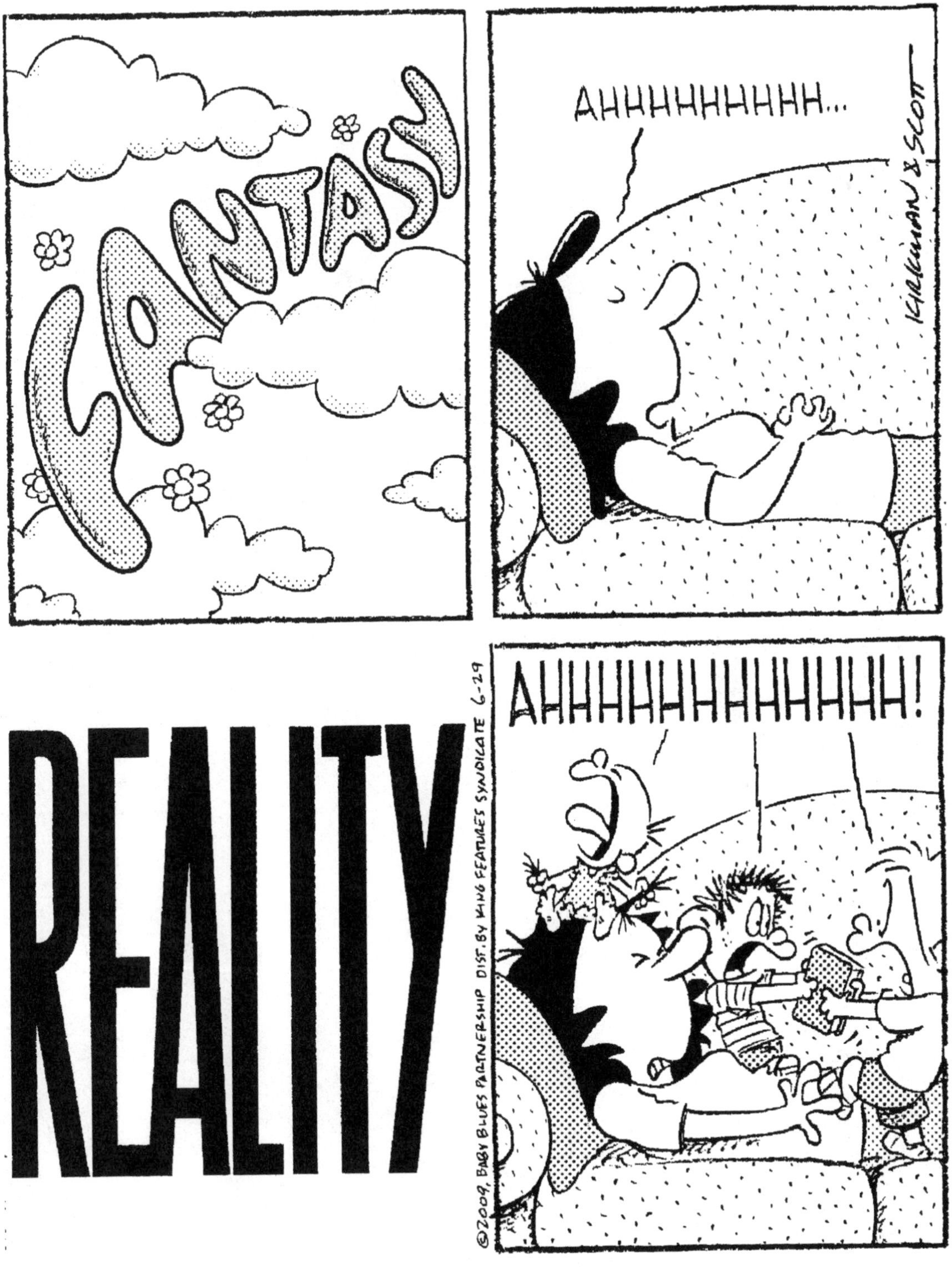
FANTASY
AHHHHHHHHH...
KIRKMAN & SCOTT
REALITY
AHHHHHHHHHHHH!
©2009, BABY BLUES PARTNERSHIP DIST. BY KING FEATURES SYNDICATE 6-29

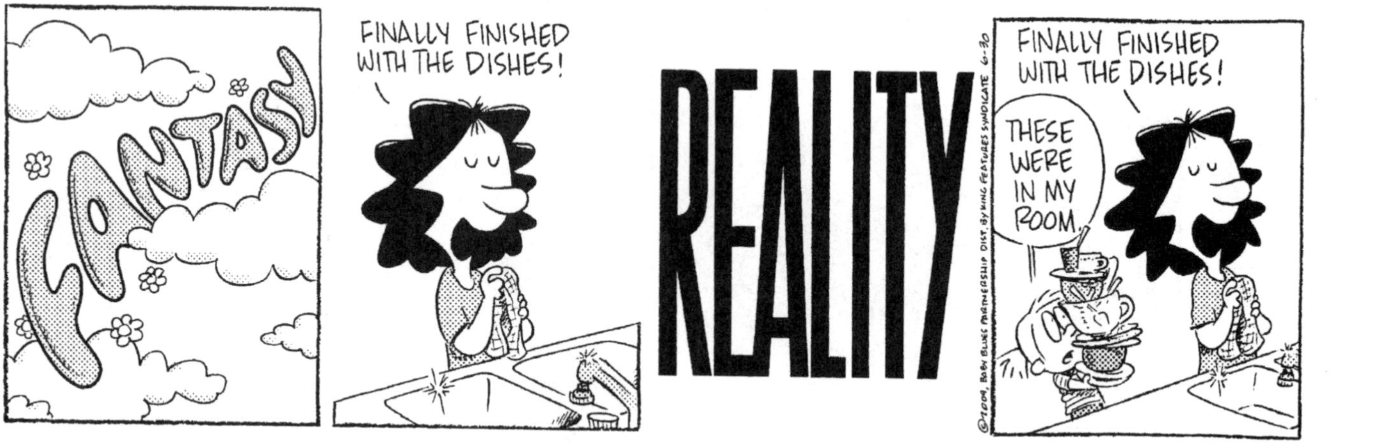
FANTASY
FINALLY FINISHED WITH THE DISHES!
REALITY
FINALLY FINISHED WITH THE DISHES!
THESE WERE IN MY ROOM.
© 2009, BABY BLUES PARTNERSHIP DIST. BY KING FEATURES SYNDICATE 6-30

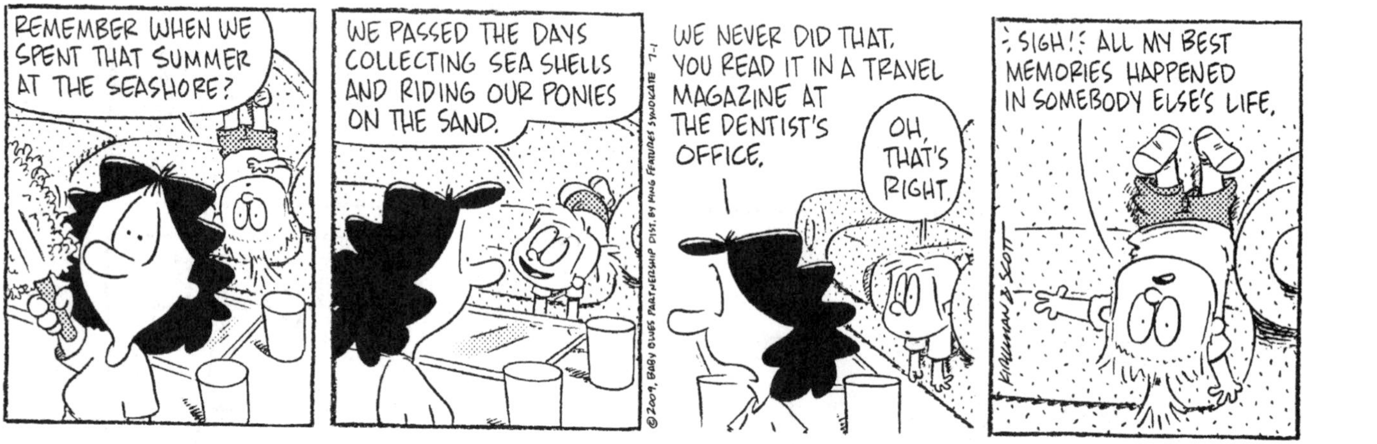
REMEMBER WHEN WE SPENT THAT SUMMER AT THE SEASHORE?
WE PASSED THE DAYS COLLECTING SEA SHELLS AND RIDING OUR PONIES ON THE SAND.
© 2009, BABY BLUES PARTNERSHIP DIST. BY KING FEATURES SYNDICATE 7-1
WE NEVER DID THAT. YOU READ IT IN A TRAVEL MAGAZINE AT THE DENTIST'S OFFICE.
OH, THAT'S RIGHT.
SIGH! ALL MY BEST MEMORIES HAPPENED IN SOMEBODY ELSE'S LIFE.
KIRKMAN & SCOTT

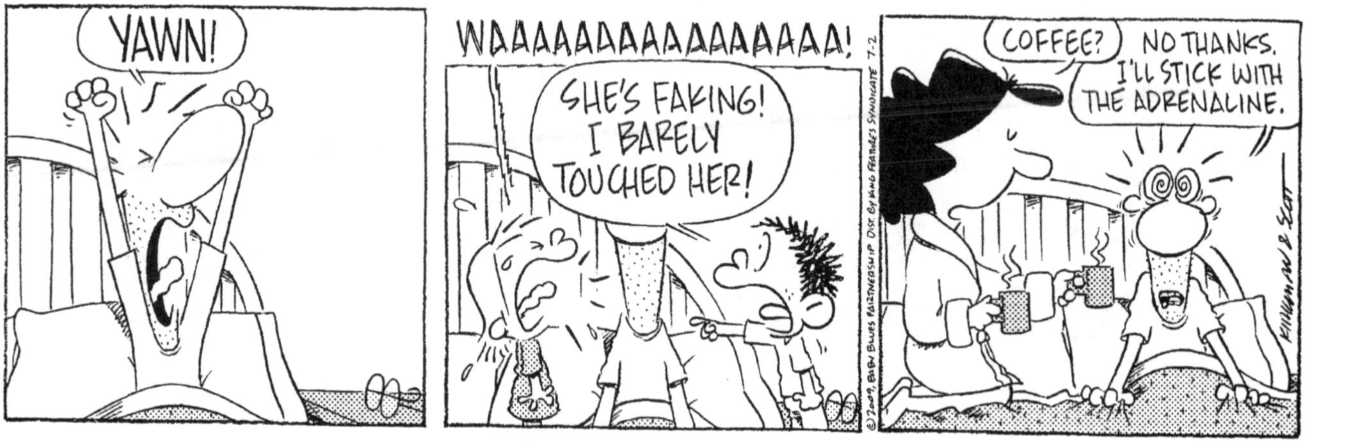
YAWN!
WAAAAAAAAAAAAAAAA!
SHE'S FAKING! I BARELY TOUCHED HER!
© 2009, BABY BLUES PARTNERSHIP DIST. BY KING FEATURES SYNDICATE 7-2
COFFEE?
NO THANKS. I'LL STICK WITH THE ADRENALINE.
KIRKMAN & SCOTT

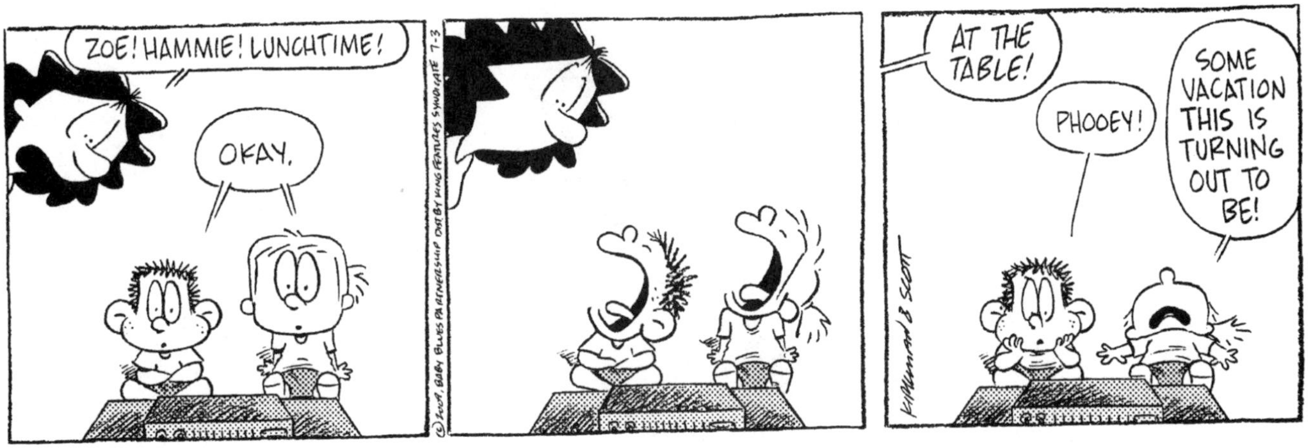
ZOE! HAMMIE! LUNCHTIME!
OKAY.
AT THE TABLE!
PHOOEY!
SOME VACATION THIS IS TURNING OUT TO BE!
© 2007, BABY BLUES PARTNERSHIP DIST. BY KING FEATURES SYNDICATE 7-3
KIRKMAN & SCOTT

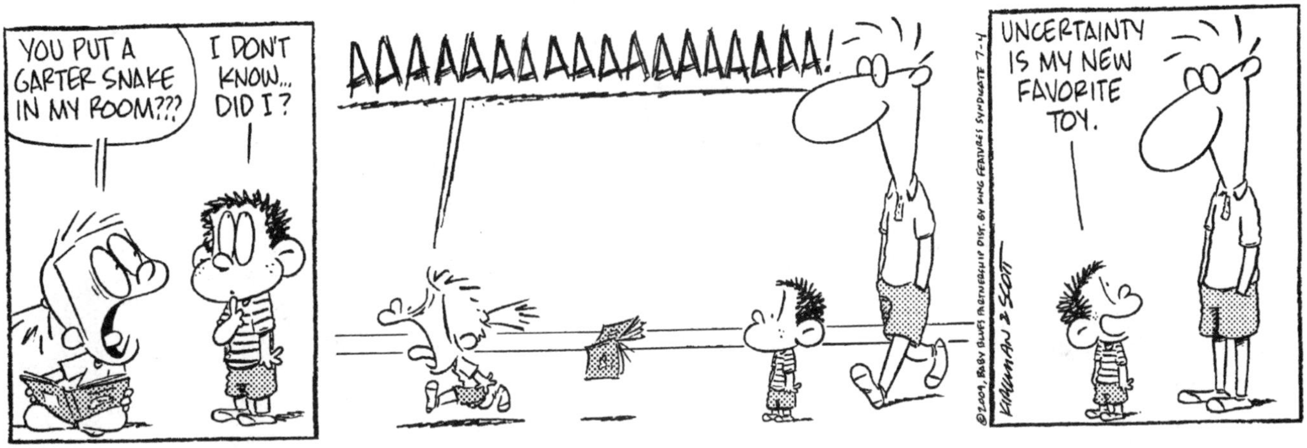
YOU PUT A GARTER SNAKE IN MY ROOM???
I DON'T KNOW... DID I?
AAAAAAAAAAAAAAAAAA!
UNCERTAINTY IS MY NEW FAVORITE TOY.
© 2009, BABY BLUES PARTNERSHIP DIST. BY KING FEATURES SYNDICATE 7-4
KIRKMAN & SCOTT

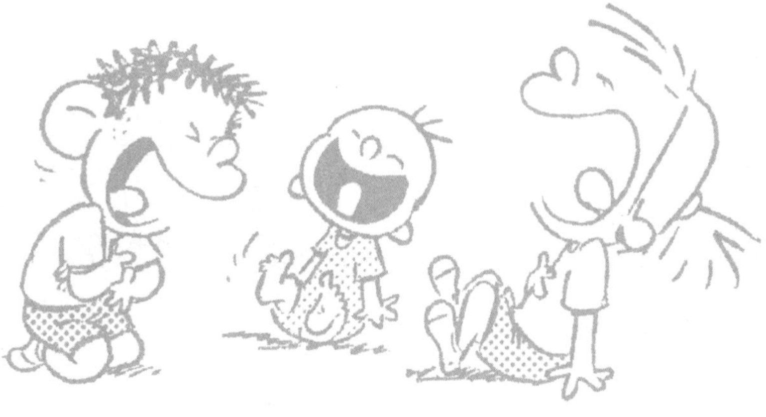

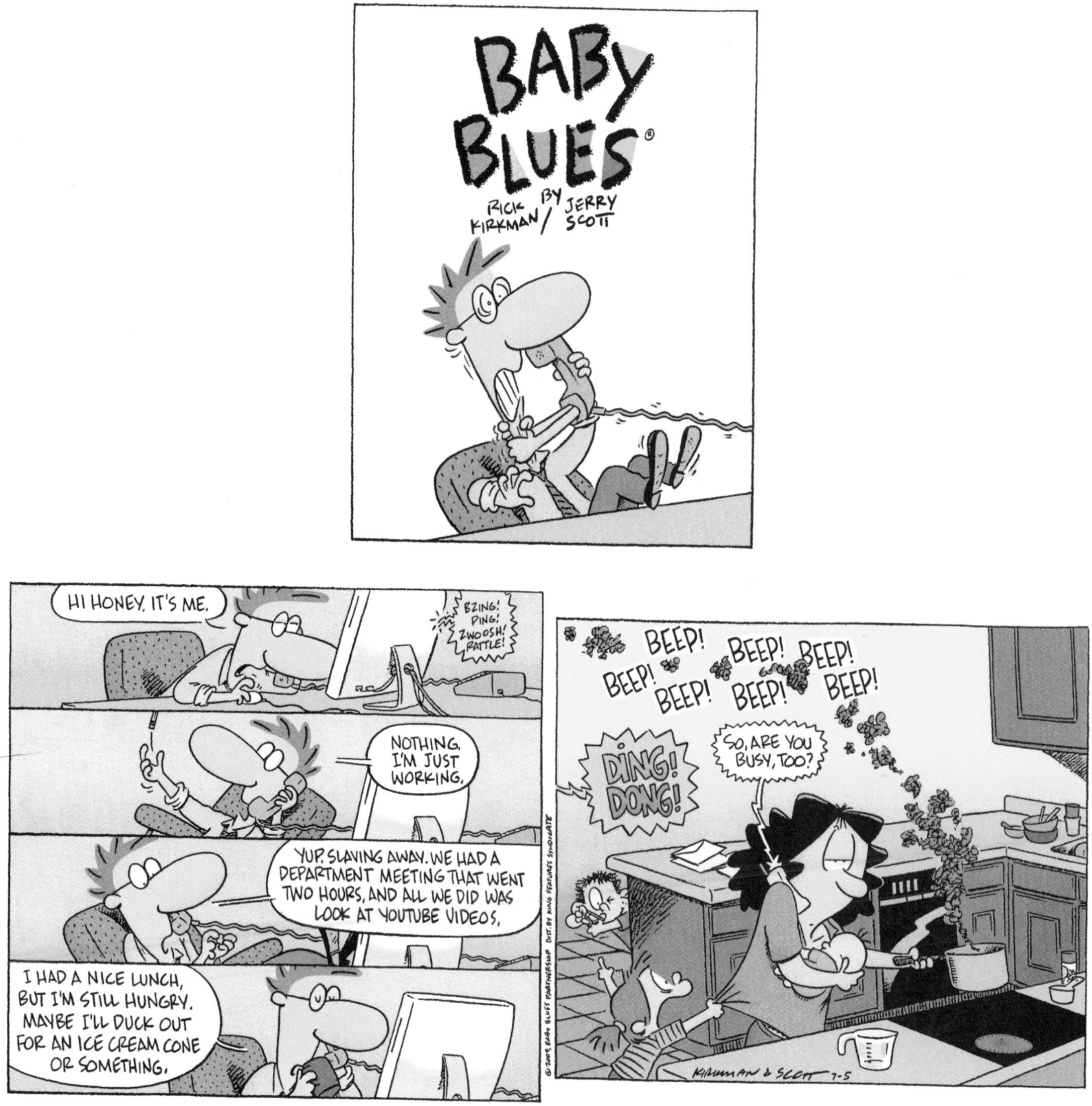
BABY BLUES®
BY RICK KIRKMAN / JERRY SCOTT
HI HONEY. IT'S ME.
BZING! PING! ZWOOSH! RATTLE!
NOTHING. I'M JUST WORKING.
YUP. SLAVING AWAY. WE HAD A DEPARTMENT MEETING THAT WENT TWO HOURS, AND ALL WE DID WAS LOOK AT YOUTUBE VIDEOS.
I HAD A NICE LUNCH, BUT I'M STILL HUNGRY. MAYBE I'LL DUCK OUT FOR AN ICE CREAM CONE OR SOMETHING.
BEEP! BEEP! BEEP! BEEP! BEEP! BEEP! BEEP!
DING! DONG!
SO, ARE YOU BUSY, TOO?
©2009, BABY BLUES PARTNERSHIP DIST. BY KING FEATURES SYNDICATE
KIRKMAN & SCOTT 7-5

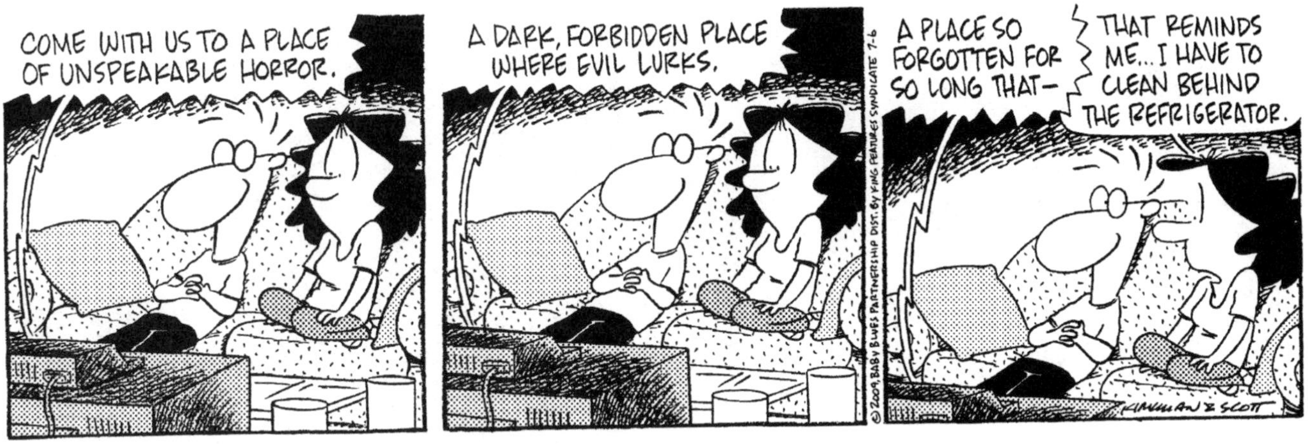
COME WITH US TO A PLACE OF UNSPEAKABLE HORROR.
A DARK, FORBIDDEN PLACE WHERE EVIL LURKS.
A PLACE SO FORGOTTEN FOR SO LONG THAT—
THAT REMINDS ME... I HAVE TO CLEAN BEHIND THE REFRIGERATOR.
© 2009, BABY BLUES PARTNERSHIP DIST. BY KING FEATURES SYNDICATE 7-6
KIRKMAN & SCOTT

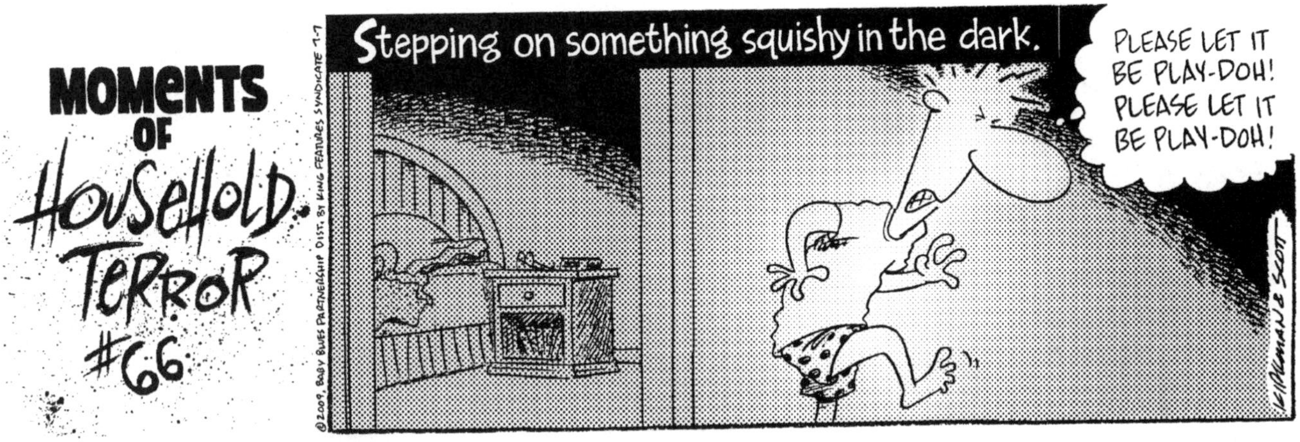
MOMENTS OF HOUSEHOLD TERROR #66
Stepping on something squishy in the dark.
PLEASE LET IT BE PLAY-DOH! PLEASE LET IT BE PLAY-DOH!
© 2009, BABY BLUES PARTNERSHIP DIST. BY KING FEATURES SYNDICATE 7-7
KIRKMAN & SCOTT

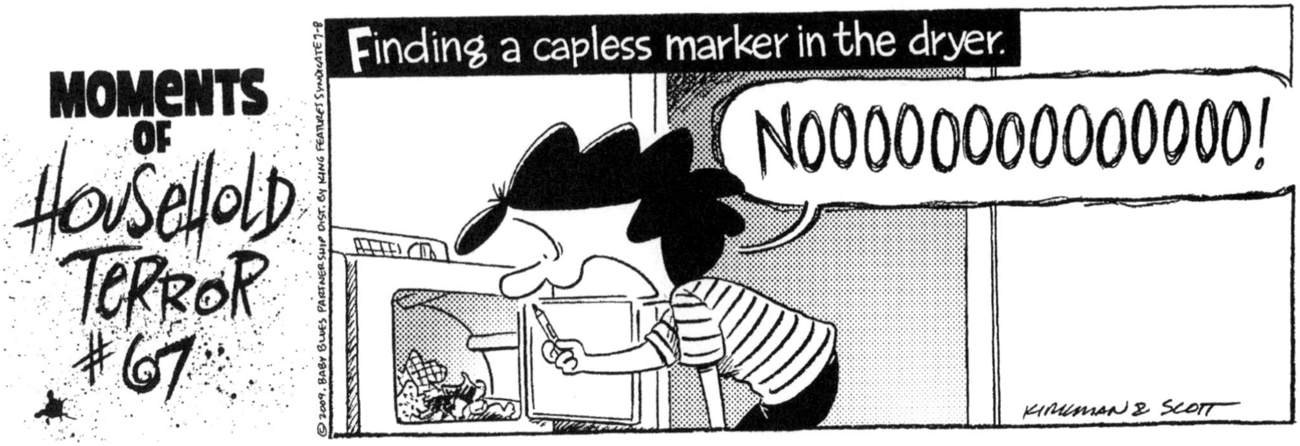
MOMENTS OF HOUSEHOLD TERROR #67
Finding a capless marker in the dryer.
NOOOOOOOOOOOOOO!
© 2009, BABY BLUES PARTNERSHIP DIST. BY KING FEATURES SYNDICATE 7-8
KIRKMAN & SCOTT

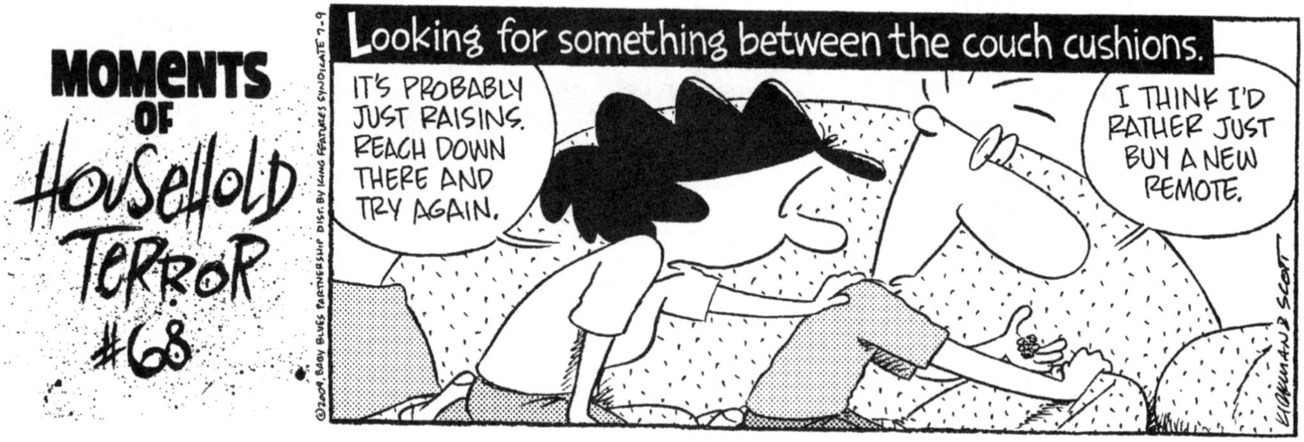
MOMENTS OF HOUSEHOLD TERROR #68
Looking for something between the couch cushions.
IT'S PROBABLY JUST RAISINS. REACH DOWN THERE AND TRY AGAIN.
I THINK I'D RATHER JUST BUY A NEW REMOTE.
©2009, BABY BLUES PARTNERSHIP DIST. BY KING FEATURES SYNDICATE 7-9
KIRKMAN & SCOTT

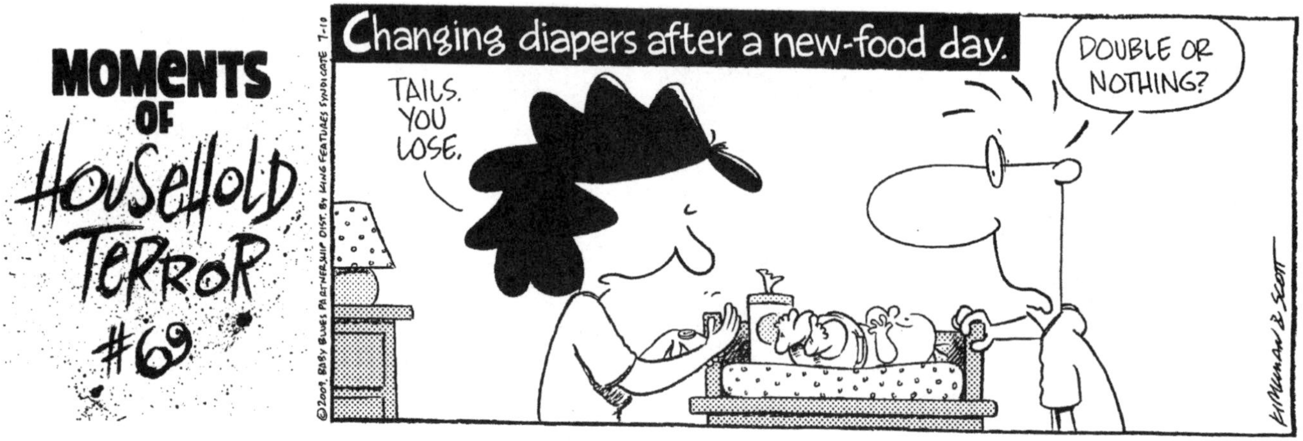
MOMENTS OF HOUSEHOLD TERROR #69
Changing diapers after a new-food day.
TAILS. YOU LOSE.
DOUBLE OR NOTHING?
©2009, BABY BLUES PARTNERSHIP DIST. BY KING FEATURES SYNDICATE 7-10
KIRKMAN & SCOTT

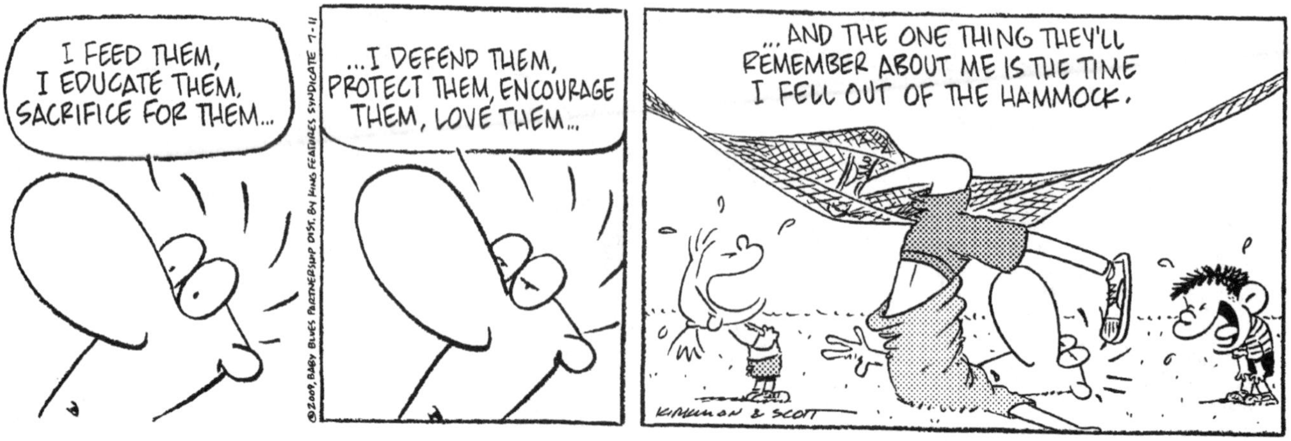
I FEED THEM, I EDUCATE THEM, SACRIFICE FOR THEM...
...I DEFEND THEM, PROTECT THEM, ENCOURAGE THEM, LOVE THEM...
...AND THE ONE THING THEY'LL REMEMBER ABOUT ME IS THE TIME I FELL OUT OF THE HAMMOCK.
©2009, BABY BLUES PARTNERSHIP DIST. BY KING FEATURES SYNDICATE 7-11
KIRKMAN & SCOTT

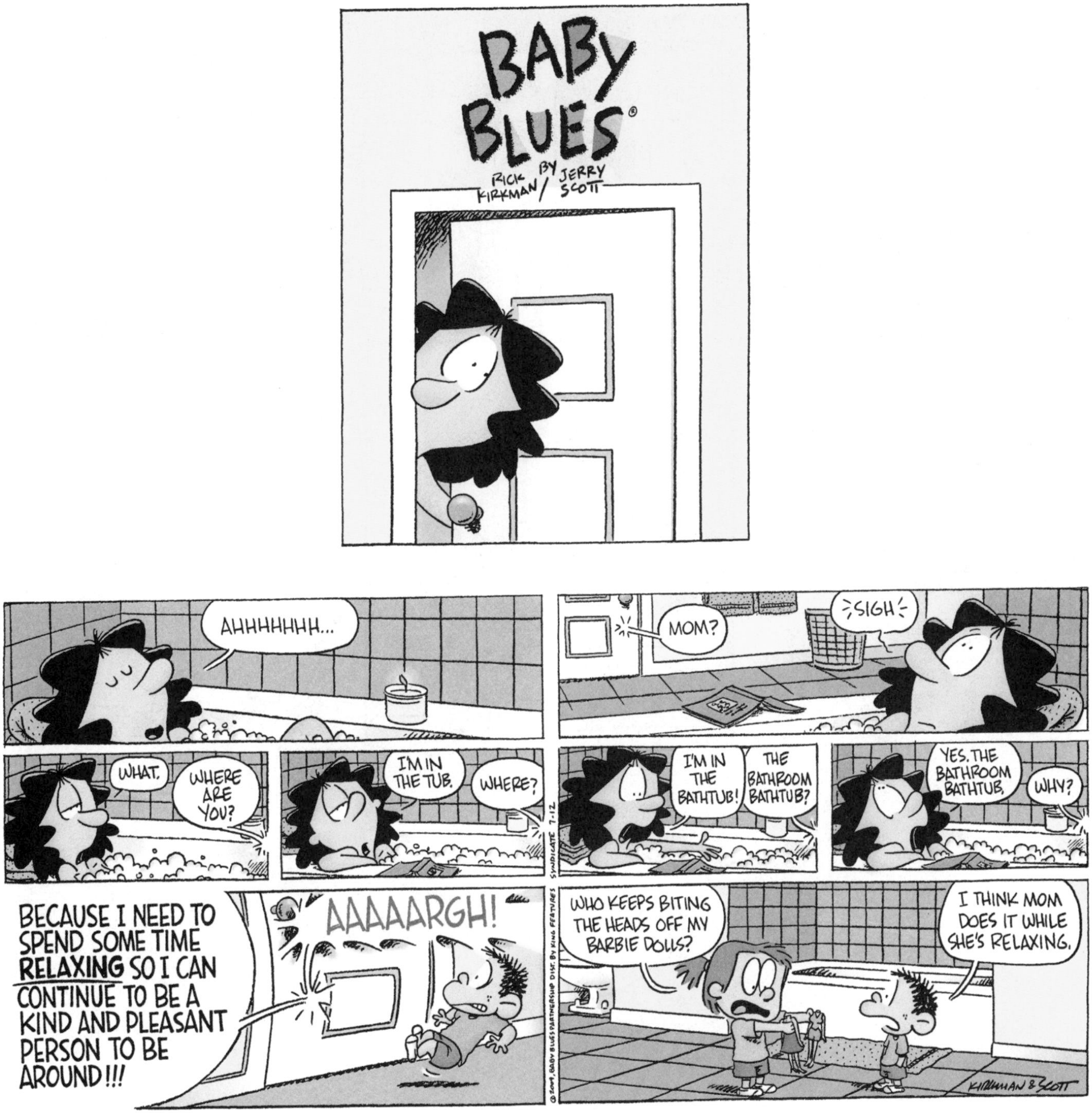
BABY BLUES®
BY RICK KIRKMAN / JERRY SCOTT
AHHHHHHH...
MOM?
SIGH
WHAT.
WHERE ARE YOU?
I'M IN THE TUB.
WHERE?
I'M IN THE BATHTUB!
THE BATHROOM BATHTUB?
YES. THE BATHROOM BATHTUB.
WHY?
BECAUSE I NEED TO SPEND SOME TIME RELAXING SO I CAN CONTINUE TO BE A KIND AND PLEASANT PERSON TO BE AROUND!!!
AAAAARGH!
WHO KEEPS BITING THE HEADS OFF MY BARBIE DOLLS?
I THINK MOM DOES IT WHILE SHE'S RELAXING.
KIRKMAN & SCOTT

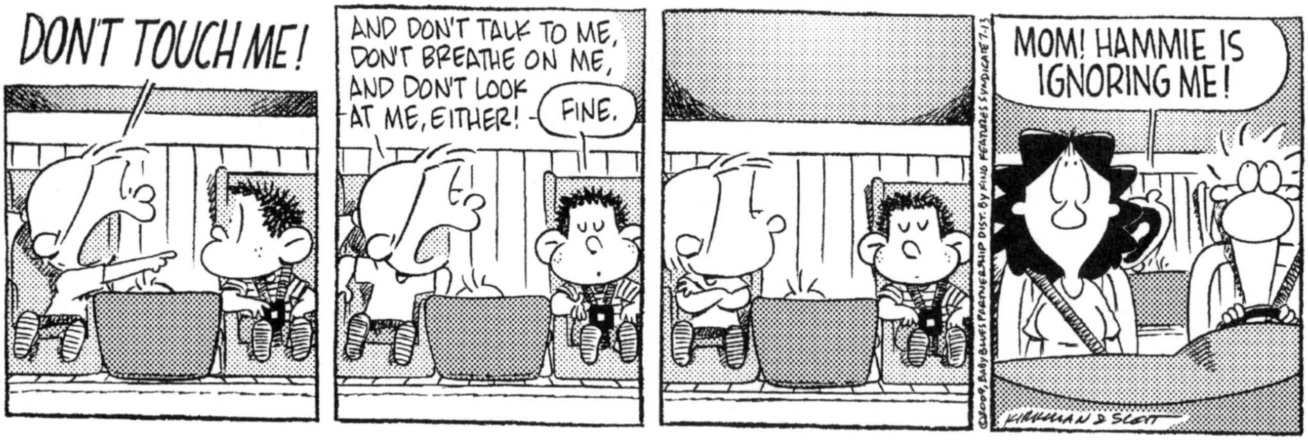
DON'T TOUCH ME!
AND DON'T TALK TO ME, DON'T BREATHE ON ME, AND DON'T LOOK AT ME, EITHER!
FINE.
©2009, BABY BLUES PARTNERSHIP DIST. BY KING FEATURES SYNDICATE 7-13
MOM! HAMMIE IS IGNORING ME!
KIRKMAN & SCOTT

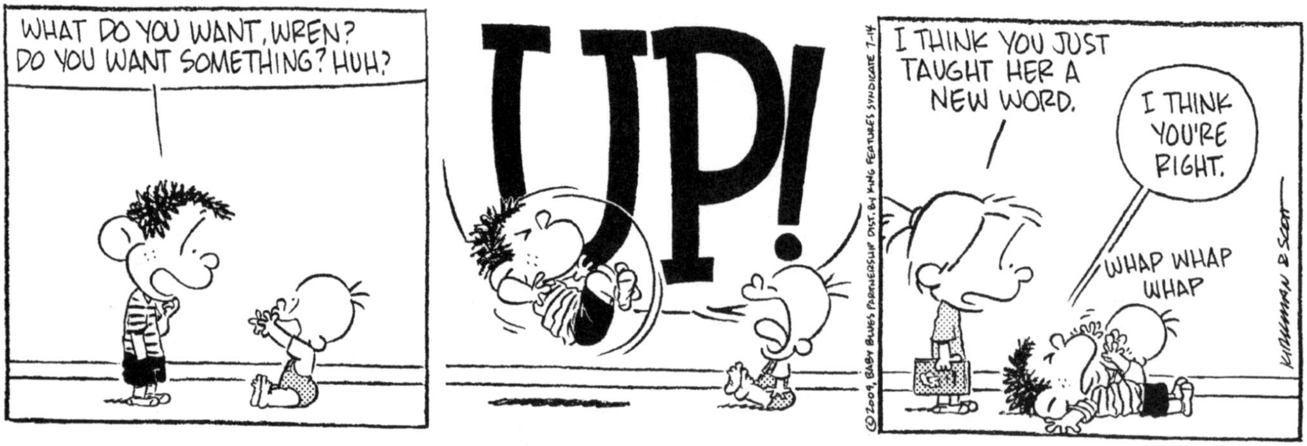
WHAT DO YOU WANT, WREN? DO YOU WANT SOMETHING? HUH?
UP!
©2009, BABY BLUES PARTNERSHIP DIST. BY KING FEATURES SYNDICATE 7-14
I THINK YOU JUST TAUGHT HER A NEW WORD.
I THINK YOU'RE RIGHT.
WHAP WHAP WHAP
KIRKMAN & SCOTT

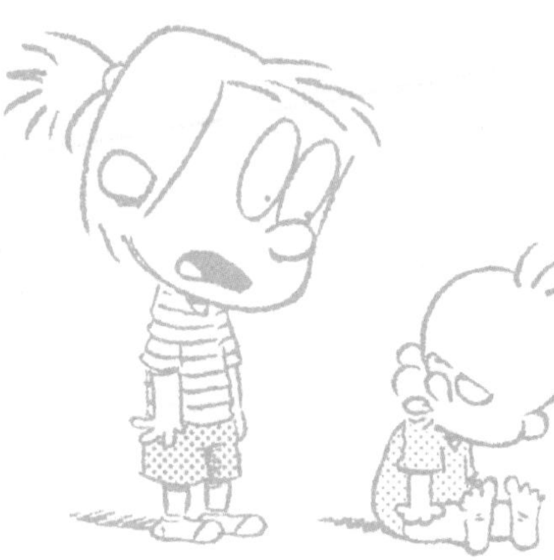

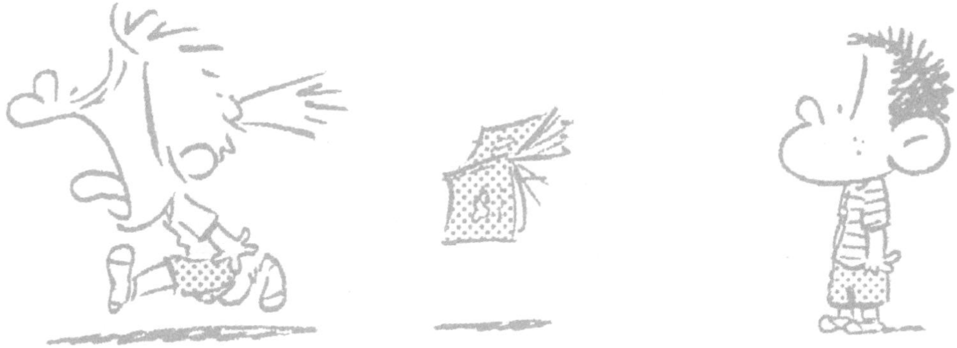

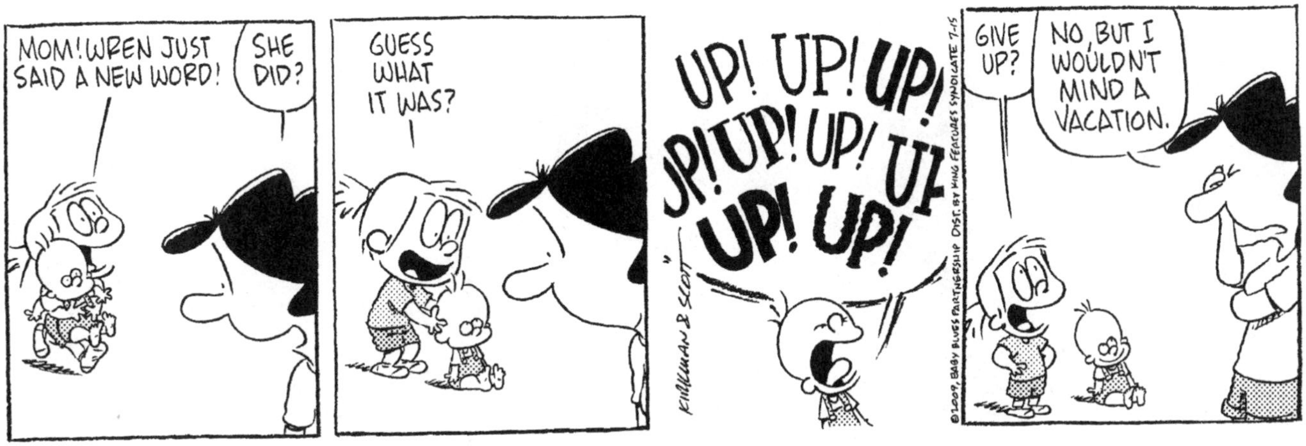
MOM! WREN JUST SAID A NEW WORD!
SHE DID?
GUESS WHAT IT WAS?
UP! UP! UP! UP! UP! UP! UP! UP! UP!
GIVE UP?
NO, BUT I WOULDN'T MIND A VACATION.
KIRKMAN & SCOTT
©2009, BABY BLUES PARTNERSHIP DIST. BY KING FEATURES SYNDICATE 7-15

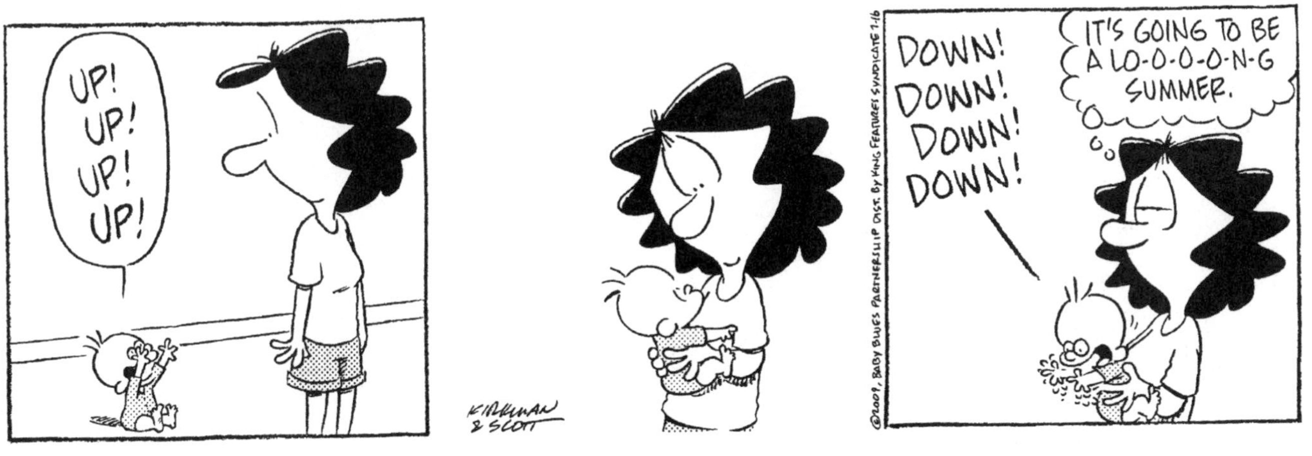
UP! UP! UP! UP!
KIRKMAN & SCOTT
©2009, BABY BLUES PARTNERSHIP DIST. BY KING FEATURES SYNDICATE 7-16
DOWN! DOWN! DOWN! DOWN!
IT'S GOING TO BE A LO-O-O-O-N-G SUMMER.

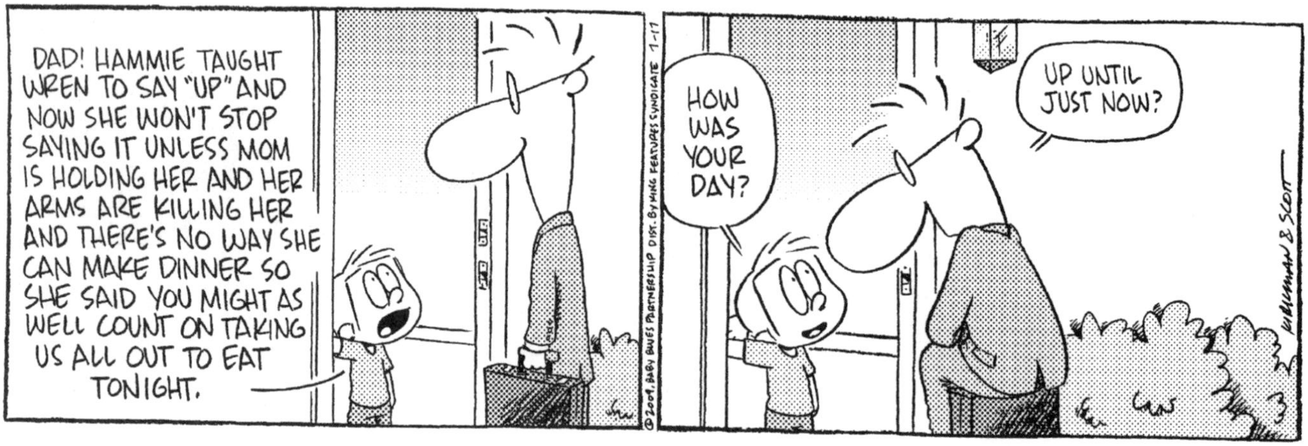
DAD! HAMMIE TAUGHT WREN TO SAY "UP" AND NOW SHE WON'T STOP SAYING IT UNLESS MOM IS HOLDING HER AND HER ARMS ARE KILLING HER AND THERE'S NO WAY SHE CAN MAKE DINNER SO SHE SAID YOU MIGHT AS WELL COUNT ON TAKING US ALL OUT TO EAT TONIGHT.
© 2009, BABY BLUES PARTNERSHIP DIST. BY KING FEATURES SYNDICATE 1-17
HOW WAS YOUR DAY?
UP UNTIL JUST NOW?
KIRKMAN & SCOTT

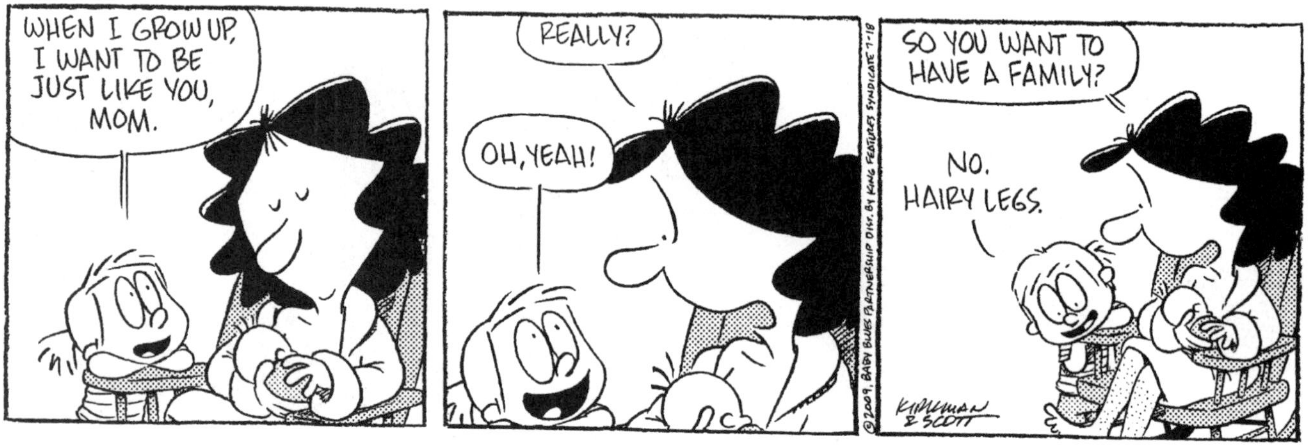
WHEN I GROW UP, I WANT TO BE JUST LIKE YOU, MOM.
REALLY?
OH, YEAH!
© 2009, BABY BLUES PARTNERSHIP DIST. BY KING FEATURES SYNDICATE 1-18
SO YOU WANT TO HAVE A FAMILY?
NO. HAIRY LEGS.
KIRKMAN & SCOTT

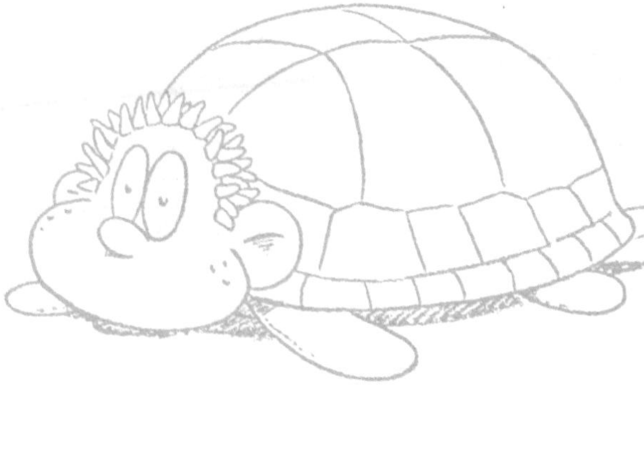

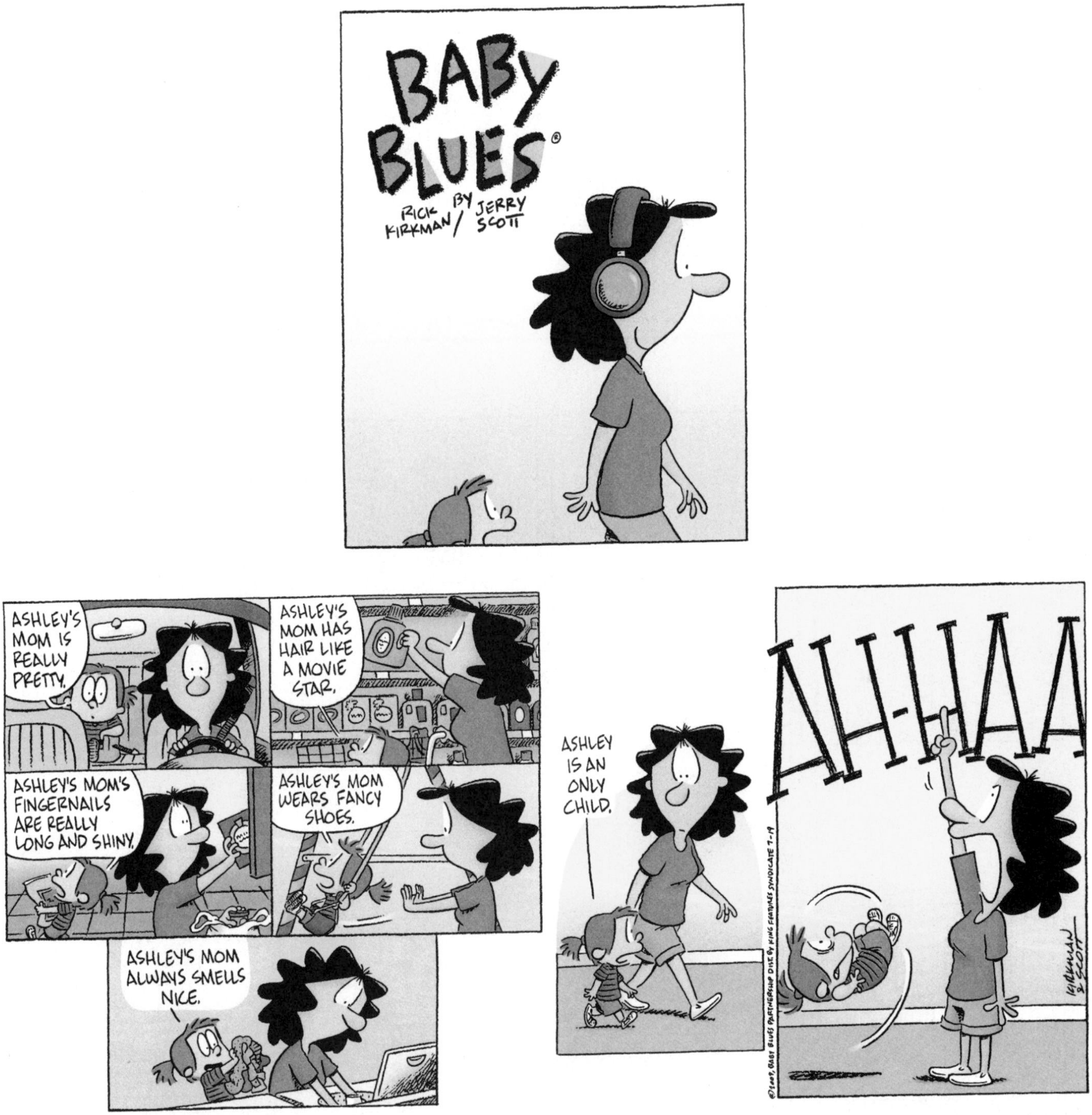
BABY BLUES®
BY RICK KIRKMAN / JERRY SCOTT
ASHLEY'S MOM IS REALLY PRETTY.
ASHLEY'S MOM HAS HAIR LIKE A MOVIE STAR.
ASHLEY'S MOM'S FINGERNAILS ARE REALLY LONG AND SHINY.
ASHLEY'S MOM WEARS FANCY SHOES.
ASHLEY'S MOM ALWAYS SMELLS NICE.
ASHLEY IS AN ONLY CHILD.
AH-HAA
©2009, BABY BLUES PARTNERSHIP DIST. BY KING FEATURES SYNDICATE 7-19
KIRKMAN & SCOTT

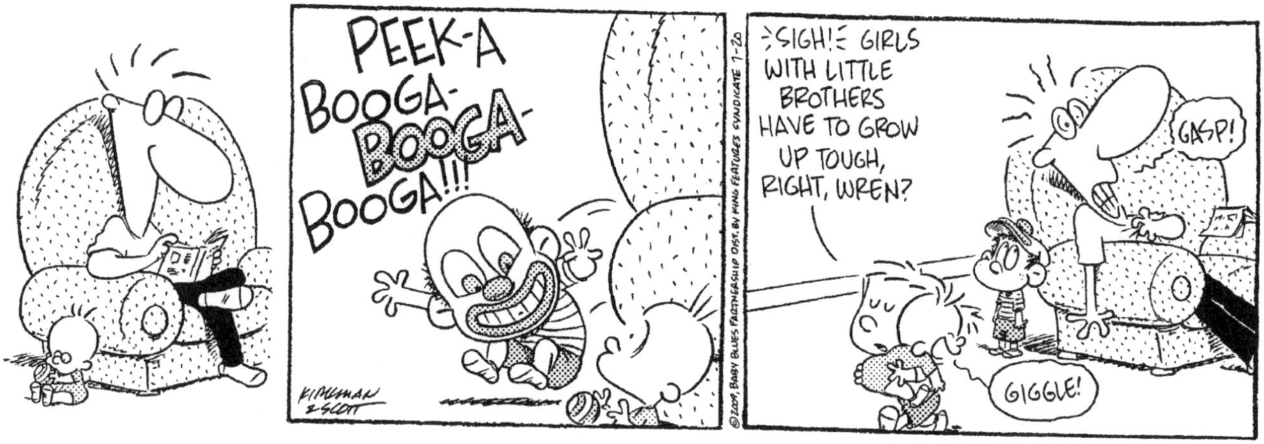
PEEK-A BOOGA-BOOGA-BOOGA!!!
KIRKMAN & SCOTT
©2009, BABY BLUES PARTNERSHIP DIST. BY KING FEATURES SYNDICATE 7-20
SIGH! GIRLS WITH LITTLE BROTHERS HAVE TO GROW UP TOUGH, RIGHT, WREN?
GASP!
GIGGLE!

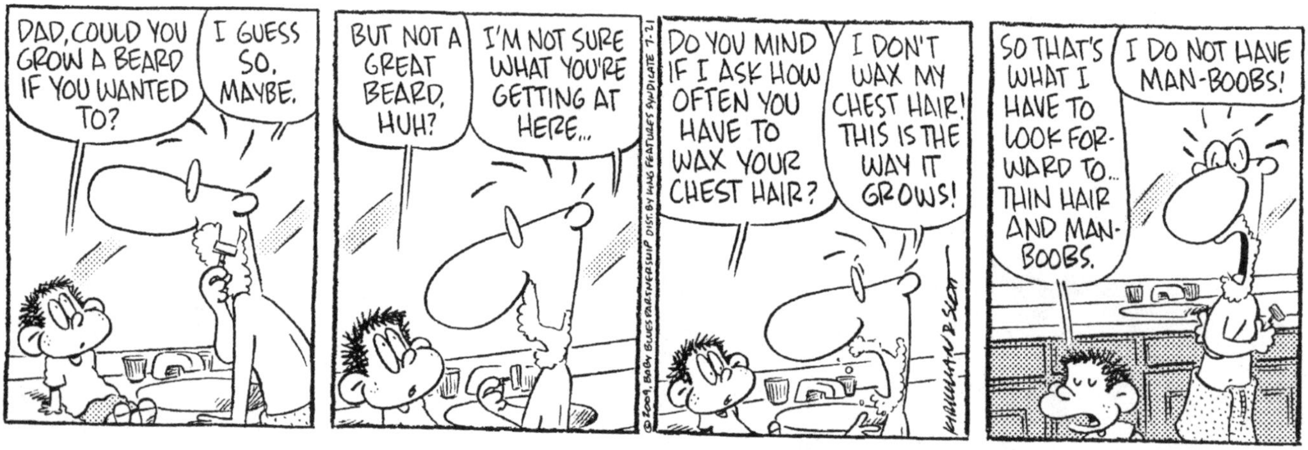
DAD, COULD YOU GROW A BEARD IF YOU WANTED TO?
I GUESS SO. MAYBE.
BUT NOT A GREAT BEARD, HUH?
I'M NOT SURE WHAT YOU'RE GETTING AT HERE...
©2009, BABY BLUES PARTNERSHIP DIST. BY KING FEATURES SYNDICATE 7-21
DO YOU MIND IF I ASK HOW OFTEN YOU HAVE TO WAX YOUR CHEST HAIR?
I DON'T WAX MY CHEST HAIR! THIS IS THE WAY IT GROWS!
KIRKMAN & SCOTT
SO THAT'S WHAT I HAVE TO LOOK FORWARD TO... THIN HAIR AND MAN-BOOBS.
I DO NOT HAVE MAN-BOOBS!

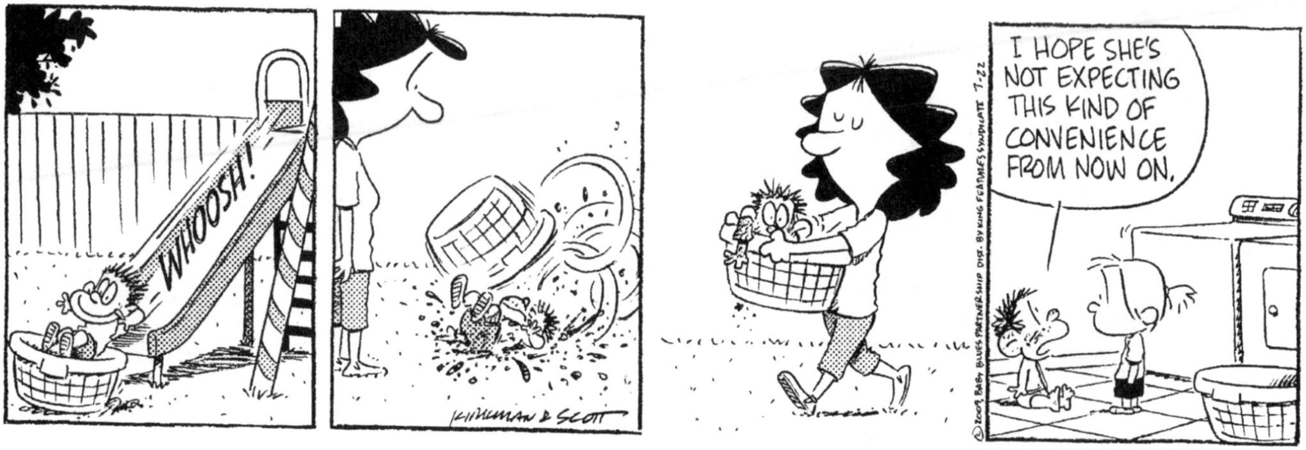
WHOOSH!
KIRKMAN & SCOTT
©2009, BABY BLUES PARTNERSHIP DIST. BY KING FEATURES SYNDICATE 7-22
I HOPE SHE'S NOT EXPECTING THIS KIND OF CONVENIENCE FROM NOW ON.

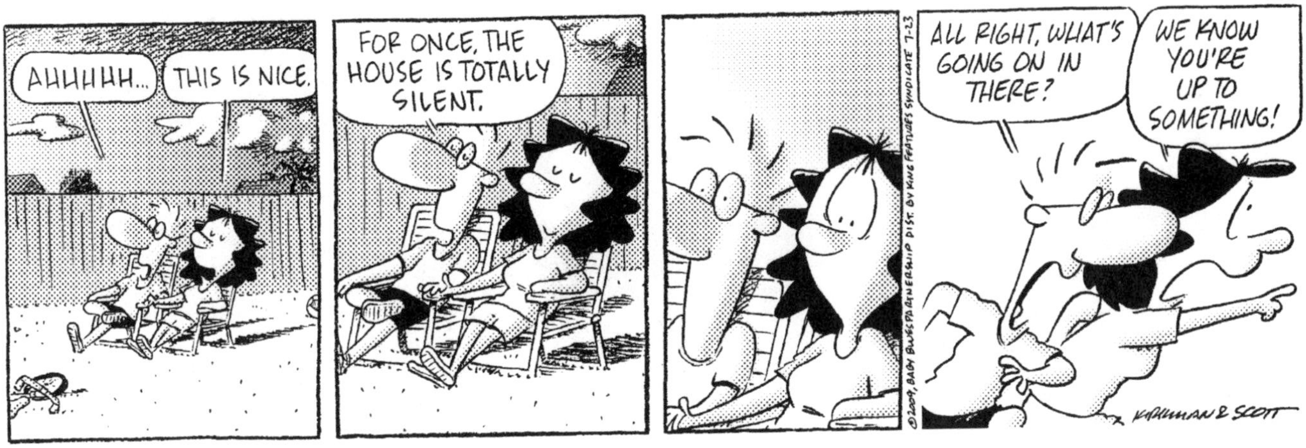
AHHHHH...
THIS IS NICE.
FOR ONCE, THE HOUSE IS TOTALLY SILENT.
©2009, BABY BLUES PARTNERSHIP DIST. BY KING FEATURES SYNDICATE 7-23
ALL RIGHT, WHAT'S GOING ON IN THERE?
WE KNOW YOU'RE UP TO SOMETHING!
KIRKMAN & SCOTT

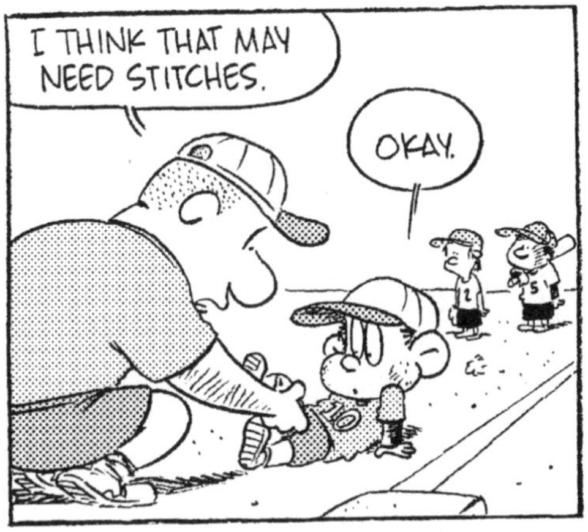
I THINK THAT MAY NEED STITCHES.
OKAY.

The tolerance for pain is in direct proportion to the proximity of the mom.

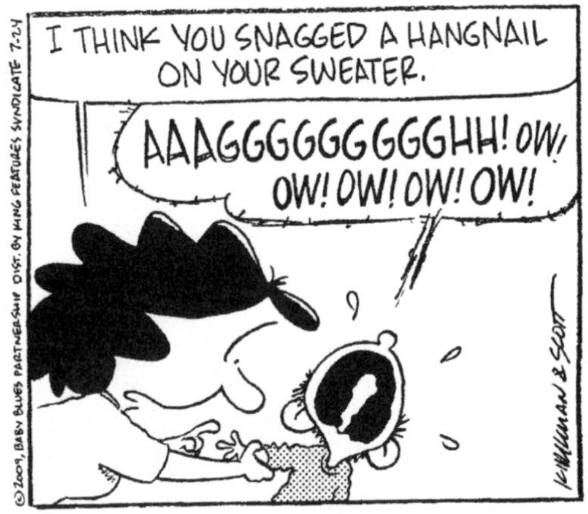
©2009, BABY BLUES PARTNERSHIP DIST. BY KING FEATURES SYNDICATE 7-24
I THINK YOU SNAGGED A HANGNAIL ON YOUR SWEATER.
AAAGGGGGGGGGHH! OW! OW! OW! OW! OW!
KIRKMAN & SCOTT

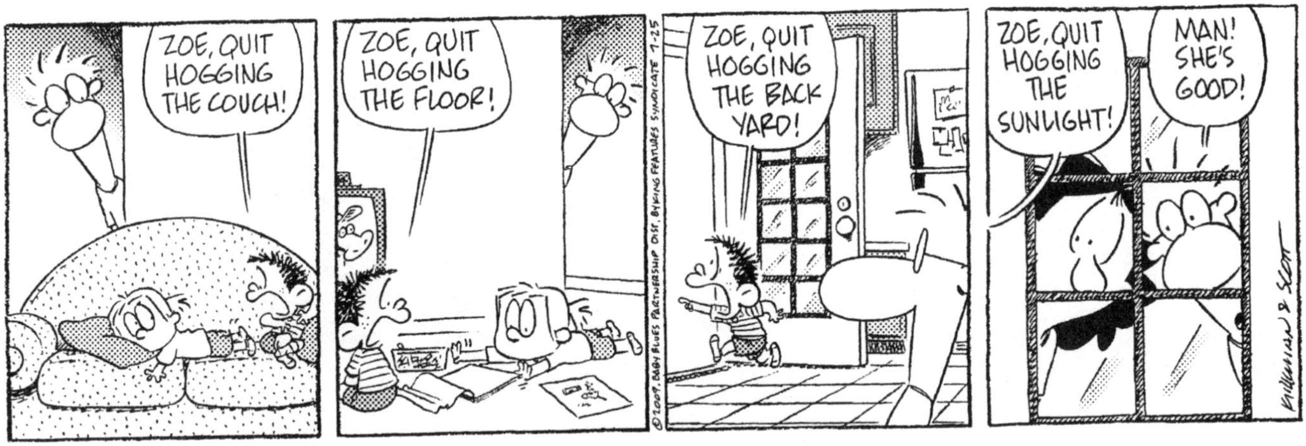
ZOE, QUIT HOGGING THE COUCH!
ZOE, QUIT HOGGING THE FLOOR!
©2009, BABY BLUES PARTNERSHIP DIST. BY KING FEATURES SYNDICATE 7-25
ZOE, QUIT HOGGING THE BACK YARD!
ZOE, QUIT HOGGING THE SUNLIGHT!
MAN! SHE'S GOOD!
KIRKMAN & SCOTT

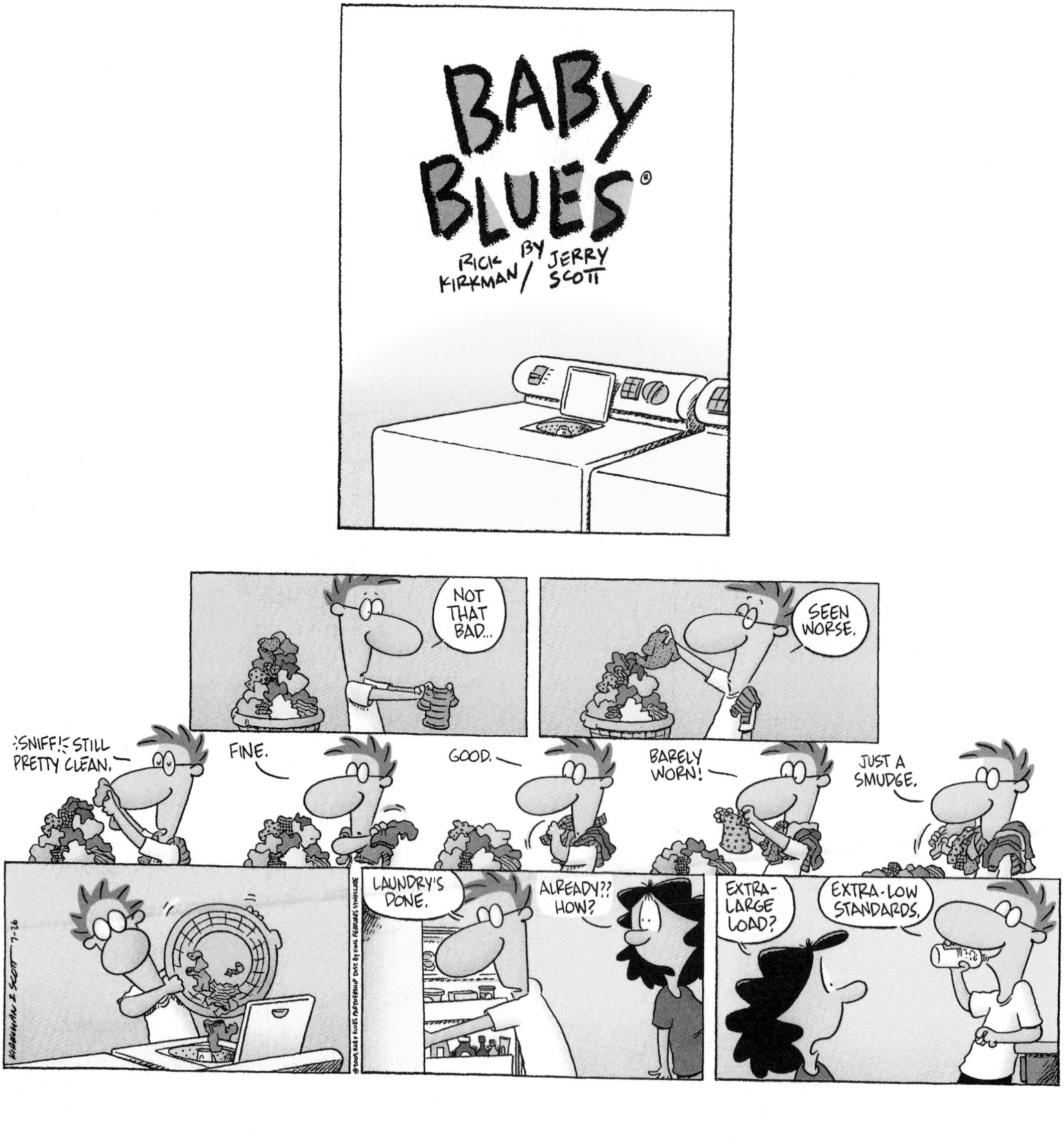
BABY BLUES®
BY RICK KIRKMAN / JERRY SCOTT
NOT THAT BAD...
SEEN WORSE.
SNIFF! STILL PRETTY CLEAN.
FINE.
GOOD.
BARELY WORN!
JUST A SMUDGE.
LAUNDRY'S DONE.
ALREADY?? HOW?
EXTRA-LARGE LOAD?
EXTRA-LOW STANDARDS.

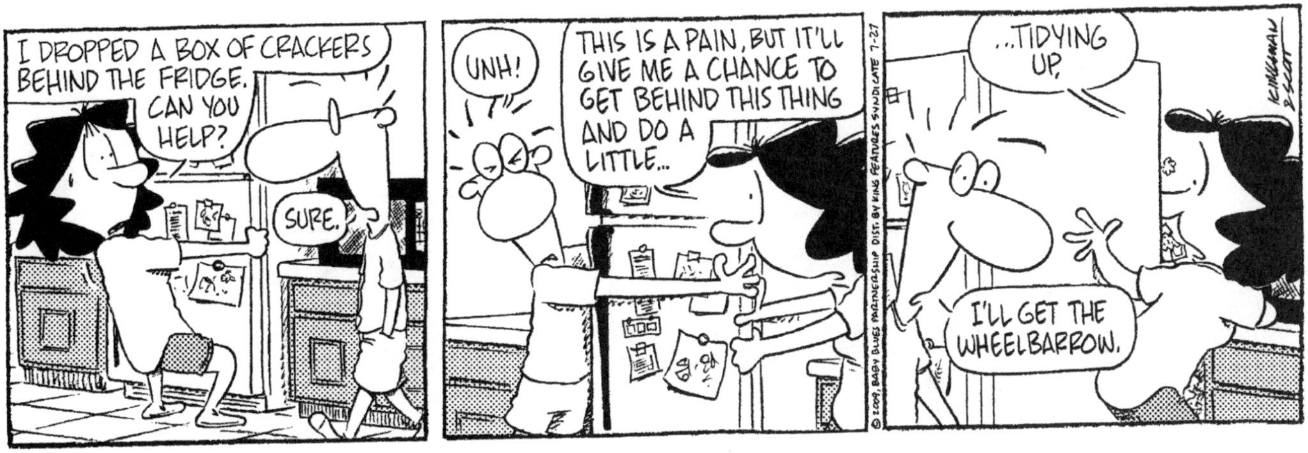
I DROPPED A BOX OF CRACKERS BEHIND THE FRIDGE.
CAN YOU HELP?
SURE.
UNH!
THIS IS A PAIN, BUT IT'LL GIVE ME A CHANCE TO GET BEHIND THIS THING AND DO A LITTLE...
...TIDYING UP.
I'LL GET THE WHEELBARROW.
KIRKMAN & SCOTT
© 2009, BABY BLUES PARTNERSHIP DIST. BY KING FEATURES SYNDICATE 7-27

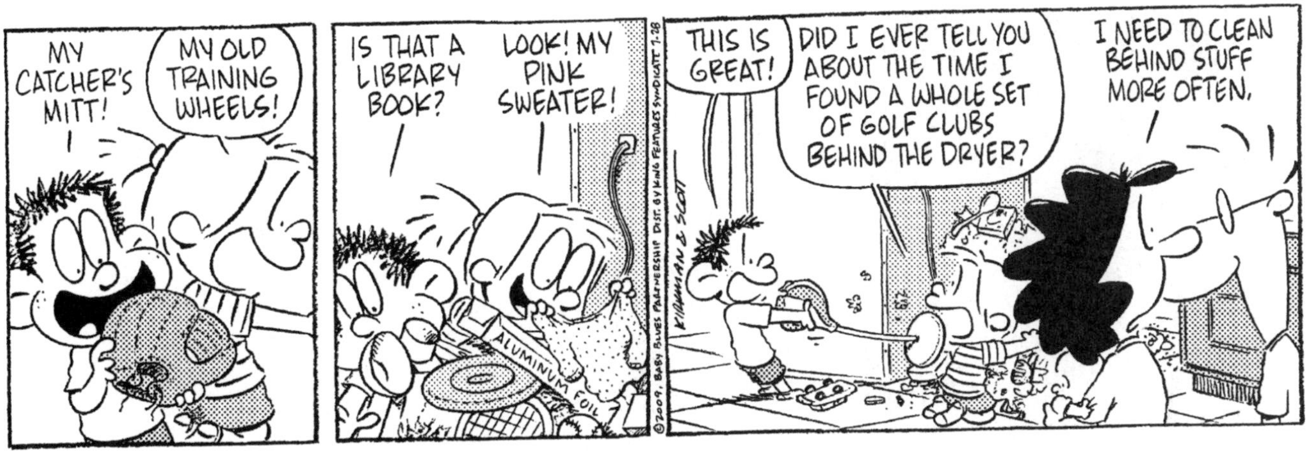
MY CATCHER'S MITT!
MY OLD TRAINING WHEELS!
IS THAT A LIBRARY BOOK?
LOOK! MY PINK SWEATER!
ALUMINUM FOIL
KIRKMAN & SCOTT
© 2009, BABY BLUES PARTNERSHIP DIST. BY KING FEATURES SYNDICATE 7-28
THIS IS GREAT!
DID I EVER TELL YOU ABOUT THE TIME I FOUND A WHOLE SET OF GOLF CLUBS BEHIND THE DRYER?
I NEED TO CLEAN BEHIND STUFF MORE OFTEN.

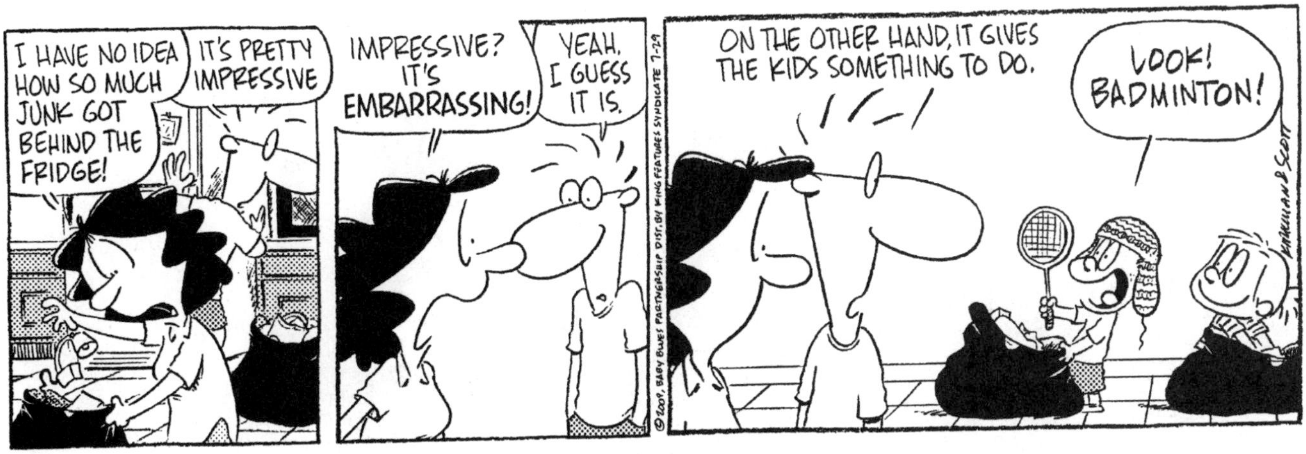
I HAVE NO IDEA HOW SO MUCH JUNK GOT BEHIND THE FRIDGE!
IT'S PRETTY IMPRESSIVE
IMPRESSIVE? IT'S EMBARRASSING!
YEAH, I GUESS IT IS.
© 2009, BABY BLUES PARTNERSHIP DIST. BY KING FEATURES SYNDICATE 7-29
ON THE OTHER HAND, IT GIVES THE KIDS SOMETHING TO DO.
LOOK! BADMINTON!
KIRKMAN & SCOTT

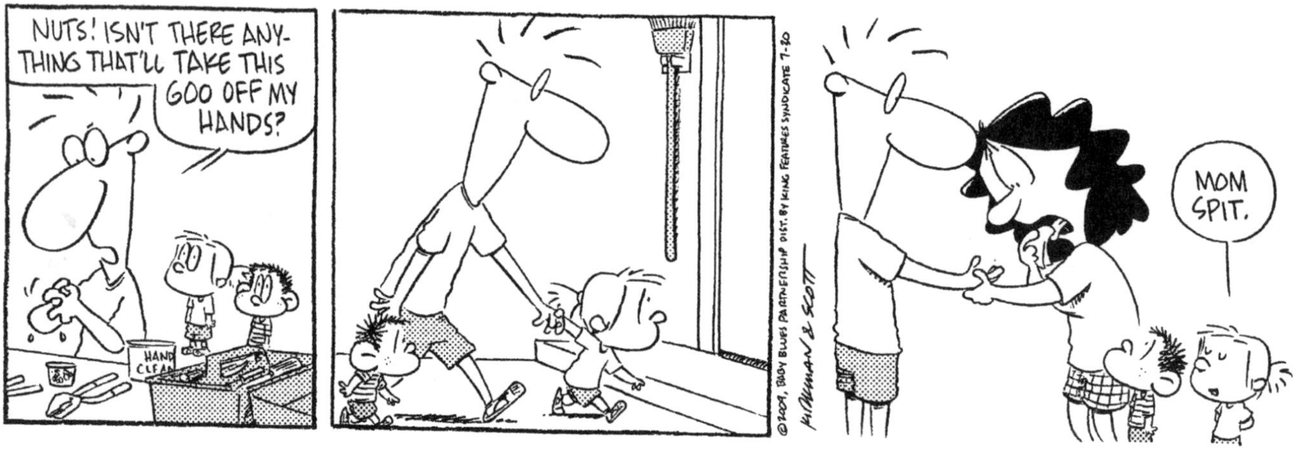
NUTS! ISN'T THERE ANYTHING THAT'LL TAKE THIS GOO OFF MY HANDS?
HAND CLEAN
© 2009, BABY BLUES PARTNERSHIP DIST. BY KING FEATURES SYNDICATE 7-30
KIRKMAN & SCOTT
MOM SPIT.

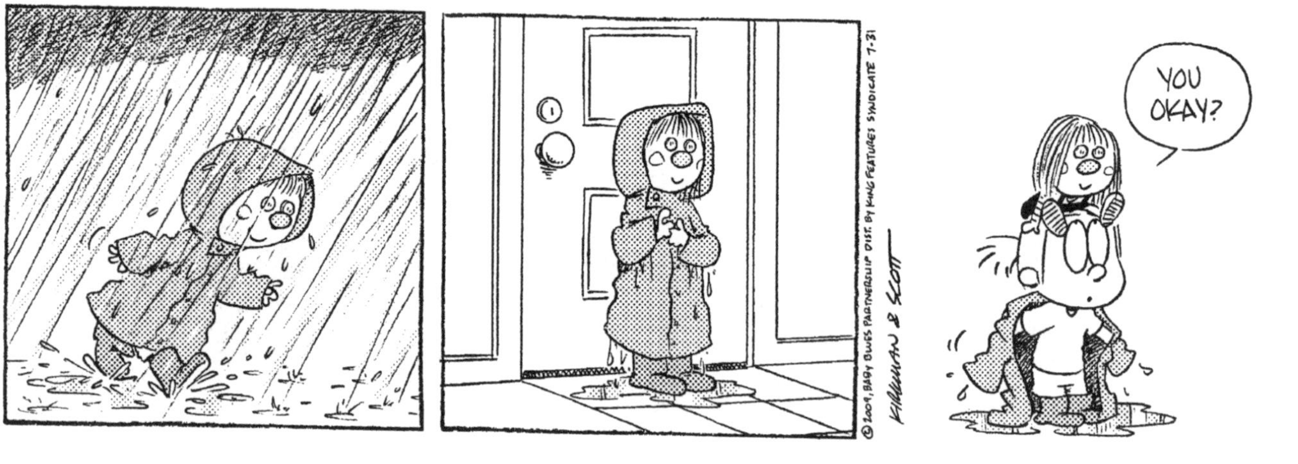
© 2009, BABY BLUES PARTNERSHIP DIST. BY KING FEATURES SYNDICATE 7-31
KIRKMAN & SCOTT
YOU OKAY?

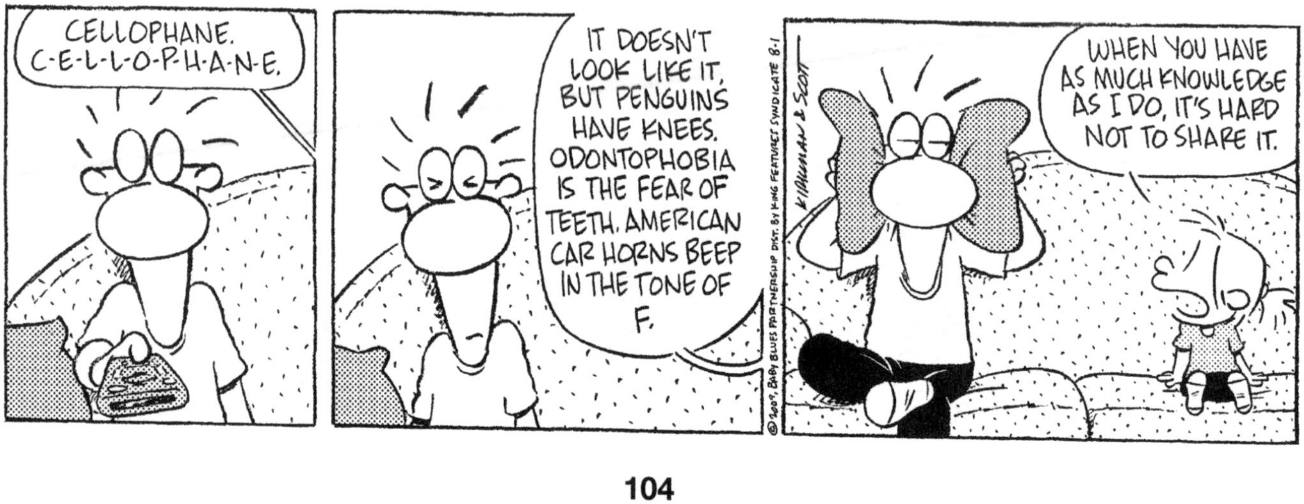
CELLOPHANE. C-E-L-L-O-P-H-A-N-E.
IT DOESN'T LOOK LIKE IT, BUT PENGUINS HAVE KNEES. ODONTOPHOBIA IS THE FEAR OF TEETH. AMERICAN CAR HORNS BEEP IN THE TONE OF F.
© 2009, BABY BLUES PARTNERSHIP DIST. BY KING FEATURES SYNDICATE 8-1
KIRKMAN & SCOTT
WHEN YOU HAVE AS MUCH KNOWLEDGE AS I DO, IT'S HARD NOT TO SHARE IT.

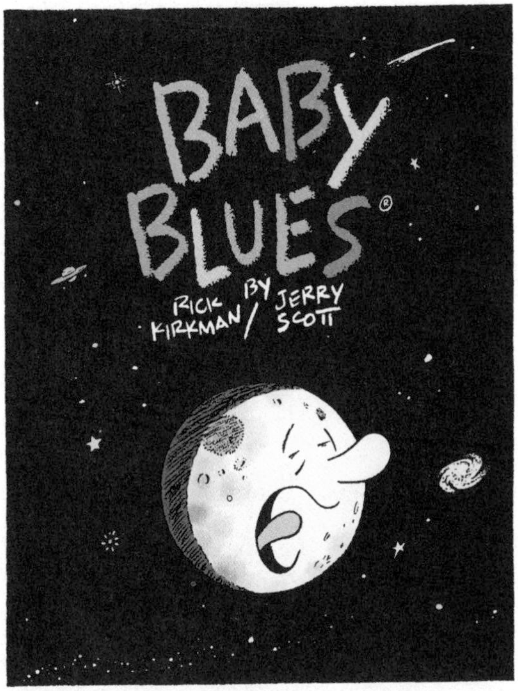
BABY BLUES®
BY RICK KIRKMAN / JERRY SCOTT

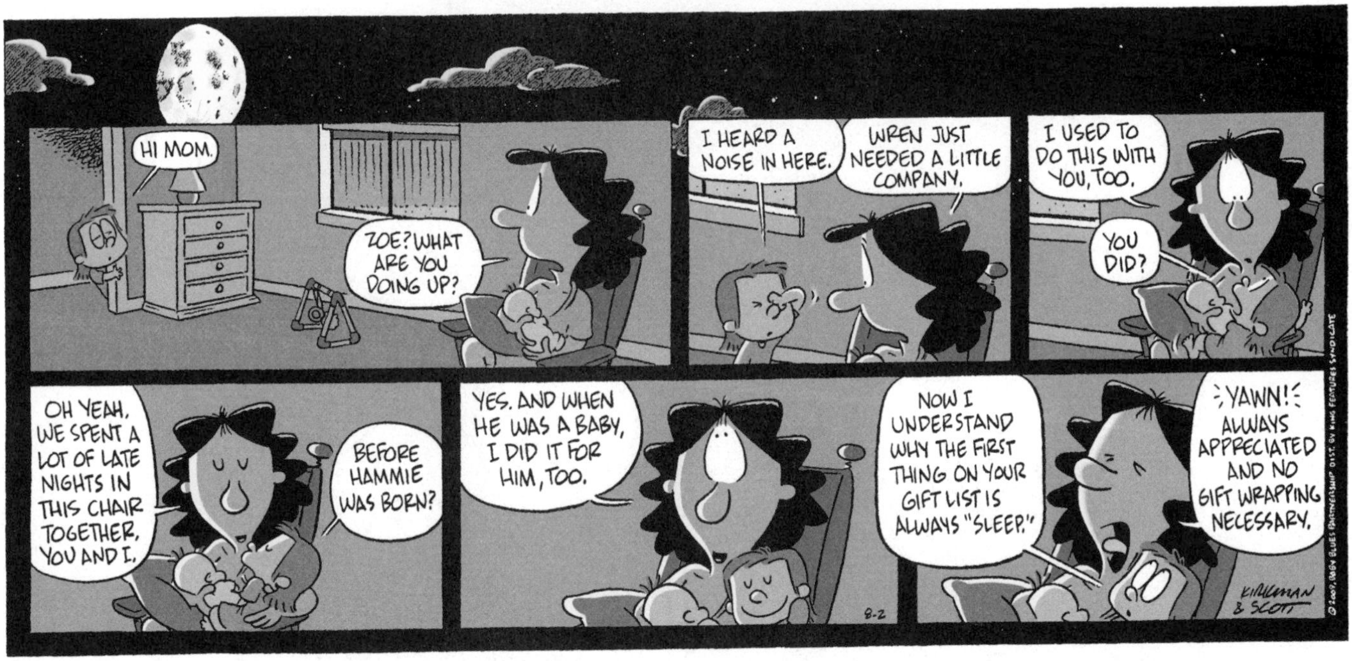
HI MOM.
ZOE? WHAT ARE YOU DOING UP?
I HEARD A NOISE IN HERE.
WREN JUST NEEDED A LITTLE COMPANY.
I USED TO DO THIS WITH YOU, TOO.
YOU DID?
OH YEAH, WE SPENT A LOT OF LATE NIGHTS IN THIS CHAIR TOGETHER, YOU AND I.
BEFORE HAMMIE WAS BORN?
YES. AND WHEN HE WAS A BABY, I DID IT FOR HIM, TOO.
8-2
NOW I UNDERSTAND WHY THE FIRST THING ON YOUR GIFT LIST IS ALWAYS "SLEEP."
YAWN!
ALWAYS APPRECIATED AND NO GIFT WRAPPING NECESSARY.
KIRKMAN & SCOTT
© 2009, BABY BLUES PARTNERSHIP DIST. BY KING FEATURES SYNDICATE

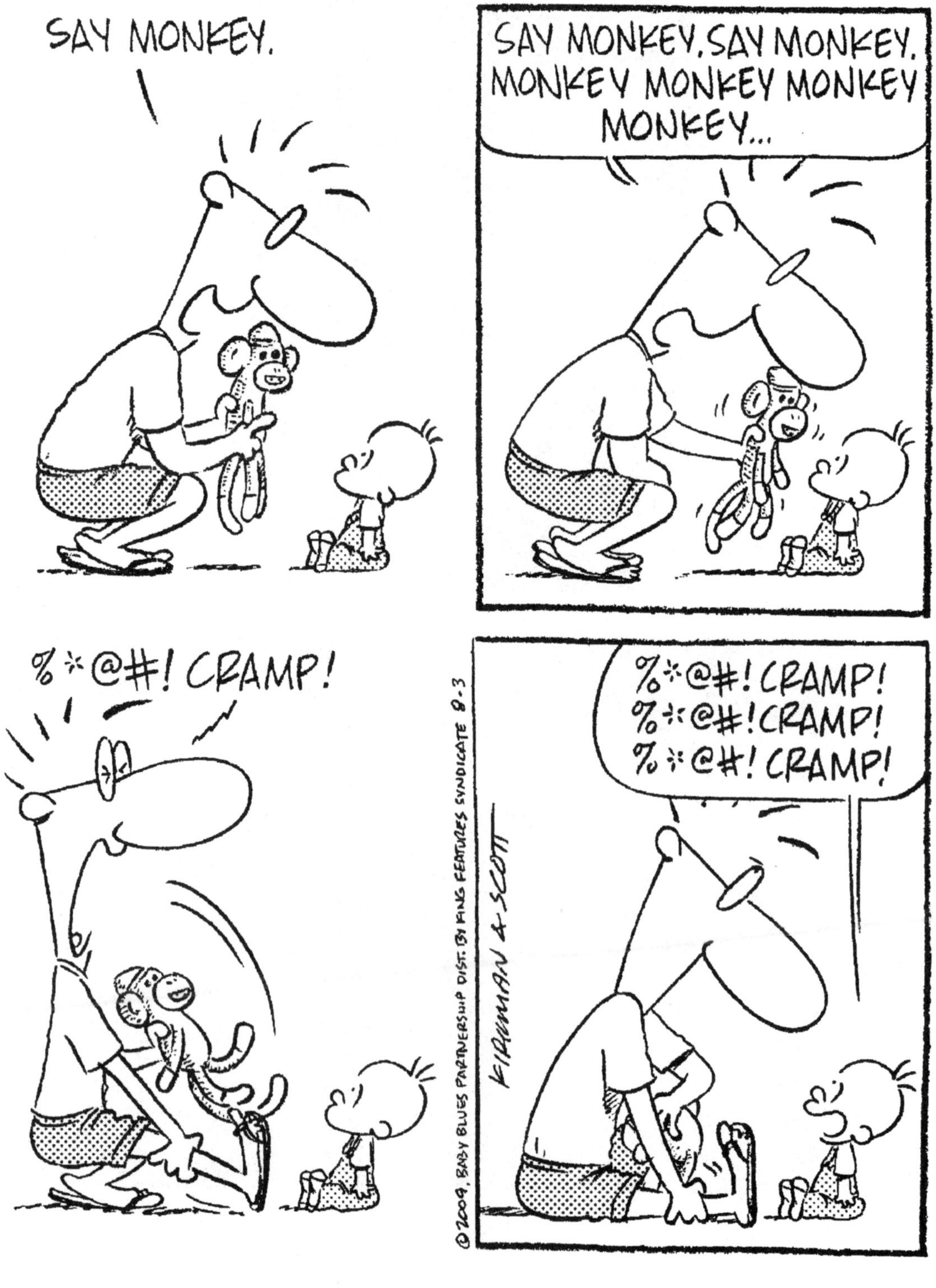
SAY MONKEY.
SAY MONKEY. SAY MONKEY. MONKEY MONKEY MONKEY MONKEY...
%*@#! CRAMP!
%*@#! CRAMP! %*@#! CRAMP! %*@#! CRAMP!
KIRKMAN & SCOTT
©2009, BABY BLUES PARTNERSHIP DIST. BY KING FEATURES SYNDICATE 8-3

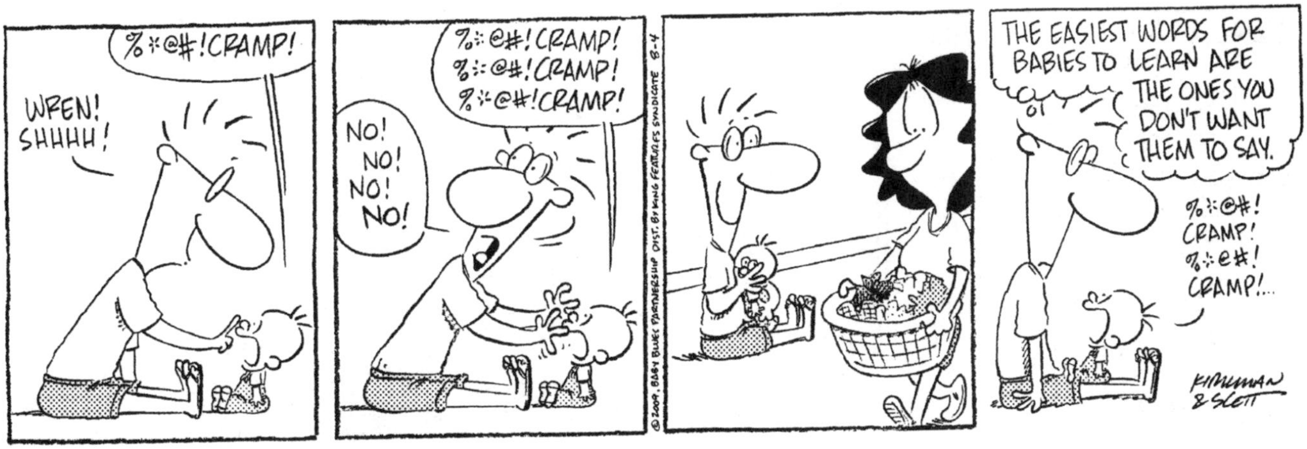
WREN! SHHHH!
%*@#!CRAMP!
NO! NO! NO! NO!
%*@#!CRAMP! %*@#!CRAMP! %*@#!CRAMP!
©2009, BABY BLUES PARTNERSHIP DIST. BY KING FEATURES SYNDICATE 8-4
THE EASIEST WORDS FOR BABIES TO LEARN ARE THE ONES YOU DON'T WANT THEM TO SAY.
%*@#! CRAMP! %*@#! CRAMP!...
KIRKMAN & SCOTT

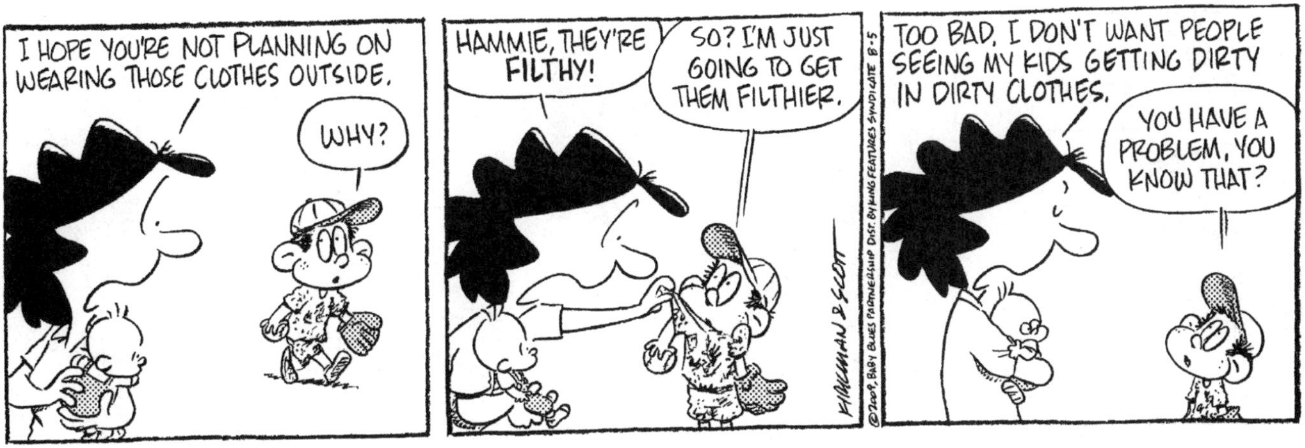
I HOPE YOU'RE NOT PLANNING ON WEARING THOSE CLOTHES OUTSIDE.
WHY?
HAMMIE, THEY'RE FILTHY!
SO? I'M JUST GOING TO GET THEM FILTHIER.
KIRKMAN & SCOTT
©2009, BABY BLUES PARTNERSHIP DIST. BY KING FEATURES SYNDICATE 8-5
TOO BAD, I DON'T WANT PEOPLE SEEING MY KIDS GETTING DIRTY IN DIRTY CLOTHES.
YOU HAVE A PROBLEM, YOU KNOW THAT?

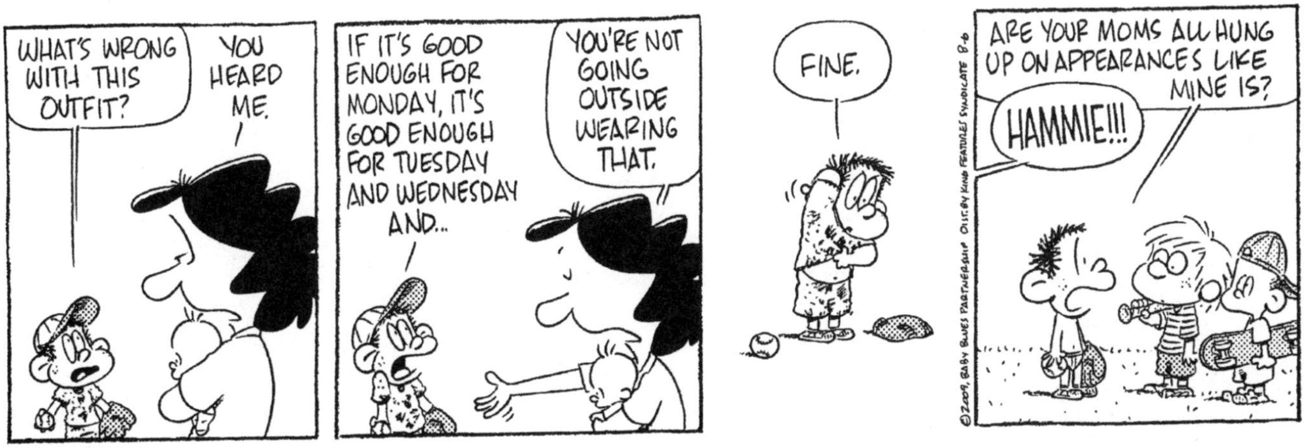
WHAT'S WRONG WITH THIS OUTFIT?
YOU HEARD ME.
IF IT'S GOOD ENOUGH FOR MONDAY, IT'S GOOD ENOUGH FOR TUESDAY AND WEDNESDAY AND...
YOU'RE NOT GOING OUTSIDE WEARING THAT.
FINE.
©2009, BABY BLUES PARTNERSHIP DIST. BY KING FEATURES SYNDICATE 8-6
ARE YOUR MOMS ALL HUNG UP ON APPEARANCES LIKE MINE IS?
HAMMIE!!!

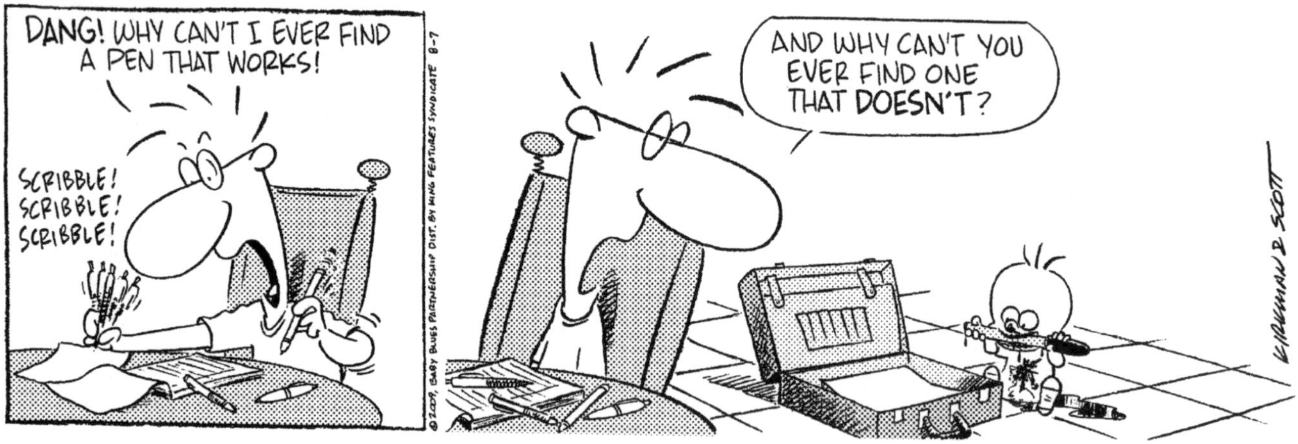
DANG! WHY CAN'T I EVER FIND A PEN THAT WORKS!
SCRIBBLE! SCRIBBLE! SCRIBBLE!
© 2009, BABY BLUES PARTNERSHIP DIST. BY KING FEATURES SYNDICATE 8-7
AND WHY CAN'T YOU EVER FIND ONE THAT DOESN'T?
KIRKMAN & SCOTT

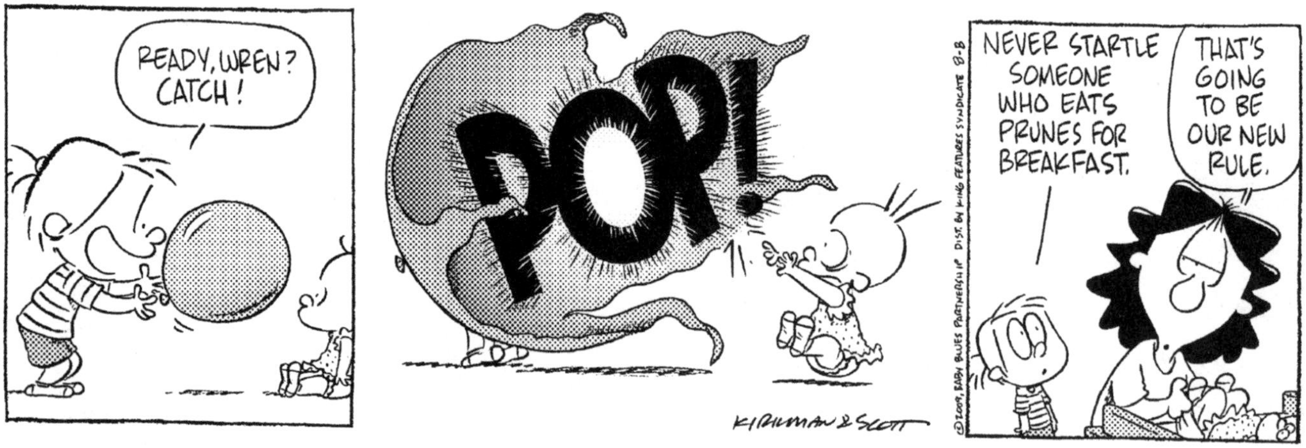
READY, WREN? CATCH!
POP!
KIRKMAN & SCOTT
© 2009, BABY BLUES PARTNERSHIP DIST. BY KING FEATURES SYNDICATE 8-8
NEVER STARTLE SOMEONE WHO EATS PRUNES FOR BREAKFAST.
THAT'S GOING TO BE OUR NEW RULE.

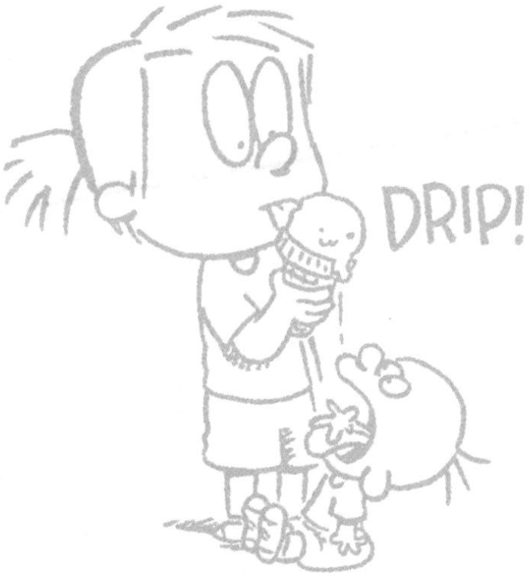
DRIP!

BABY BLUES®
BY RICK KIRKMAN / JERRY SCOTT

THAT'S IT? I THOUGHT YOU WERE GOING TO BUILD SOMETHING BIG.
I'M NOT FINISHED YET.
8-9
KIRKMAN & SCOTT

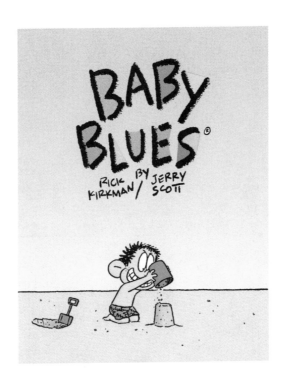

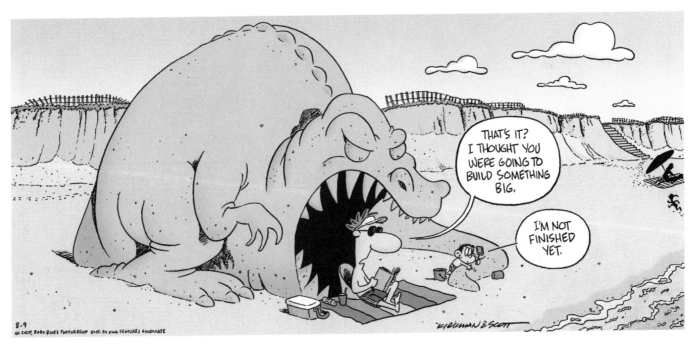

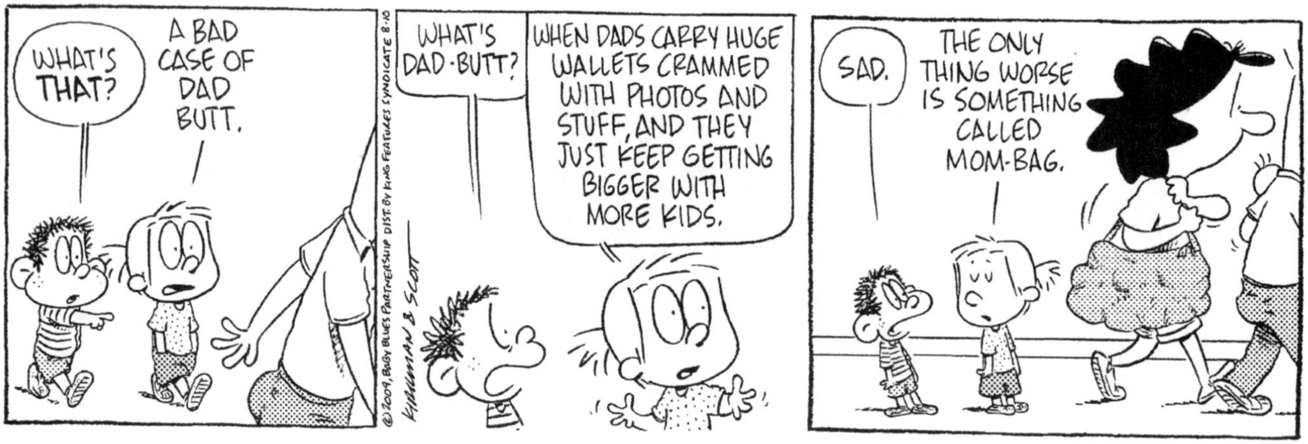
WHAT'S THAT?
A BAD CASE OF DAD BUTT.
© 2009, BABY BLUES PARTNERSHIP DIST. BY KING FEATURES SYNDICATE 8-10
KIRKMAN & SCOTT
WHAT'S DAD-BUTT?
WHEN DADS CARRY HUGE WALLETS CRAMMED WITH PHOTOS AND STUFF, AND THEY JUST KEEP GETTING BIGGER WITH MORE KIDS.
SAD.
THE ONLY THING WORSE IS SOMETHING CALLED MOM-BAG.

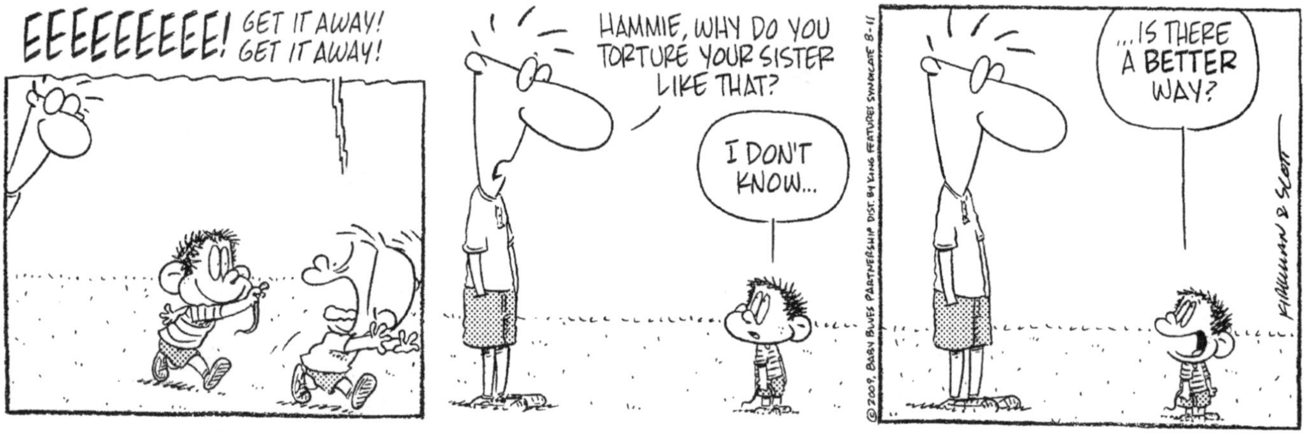
EEEEEEEEE! GET IT AWAY! GET IT AWAY!
HAMMIE, WHY DO YOU TORTURE YOUR SISTER LIKE THAT?
I DON'T KNOW...
© 2009, BABY BLUES PARTNERSHIP DIST. BY KING FEATURES SYNDICATE 8-11
...IS THERE A BETTER WAY?
KIRKMAN & SCOTT

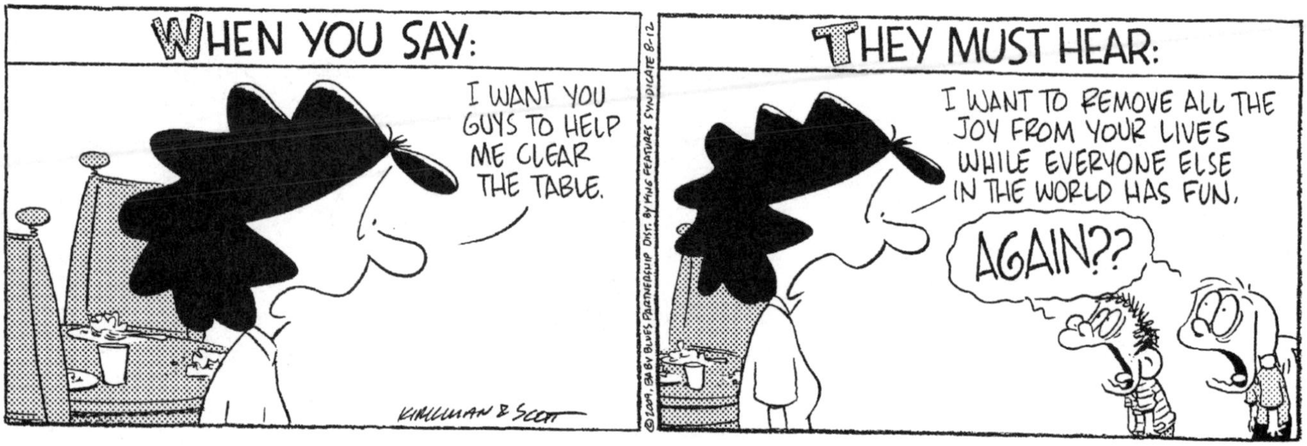
WHEN YOU SAY:
I WANT YOU GUYS TO HELP ME CLEAR THE TABLE.
KIRKMAN & SCOTT
© 2009, BABY BLUES PARTNERSHIP DIST. BY KING FEATURES SYNDICATE 8-12
THEY MUST HEAR:
I WANT TO REMOVE ALL THE JOY FROM YOUR LIVES WHILE EVERYONE ELSE IN THE WORLD HAS FUN.
AGAIN??

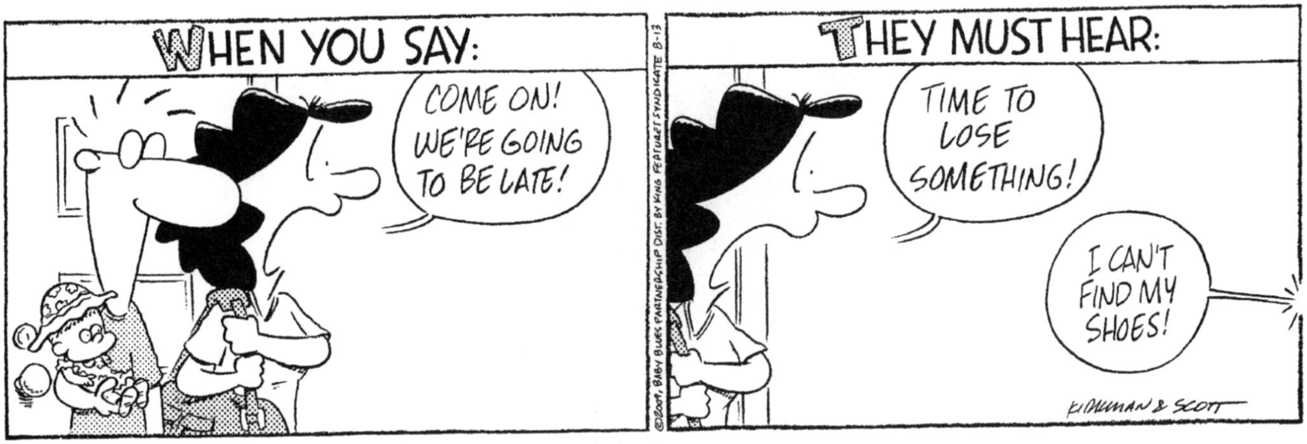
WHEN YOU SAY:
COME ON! WE'RE GOING TO BE LATE!
THEY MUST HEAR:
TIME TO LOSE SOMETHING!
I CAN'T FIND MY SHOES!
©2009, BABY BLUES PARTNERSHIP DIST. BY KING FEATURES SYNDICATE 8-13
KIRKMAN & SCOTT

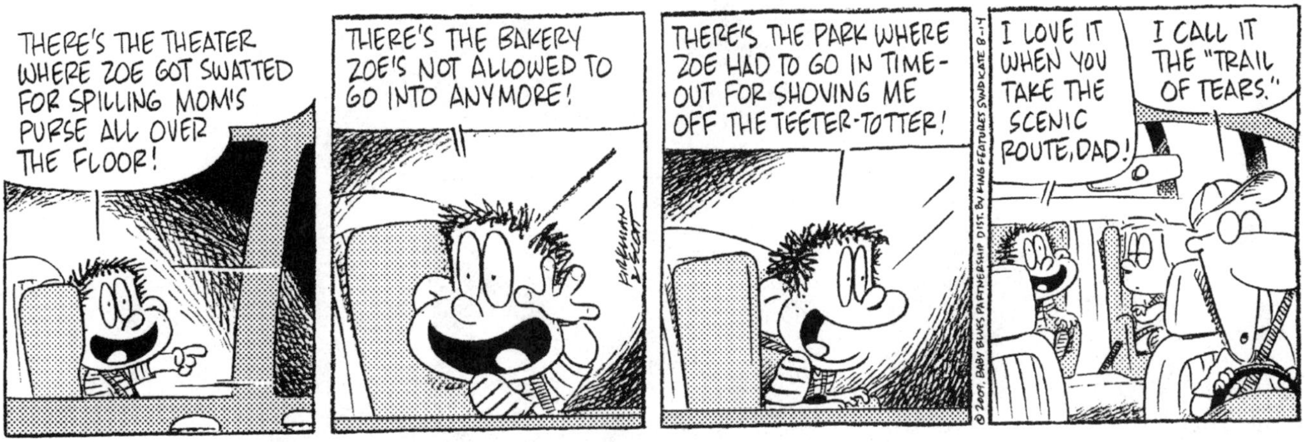
THERE'S THE THEATER WHERE ZOE GOT SWATTED FOR SPILLING MOM'S PURSE ALL OVER THE FLOOR!
THERE'S THE BAKERY ZOE'S NOT ALLOWED TO GO INTO ANYMORE!
KIRKMAN & SCOTT
THERE'S THE PARK WHERE ZOE HAD TO GO IN TIME-OUT FOR SHOVING ME OFF THE TEETER-TOTTER!
©2009, BABY BLUES PARTNERSHIP DIST. BY KING FEATURES SYNDICATE 8-14
I LOVE IT WHEN YOU TAKE THE SCENIC ROUTE, DAD!
I CALL IT THE "TRAIL OF TEARS."

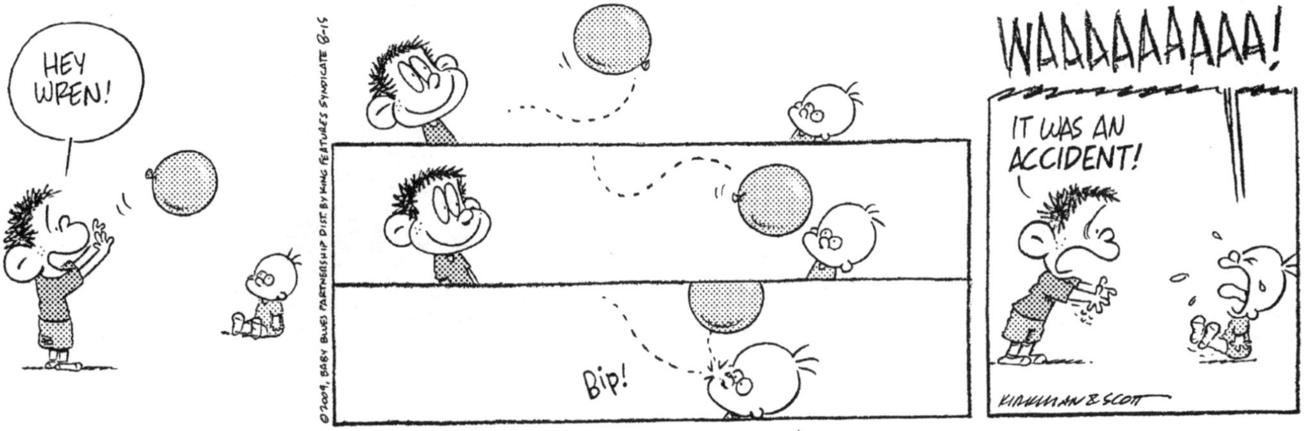
HEY WREN!
©2009, BABY BLUES PARTNERSHIP DIST. BY KING FEATURES SYNDICATE 8-15
Bip!
WAAAAAAAAA!
IT WAS AN ACCIDENT!
KIRKMAN & SCOTT

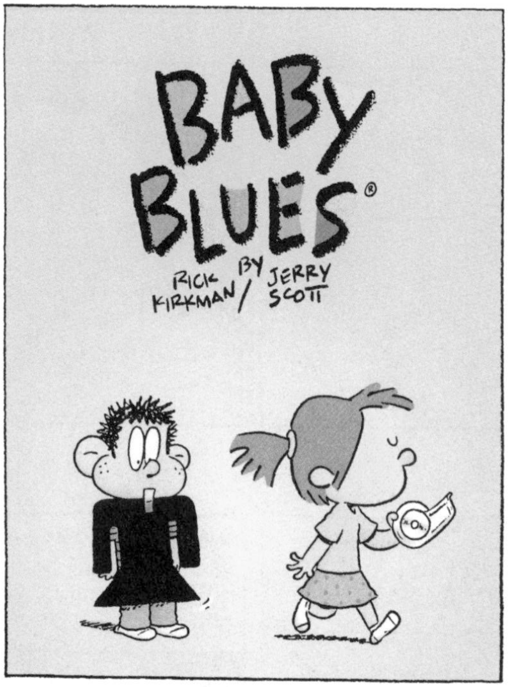
BABY BLUES®
BY RICK KIRKMAN / JERRY SCOTT

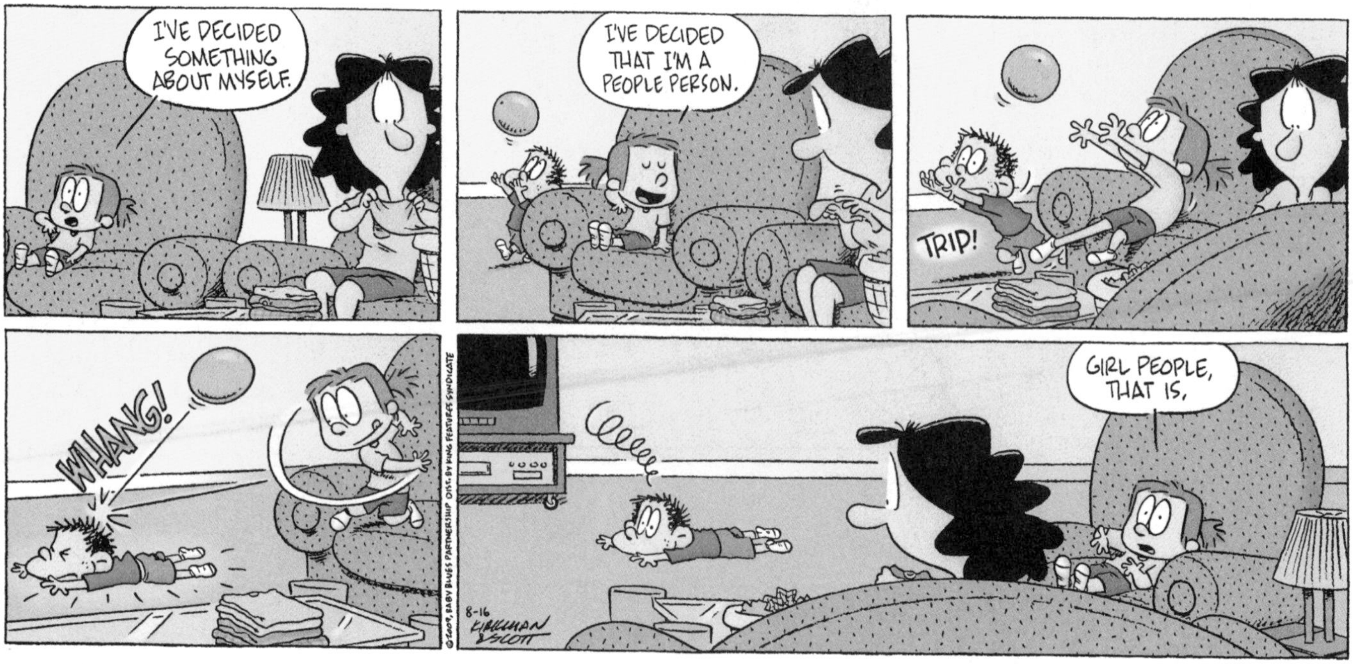
I'VE DECIDED SOMETHING ABOUT MYSELF.
I'VE DECIDED THAT I'M A PEOPLE PERSON.
TRIP!
WHANG!
GIRL PEOPLE, THAT IS.
8-16
KIRKMAN & SCOTT

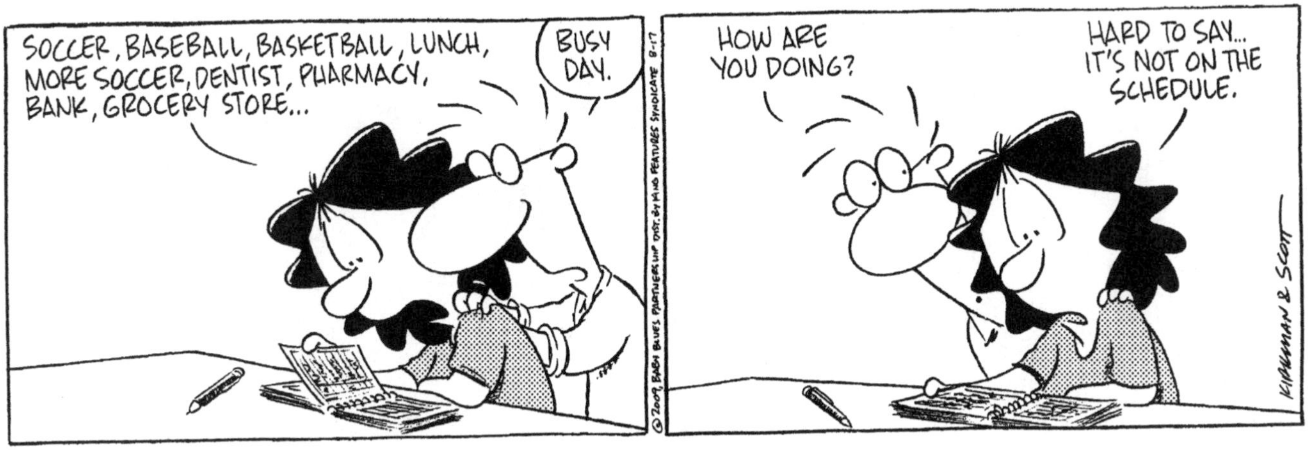
SOCCER, BASEBALL, BASKETBALL, LUNCH, MORE SOCCER, DENTIST, PHARMACY, BANK, GROCERY STORE...
BUSY DAY.
HOW ARE YOU DOING?
HARD TO SAY... IT'S NOT ON THE SCHEDULE.
KIRKMAN & SCOTT

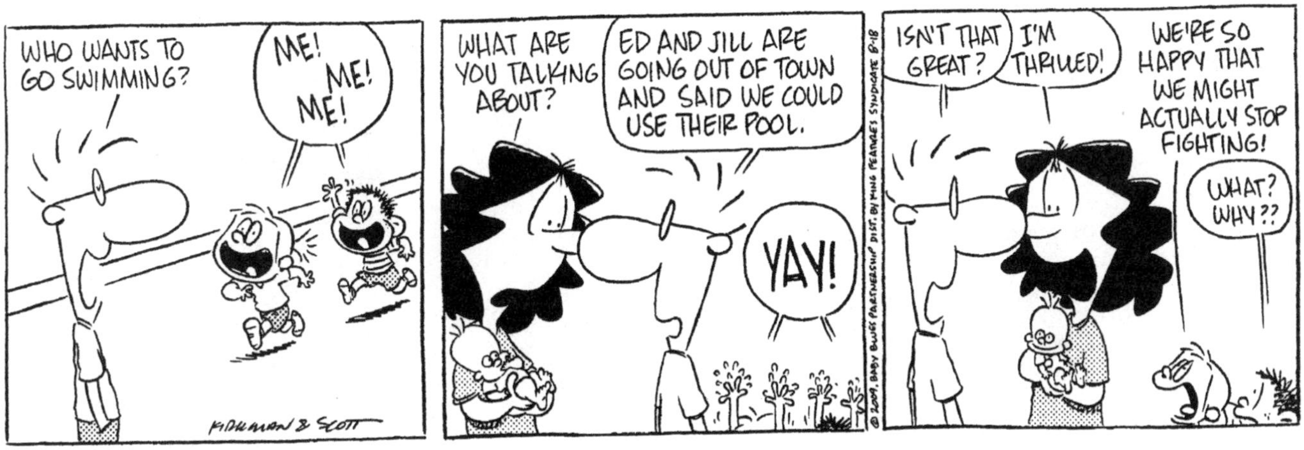
WHO WANTS TO GO SWIMMING?
ME! ME! ME!
KIRKMAN & SCOTT
WHAT ARE YOU TALKING ABOUT?
ED AND JILL ARE GOING OUT OF TOWN AND SAID WE COULD USE THEIR POOL.
YAY!
ISN'T THAT GREAT?
I'M THRILLED!
WE'RE SO HAPPY THAT WE MIGHT ACTUALLY STOP FIGHTING!
WHAT? WHY??

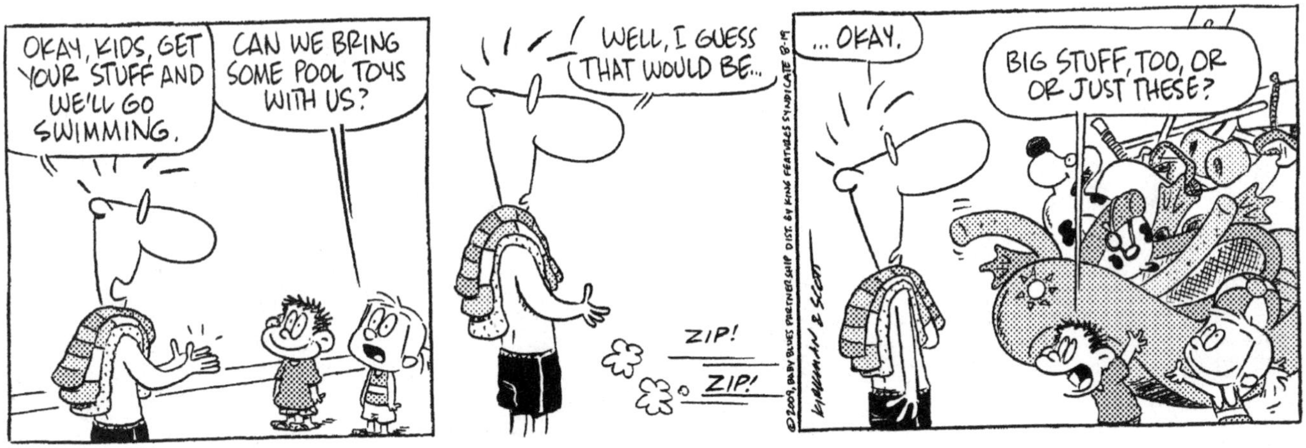
OKAY, KIDS, GET YOUR STUFF AND WE'LL GO SWIMMING.
CAN WE BRING SOME POOL TOYS WITH US?
WELL, I GUESS THAT WOULD BE...
ZIP!
ZIP!
...OKAY.
BIG STUFF, TOO, OR OR JUST THESE?
KIRKMAN & SCOTT

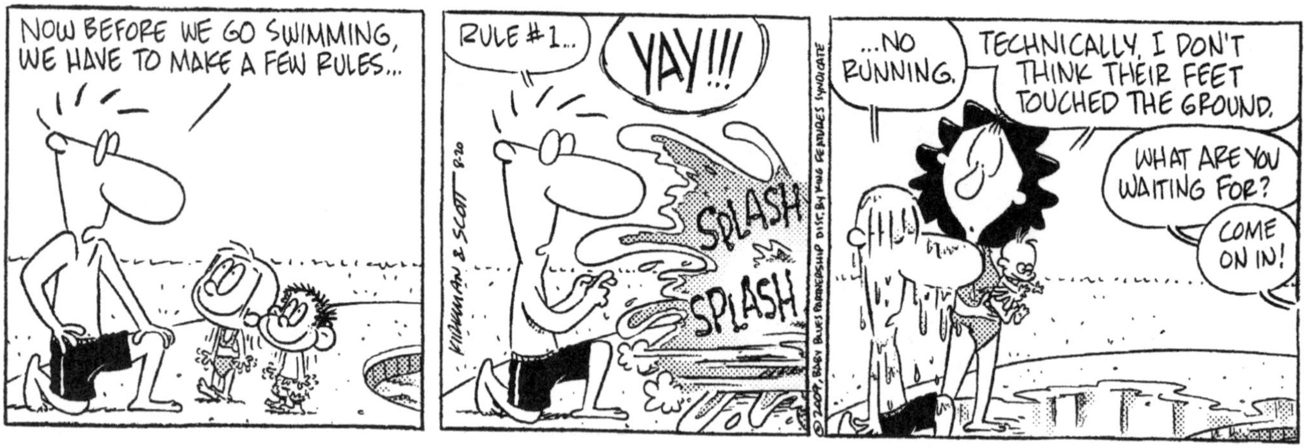
NOW BEFORE WE GO SWIMMING, WE HAVE TO MAKE A FEW RULES...
RULE #1...
YAY!!!
SPLASH
SPLASH
...NO RUNNING.
TECHNICALLY, I DON'T THINK THEIR FEET TOUCHED THE GROUND.
WHAT ARE YOU WAITING FOR?
COME ON IN!

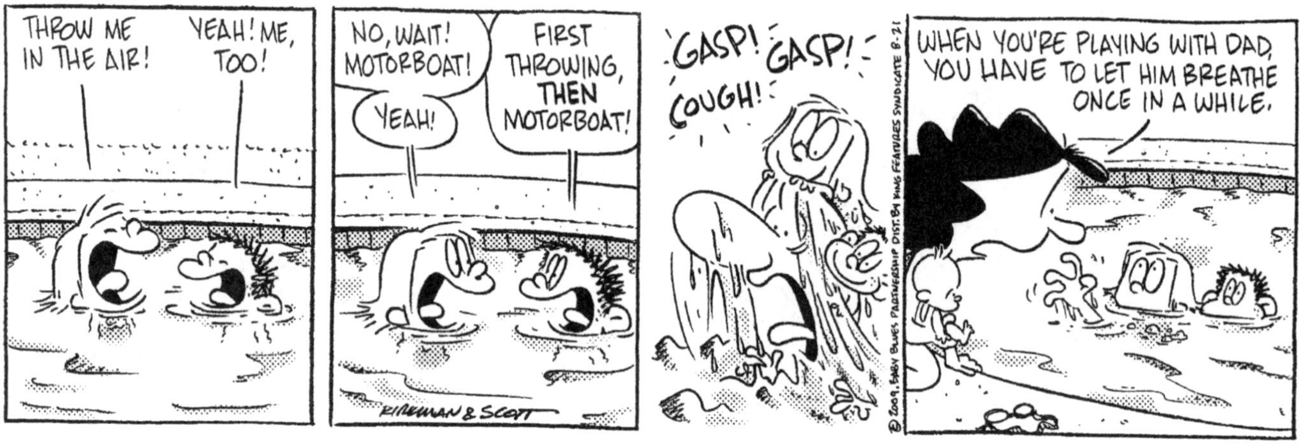
THROW ME IN THE AIR!
YEAH! ME, TOO!
NO, WAIT! MOTORBOAT!
YEAH!
FIRST THROWING, THEN MOTORBOAT!
GASP!
GASP!
COUGH!
WHEN YOU'RE PLAYING WITH DAD, YOU HAVE TO LET HIM BREATHE ONCE IN A WHILE.

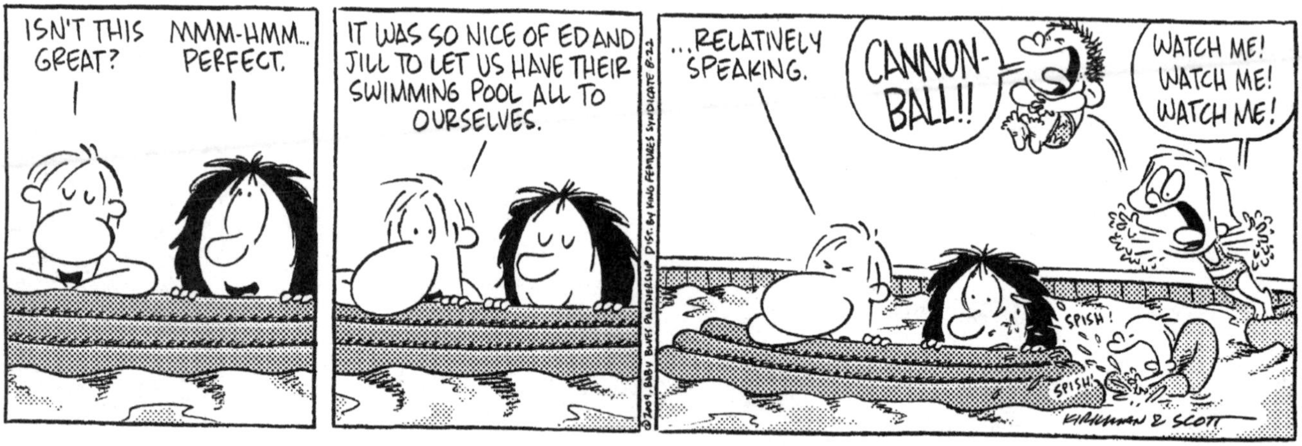
ISN'T THIS GREAT?
MMM-HMM.. PERFECT.
IT WAS SO NICE OF ED AND JILL TO LET US HAVE THEIR SWIMMING POOL ALL TO OURSELVES.
...RELATIVELY SPEAKING.
CANNON-BALL!!
WATCH ME! WATCH ME! WATCH ME!
SPISH!
SPISH!

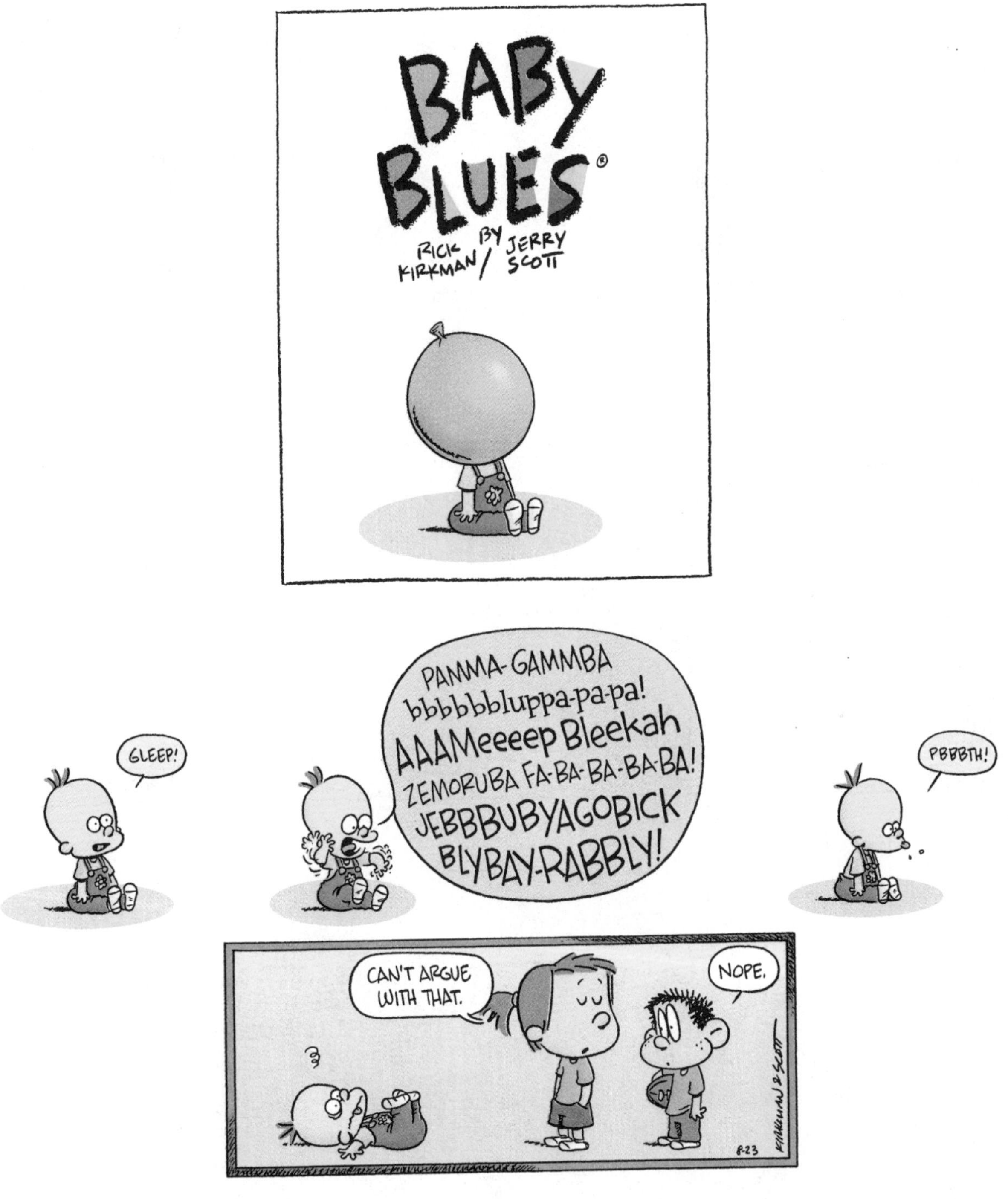
BABY BLUES®
RICK KIRKMAN / BY JERRY SCOTT
GLEEP!
PAMMA-GAMMBA bbbbbbluppa-pa-pa! AAAMeeeep Bleekah ZEMORUBA FA-BA-BA-BA-BA! JEBBBUBYAGOBICK BLYBAY-RABBLY!
PBBBTH!
CAN'T ARGUE WITH THAT.
NOPE.
KIRKMAN & SCOTT
8-23

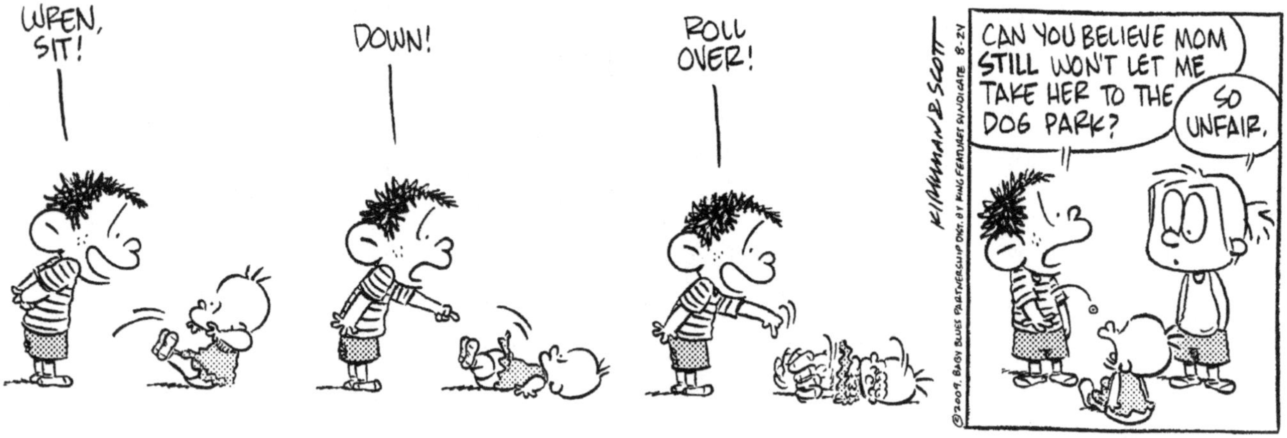
WREN, SIT!
DOWN!
ROLL OVER!
CAN YOU BELIEVE MOM STILL WON'T LET ME TAKE HER TO THE DOG PARK?
SO UNFAIR.
KIRKMAN & SCOTT
©2009, BABY BLUES PARTNERSHIP DIST. BY KING FEATURES SYNDICATE 8-24

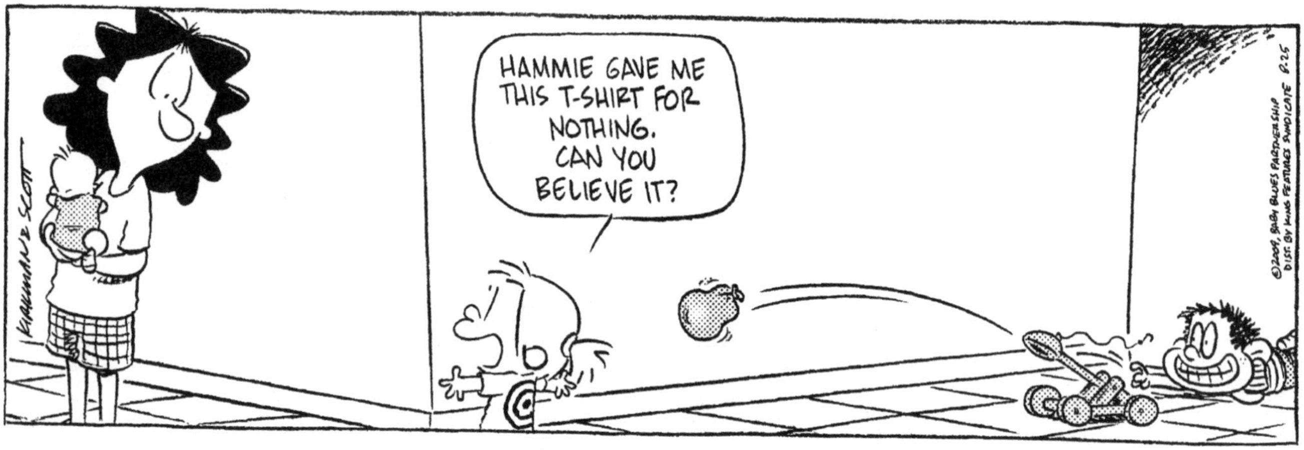
HAMMIE GAVE ME THIS T-SHIRT FOR NOTHING. CAN YOU BELIEVE IT?
KIRKMAN & SCOTT
©2009, BABY BLUES PARTNERSHIP DIST. BY KING FEATURES SYNDICATE 8-25

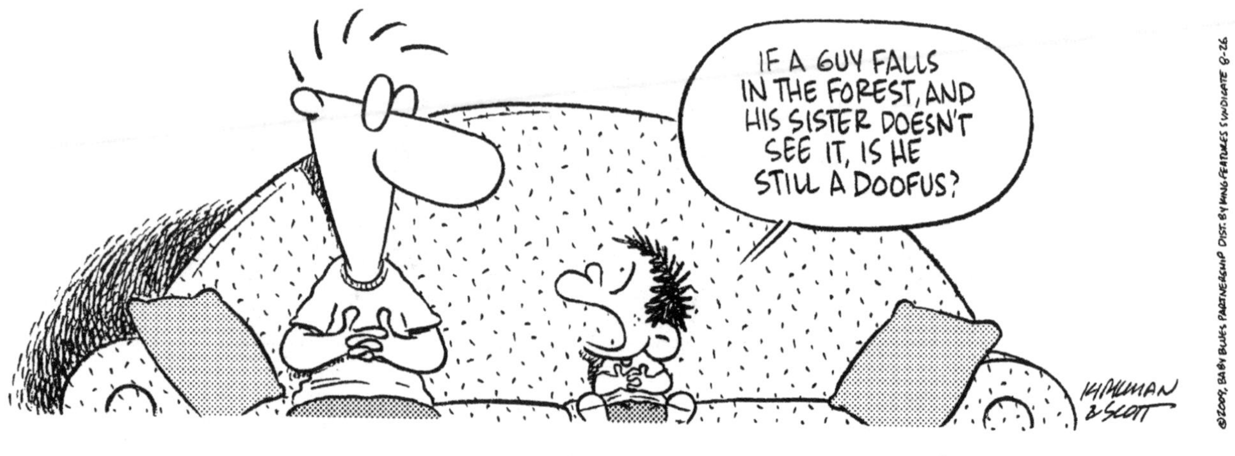
IF A GUY FALLS IN THE FOREST, AND HIS SISTER DOESN'T SEE IT, IS HE STILL A DOOFUS?
KIRKMAN & SCOTT
©2009, BABY BLUES PARTNERSHIP DIST. BY KING FEATURES SYNDICATE 8-26

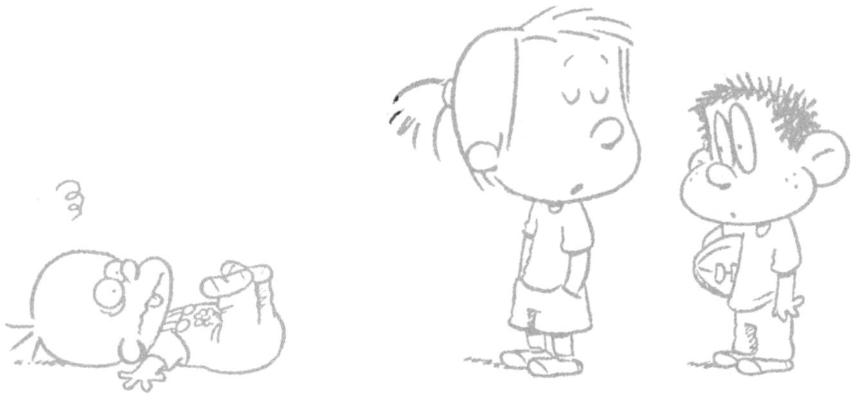

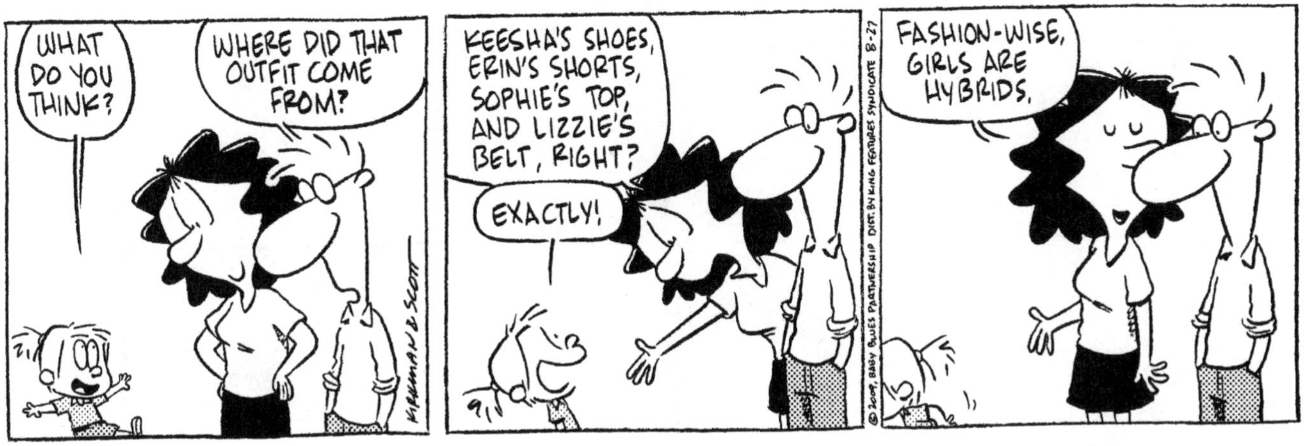

WHAT DO YOU THINK?
WHERE DID THAT OUTFIT COME FROM?
KIRKMAN & SCOTT
KEESHA'S SHOES, ERIN'S SHORTS, SOPHIE'S TOP, AND LIZZIE'S BELT, RIGHT?
EXACTLY!
© 2009, BABY BLUES PARTNERSHIP DIST. BY KING FEATURES SYNDICATE 8-27
FASHION-WISE, GIRLS ARE HYBRIDS.

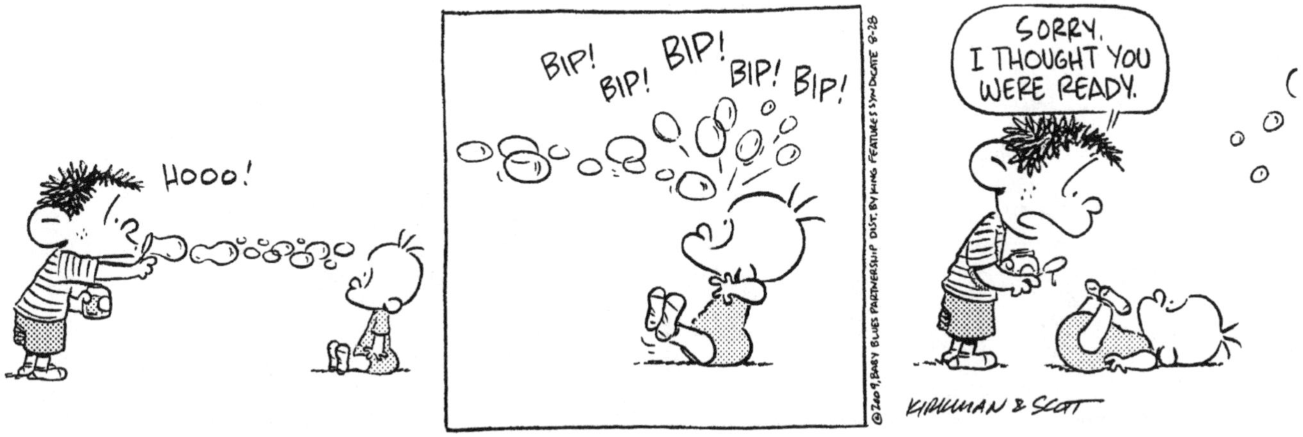

HOOO!
BIP! BIP! BIP! BIP! BIP!
© 2009, BABY BLUES PARTNERSHIP DIST. BY KING FEATURES SYNDICATE 8-28
SORRY. I THOUGHT YOU WERE READY.
KIRKMAN & SCOTT

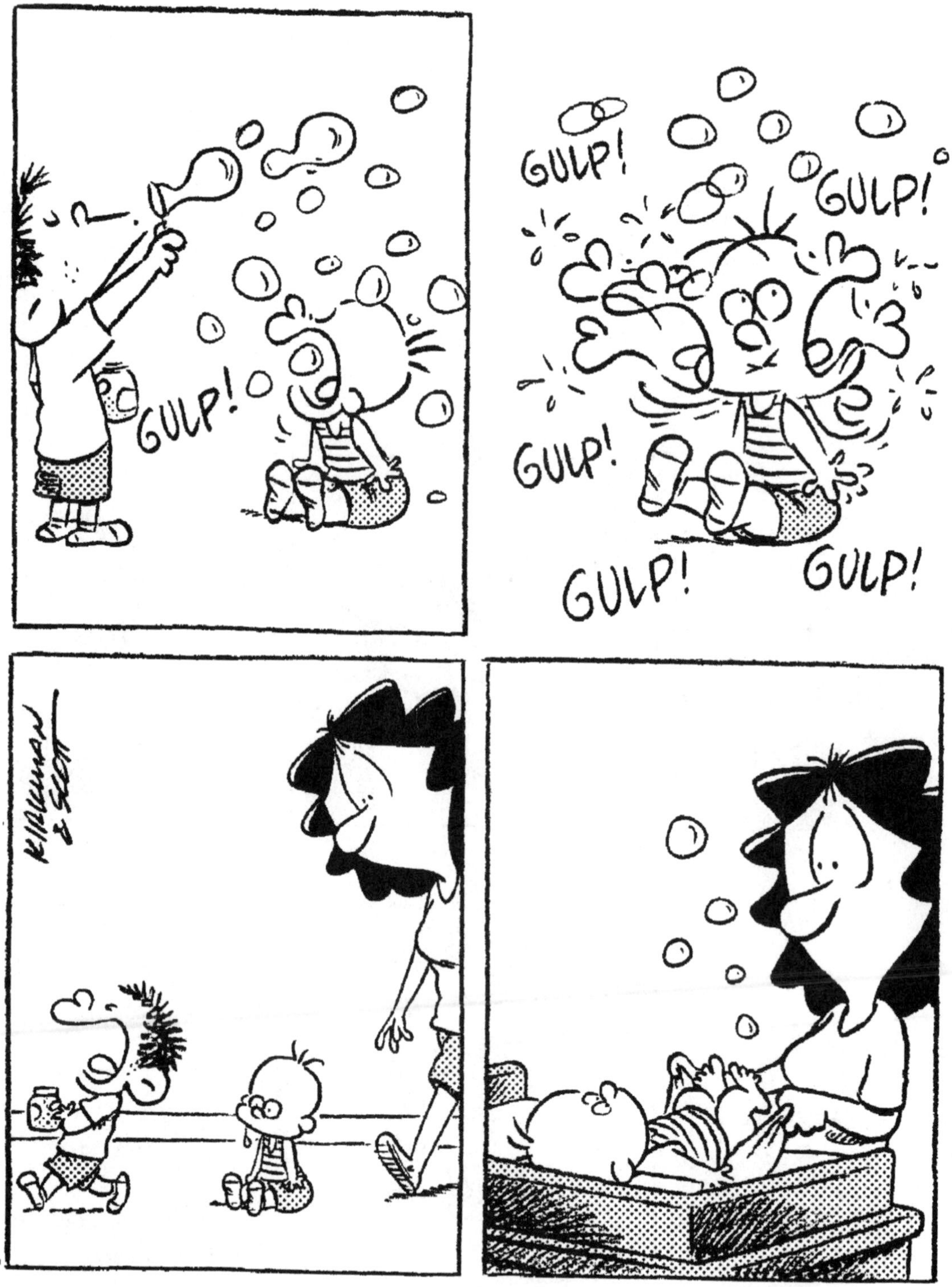
GULP!
GULP!
GULP!
GULP!
GULP!
GULP!
KIRKMAN & SCOTT

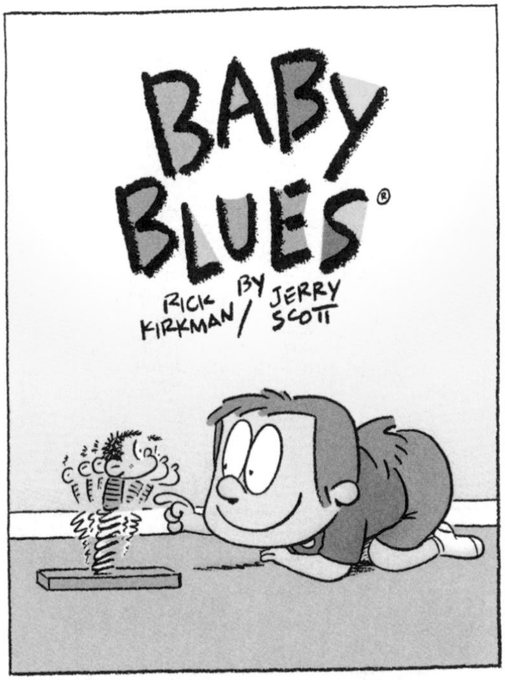
BABY BLUES®
BY RICK KIRKMAN / JERRY SCOTT

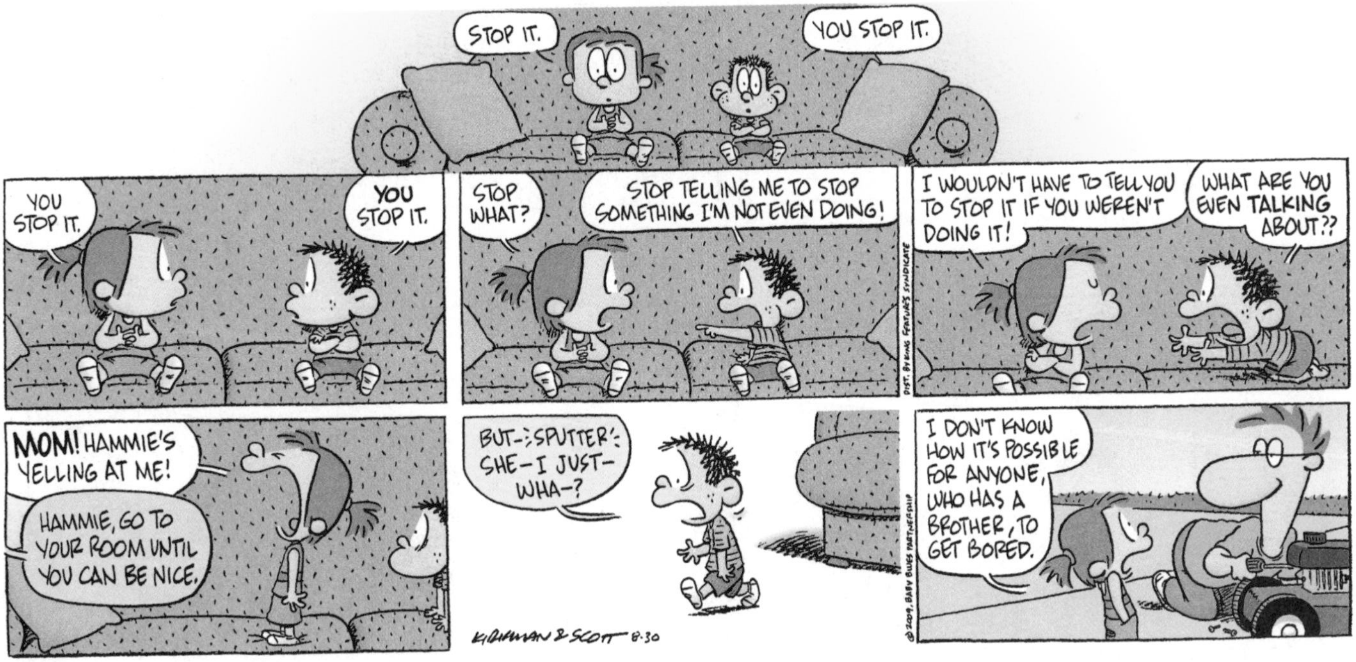
STOP IT.
YOU STOP IT.
YOU STOP IT.
YOU STOP IT.
STOP WHAT?
STOP TELLING ME TO STOP SOMETHING I'M NOT EVEN DOING!
DIST. BY KING FEATURES SYNDICATE
I WOULDN'T HAVE TO TELL YOU TO STOP IT IF YOU WEREN'T DOING IT!
WHAT ARE YOU EVEN TALKING ABOUT??
MOM! HAMMIE'S YELLING AT ME!
HAMMIE, GO TO YOUR ROOM UNTIL YOU CAN BE NICE.
BUT- SPUTTER - SHE- I JUST- WHA-?
KIRKMAN & SCOTT 8-30
©2009, BABY BLUES PARTNERSHIP
I DON'T KNOW HOW IT'S POSSIBLE FOR ANYONE, WHO HAS A BROTHER, TO GET BORED.

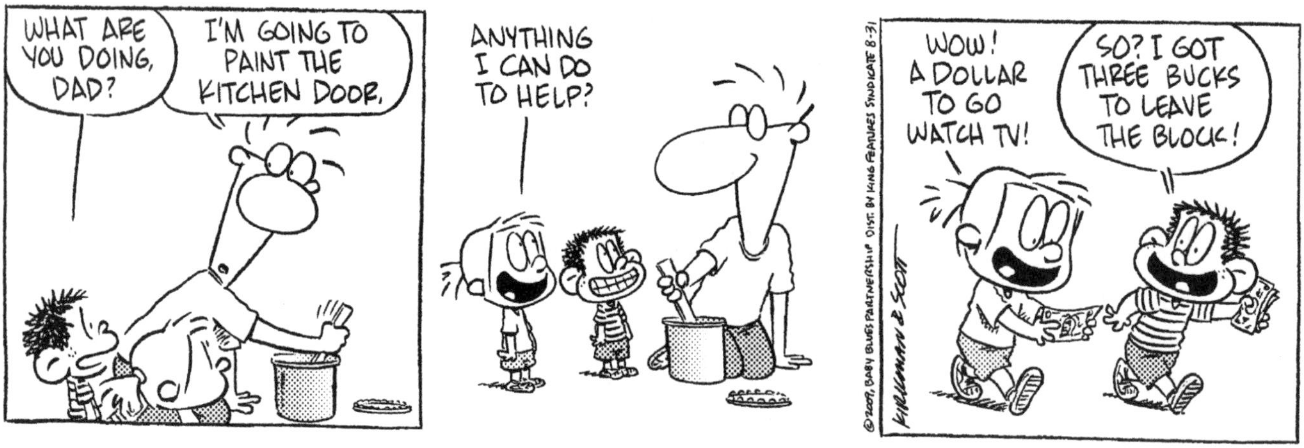
WHAT ARE YOU DOING, DAD?
I'M GOING TO PAINT THE KITCHEN DOOR.
ANYTHING I CAN DO TO HELP?
WOW! A DOLLAR TO GO WATCH TV!
SO? I GOT THREE BUCKS TO LEAVE THE BLOCK!
© 2009, BABY BLUES PARTNERSHIP DIST. BY KING FEATURES SYNDICATE 8-31
KIRKMAN & SCOTT

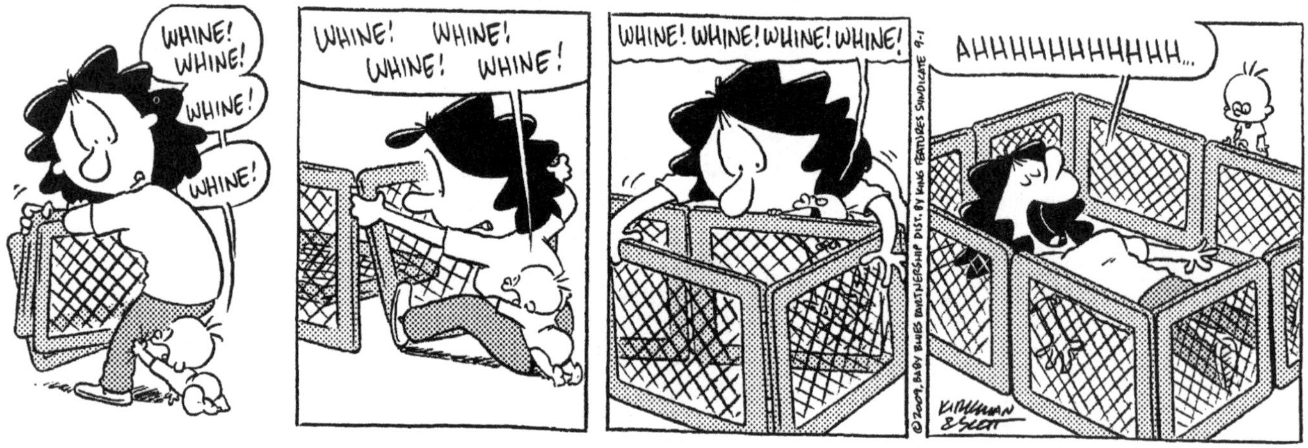
WHINE! WHINE!
WHINE!
WHINE!
WHINE! WHINE! WHINE! WHINE!
WHINE! WHINE! WHINE! WHINE!
© 2009, BABY BLUES PARTNERSHIP DIST. BY KING FEATURES SYNDICATE 9-1
AHHHHHHHHHHH...
KIRKMAN & SCOTT

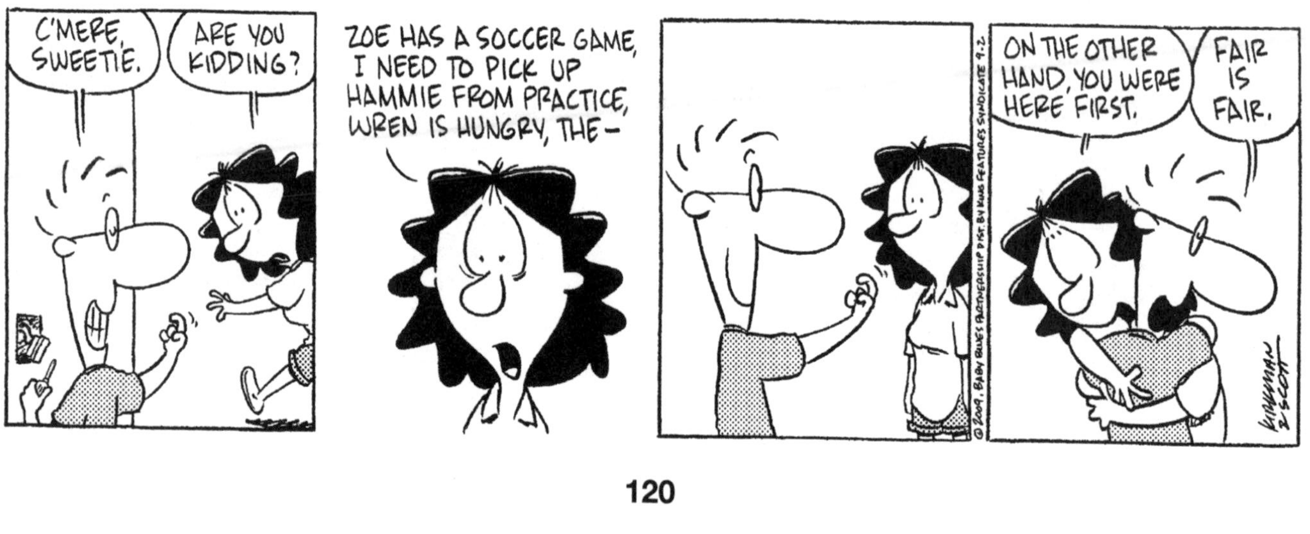
C'MERE, SWEETIE.
ARE YOU KIDDING?
ZOE HAS A SOCCER GAME, I NEED TO PICK UP HAMMIE FROM PRACTICE, WREN IS HUNGRY, THE–
© 2009, BABY BLUES PARTNERSHIP DIST. BY KING FEATURES SYNDICATE 9-2
ON THE OTHER HAND, YOU WERE HERE FIRST.
FAIR IS FAIR.
KIRKMAN & SCOTT

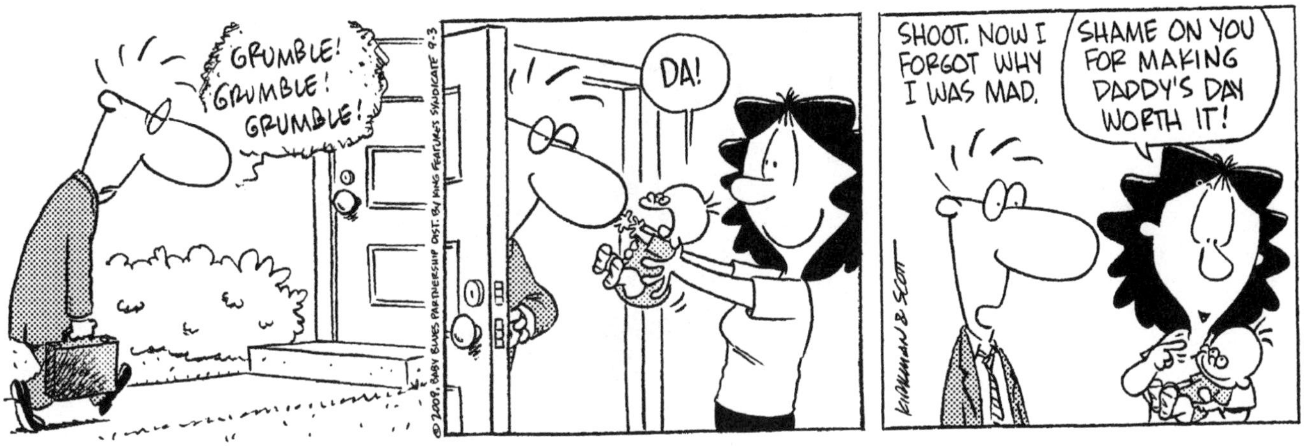
GRUMBLE! GRUMBLE! GRUMBLE!
DA!
SHOOT. NOW I FORGOT WHY I WAS MAD.
SHAME ON YOU FOR MAKING DADDY'S DAY WORTH IT!
KIRKMAN & SCOTT
© 2009, BABY BLUES PARTNERSHIP DIST. BY KING FEATURES SYNDICATE 9-3

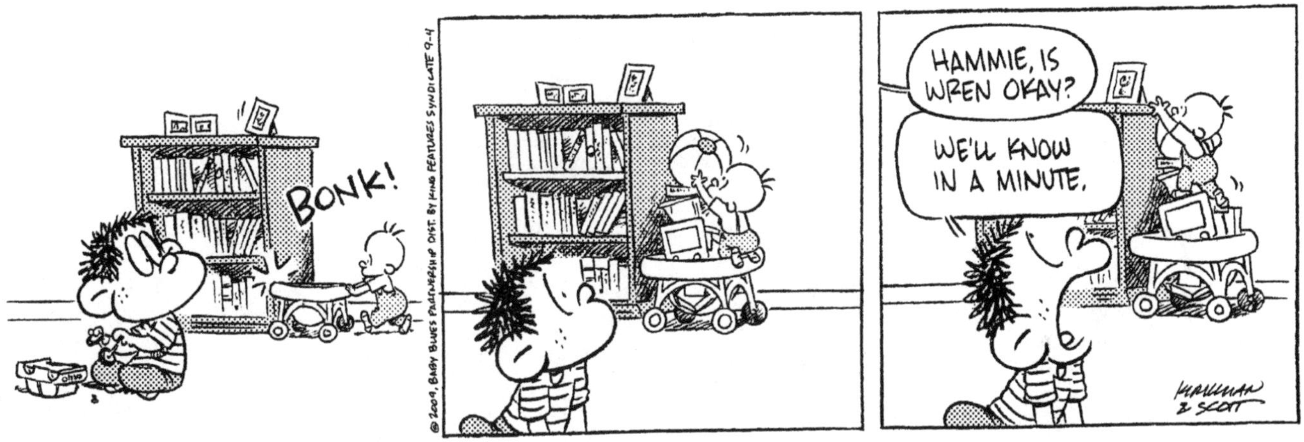
BONK!
HAMMIE, IS WREN OKAY?
WE'LL KNOW IN A MINUTE.
KIRKMAN & SCOTT
© 2009, BABY BLUES PARTNERSHIP DIST. BY KING FEATURES SYNDICATE 9-4

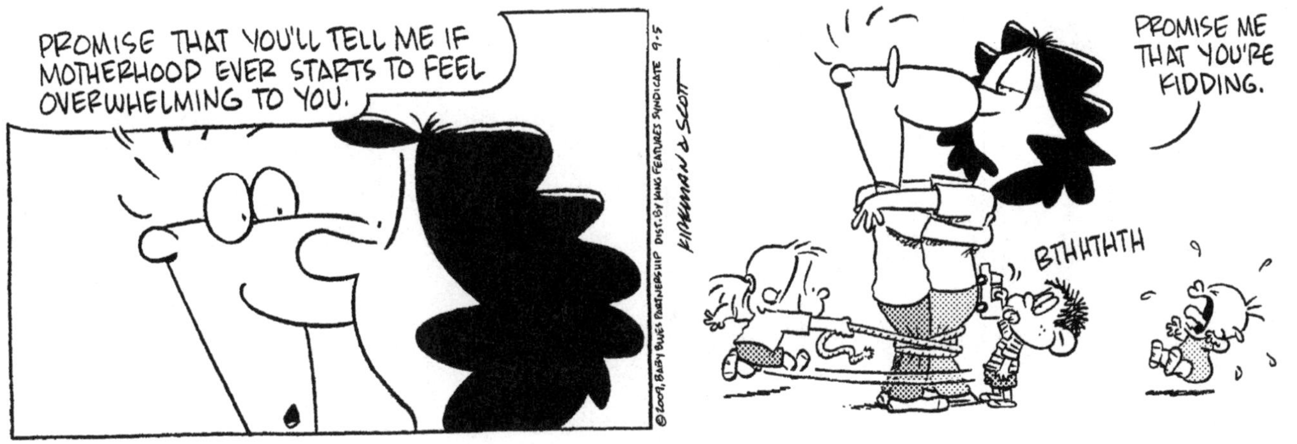
PROMISE THAT YOU'LL TELL ME IF MOTHERHOOD EVER STARTS TO FEEL OVERWHELMING TO YOU.
PROMISE ME THAT YOU'RE KIDDING.
BTHHTHTH
KIRKMAN & SCOTT
© 2009, BABY BLUES PARTNERSHIP DIST. BY KING FEATURES SYNDICATE 9-5

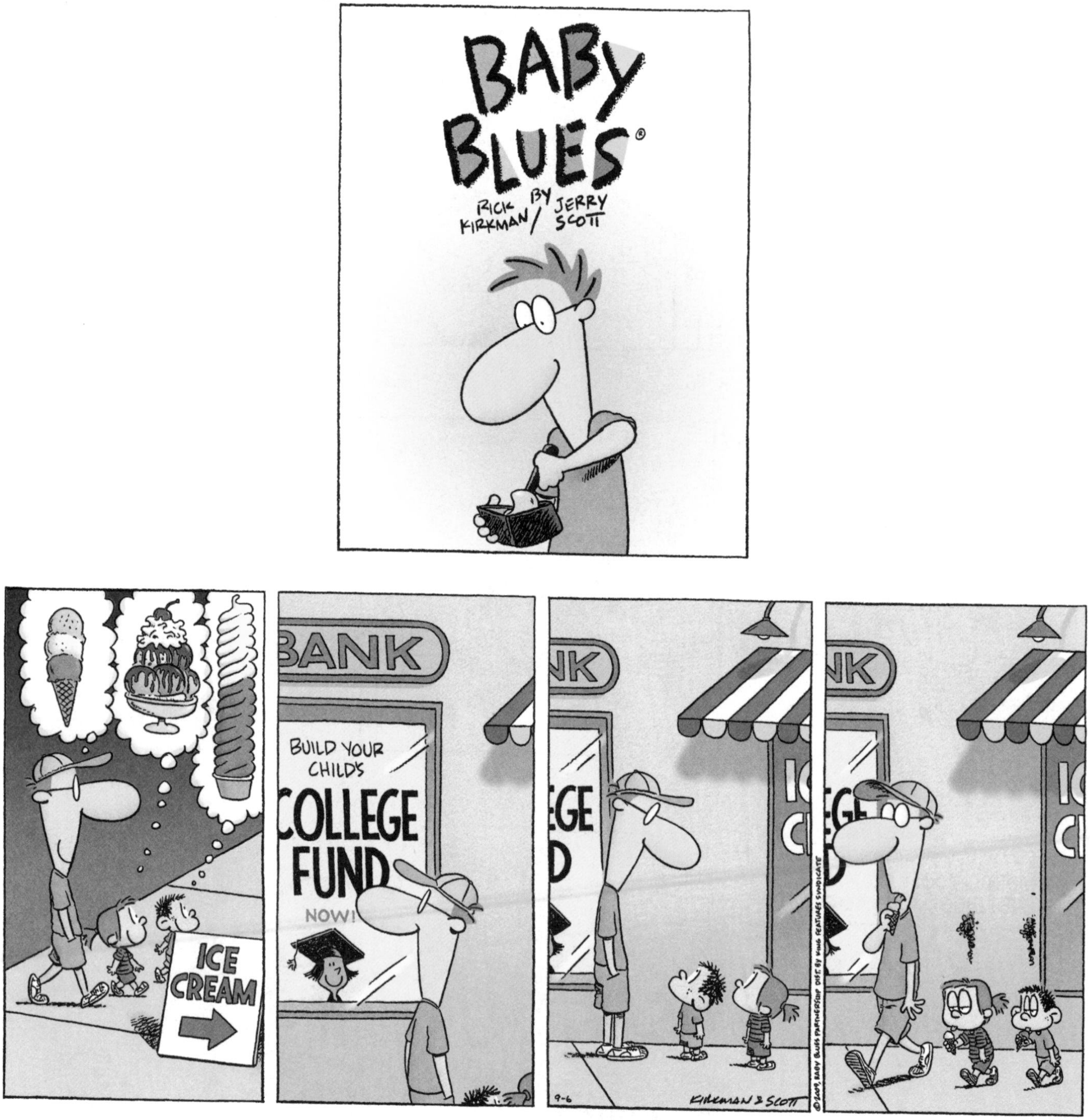
BABY BLUES®
BY RICK KIRKMAN / JERRY SCOTT
BANK
ICE CREAM
BUILD YOUR CHILD'S COLLEGE FUND NOW!
9-6
KIRKMAN & SCOTT
©2009, BABY BLUES PARTNERSHIP DIST. BY KING FEATURES SYNDICATE

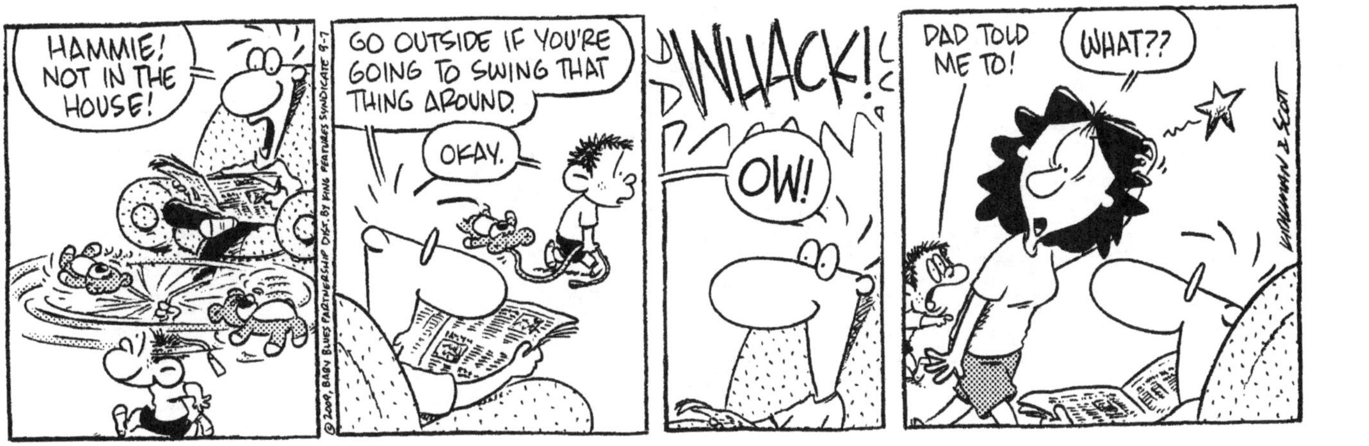
HAMMIE! NOT IN THE HOUSE!
©2009, BABY BLUES PARTNERSHIP DIST. BY KING FEATURES SYNDICATE 9-7
GO OUTSIDE IF YOU'RE GOING TO SWING THAT THING AROUND.
OKAY.
WHACK!
OW!
DAD TOLD ME TO!
WHAT??
KIRKMAN & SCOTT

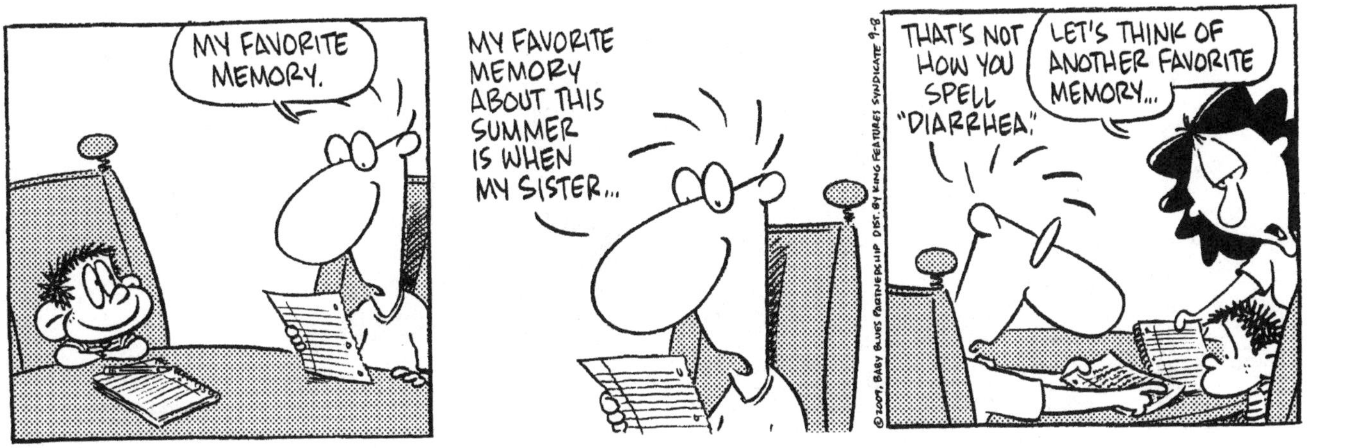
MY FAVORITE MEMORY.
MY FAVORITE MEMORY ABOUT THIS SUMMER IS WHEN MY SISTER...
©2009, BABY BLUES PARTNERSHIP DIST. BY KING FEATURES SYNDICATE 9-8
THAT'S NOT HOW YOU SPELL "DIARRHEA."
LET'S THINK OF ANOTHER FAVORITE MEMORY...

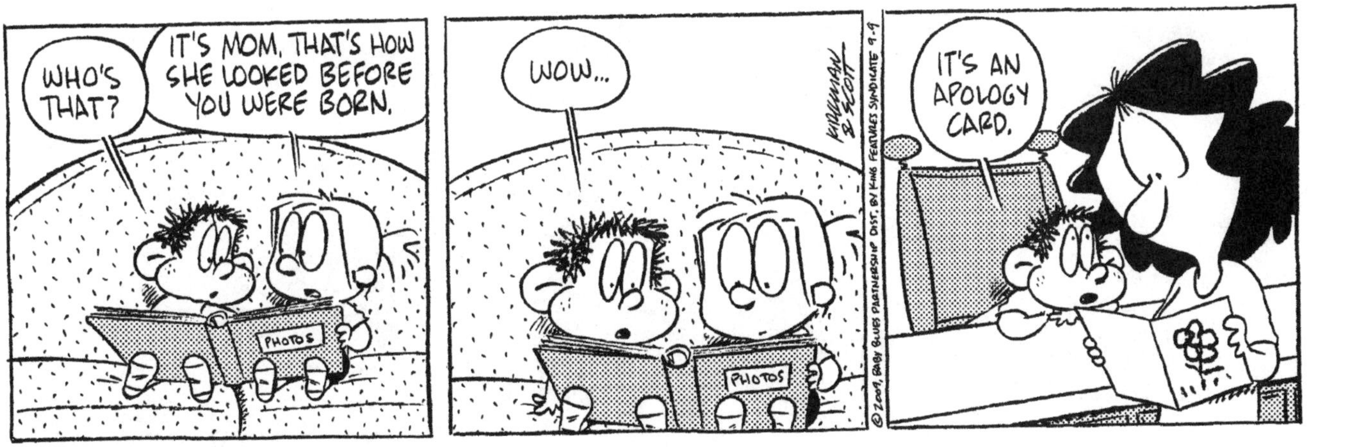
WHO'S THAT?
IT'S MOM. THAT'S HOW SHE LOOKED BEFORE YOU WERE BORN.
PHOTOS
WOW...
PHOTOS
KIRKMAN & SCOTT
©2009, BABY BLUES PARTNERSHIP DIST. BY KING FEATURES SYNDICATE 9-9
IT'S AN APOLOGY CARD.

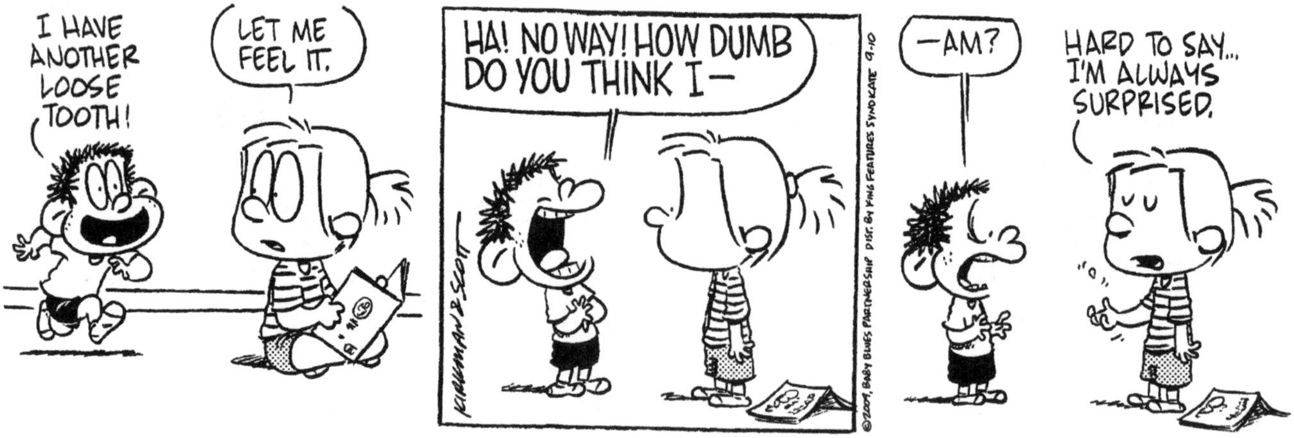
I HAVE ANOTHER LOOSE TOOTH!
LET ME FEEL IT.
HA! NO WAY! HOW DUMB DO YOU THINK I—
—AM?
HARD TO SAY... I'M ALWAYS SURPRISED.
KIRKMAN & SCOTT
©2009, BABY BLUES PARTNERSHIP DIST. BY KING FEATURES SYNDICATE 9-10

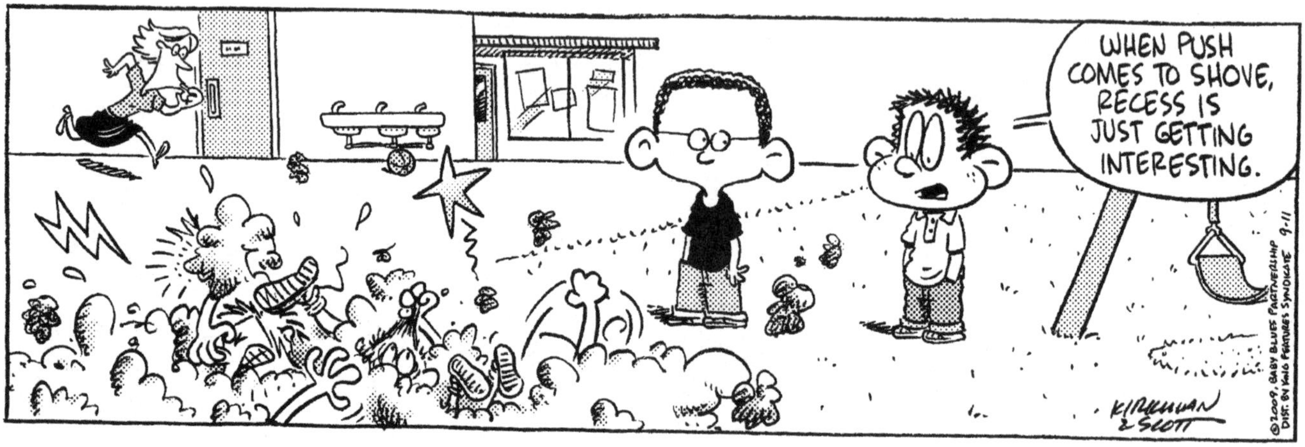
WHEN PUSH COMES TO SHOVE, RECESS IS JUST GETTING INTERESTING.
KIRKMAN & SCOTT
©2009, BABY BLUES PARTNERSHIP DIST. BY KING FEATURES SYNDICATE 9-11

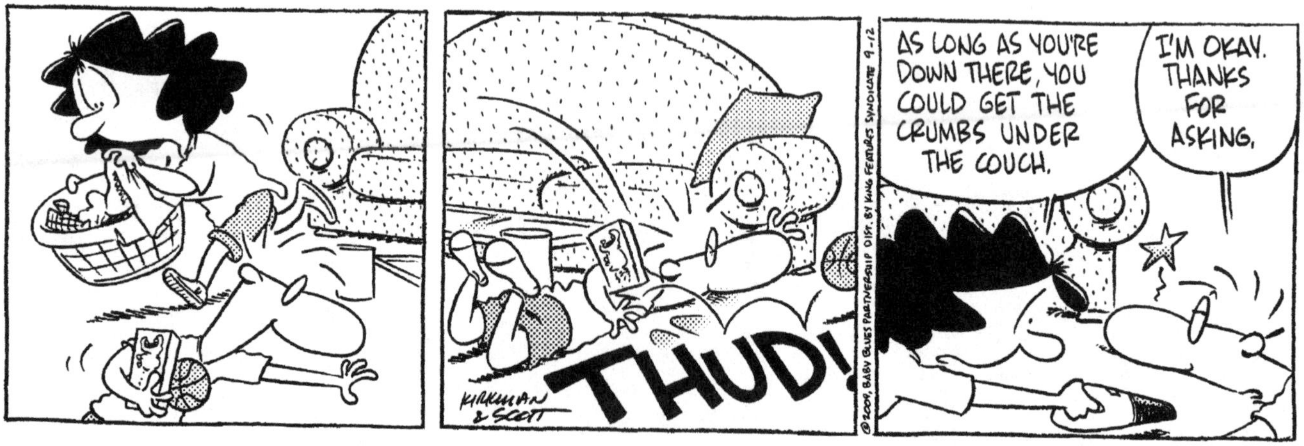
KIRKMAN & SCOTT
THUD!
©2009, BABY BLUES PARTNERSHIP DIST. BY KING FEATURES SYNDICATE 9-12
AS LONG AS YOU'RE DOWN THERE, YOU COULD GET THE CRUMBS UNDER THE COUCH.
I'M OKAY. THANKS FOR ASKING.

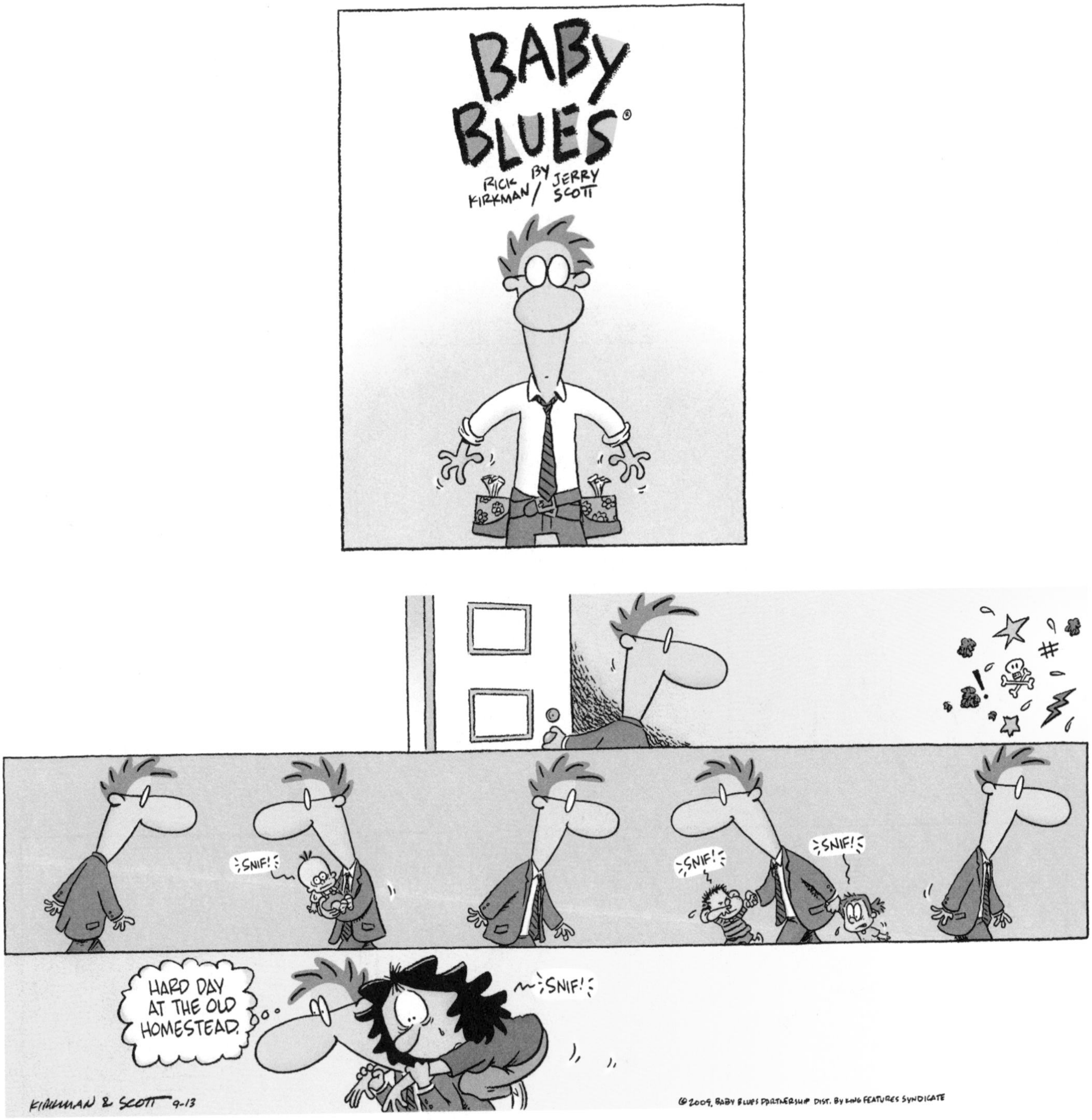
BABY BLUES®
BY RICK KIRKMAN / JERRY SCOTT
SNIF!
SNIF!
SNIF!
HARD DAY AT THE OLD HOMESTEAD.
SNIF!
KIRKMAN & SCOTT 9-13
©2009, BABY BLUES PARTNERSHIP DIST. BY KING FEATURES SYNDICATE

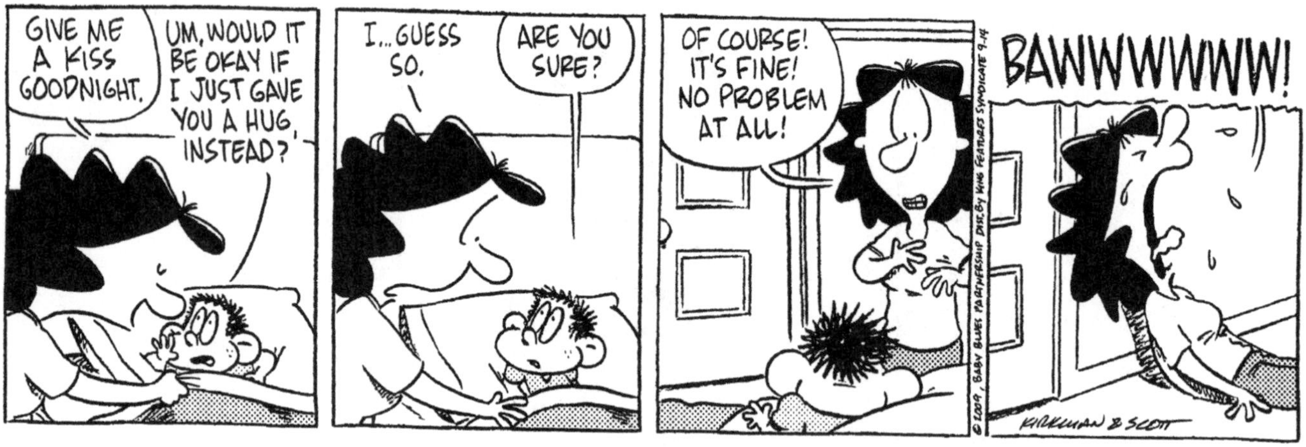
GIVE ME A KISS GOODNIGHT.
UM, WOULD IT BE OKAY IF I JUST GAVE YOU A HUG, INSTEAD?
I... GUESS SO.
ARE YOU SURE?
OF COURSE! IT'S FINE! NO PROBLEM AT ALL!
© 2009, BABY BLUES PARTNERSHIP DIST. BY KING FEATURES SYNDICATE 9-14
BAWWWWWW!
KIRKMAN & SCOTT

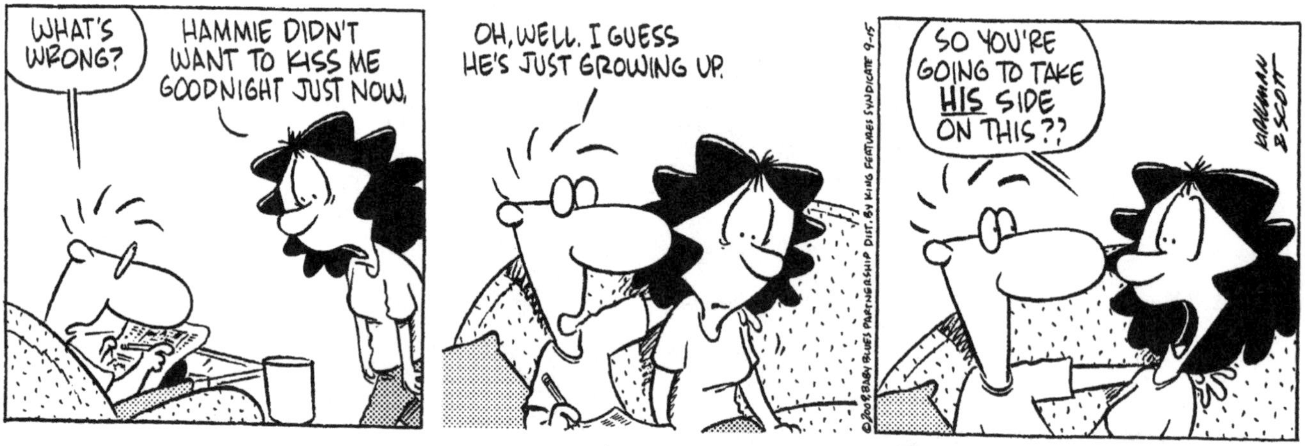
WHAT'S WRONG?
HAMMIE DIDN'T WANT TO KISS ME GOODNIGHT JUST NOW.
OH, WELL. I GUESS HE'S JUST GROWING UP.
© 2009 BABY BLUES PARTNERSHIP DIST. BY KING FEATURES SYNDICATE 9-15
SO YOU'RE GOING TO TAKE HIS SIDE ON THIS??
KIRKMAN & SCOTT

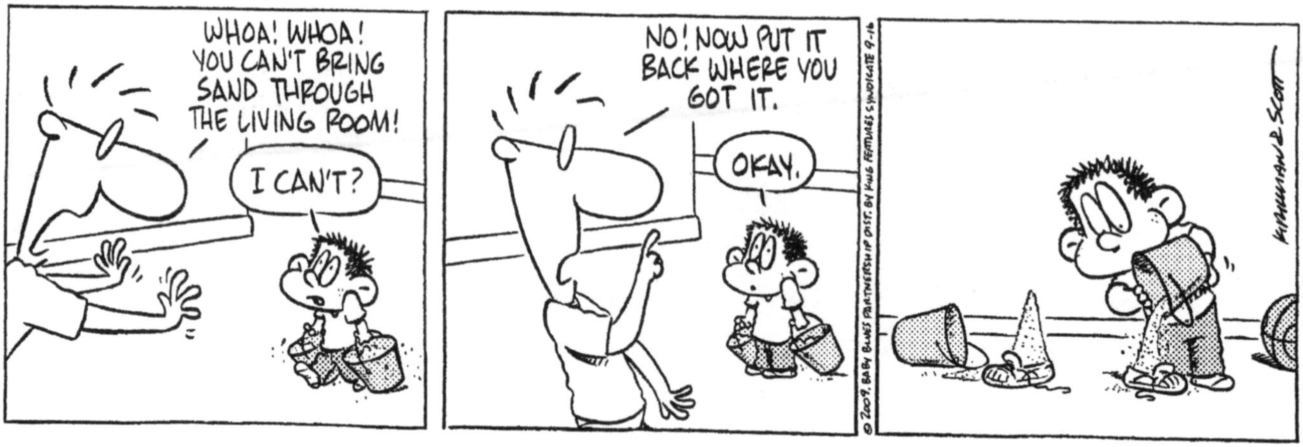
WHOA! WHOA! YOU CAN'T BRING SAND THROUGH THE LIVING ROOM!
I CAN'T?
NO! NOW PUT IT BACK WHERE YOU GOT IT.
OKAY.
© 2009, BABY BLUES PARTNERSHIP DIST. BY KING FEATURES SYNDICATE 9-16
KIRKMAN & SCOTT

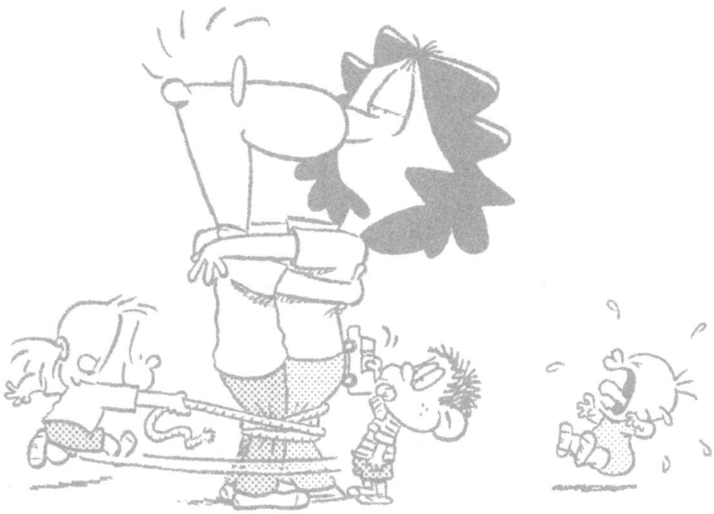

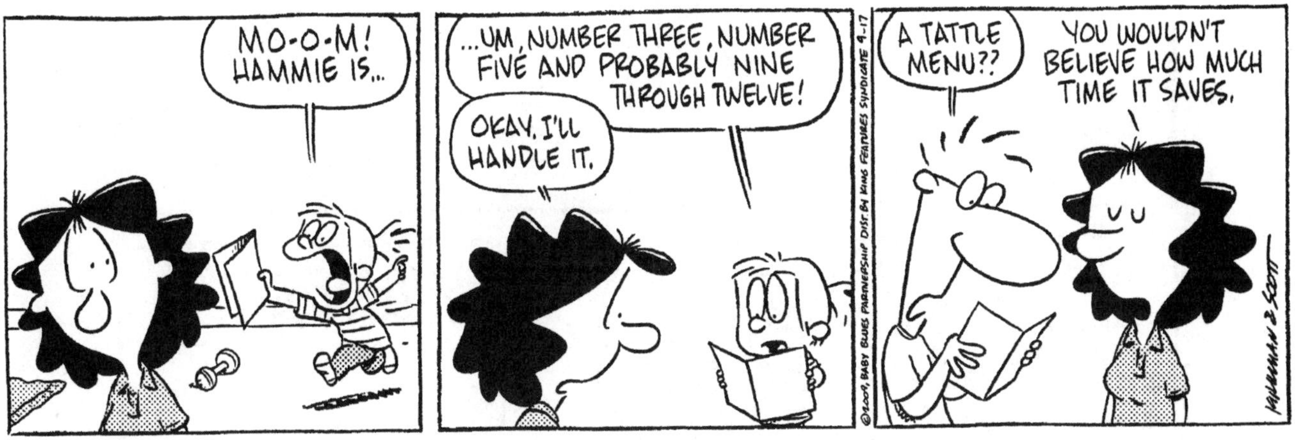

MO-O-M! HAMMIE IS...
...UM, NUMBER THREE, NUMBER FIVE AND PROBABLY NINE THROUGH TWELVE!
OKAY. I'LL HANDLE IT.
©2009, BABY BLUES PARTNERSHIP DIST. BY KING FEATURES SYNDICATE 9-17
A TATTLE MENU??
YOU WOULDN'T BELIEVE HOW MUCH TIME IT SAVES.
KIRKMAN & SCOTT

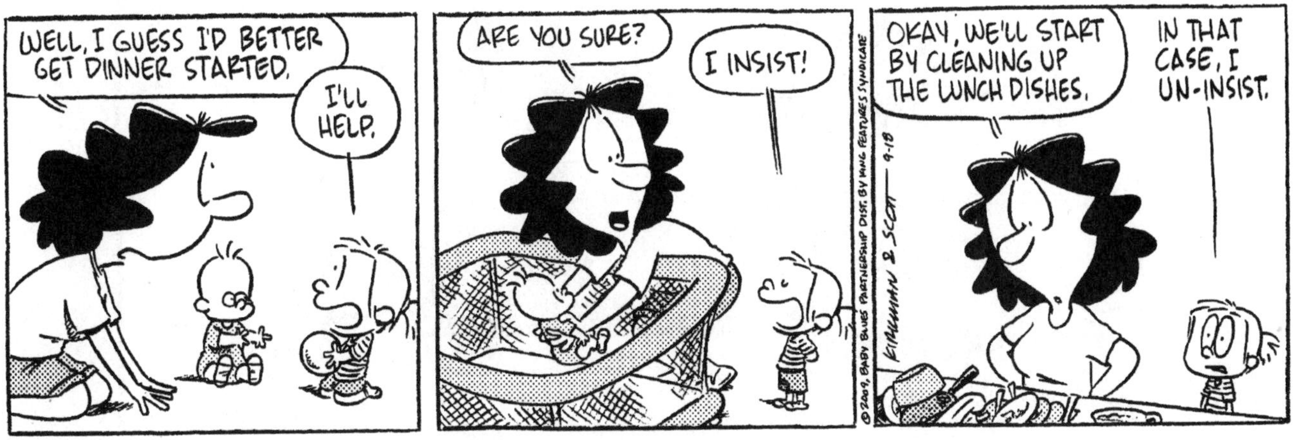

WELL, I GUESS I'D BETTER GET DINNER STARTED.
I'LL HELP.
ARE YOU SURE?
I INSIST!
©2009, BABY BLUES PARTNERSHIP DIST. BY KING FEATURES SYNDICATE
KIRKMAN & SCOTT 9-18
OKAY, WE'LL START BY CLEANING UP THE LUNCH DISHES.
IN THAT CASE, I UN-INSIST.

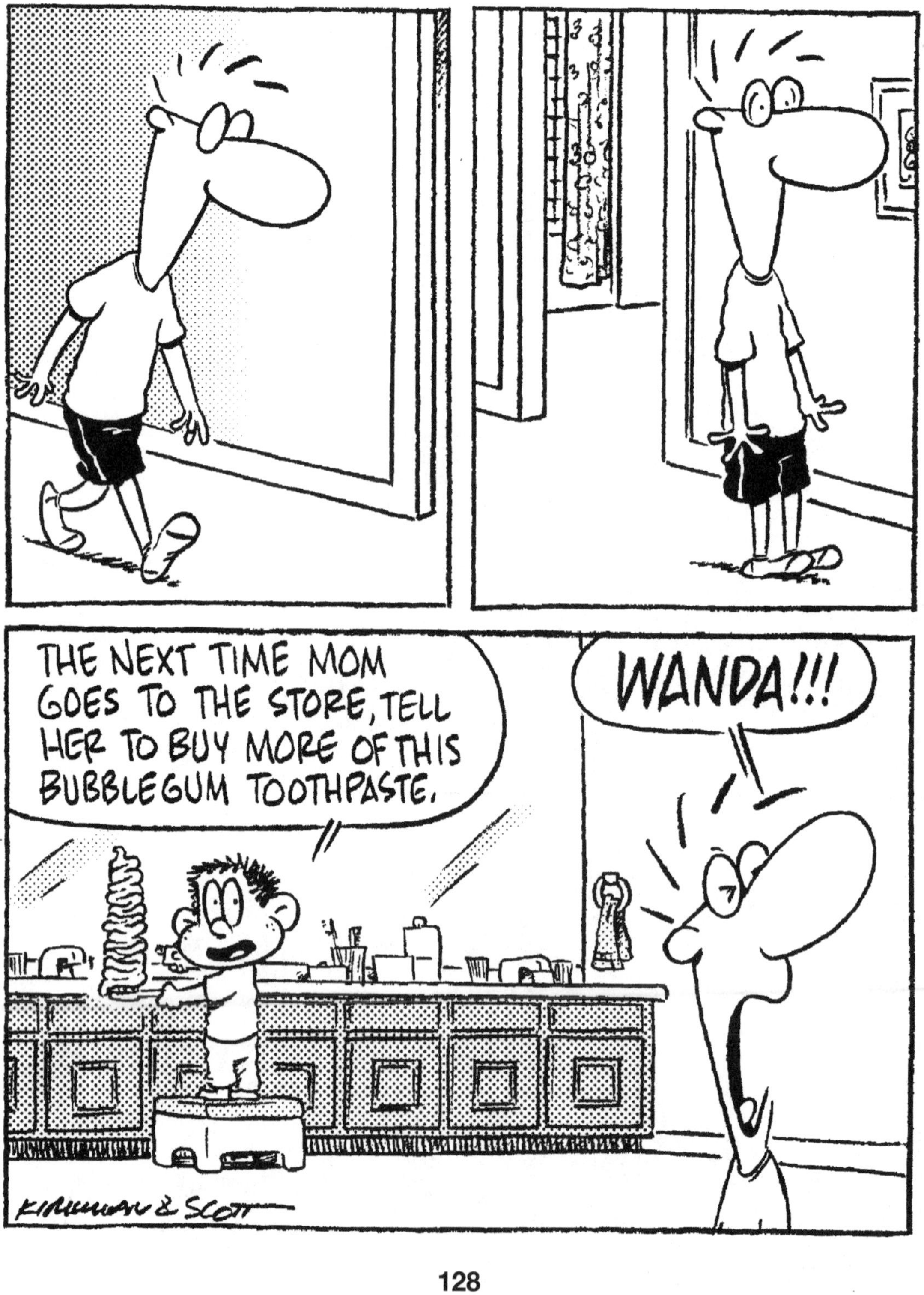
THE NEXT TIME MOM GOES TO THE STORE, TELL HER TO BUY MORE OF THIS BUBBLEGUM TOOTHPASTE.
WANDA!!!
KIRKMAN & SCOTT